COMPOUND INTEREST
AND
ANNUITIES-CERTAIN

COMPOUND INTEREST
AND
ANNUITIES-CERTAIN

BY

D. W. A. DONALD

O.B.E., T.D., F.F.A.

SECOND EDITION

CAMBRIDGE

Published for the Institute of Actuaries and the Faculty of Actuaries

AT THE UNIVERSITY PRESS

1970

Published by the Syndics of the Cambridge University Press
Bentley House, 200 Euston Road, London N.W.1
American Branch: 32 East 57th Street, New York, N.Y. 10022

Standard Book Number: 521 08011 8

Library of Congress Catalogue Card Number: 71-130908

First Published	1953
Reprinted with Corrections	1956
Reprinted	1963
Second Edition	1970

Printed in Great Britain
at the University Printing House, Cambridge
(Brooke Crutchley, University Printer)

CONTENTS

PREFACE

The subject of 'Compound Interest' and the name 'Todhunter' have been indissolubly linked in the minds of actuaries and of actuarial students for over fifty years. In preparing a new text-book on this subject I have been very conscious of the comparison that will necessarily be made with a work which has so well withstood the passage of time. It would be idle to challenge comparison with a text-book which for its completeness and its value as a work of reference could hardly be improved. Experience as a tutor has, however, led me to wonder whether its very completeness has not sometimes been a stumbling-block to the student approaching the subject for the first time. His needs may at times best be served by a strictly practical and even numerical method of approach, and from his point of view some aspects of the application of the theory of compound interest found in the previous text-book might well be left for study at a later stage of his career. I have not hesitated to exclude from this book anything which is not of direct use to the student, even though this has meant a limitation of its scope as compared with the previous work.

Perhaps the main difficulty in studying compound interest is the relative unfamiliarity of the types of transactions on the Stock Exchange which give rise to most of the problems encountered in practice. At the risk of seeming to labour the obvious I have therefore tried to explain what the basic nature of each problem really is, and to focus attention on the application of general principles to its solution. In the earlier stages I have tried to avoid undue complications, and for that reason have deferred all consideration of the effect of income tax to one chapter occurring towards the end of the book.

Compound interest is essentially a practical subject, and it is only by practice in numerical work that confidence can be obtained. Numerous illustrative examples have been included in each chapter. These should be studied carefully. Once the points of principle have been grasped the numerical working should be checked. In addition to the illustrative examples a certain number of exercises have been provided. In the early stages these are intended mainly to give practice in handling compound interest tables, but some of the later questions have been selected from examination papers of the Institute and the Faculty. It is hoped they will be useful to the student both in consolidating knowledge already gained and in helping him in the revision stages of his work.

My indebtedness to Todhunter is obvious. I have had the benefit of access to the notes provided for students by the Actuarial Tuition Service and I must also record my thanks to a number of my professional colleagues who have helped with advice and criticism—particularly to Mr A. F. Ross, who, apart from much useful general comment, undertook the laborious task of checking the solutions to the illustrative examples. For any ambiguities, errors or imperfections which remain I am, however, entirely responsible.

D.W.A.D.

CHAPTER I

BASIC CONCEPTIONS AND GENERAL IDEAS

1·1. The payment of interest as a reward for the use of capital is an established part of our economic life. In a sense interest may be regarded as a reward paid by a person, who is given the use of a sum of capital, to the owner of the capital. In theory the two items, the capital which is being used and the interest which is being paid, need not be expressed in terms of the same commodity. For example, if a farmer lends his neighbour a tractor for his harvest in return for a proportion of the corn reaped, the tractor could be considered as the capital lent and the corn as the interest paid. In financial and actuarial theory, however, it is necessary to consider only the case where both capital and interest are expressed in terms of money. The theory of compound interest is concerned with the continued growth of a sum of money under the operation of interest.

1·2. Rate of interest

In practice the interest which it has been agreed will be paid for the use of the capital is payable at stated intervals of time. The rate of interest which operates during one of these intervals is found by considering the amount of interest agreed to be paid in relation to the capital invested. Thus the strict definition of a rate of interest is

> *The amount contracted to be paid in one unit interval of time for each unit of capital invested.*

The general financial practice is to make the unit interval of time a year, and this unfortunately tends to induce the preconceived idea that rates of interest must be annual rates, and still more unfortunately it is customary, as will be seen below, to describe certain rates of interest as 'rates per annum' when in fact they are not. For example, one of the best known British Government

Securities is referred to as '$3\frac{1}{2}$% War Loan'. The actual rate of interest paid on this security is not, however, $3\frac{1}{2}$% per annum because it is paid twice yearly in June and December, and in terms of the definition above the rate of interest is $1\frac{3}{4}$% per half-year. As will be seen later, this is not the same as $3\frac{1}{2}$% per annum, and it is important, especially in considering first principles, that this distinction should be clearly grasped at the outset.

1·3. Compound interest

By definition, if a stated rate of interest is to be paid it means that at the end of a stated interval of time the lender or investor will receive a fixed sum of money for the use of his capital during that period. In the theory of compound interest it is assumed that when the lender receives this sum he can immediately use it as capital and invest it so that it earns interest in the same way as the original loan. The accumulated amount of the original capital invested or 'principal', plus the interest paid on it and similarly invested, is called the 'amount' of the principal. In the theory of compound interest it is a fundamental hypothesis that the amount of a given principal is a continuous function of time. In actual practice, of course, interest is added only at stated intervals of time, with the result that the amount of the principal displays sudden jumps at the end of each interval. But in the theoretical aspect of the subject interest is regarded as accruing continuously throughout the interval so that the amount of the principal is subject to a process of continuous growth. In other words if, in Fig. 1, AA_1, BB_1, CC_1, etc., represent the amounts of interest paid after 1, 2, 3, ... intervals, the graph of the amount of principal invested is represented by the continuous curve and not the dotted line.

1·4. Analogy with natural processes

The accumulation of a sum of money at compound interest may in fact be compared with the natural process of a plant or tree growing. When a tree grows the stem puts forth branches. These branches are like interest being added to the principal. They in turn throw off twigs, which also grow and are like the interest, which it has been postulated can be earned on the original interest, once it has been invested and thus become capital. The total amount by which the tree has increased over its original size in a given period is equivalent to the total interest which the principal has earned in that period. The obvious difference is that in natural growth there is no doubt about the continuity of the process, and it may therefore help to give a clearer picture if the analogy is considered in greater detail.

For the sake of simplicity let it be assumed that there is a tree whose branches grow only lengthwise and that it is desired to measure the rate of longitudinal growth of one of its branches. The

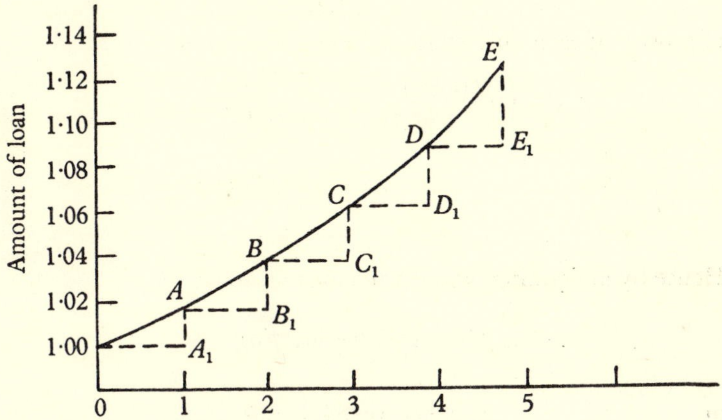

Fig. 1.

obvious method would be to measure its length at the start of some interval of time and to measure it again at the end of the interval. The difference expressed per unit length of the original branch would then be the average rate of growth of the branch for that given period. It is clear that this rate is the result of the continuous process by which the branch grows, and that by reducing the time interval over which the length of the branch is measured it would be possible to approximate more and more closely to the instantaneous rate of growth. It should also be clear that the instantaneous rate is the fundamental rate, and that a rate found by measurement for any other period of time is only a way of expressing the results of the instantaneous rate by relating the effect of its operation to a given interval of time. The same is true of principal accumulating at compound interest.

1·5. Application of the calculus

Still considering the natural process of a branch of a tree growing, let the initial length be $f(0)$ and the length after time t be $f(t)$. Then the amount by which the length of the branch increases between time t and time $t+h$ is $f(t+h)-f(t)$. The rate of growth per unit interval of time is therefore $\{f(t+h)-f(t)\}/h$, and the rate of growth for each unit length of $f(t)$ is $\dfrac{f(t+h)-f(t)}{hf(t)}$. The instantaneous rate of growth of each unit length at time t is therefore

$$\lim_{h\to 0}\frac{f(t+h)-f(t)}{hf(t)}=\frac{1}{f(t)}\frac{d}{dt}f(t)$$

$$=\frac{d}{dt}\log_e f(t)$$

$$=\delta_t \text{ say.}$$

Hence by integrating between the limits 0 and t,

$$\log_e f(t)=\int_0^t \delta_t\,dt+\log_e f(0)$$

or

$$f(t)=f(0)\exp\left[\int_0^t \delta_t\,dt\right].$$

1·6. Numerical example based on natural growth

Suppose that the initial length of the branch is 10 m and that it is found to be 10·5 m after 1 year. The average rate of growth is therefore 50 cm per 10 m per annum, i.e. 5% per annum. If the branch grows continuously then the continuous rate of growth per annum is δ_t, where

$$f(1)=10\cdot 5=f(0)\exp\left[\int_0^1 \delta_t\,dt\right].$$

If it is assumed that the continuous rate of growth is δ, where δ is constant throughout the period, then

$$\delta=\log_e 1\cdot 05$$

$$=\cdot 04879,$$

i.e. the statement that the branch grows 50 cm in 1 year is merely expressing the result in 1 year of the effect of a constant continuous rate of growth of 4·879% per annum. For this reason the statement might be made that the effective rate of growth is 5% per annum, and this statement gives without further calculation the information that the increase which would be found in the branch if it were measured after 1 year would be 5% of 10 m or 50 cm.

1·7. Consideration of intermediate points

If it were desired, given that the constant instantaneous rate of growth is 4·879% per annum, to find how much the branch would grow in 6 months, the process would be

$$f(\tfrac{1}{2}) = f(0)\exp\left[\int_0^{\frac{1}{2}} \cdot 04879\, dt\right]$$
$$= 10e^{\cdot 02439}$$
$$= 10\cdot 247 \text{ m}$$

The increase would be ·247 m, or 24·7 cm. This is of course less than half the increase for the year because the 24·7 cm which have grown in the first 6 months will themselves grow further in the second 6 months and will make up the total growth to 50 cm. To investigate the result of this let it be assumed:

(*a*) that, if the increase in length at any time is cut off, the original branch will grow at the same rate as before;

(*b*) that, if the increase is planted, it will grow at the same rate as the parent stem, but, if it is not planted, it is unable to grow.

Thus if, after 6 months, the increase in length of 24·7 cm is removed, the original 10 m of branch will grow a further 24·7 cm as before in the next 6 months. If the portion cut off is replanted it will increase, as before, to

$$24\cdot 7\exp\left[\int_0^{\frac{1}{2}} \cdot 04879\, dt\right] = 24\cdot 7 \times 1\cdot 0247$$
$$= 25\cdot 3 \text{ cm.}$$

The total growth is therefore 24·7 + 25·3 = 50 cm, as before.

In other words the effect of a continuous rate of growth of 4·879% per annum could be stated either as an actual increase of 5% per annum, or as 2·47% per 6 months. Now if the amount of the increase after 6 months had not been replanted, the increase in the second 6 months would have been only 24·7 cm, and the total growth would have been 49·4 cm, or at the rate of 4·94%. This assumption, however, implies that at the end of 6 months the increase in the length of the branch is cut off and prevented from growing further. If it is left to follow its own natural processes it will grow and the effect of the given rate will still be to add 50 cm to the length of the branch in 1 year.

1·8. Application to compound interest

Exactly the same arguments hold good for a sum of money accumulating at interest. It so happens that because most financial transactions are viewed on a year-to-year basis, the most common way of stating the rate of growth is as a percentage per annum, i.e. it is more common to state the effect in the course of a year of a continuous rate of growth than it is to state the continuous rate of growth itself. But this should not obscure the fact that the basic force giving rise to the effect is the continuous rate of growth. It is this function which lies at the root of all the theory of compound interest and the natural emphasis laid in practice on the expression of rates of interest as yearly rates must not be allowed to obscure this fundamental fact. In actuarial language the continuous rate at which a sum of money grows under the operation of interest is called the 'force of interest' and the increase per unit due to the effect of the operation of this force of interest in any given period is called the 'effective rate of interest' for that period. The relations between these, and other rates of interest, will be discussed in the following chapter.

CHAPTER 2

DEFINITIONS AND ELEMENTARY PROPOSITIONS

2·1. In Chapter 1 the general theory of compound interest was stated as the continuous growth of money under the operation of a force of interest. It is necessary now to consider the application of this theory to the problems which arise in practice. Normally, rates of interest are stated in terms of an interval of one year, or sometimes a submultiple of a year. They may be true effective rates for the period stated, or, as has been mentioned in § 1·2, they may be rates per annum in name only. There will be no difficulty in understanding these differences if the stated rate is always related to the underlying force of interest.

2·2. Effective rate of interest

The effective rate of interest during any period has already been defined as the actual rate of increase per unit invested during that time. In Chapter 1 it was seen that the effect in 1 year of a continuous rate of increase of 4·879 % during the period was to increase the length of the branch by 5 %, or in other words to add 5 % to the value of a unit invested at the beginning of the period. In this case the effective rate of interest is 5 % per annum. It was also seen that the effect of the same rate of continuous increase was to add 2·47 % after 6 months to the value of a unit invested at the start of the 6 months. The effective rate of interest might be stated in this case as 2·47 % per half-year.

2·3. Nominal rate of interest

As has been mentioned in Chapter 1, the common financial practice is to express rates of interest as rates per annum, and sometimes a rate is stated as so much per annum, even though the interest is paid more frequently than once per year. Thus an effective rate of 2·47 % per half-year might be expressed as a rate of 4·94 % per annum, payable half-yearly. But in §2·2 it was shown that the effect in 1 year of an effective rate of interest of 2·47 % per half-year was to add 5 % to the value of a unit invested. The rate stated as 4·94 % per annum is therefore not an effective rate. It is a rate of interest in name only, and for this reason it is called a 'nominal' rate of interest. It merely expresses *the total interest which is payable in a year on a unit invested at the beginning of the year assuming that any interest paid during the year is not reinvested.* To complete the definition the number of times the interest is payable during the year must be stated. This is done by employing one of the following phrases which have identical meanings:

payable half-yearly, quarterly, monthly or, generally, m times per annum;

or convertible half-yearly, quarterly, monthly or, generally, m times per annum;

or payable with half-yearly, quarterly, monthly or, generally, $1/m$thly rests.

If the number of times a year that interest is convertible is increased indefinitely the nominal rate becomes the annual rate of continuous growth, which, as already mentioned, is known as the 'force of interest'.

2·4. Analogy with Chapter 1

It is now possible to translate the results of Chapter 1 into terms of rates of interest. The continuous rate of increase corresponds to the force of interest. The amount by which the branch grows in a given period under the operation of the continuous rate for that period corresponds to the effective rate of interest for the period concerned. A nominal rate of interest payable more frequently than once during the given period corresponds to the result of cutting off the amount by which the branch has grown after part of the period and not replanting it. This process is repeated after each part of the period, and the sum of the measurements of the portions thus detached and not replanted would correspond to the nominal rate of interest for the period concerned. If these portions had been free to grow, the total at the end of the period would have been the same as the effective rate of interest for that period.

2·5. Symbolic representation of rates of interest

The generally accepted symbols for the rates of interest are

(a) The force of interest per annum is represented by δ.

(b) An effective rate of interest per annum is represented by i.

(c) A nominal rate of interest per annum payable m times a year is represented by $i^{(m)}$.*

2·6. Relations between i, $i^{(m)}$ and δ

By definition

$$\delta = \lim_{h\to 0} \frac{1}{h} \frac{f(t+h)-f(t)}{f(t)},$$

where $f(t)$ is the amount of a unit of principal at time t.

$$\therefore\ \delta = \frac{1}{f(t)} \frac{d}{dt} f(t)$$

$$= \frac{d}{dt} \log_e f(t),$$

$$\therefore\ \log_e f(1) = \int_0^1 \delta\, dt$$

$$= \delta.$$

But the amount of a unit after one year at an effective rate of i per annum is clearly $(1+i)$, since the original unit is intact and the interest paid at the end of a year is i.

$$\therefore\ \delta = \log_e (1+i) \qquad (2\cdot 1)$$

or

$$i = e^{\delta} - 1. \qquad (2\cdot 2)$$

Also

$$\log_e f\left(\frac{1}{m}\right) = \int_0^{1/m} \delta\, dt$$

$$= \frac{1}{m}\delta$$

$$= \frac{1}{m} \log_e (1+i).$$

$$\therefore\ f\left(\frac{1}{m}\right) = (1+i)^{(1/m)}.$$

* In older actuarial works the symbol used is $j_{(m)}$.

But the amount of 1 after $1/m$th of a year at a nominal rate of $i^{(m)}$ is also $1+\frac{i^{(m)}}{m}$, since the effective rate of interest is $\frac{i^{(m)}}{m}$ per interval.

$$\therefore \quad \left(1+\frac{i^{(m)}}{m}\right)=(1+i)^{1/m}, \tag{2·3}$$

or

$$i=\left(1+\frac{i^{(m)}}{m}\right)^m-1. \tag{2·4}$$

Equation (2·4) merely expresses symbolically what should be apparent from general reasoning. If a unit is invested at a nominal rate $i^{(m)}$ per annum the interest received after $1/m$th of a year is $\frac{i^{(m)}}{m}$ and, if this is invested also, the capital becomes $\left(1+\frac{i^{(m)}}{m}\right)$. In the next interval the interest is $\frac{i^{(m)}}{m}\left(1+\frac{i^{(m)}}{m}\right)$ and the amount of the capital becomes

$$\left(1+\frac{i^{(m)}}{m}\right)+\frac{i^{(m)}}{m}\left(1+\frac{i^{(m)}}{m}\right)=\left(1+\frac{i^{(m)}}{m}\right)^2.$$

In the next interval the interest will be $\frac{i^{(m)}}{m}\left(1+\frac{i^{(m)}}{m}\right)^2$, and the amount of the capital at the end of the interval will be

$$\left(1+\frac{i^{(m)}}{m}\right)^2+\frac{i^{(m)}}{m}\left(1+\frac{i^{(m)}}{m}\right)^2=\left(1+\frac{i^{(m)}}{m}\right)^3.$$

After m intervals, i.e. after 1 year, the amount of the capital is similarly $\left(1+\frac{i^{(m)}}{m}\right)^m$, and the total interest earned in the year, which by definition is the effective rate of interest per annum, is therefore

$$\left(1+\frac{i^{(m)}}{m}\right)^m-1.$$

Equation (2·2) could also be obtained by algebraic means as follows:

$$\begin{aligned} i&=\left(1+\frac{i^{(m)}}{m}\right)^m-1 \\ &=1+i^{(m)}+\frac{m(m-1)}{2!}\left(\frac{i^{(m)}}{m}\right)^2+\ldots-1. \end{aligned}$$

In the limit where $m \to \infty$, $i^{(m)}$ becomes δ and we have

$$i = 1 + \delta + \frac{\delta^2}{2!} + \frac{\delta^3}{3!} + \dots - 1$$
$$= e^\delta - 1 \quad \text{as before.}$$

It will be seen therefore that the basis on which interest is calculated in any given transaction may be defined by means of either

a force of interest δ,

or *an effective rate of interest per annum of* i,

or *a nominal rate of interest per annum payable m times a year of* $i^{(m)}$,

and that if one of these is defined the corresponding values of the others can be found from the equations

$$e^\delta = (1+i) = \left(1 + \frac{i^{(m)}}{m}\right)^m. \tag{2·5}$$

2·7. Accumulation at compound interest

So far the effect of the investment of a sum of money at compound interest has been investigated only for periods of one year or less. To find the effect of investing a sum for a longer period it is necessary to consider only the fundamental equation

$$\delta = \frac{d}{dt} \log_e f(t),$$

or

$$f(t) = f(0) \exp\left[\int_0^t \delta\, dt\right]$$
$$= f(0)\, e^{t\delta} \tag{2·6}$$
$$= f(0)\,(1+i)^t \tag{2·7}$$
$$= f(0) \left(1 + \frac{i^{(m)}}{m}\right)^{tm}, \tag{2·8}$$

by substitution from equation (2·5).

The identity $f(t) = f(0)\,(1+i)^t$ can readily be deduced by general reasoning if t is integral, by a process exactly similar to that followed in proving that $(1+i) = \left(1 + \frac{i^{(m)}}{m}\right)^m$ in § 2·6. It is apparent that the amounts of the principal in successive years must form a geometric progression with common ratio $(1+i)$, and therefore the amount after t years must be $f(0)(1+i)^t$.

The approach through the force of interest is, however, preferable, since it makes it clear that the identity holds even though t is not an integral number of years.

2·8. Numerical example of rates of interest

It may serve to illustrate more readily the principles above if an actual numerical example be considered:

Find the amount of a unit after 10 years if the rate of interest be

(*a*) 5 % per annum convertible momently,
(*b*) 5 % per annum effective,
(*c*) 5 % per annum payable with quarterly rests.

In symbols these statements mean (*a*) $\delta = \cdot 05$, (*b*) $i = \cdot 05$ and (*c*) $i^{(4)} = \cdot 05$.

It would be possible to work from equation (2·5) and to calculate the value of i corresponding to these rates, i.e. in (*a*)

$$i = e^{\cdot 05} - 1 = \cdot 051271$$

and in (*c*) $$i = (1\cdot 0125)^4 - 1 = \cdot 05095.$$

These effective rates might then be used in the formula $(1+i)^{10}$, i.e in (*a*) the amount would be $(1\cdot 051271)^{10}$, in (*b*) $(1\cdot 05)^{10}$ and in (*c*) $(1\cdot 05095)^{10}$. This intermediate process, however, has no real advantage; it merely introduces another operation into the calculation, it increases the liability to arithmetical error, and it is far easier to work direct from first principles. Thus in (*a*) the value is $e^{10\delta} = e^{\cdot 5} = 1\cdot 6487$ (either by logarithms or by direct expansion of the exponential series). In (*b*) the value is $(1\cdot 05)^{10} = 1\cdot 6289$ (by logarithms) and in (*c*) the value is $\left(1 + \frac{\cdot 05}{4}\right)^{40} = 1\cdot 6436$ (by logarithms). In effect what has been done in (*a*) and (*c*) has been the replacement of the time interval of a year by a more convenient interval. The choice of interval is conditioned by the rate of interest. In (*a*) it is stated as a continuous rate, and therefore the time interval best suited for the work is the interval dt, and the methods of the calculus will clearly give the easiest solution. In (*c*) interest is payable four times a year, and a period of three months is therefore the most appropriate. Considered in this way the problem becomes one involving an effective rate of interest of $1\frac{1}{4}\%$ per quarter for a period of 40 quarter years.

2·9. Present values

So far the problem considered has been of finding to what amount a sum of money will accumulate after a given period under the operation of a given rate of interest. The cognate problem of finding what sum of money must be invested to accumulate after a specified time at a specified rate of interest to a given sum must also be considered. This process is called finding the 'present value' of a given sum, and the process involved is called 'discounting' a given sum, as opposed to its accumulation.

2·10. Obvious relationships

If the sum to be discounted is 1, its present value at any given rate of interest is readily found by simple proportion from the results of § 2·7. Since the amount after a period of time t of a unit invested now at a force of interest δ, a corresponding effective rate per annum of i, or a corresponding nominal rate of $\dfrac{i^{(m)}}{m}$ is $e^{t\delta}$, $(1+i)^t$ or $\left(1+\dfrac{i^{(m)}}{m}\right)^{tm}$ respectively, the sum which must be invested to amount to 1 at the same rates must be in each case

$$\frac{1}{e^{t\delta}}, \quad \frac{1}{(1+i)^t} \quad \text{and} \quad \frac{1}{\left(1+\dfrac{i^{(m)}}{m}\right)^{tm}},$$

i.e. if $\phi(t)$ denotes the present value of 1 due after a period of time t

$$\phi(t) = e^{-t\delta}, \tag{2·9}$$

$$= (1+i)^{-t}, \tag{2·10}$$

$$= \left(1+\frac{i^{(m)}}{m}\right)^{-tm}. \tag{2·11}$$

It is convenient to have a symbol to represent $(1+i)^{-1}$, and this is generally written as v, so that $\phi(t)=v^t$.

2·11. Rates of discount

In § 2·10 the present value of a unit was found at a given rate of interest. It would be equally possible, and in some connexions it is more convenient, to work with a rate of discount. Interest was defined as the reward for the use of capital, and the payment of interest postulates the idea that a borrower will be prepared to pay sums of money at the end of stated intervals in return for the privilege of having had the loan. The idea of discount is exactly similar except that the payments are made in advance, at the start of each stated interval. In practice the problem arises mainly in connexion with transactions of the type where a person is entitled to a sum payable at the end of some interval of time and wishes to have the use of his money immediately. In return for the surrender of his right to the future sum he receives a cash payment now. If S is the sum due in the future and P is the sum which he is offered for it now, the transaction could be considered in two ways:

(*a*) the difference he pays for receiving his money at once is $S-P$, and this is defined as the discount. The rate of discount for the time interval in question is therefore $\dfrac{S-P}{S}$ per unit of capital to be received.

(*b*) on the other hand, viewing the transaction as one of interest he borrows a sum of P now and repays a sum of S at the end of the stated time. The interest he pays is therefore $(S-P)$, and the rate of interest for the period is $\dfrac{S-P}{P}$ per unit of capital borrowed.

The two methods are merely different ways of looking at the same transaction, and the theory of discount may be considered in exactly the same way as the theory of interest.

2·12. Force of discount

Let δ' be the 'Force of Discount', and as before let $\phi(t)$ be the present value of a sum of 1 due after an interval of time t. Then by definition

$$\delta' = \lim_{h\to 0} \frac{\phi(t)-\phi(t+h)}{h\phi(t)}$$

$$= -\frac{1}{\phi(t)}\frac{d}{dt}\phi(t)$$

$$= -\frac{d}{dt}\log_e \phi(t).$$

Now if $f(t)$ is the amount of a sum of 1 after an interval of time t at the corresponding rate of interest, then by simple proportion

$$\phi(t) = \frac{1}{f(t)}.$$

$$\therefore\ \delta' = -\frac{d}{dt}\log_e \phi(t) = \frac{d}{dt}\log_e f(t) = \delta,$$

the corresponding force of interest.

This result may be confirmed by general reasoning. In the notation of §2·11 the ratio of the rate of discount to the rate of interest is $\frac{S-P}{S}\bigg/\frac{S-P}{P} = \frac{P}{S}$. If the time interval is infinitesimally small P and S will become identical and the two rates become the force of discount and force of interest respectively, which must therefore be identical.

2·13. Effective and nominal rates of discount

As before let δ be the force of discount. Then in one year the total discount, in the notation of §2·12, is $1-\phi(1)$.

But

$$\delta = -\frac{d}{dt}\log_e \phi(t)$$

or

$$\phi(t) = \exp\left[-\int_0^t \delta\, dt\right]$$

$$= e^{-t\delta}.$$

The total discount is therefore $1-e^{-\delta}$, and this, by definition, is the effective rate of discount usually denoted by d.

Hence $d = 1 - e^{-\delta}$ or $e^{-\delta} = (1-d)$.

Since the present value of 1 due after a period t is $e^{-t\delta}$ it is equally $(1-d)^t$.

This result can also be established, where t is integral, by general reasoning. Considering each interval of time separately it will be seen that the ratio between the present values of the sum due at the beginning and the end of the interval must be $(1-d):1$. Hence the present values form a geometric progression with common ratio $(1-d)$, and the present value of a unit due after t intervals is $(1-d)^t$.

On the same lines as were followed in § 2·3 for a nominal rate of interest it is possible to understand what is meant by a nominal rate of discount. Such a rate merely expresses the annual rate of discount, irrespective of how often during the year the operation of discounting is performed. Naturally, if this operation is performed more than once during the year, the effective rate of discount for the year will not be the same as the nominal rate, and the relationship between the two will be analogous to that connecting i and $i^{(m)}$. The symbol used for a nominal rate of discount is $d^{(m)}$, and the relationship between d and $d^{(m)}$ is established as follows:

By definition
$$\frac{d^{(m)}}{m} = 1 - e^{-\delta/m}$$
$$= 1 - (1-d)^{1/m}$$

or
$$1 - d = \left(1 - \frac{d^{(m)}}{m}\right)^m,$$

and hence
$$e^{-\delta} = 1 - d = \left(1 - \frac{d^{(m)}}{m}\right)^m \qquad (2·12)$$

2·14. Relation between interest and discount

Since interest and discount are merely different ways of looking at the same problem, it follows that for every given rate of interest there is a corresponding rate of discount and vice versa. It is instructive to examine the relationship. First, since i and d are the respective effective rates of interest and discount, then in respect of a loan of 1 the payment of i at the *end* of the year corresponds to the payment of d at the *beginning* of the year. Hence d invested for a year at the effective rate of interest concerned must amount to i at the end of the year or

$$d(1+i)=i. \tag{2·13}$$

Equally i discounted for a year at rate d must be equal to d or

$$i(1-d)=d. \tag{2·14}$$

And lastly as the present value of 1 due in a year's time is either v or $1-d$, and, as these are equivalent,

$$1-d=v. \tag{2·15}$$

These results, of course, also follow algebraically from the equation in §2·12, since

$$1-d=e^{-\delta}=(1+i)^{-1}=v.$$

$$\therefore\ d=1-v=\frac{i}{1+i}=iv=i(1-d) \tag{2·16}$$

and

$$i-d=id. \tag{2·17}$$

Equation (2·17) may also be used to show that the force of interest and the force of discount are identical. They are respectively

$$\lim_{m\to\infty} i^{(m)} \quad \text{and} \quad \lim_{m\to\infty} d^{(m)}.$$

Now $\dfrac{i^{(m)}}{m}-\dfrac{d^{(m)}}{m}=\dfrac{i^{(m)}}{m}\times\dfrac{d^{(m)}}{m}$ by the same argument as led to equation (2·17), and hence in the limit

$$\lim_{m\to\infty}(i^{(m)}-d^{(m)})=\lim_{m\to\infty}\frac{i^{(m)}\times d^{(m)}}{m}=0,$$

i.e. the force of interest and the force of discount are identical.

The relationships connecting interest and discount can be shown very clearly by an extension of Fig. 1 in Chapter 1 as follows.

The curve *PQRST* (Fig. 2) represents the accumulation of a sum at compound interest, the amount of the sum at the origin *O* being unity. Points on the curve to the right of the origin therefore represent the accumulation of the unit sum at interest, and points on the curve to the left of the origin represent the discounting of the unit sum at the same rate of interest, or at the corresponding rate of discount. From a study of the diagram the following relationships are apparent:

$$X_{-1}P = v = 1 - d,$$

$$AP = d,$$

$$X_{-\frac{1}{2}}Q = v^{\frac{1}{2}} = (1-d)^{\frac{1}{2}},$$

$$BQ = \frac{d^{(2)}}{2},$$

$$OF = 1 - d,$$

$$RF = i(1-d) = iv,$$

$$X_{\frac{1}{2}}S = (1+i)^{\frac{1}{2}},$$

$$SC = \frac{i^{(2)}}{2},$$

$$X_1 T = 1 + i,$$

$$TD = i.$$

Formulae analogous to the general formulae (2·13) to (2·17) may be deduced immediately from these relationships.

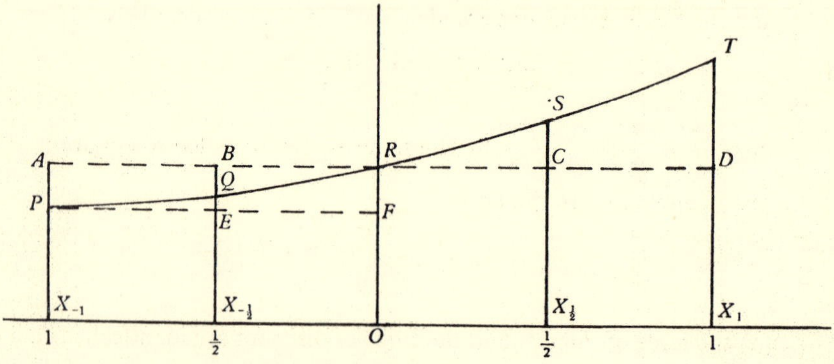

Fig. 2.

2·15. Commercial discount

In commercial practice the operation of discounting is frequently met with in the business of discounting bills. A 'bill' or 'bill of exchange' is simply a promise to pay a fixed sum after a specified time, usually less than 1 year. A 'Bill Broker' is a man who is prepared to buy bills for cash now, in return for the proceeds of the bills when they fall due. The difference between the face value of the bill (or the sum which is due to be paid when the bill matures), and the sum the broker offers for it is, of course, the discount. Bill brokers normally quote their terms as a certain rate of discount, and the practice is to treat this as a nominal rate convertible with the same frequency as the period of the bill. Thus if the commercial rate of discount were 3 %, the discount on a three months bill for £100 would be $100 \times \cdot 03/4$ or for a six months bill $100 \times \cdot 03/2$ and so on. It will be seen that in fact this means that the effective rate of discount per annum involved in the two transactions is not the same. In the first case it is $1-(1-\cdot 03/4)^4$ and in the second $1-(1-\cdot 03/2)^2$, but this refinement is disregarded by the broker who simply quotes a rate and treats it as a nominal one whatever the period of the bill.

2·16. Summary of results

It may be convenient to summarize the results so far established in this chapter. It is assumed that the rates of interest, discount, etc., below correspond to one another.

Rate of interest or discount concerned

	Force of interest or discount δ	Effective rate of interest i	Nominal rate of interest $i^{(m)}$	Effective rate of discount d	Nominal rate of discount $d^{(m)}$
(*a*) The amount of 1 after time *t* is	$e^{t\delta}$	$(1+i)^t$	$\left(1+\frac{i^{(m)}}{m}\right)^{tm}$	$(1-d)^{-t}$	$\left(1-\frac{d^{(m)}}{m}\right)^{-tm}$
(*b*) The present value of 1 due after time *t* is	$e^{-t\delta}$	v^t $[\equiv(1+i)^{-t}]$	$\left(1+\frac{i^{(m)}}{m}\right)^{-tm}$	$(1-d)^t$	$\left(1-\frac{d^{(m)}}{m}\right)^{tm}$

2·17. Interest tables

It would obviously be possible by the use of logarithms to evaluate the expressions $(1+i)^t$ and v^t, but as these functions are required frequently their values have been worked out for the rates of interest and for values of t likely to be met with in practice. Examples of interest tables are given at the end of this book, and these tables are used in the solution of the various examples given in the book.

2·18. Varying rates of interest

It has been assumed in this chapter that during the period of time under consideration the force of interest remains constant. This, of course, is unnecessary, and the fundamental relations that δ_t, the force of interest, at time t equals

$$\lim_{h\to 0} \frac{f(t+h)-f(t)}{hf(t)},$$

or that $f(t)$, the amount of 1 after time $t = \exp\left[\int_0^t \delta_t\,dt\right]$, hold equally whether δ_t is constant or not. The general theory of varying rates of interest will be considered in Chapter 11, but for the present it should be noted, apart from the question of a continuously varying force of interest, that in practice it is often necessary to consider problems involving an effective rate of interest which varies from year to year. Such problems need cause no difficulty. If, for example, it be desired to find the amount of 1 after t years when the effective rate of interest is i_1 in the first year, i_2 in the second and so on, the transaction can be considered from year to year. After 1 year the amount is $(1+i_1)$ and this is invested at rate i_2. After 2 years the amount is therefore $(1+i_1)+i_2(1+i_1)=(1+i_1)\,(1+i_2)$ and so on, leading to the general result that the amount after t years is

$$(1+i_1)(1+i_2)\ldots(1+i_t). \qquad (2\cdot18)$$

If $i_1=i_2=\ldots=i_t=i$, the result becomes of course $(1+i)^t$ as in formula (2·7).

2·19. Examples

The following examples illustrate the work of this chapter.

Example 2·1

(*a*) Find the amount to which £100 will accumulate as follows:

(i) At 4% per annum convertible quarterly for 10 years.
(ii) At 6% per annum convertible half-yearly for 5 years.
(iii) At the rate of interest corresponding to an effective rate of discount of 3% per annum for 8 years.

(iv) At 5% effective for 10 years, 4% effective for 5 years and $2\frac{1}{2}$% effective for 3 years.

(v) At a force of interest of 4% per annum for $3\frac{3}{4}$ years.

(*b*) What constant force of interest would produce the same result as the rates of interest in (iv) above?

(*a*) (i) The effective rate of interest is $\frac{\cdot 04}{4}$ per quarter and the money is invested for 40 quarters, hence the answer is

$$100(1\cdot01)^{40} = 148\cdot89 \quad \text{or} \quad £148\cdot89$$

(ii) As above $100(1\cdot03)^{10} = 134\cdot39$ or £134·39.

(iii) The effective rate of interest is i, where

$$\frac{1}{1+i} = 1 - \cdot 03 \quad (\text{since } 1-d=v)$$

or
$$(1+i) = \frac{1}{\cdot 97}.$$

The result is therefore

$$100\left(\frac{1}{\cdot 97}\right)^8 = 127\cdot59$$
$$= £127\cdot59.$$

(As a check the result should be more than

$$100(1\cdot03)^8 = £126\cdot68).$$

(iv) After 10 years the amount is $100(1\cdot05)^{10}$. This accumulates for 5 years at 4% and therefore becomes $100(1\cdot05)^{10}(1\cdot04)^5$. This accumulates for 3 years at $2\frac{1}{2}$% and therefore amounts to

$$100(1\cdot05)^{10}(1\cdot04)^5(1\cdot025)^3 = 100 \times 1\cdot62889 \times 1\cdot21665 \times 1\cdot07689$$
$$= 213\cdot42$$
$$= £213\cdot42.$$

(v) Since $f(t) = 100\exp\left[\int_0^t \delta_t\, dt\right]$ and in this case δ_t is constant

$$f(t) = 100e^{t\delta}$$
$$= 100e^{3\frac{3}{4} \times \cdot 04}.$$
$$= 100e^{\cdot 15}$$
$$= 116\cdot18$$
$$= £116\cdot18.$$

(*b*) If the constant force of interest for 18 years is δ, the amount of 100 will be $100e^{18\delta}$. Therefore, by the terms of the question,

$$100e^{18\delta} = 213{\cdot}42$$

or

$$\delta = \frac{\log_{10} 2{\cdot}1342}{18 \log_{10} e}$$

$$= \frac{{\cdot}32923}{18 \times {\cdot}43429}$$

$$= {\cdot}04212.$$

Example 2·2

A moneylender lends small sums and charges interest at the rate of 1p. per 12p. per month, payable in advance. After 1 month the loan may be renewed for a further month on payment of a further 1p. per 12p., and so on till the loan is repaid. What effective rate of interest does he charge per annum?

Consider a loan of 12p. The amount actually lent by the lender is 11p. and, after a month, this has amounted to 12p. Hence if $i^{(12)}$ is the nominal rate convertible monthly

$$11\left(1 + \frac{i^{(12)}}{12}\right) = 12$$

or

$$\left(1 + \frac{i^{(12)}}{12}\right) = \frac{12}{11}.$$

The corresponding effective rate is

$$\left(1 + \frac{i^{(12)}}{12}\right)^{12} - 1 = \left(\frac{12}{11}\right)^{12} - 1$$

$$= 2{\cdot}8406 - 1$$

$$= 1{\cdot}8406$$

or

$$184{\cdot}06\%.$$

Example 2·3

Show that a bill broker realizes a higher effective rate of discount on long-term than on short-term bills.

If the rate of commercial discount is f per annum and a bill is due in $1/n$ of a year, the bill broker treats the rate of discount as a nominal one convertible n times per annum and charges discount of f/n.

The effective rate of discount he realizes is d, where

$$1-d=\left[1-\frac{f}{n}\right]^n=e^{-\delta}.$$

$$\therefore\ \log(1-d)=n\log\left(1-\frac{f}{n}\right)=-\delta$$

or
$$\delta=f+\frac{f^2}{2n}+\frac{f^3}{3n^2}+\dots.$$

It will be seen that as n increases δ diminishes, hence $e^{-\delta}$ increases and $d\,(=1-e^{-\delta})$ must also diminish, i.e. the effective rate is higher for longer term bills.

Example 2·4

Show that
$$\frac{d^n}{dv^n}(v^{n-1}\delta)=-\frac{(n-1)!}{v},$$

$$\frac{d}{dv}(v^{n-1}\delta)=(n-1)\,v^{n-2}\delta+v^{n-1}\frac{d\delta}{dv}.$$

But
$$\frac{d\delta}{dv}=\frac{d}{dv}\log_e(1+i)=-\frac{d}{dv}\log v.$$
$$=-(1+i).$$

$$\therefore\ \frac{d}{dv}(v^{n-1}\delta)=(n-1)\,v^{n-2}\delta-v^{n-2}.$$

Similarly

$$\frac{d^2}{dv^2}(v^{n-1}\delta)=(n-1)(n-2)\,v^{n-3}\delta-(n-1)\,v^{n-3}-(n-2)\,v^{n-3}$$
$$=(n-1)(n-2)\,v^{n-3}\delta-(2n-3)\,v^{n-3},$$

and in general, for values of $r<n$,

$$\frac{d^r}{dv^r}(v^{n-1}\delta)=(n-1)(n-2)\dots(n-r)\,v^{n-r-1}\delta-K_r v^{n-r-1},$$

where K_r is independent of v.

$$\therefore\ \frac{d^{n-1}}{dv^{n-1}}(v^{n-1}\delta)=(n-1)(n-2)\dots(2)(1)\,v^0\delta-K_{n-1}v^0.$$

$$\therefore\ \frac{d^n}{dv^n}(v^{n-1}\delta)=(n-1)!\frac{d\delta}{dv}=-\frac{(n-1)!}{v}.$$

Example 2·5

Prove that if $i^{(m)}$ and $d^{(m)}$ are respectively the nominal rates of interest and discount convertible m times a year and δ is the corresponding force of interest, then approximately

$$\delta=\frac{i^{(m)}+d^{(m)}}{2},$$

and find correct to 8 decimal places the error involved when $m=5$ and the effective rate of interest is 3 %.

Since

$$e^{\delta}=\left(1+\frac{i^{(m)}}{m}\right)^{m}$$

and

$$e^{-\delta}=\left(1-\frac{d^{(m)}}{m}\right)^{m},$$

then

$$1+\delta+\frac{\delta^2}{2!}+\ldots=1+i^{(m)}+m(2)\left(\frac{i^{(m)}}{m}\right)^2+\ldots,$$

and

$$1-\delta+\frac{\delta^2}{2!}-\ldots=1-d^{(m)}+m(2)\left(\frac{d^{(m)}}{m}\right)^2+\ldots.$$

Subtracting the second equation from the first and neglecting powers of δ, $i^{(m)}$ and $d^{(m)}$ higher than the first

$$2\delta=i^{(m)}+d^{(m)}$$

or

$$\delta=\frac{i^{(m)}+d^{(m)}}{2}\quad\text{approx.}$$

When $m=5$ and $i=\cdot 03$

$$i^{(5)}=5\left[(1\cdot 03)^{1/5}-1\right]$$

$$=\cdot 029646347 \quad \text{by calculation from the binomial expansion,}$$

$$d^{(5)}=5\left[1-(1\cdot 03)^{-1/5}\right]$$

$$=\cdot 029471602 \quad \text{by calculation as before.}$$

$\therefore$ Approximately $\delta=\cdot 029558975$.

The true value of δ is $\log_e(1\cdot 03)$

$$=\cdot 029558802 \quad \text{by calculation from the logarithmic series.}$$

The error is therefore ·00000017 in excess.

Example 2·6

For a certain purpose it is required to calculate a table of the values of $i/i^{(2)}$, and it is suggested that the value should be taken as $1+\frac{1}{4}i$. Show this is approximately true and calculate the error involved to 5 places of decimals when $i = \cdot 04$.

$$\frac{i}{i^{(2)}} = \frac{i}{2[(1+i)^{1/2}-1]}$$

$$= \frac{i}{2[1+\frac{1}{2}i-\frac{1}{8}i^2+\frac{1}{16}i^3-\ldots-1]}$$

$$= \frac{i}{i-\frac{1}{4}i^2+\frac{1}{8}i^3-\ldots}$$

$$= \frac{1}{1-\frac{1}{4}i+\frac{1}{8}i^2-\ldots}.$$

Assuming that terms involving i^2 and above may be ignored, we have

$$\frac{i}{i^{(2)}} = \frac{1}{1-\frac{1}{4}i}$$

$$= 1+\frac{1}{4}i \quad \text{approximately.}$$

The true value is $\quad 1+\frac{1}{4}i-\frac{1}{16}i^2+\frac{1}{32}i^3.$

When $i = \cdot 04$ this is 1·009902, and the error is therefore ·00010 in excess.

Example 2·7

In how many years will a sum of money double itself at compound interest?

If the effective rate be i the value of n is given by the equation

$$(1+i)^n = 2$$

and hence $\quad n = \dfrac{\log 2}{\log(1+i)}.$

If natural logarithms are taken

$$n = \frac{\log_e 2}{\log_e(1+i)}$$

$$= \frac{\log_e 2}{i-\frac{1}{2}i^2+\frac{1}{3}i^3-\ldots},$$

or, if powers of i above the first are neglected,

$$=\frac{\log_e 2}{i}[1+\tfrac{1}{2}i]$$

$$=\frac{\cdot 69315}{i}+\cdot 35 \quad \text{approximately.}$$

In practice the value of n would be found by using ordinary logarithms, or by inspection of an interest table at the appropriate rate, but the above is an interesting confirmation of a practical approximation often used, viz. 'Divide 70 by the rate of interest per cent.'

Example 2·8

The sum of the amount of 1 in 2 years at a certain nominal rate of interest and of the present value of 1 due in 2 years at the same nominal rate of discount, both rates convertible half-yearly, is 2·00480032. Find the rate.

Let $2r$ be the rate per annum.

Then
$$\left(1+\frac{2r}{2}\right)^4+\left(1-\frac{2r}{2}\right)^4=2\cdot 00480032$$

or
$$2+12r^2+2r^4=2\cdot 00480032$$

or
$$r^4+6r^2-\cdot 00240016=0$$

or
$$(r^2-\cdot 0004)(r^2+6\cdot 0004)=0,$$

giving, as a practical solution, $r=\cdot 02$ and $2r=\cdot 04$.

Example 2·9

During the year 1969 a fund accumulated under the operation of a force of interest which varied continuously in such a way that at any time the fund was a rational integral function of the fourth degree in t. The following rates were each 4% per annum:

(i) The effective rate of interest over the whole year.
(ii) The nominal rate of interest convertible quarterly from July to September.
(iii) The nominal rate of discount convertible half-yearly from April to September.
(iv) The nominal rate of discount convertible quarterly from January to March.

Assuming the year to consist of 12 months of equal length find the force of interest at midnight on 30 June 1969.

Let the fund at time t be $f(t)$ and work in quarter years so that the fund on 1 January is $f(0)$, 1 April $f(1)$ and so on.

The data given lead to the following equations:

$$\text{(i)}\quad f(4) = 1{\cdot}04 f(0),$$

$$\text{(ii)}\quad f(3) = 1{\cdot}01 f(2),$$

$$\text{(iii)}\quad f(1) = {\cdot}98 f(3),$$

$$\text{(iv)}\quad f(0) = {\cdot}99 f(1).$$

The force of interest at midnight on 30 June 1969 is the continuous rate *per annum* at which the fund is increasing at that moment. Since the values of $f(t)$ relate to periods of one quarter-year the value $\frac{1}{f(t)}\frac{d}{dt}f(t)$ will give the force of interest at time t per quarter-year and the value required is therefore $\frac{4}{f(t)}\frac{d}{dt}f(t)$ when $t=2$.

Now writing $\quad f(t) = f(0) + t\Delta f(0) + t(2)\Delta^2 f(0) + \dots$

$$\frac{d}{dt}f(t) = \Delta f(0) + \Delta^2 f(0)\frac{d}{dt}t(2) + \dots.$$

Differentiating and putting $t=2$

$$= \Delta f(0) + \tfrac{3}{2}\Delta^2 f(0) + \tfrac{1}{3}\Delta^3 f(0) - \tfrac{1}{12}\Delta^4 f(0)$$

$$= f(1) - f(0) + \tfrac{3}{2}[f(2) - 2f(1) + f(0)] + \tfrac{1}{3}[f(3) - 3f(2) + 3f(1) - f(0)]$$
$$- \tfrac{1}{12}[f(4) - 4f(3) + 6f(2) - 4f(1) + f(0)]$$

$$= \tfrac{1}{12}f(0) - \tfrac{2}{3}f(1) + \tfrac{2}{3}f(3) - \tfrac{1}{12}f(4),$$

and substituting the values from equations (i)–(iv) above

$$= \frac{f(2)}{12}[{\cdot}99 \times {\cdot}98 \times 1{\cdot}01 - 8$$
$$\times {\cdot}98 \times 1{\cdot}01 + 8 \times 1{\cdot}01 - 1{\cdot}04 \times {\cdot}98 \times {\cdot}99 \times 1{\cdot}01]$$

$$= \frac{f(2)}{12}[{\cdot}02 \times 8 \times 1{\cdot}01 - {\cdot}04 \times {\cdot}98 \times {\cdot}99 \times 1{\cdot}01]$$

$$= {\cdot}0102003 f(2).$$

$$\therefore\ 4\left[\frac{1}{f(t)}\frac{d}{dt}f(t)\right]_{t=2} = 4 \times {\cdot}0102003 = {\cdot}0408012.$$

EXERCISES 2

2·1 Find the present value of £100 due at the end of 20 years, at the following annual rates of interest:

(a) 5% convertible half-yearly.
(b) 5% convertible momently.
(c) 4% convertible quarterly for the first 10 years, thereafter 3% effective.

2·2 Find the amount of £100 accumulated for 20 years at the following rates of interest:

(a) The effective rate of interest corresponding to a nominal rate of discount of 4% per annum convertible half-yearly.
(b) 6% per annum convertible 3 times per annum for 12 years, thereafter $3\frac{1}{2}$% per annum convertible every second year.
(c) The rate of interest per annum at which a sum of money will treble itself in 21 years.

2·3 Show that, approximately, $i/\delta = 1 + \frac{1}{2}i$, and find, to 5 decimal places, the error involved when $\delta = {\cdot}04$.

2·4 Fund A accumulates at a rate of interest of 2% effective per annum and fund B at 3% effective per annum. At the end of 20 years the total of the two funds is £1000. At the end of 10 years the amount of fund A is half that of fund B. What is the amount of the combined funds after 5 years?

2·5 A calculator, who wished to find the amount at the end of 20 years of £100 accumulating at a force of interest of 5% per annum, obtained the effective rate of interest, i per annum, corresponding to the given force of interest and assumed that values of $(1+i)^n$ could be found by first difference interpolation between the tabular values of $(1{\cdot}05)^n$ and $(1{\cdot}06)^n$. Find to the nearest penny the error involved in his assumption.

2·6 Given
$$\sum_{1}^{\infty} (-1)^{m-1} \left(\frac{i^m}{d^{(m)}} - \frac{i^m}{i^{(m)}}\right) = {\cdot}041622,$$
find i.

CHAPTER 3

ON THE SOLUTION OF PROBLEMS IN COMPOUND INTEREST

3·1. General considerations

The basic principles of compound interest are so simple that it is not easy to understand the undoubted difficulties which many students experience on coming to the subject for the first time. Experience has, however, shown that these difficulties usually arise from a neglect of first principles and from a too slavish attempt to solve problems by a mechanical application of formulae. It is important therefore that it should be realized that with the basic ideas of Chapter 2 it is possible to solve any problem in compound interest. The remainder of this text-book, and the formulae it contains, are only extensions of these basic ideas and merely present a technique of shortening the labour of arithmetical work. In order to acquire fluency in handling compound interest problems it is essential that this technique be mastered, but it must always be remembered that the intelligent application of the technique can be made only if there is a solid understanding of the underlying basic principles. This chapter, therefore, is devoted to stating the principles which must be followed in dealing with compound interest problems.

3·2. Essentials of the problem

In its simplest terms every compound interest problem involves three elements:

(*a*) the sum invested,
(*b*) the rate of interest,
(*c*) the sum to be received after a specified time.

If any two of these are given, the value of the third may be deduced. The simplest problems, such as are dealt with in elementary arithmetic text-books, involve as a rule only a single sum of money.

The theory is readily extended to cover problems involving series of payments, and the various broad types of problem are discussed below.

3·3. Problems involving a known rate of interest

Such problems may be elementary, as in Example 1 of Chapter 2, or considerably more complicated as in later chapters. The essential problem, however, the rate of interest being known, is either in finding the amount to which a given sum will accumulate, or in determining the present value of a sum payable in the future. The more complicated cases are usually those involving a series of payments instead of one isolated transaction, but the principle is the same.

3·4. Problems involving an unknown rate of interest

In such cases the principal and its amount, or the future sum and its present value, are given, and it is required to find the rate of interest involved. In simple cases, such as Example 1 (*b*) of Chapter 2, it is possible by solving an equation of the type

$$S = Pe^{n\delta} = P(1+i)^n,$$

by algebraic or other means to find the rate of interest. In more complicated cases where series of payments are involved, this method of solution may not be possible. The general theory will be discussed later in this book, and for the present it is sufficient to say that the most generally adopted method of solving the equation $f(i)=k$ is to evaluate $f(i)$ at two adjacent tabular rates of interest, and then to find the value of i which satisfies the given equation by inverse first difference interpolation.

3·5. Equation of value

The principle of the equation of value is best illustrated by an example:

In return for a promise to pay £500 at the end of 10 years, a man agrees to pay £100 now, £200 at the end of 6 years and a further sum at the end of 12 years. If interest is 3% per annum effective what should the final sum be?

The statement that interest is 3 % effective means that, if the payments under either transaction are valued at any time at 3 % effective, the two values must be the same.

If X be the final payment, the value of the series of payments at the present time is

$$100+200v^6+Xv^{12} \text{ at } 3\,\%.$$

The value of the payment due at the end of 10 years is $500v^{10}$, and the equation of value is therefore

$$100+200v^6+Xv^{12}=500v^{10},$$

whence
$$X=\frac{500v^{10}-200v^6-100}{v^{12}}$$

$$=£149 \text{ to the nearest } £1.$$

It would have been equally possible to consider the transaction at the end of 12 years. The accumulated value of the series of payments at that time is
$$100(1{\cdot}03)^{12}+200(1{\cdot}03)^6+X.$$

The accumulated value of £500, 2 years after it has been paid (i.e. in 12 years from now), is $500(1{\cdot}03)^2$, and in this case the equation of value is

$$100(1{\cdot}03)^{12}+200(1{\cdot}03)^6+X=500(1{\cdot}03)^2,$$

whence
$$X=500(1{\cdot}03)^2-100(1{\cdot}03)^{12}-200(1{\cdot}03)^6$$

$$=£149 \text{ to the nearest } £1.$$

The fundamental principle is that, at the rate of interest involved in any given transaction, the value at any time of all the payments which one party to the transaction must make, and the value, at the same time, of all the payments he will receive, must be equal. Any such problem may therefore be reduced to an expression of the type

$$\sum_1^n K_t(1+i)^t=X,$$

where it is required either to find X given the values of K_t and i, or to find i given the values of K_t and X.

3·6. General principles

Certain general principles may be stated under the following categories, and their intelligent application will materially lighten the labour of solving compound interest problems. They all concern the form which the equation of value may take.

(*a*) *Choice of time at which the equation of value is made*

In the example above it was immaterial whether the equation of value was written as

$$100+200v^6+Xv^{12}=500v^{10}$$

or as $$100(1\cdot03)^{12}+200(1\cdot03)^6+X=500(1\cdot03)^2,$$

but by choosing the second form the arithmetical work was reduced, since X was found directly without the necessity of dividing by v^{12}. It is therefore important to try to draw up the equation of value at the particular time which gives the required result in the simplest form. This ability can come only with practice, but there is considerable scope for ingenuity in cutting down arithmetical work in this way.

(*b*) *Choice of time interval in the equation of value*

In the example above there was no choice. The given rate was an effective one and it was natural to work in terms of years. But suppose interest had been at the rate of 3 % per annum convertible half-yearly, two courses would have been open. If i is the effective rate per annum corresponding to 3 % per annum convertible half-yearly then

$$1+i=(1\cdot015)^2,$$

or $$i=\cdot030225.$$

Hence the equation of value could be written in the form

$$X=500(1\cdot030225)^2-100(1\cdot030225)^{12}-200(1\cdot030225)^6.$$

This, however, would be a clumsy process, as the values of the powers of (1·030225) would have to be found by logarithms instead of direct from an interest table. In this case, therefore, the interval of a year is not a convenient one.

But a nominal rate of 3 % convertible half-yearly is the same as an effective rate of $1\frac{1}{2}$ % per half-year, and if therefore the interval is taken as half a year the equation can be written as

$$X = 500(1{\cdot}015)^4 - 100(1{\cdot}015)^{24} - 200(1{\cdot}015)^{12}$$
$$= 148{\cdot}61.$$

By this method the work is shortened, since the values of powers of (1·015) are available in interest tables. It will also be noted that it would not be accurate enough to convert the nominal rate to a corresponding effective rate approximately and to use the approximation (in this case ·03) as an effective rate. The solution lies in the choice of a time interval which will make tabular values available.

(*c*) *Choice of interest function on which to operate*

The choice of the time interval will generally result in the problem becoming one involving an effective rate of interest for the time interval chosen. In numerical work it will generally be best to use expressions of the form $(1+i)^n$, but in analytical work and in exploration of the general theory it is often convenient to use expressions of the form $e^{n\delta}$ for the amount of 1 after n intervals of time, and this device should not be overlooked in dealing with such questions.

3·7. Further points

Two further points may be mentioned. First, it must always be remembered that as soon as any transaction is completed, the rate of interest for that period is determined absolutely, and nothing that happens thereafter can affect the rate of interest in the period being considered. Thus in Example 2 of Chapter 2 the effective rate charged by the moneylender was found by considering the effect of the transaction for a period of one month. The effective rate *per month* so found was then expressed as an effective rate *per annum*, and it should be realized that this rate merely expresses what the result in one year would be, if the conditions that prevailed for the period of one month continued unaltered for the balance of the year. The actual amount of interest which the moneylender will receive in a year on each unit invested will be the same as the effective rate of interest per annum found in the solution of

Example 2 of Chapter 2, only if he is able to reinvest his money on the same terms at the end of each month for the balance of the year. In the example this is true, and it is therefore immaterial whether the transaction is considered as extending over one month or several. The solution in this case was most readily found by considering only one month, and a similar device can often be used with advantage in more complicated questions (for example, in a type of problem which will be discussed in Chapter 6).

The remaining point, which may cause some trouble, is that every interest transaction can be considered from two points of view. For example, consider the question: 'In return for an immediate payment of £100, what sum can be paid at the end of each of the next 10 years assuming an effective rate of interest of $2\frac{1}{2}\%$ per annum?'

Let the sum be X.

Then the present value of all the future payments is

$$Xv + Xv^2 + \dots + Xv^{10} = Xv\frac{1-v^{10}}{1-v}$$

$$= X\frac{1-v^{10}}{i}.$$

The present value of the sum paid in return for these payments is of course 100, and the equation of value at $2\frac{1}{2}\%$ is therefore

$$X\left[\frac{1-v^{10}}{i}\right] = 100$$

$$\therefore\ X = \frac{2\cdot5}{\cdot2188}$$

$$= 11\cdot43.$$

This transaction could be viewed as the purchase of ten payments of £11·43, at successive yearly intervals, for a purchase price of £100. Equally, however, it could be said that if a man borrows £100 the payments to be made each year to liquidate the debt in ten years would be £11·43. The first method considers the transaction from the purchaser's point of view. He is of course mainly concerned with the sums which he is to receive in return for his capital. The second method considers the transaction as a loan, and looks at it from the borrower's point of view. He is mainly concerned with the payments he will have to make to repay the amount borrowed. In the course of this book, transactions will be considered sometimes from the one side and sometimes from the other, but it must be realized that the basic problem is the same in either case.

3·8. The following examples illustrate the principles discussed in this chapter:

Example 3·1

A is under an obligation to pay *B* £50 in three months and £100 in nine months. *B* offers instead to accept either (*a*) an immediate payment of £146·60 or (*b*) four payments of £37·20, the first due now and the others at intervals of three months.

Which offer should *A* accept?

Under method (*a*) if the rate of interest is i per quarter the equation of value is

$$146{\cdot}6 = 50(1+i)^{-1} + 100(1+i)^{-3},$$

or

$$146{\cdot}6(1+i)^3 - 50(1+i)^2 - 100 = 0.$$

As a first approximation, neglecting terms involving i^2 and i^3,

$$146{\cdot}6(1+3i) - 50(1+2i) - 100 = 0,$$

whence

$$i = \frac{3{\cdot}4}{339{\cdot}8}$$

$$= {\cdot}01 \quad \text{very nearly.}$$

At 1%

$$\begin{aligned} 50v &= 49{\cdot}505, \\ 100v^3 &= 97{\cdot}059 \\ & \overline{146{\cdot}564}, \end{aligned}$$

hence for practical purposes the rate of interest involved in method (*a*) is 1% per quarter.

Under method (*b*) the equation of value is

$$37{\cdot}2 + 37{\cdot}2v + 37{\cdot}2v^2 + 37{\cdot}2v^3 = 50v + 100v^3.$$

Now at 1% per quarter the left-hand side is

$$37{\cdot}2\frac{(1-v^4)}{1-v} = 37{\cdot}2 \times \frac{{\cdot}03902}{{\cdot}0099}$$

$$= 146{\cdot}621,$$

and the right-hand side is 146·564.

Hence the present values of the alternative offers made by B are

(a) 146·600,

(b) 146·621.

For all practical purposes, therefore, there is nothing to choose between method (a) and method (b), both of which involve a rate of interest of 4% per annum convertible quarterly.

Example 3·2

The shareholders of an industrial company receive fixed dividends at the rate of 3% per annum payable on 30 June and 31 December in each year. An additional dividend, depending on profits earned, is paid yearly on 31 December. What rate of interest is earned by an investor who purchases one £100 share for £95 on 1 January, assuming the additional dividends to be at the rate of 1% per annum?

This is an example of a Stock Exchange transaction, and it is important to define what the terms mean. The description of a share as being a '£100 share' is only a statement of the nominal value of the share, and its purpose is to fix the nominal amount of capital on which dividends are calculated. The holder of such a share is in fact entitled to a series of payments, the amount of which depends on the nominal value of his share. The real value of the share is the present value of these payments at an appropriate rate of interest.

In the present example let i be the rate of interest earned per half-year. The present value of all future payments for a £100 share is

$$1{\cdot}5\,(v+v^2+\ldots)+1\,(v^2+v^4+v^6+\ldots)=1{\cdot}5\frac{v}{1-v}+\frac{v^2}{1-v^2},$$

and the present value of the sum paid for this series is, of course, 95.

$$\therefore\ 95=\frac{1{\cdot}5}{i}+\frac{1}{i^2+2i},$$

whence $$190i^2+377i-8=0,$$

and $i=\cdot021$, approximately, on solving the equation.

This method of solution took the equation of value at the present time. It would, however, be equally possible to consider the transaction on the basis of one year's operation, and to write down the equation of value after one year. The accumulation of the price 95 to the end of the year is $95\,(1+i)^2$. The accumulation of the payments received is

$$1{\cdot}5\{(1+i)+1\}+1,$$

and if the same rate of interest is to be earned in future the share is still worth £95, so the amount invested is intact. Hence

$$95 + 1\cdot 5\{(1+i)+1\}+1 = 95(1+i)^2,$$

whence

$$95i^2 + 188\cdot 5i - 4 = 0,$$

which is, of course, the same equation as before.

The yield is therefore 4·2% per annum convertible half-yearly.

This example illustrates the point made in § 3·7 above.

Example 3·3

The sums $s_1, s_2, \ldots, s_t$ are due to be paid at the end of $n_1, n_2, \ldots, n_t$ years respectively. It is proposed to replace this series by a single sum of $(s_1+s_2+\ldots+s_t)$ at the end of n years. If the rate of interest involved is i per annum show how to determine n.

The equation of value is

$$(s_1+s_2+\ldots+s_t)\,v^n = s_1 v^{n_1} + s_2 v^{n_2} + \ldots + s_t v^{n_t}.$$

$$\therefore\ v^n = \frac{s_1 v^{n_1} + s_2 v^{n_2} + \ldots + s_t v^{n_t}}{s_1+s_2+\ldots+s_t},$$

hence

$$n = \frac{\log(s_1 v^{n_1} + s_2 v^{n_2} + \ldots + s_t v^{n_t}) - \log(s_1+s_2+\ldots+s_t)}{\log v},$$

the value of n can thus be obtained by the use of interest tables.

It is possible, however, to obtain an approximate expression for n without the use of interest tables as follows:

The equation of value may be written

$$(s_1+s_2+\ldots+s_t)\,e^{-n\delta} = s_1 e^{-n_1\delta} + s_2 e^{-n_2\delta} + \ldots + s_t e^{-n_t\delta},$$

i.e.

$$\begin{aligned}(s_1+s_2+\ldots+s_t)\left(1-n\delta+\frac{n^2\delta^2}{2}-\ldots\right) = {} & s_1\left(1-n_1\delta+\frac{n_1^2\delta^2}{2}-\ldots\right)\\ & +s_2\left(1-n_2\delta+\frac{n_2^2\delta^2}{2}-\ldots\right)\\ & +\ldots\\ & +s_t\left(1-n_t\delta+\frac{n_t^2\delta^2}{2}-\ldots\right).\end{aligned}$$

Writing Σs for $s_1+s_2+\ldots+s_t$,

$\Sigma(ns)$ for $n_1 s_1 + n_2 s_2 + \ldots + n_t s_t$

and $\Sigma(n^2 s)$ for $n_1^2 s_1 + n_2^2 s_2 + \ldots + n_t^2 s_t$, and ignoring powers of δ above δ^2, the equation becomes

$$\Sigma s - n\delta\Sigma s + \frac{n^2\delta^2}{2}\Sigma s = \Sigma s - \delta\Sigma(ns) + \frac{\delta^2}{2}\Sigma(n^2 s).$$

$$\therefore\ n\Sigma s = \Sigma(ns) - \frac{\delta}{2}[\Sigma(n^2 s) - n^2\Sigma s],$$

i.e.

$$n = \frac{\Sigma(ns)}{\Sigma s} - \frac{\delta}{2}\left[\frac{\Sigma(n^2 s)}{\Sigma s} - n^2\right],$$

as a first approximation,

$$n = \frac{\Sigma(ns)}{\Sigma s},$$

and by substituting this value for n in the square bracket we get as a second approximation

$$n = \frac{\Sigma(ns)}{\Sigma s} - \frac{\delta}{2}\left[\frac{\Sigma(n^2 s)}{\Sigma s} - \left(\frac{\Sigma(ns)}{\Sigma s}\right)^2\right].$$

The period n is defined as the 'equated time' of the individual sums and the first approximation above expresses the common rule for finding the equated time of payment: 'Multiply each amount by the number of years to elapse before it falls due and divide the total by the sum of the amounts to be paid.'

The value of n found in this way may be shown to be too great, and the common rule is therefore to the debtor's advantage, since the aggregate sum he pays is paid later than is strictly correct. The following proof that this is so is taken from *J.I.A.* vol. 33.

Let there be s_1 quantities each equal to v^{n_1}, s_2 quantities each equal to v^{n_2} and so on.

The arithmetic mean of these quantities is

$$\frac{\sum_1^t s_t v^{n_t}}{\sum_1^t s_t}.$$

The geometric mean is

$$v^{\sum_1^t n_r s_r / \sum_1^t s_r}.$$

The arithmetic mean is greater than the geometric mean and hence

$$\frac{\sum_1^t s_t v^{n_t}}{\sum_1^t s_t} > v^{\sum_1^t n_t s_t \big/ \sum_1^t s_t},$$

or

$$\sum_1^t s_t v^{n_t} > \left(\sum_1^t s_t\right) v^n,$$

where n is the equated time found by the rule above. Hence the true present value of the sums is greater than the present value of the total sum paid at the equated time found by the rule, which is equivalent to saying that the equated time so found must be greater than the true equated time, or that the rule favours the debtor.

Example 3·4

A banker is offered bills for £100 due in 2 months, £200 due in 3 months, and £500 due in 8 months, or alternatively one bill for £800 due in 6 months. The same rate of commercial discount is to apply in each case. Which offer should he accept?

The sum the banker will give for the three bills is

$$100(1-\tfrac{1}{6}f)+200(1-\tfrac{1}{4}f)+500(1-\tfrac{2}{3}f),$$

where f is the rate of commercial discount

$$=800(1-\tfrac{1}{2}f).$$

The sum the banker will give for the 6 months bill is $800(1-\frac{1}{2}f)$; therefore the same cash payment will secure either offer. It is therefore a question whether the three bills are worth more or less than the one bill. The value of the three bills, at an effective rate i per month, is

$$100v^2+200v^3+500v^8,$$

and according as this is greater or less than $800v^6$ it will be to the banker's advantage to accept the offer of the three bills or the offer of the one bill.

Now
$$\begin{aligned}&100v^2+200v^3+500v^8\\ &=100(1+i)^{-8}[(1+i)^6+2(1+i)^5+5]\\ &>100(1+i)^{-8}[(1+6i+15i^2)+(2+10i+20i^2)+5],\end{aligned}$$

since i must be positive

$$>100(1+i)^{-8}[8+16i+35i^2]$$

Now
$$800v^6 = 800(1+i)^{-8}(1+i)^2$$
$$= 800(1+i)^{-8}(1+2i+i^2)$$
$$< 800(1+i)^{-8}(1+2i+\tfrac{35}{8}i^2).$$
$$\therefore\ 100v^2 + 200v^3 + 500v^8 > 800v^6,$$

and hence the offer of the three bills should be accepted.

It will be noted that the 'equated time' of the three bills found by the common rule is

$$\frac{(100\times 2)+(200\times 3)+(500\times 8)}{100+200+500} = 6 \text{ months},$$

and, as has been shown in Example 3, this favours the borrower which confirms the result just proved.

CHAPTER 4

THE VALUATION OF ANNUITIES-CERTAIN

4·1. As was mentioned in Chapter 3 much of the practical application of the theory of compound interest is devoted to the valuation of series of payments. It is therefore desirable to consider this problem in more detail and, if possible, to deduce expressions which will facilitate the work.

4·2. Annuities

In general an annuity is a series of payments at fixed intervals of time continuing during the existence of a given status—for example, during the lifetime of a given person, or to a widow so long as she has children under the age of 21, or, more simply, for a fixed period of years, independent of any other contingency. Annuities payable for a fixed period of years are called 'annuities-certain', and it is with them that the theory of compound interest is concerned. The payments may be uniform or they may vary. They may be made yearly or more frequently than yearly, but generally the amount of the payment is expressed as so much per annum, and this amount is called the annual rent of the annuity. Thus an annuity of £40 per annum payable half-yearly for 20 years certain denotes a series of payments of £20 each made at 6-monthly intervals for 40 half-years. The annual rent is £40, but this merely fixes the total amount paid in the year, irrespective of how often it is paid (cf. a nominal rate of interest).

4·3. Symbols

The general symbol for the *present value* of a uniform annuity is a. The addition of a suffix denotes the status during which it is to be paid, thus:

a_x denotes the present value of an annuity of 1 per annum payable yearly during the lifetime of a life aged (x) years, the first payment being made one year from now, and

$a_{\overline{n}|}$ denotes the present value of an annuity of 1 per annum—payable for a term certain of n years—the symbol $\urcorner$ being used to denote a fixed period of time. Such an annuity is called an 'immediate' annuity.

The frequency with which payments are made is denoted by the addition of a further suffix thus:

$a_{\overline{n}|}^{(p)}$ denotes the present value of an annuity of 1 per annum payable p times per annum for n years certain. If the annuity is payable continuously, i.e. if it is assumed to be payable momently by infinitely small instalments, the special symbol $\bar{a}_{\overline{n}|}$ is used in place of $a_{\overline{n}|}^{(\infty)}$. If the first payment of the annuity is not to be made at the end of the first $1/p$th of a year but is to be deferred for say (m) years from the present time the annuity is called a 'deferred' annuity, to distinguish it from an immediate annuity, and the symbol used is ${}_{m|}a_{\overline{n}|}^{(p)}$. If the first payment is to be made at once, instead of at the end of the first $1/p$th of a year, the annuity is called an 'annuity-due' and the symbol used is $\ddot{a}_{\overline{n}|}^{(p)}$.*

These expressions are merely a convenient shorthand way of expressing certain series, as follows:

$$a_{\overline{n}|}^{(p)} = \frac{1}{p}v^{1/p} + \frac{1}{p}v^{2/p} + \dots + \frac{1}{p}v^{n},$$

$$_{m|}a_{\overline{n}|}^{(p)} = \frac{1}{p}v^{m+1/p} + \frac{1}{p}v^{m+2/p} + \dots + \frac{1}{p}v^{m+n},$$

$$\bar{a}_{\overline{n}|} = \int_0^n v^t\,dt,$$

$$\ddot{a}_{\overline{n}|}^{(p)} = \frac{1}{p} + \frac{1}{p}v^{1/p} + \dots + \frac{1}{p}v^{n-1/p}.$$

Instead of considering the value at the present time it might be desired to consider the *amount* to which all the payments would accumulate at a given rate of interest. The general symbol for this

* In older actuarial literature the symbol $\mathrm{a}_{\overline{n}|}^{(p)}$ is used with the same meaning.

is s, and the same process of adding suffixes may be followed so that

$$s_{\overline{n}|}^{(p)} = \frac{1}{p}(1+i)^{n-1/p} + \frac{1}{p}(1+i)^{n-2/p} + \dots + \frac{1}{p},$$

$$\bar{s}_{\overline{n}|} = \int_0^n (1+i)^t \, dt,$$

$$\ddot{s}_{\overline{n}|}^{(p)} = \frac{1}{p}(1+i)^n + \frac{1}{p}(1+i)^{n-1/p} + \dots + \frac{1}{p}(1+i)^{1/p}.$$

4·4. Elementary relationships

It should be clear that an immediate annuity represents a series of payments made at the *end* of stated intervals of time, whereas an annuity-due represents the same series of payments, the payments, however, being made at the *start* of each stated interval. The relationship between the present value of an immediate annuity payable for n years and an annuity-due payable for n years is, therefore, the same as the relationship between the present value of a payment of 1 due at the end of one year and of a payment of 1 due at once, i.e.

$$a_{\overline{n}|} = v\ddot{a}_{\overline{n}|},$$

or, by transposition,

$$\ddot{a}_{\overline{n}|} = (1+i)\,a_{\overline{n}|}.$$

A similar argument may be applied to the respective amounts of these annuities, from which it follows that

$$\ddot{s}_{\overline{n}|} = (1+i)\,s_{\overline{n}|}.$$

From another point of view the series represented by the present value of an annuity-due of 1 per annum for n years is the same as the series represented by a payment of 1 at once followed by an immediate annuity for $(n-1)$ years, i.e.

$$\ddot{a}_{\overline{n}|} = 1 + a_{\overline{n-1}|},$$

and similarly

$$\ddot{s}_{\overline{n}|} = s_{\overline{n+1}|} - 1.$$

It is also apparent that since $a_{\overline{n}|}$ represents the present value of n payments of 1 per period and $s_{\overline{n}|}$ represents the accumulation of the same series of payments for n periods, $a_{\overline{n}|}$ and $s_{\overline{n}|}$ must be connected by the same relationship as holds good for a single sum of money and its amount after a stated period at compound interest, i.e.

$$a_{\overline{n}|} = v^n s_{\overline{n}|}$$

or

$$s_{\overline{n}|} = (1+i)^n\,a_{\overline{n}|}.$$

The value of an annuity-certain for n years deferred m years may be considered either as the present value of the single sum which represents the value of the annuity at the moment it is entered upon, i.e. in m years from the present, or as the difference between the present value of an annuity-certain for $(m+n)$ years less the present value of the payments in the first (m) years which are not received, i.e.

$$_{m|}a_{\overline{n|}} = v^m a_{\overline{n|}}$$
$$= a_{\overline{m+n|}} - a_{\overline{m|}}.$$

All these relationships may be deduced algebraically from the series in §4·3, and corresponding relationships hold for annuities payable p times a year as follows:

$$a_{\overline{n|}}^{(p)} = v^{1/p}\ddot{a}_{\overline{n|}}^{(p)},$$

or

$$\ddot{a}_{\overline{n|}}^{(p)} = (1+i)^{1/p}\, a_{\overline{n|}}^{(p)} = \frac{1}{p} + a_{\overline{n-1/p|}}^{(p)},$$

$$\ddot{s}_{\overline{n|}}^{(p)} = (1+i)^{1/p}\, s_{\overline{n|}}^{(p)} = s_{\overline{n+1/p|}}^{(p)} - \frac{1}{p},$$

$$a_{\overline{n|}}^{(p)} = v^n s_{\overline{n|}}^{(p)},$$

or

$$s_{\overline{n|}}^{(p)} = (1+i)^n\, a_{\overline{n|}}^{(p)},$$

$$_{m|}a_{\overline{n|}}^{(p)} = v^m a_{\overline{n|}}^{(p)} = a_{\overline{m+n|}}^{(p)} - a_{\overline{m|}}^{(p)}.$$

4·5. Present values of annuities

Consider first the simplest case of the value at an effective rate of interest of an immediate annuity payable yearly for n years certain. The present value of the first payment is v, of the next v^2 and so on. Hence as above

$$a_{\overline{n|}} = v + v^2 + \ldots + v^n$$
$$= \frac{v(1-v^n)}{1-v}$$
$$= \frac{v(1-v^n)}{iv}$$
$$= \frac{1-v^n}{i}. \qquad (4·1)$$

This could readily be evaluated from interest tables in which v^n is tabulated but, as the values of $a_{\overline{n|}}$ are constantly required in the solution of problems involving compound interest, it is customary to tabulate values of $a_{\overline{n}|}$ at common rates of interest for the terms likely to arise in practice.

4·6. If the annuity is payable p times a year instead of yearly its present value becomes

$$a_{\overline{n}|}^{(p)} = \frac{1}{p}v^{1/p} + \frac{1}{p}v^{2/p} + \dots + \frac{1}{p}v^n$$

$$= \frac{1}{p}v^{1/p}\frac{1-v^n}{1-v^{1/p}}.$$

$$= \frac{1-v^n}{p\{(1+i)^{1/p}-1\}}. \qquad (4{\cdot}2)$$

This, however, is not a particularly convenient form, since values of $(1+i)^{1/p}$ may not readily be available, and it is hardly worth while to produce the number of tables which would be required in practice to cover all possible combinations of p, n and i. The reason that this result is somewhat unwieldy is that the time interval for the interest is a year, and for the annuity payment is $(1/p)$th of a year. As the two do not coincide it is difficult to apply the principles of Chapter 3 and to choose the most suitable time interval. This difficulty would vanish if the annuity payments were made to coincide with the intervals by which the interest is reckoned, i.e. if, instead of valuing a series of $1/p$ at intervals of $1/p$ of a year, the value was found of the payment which, if made at the end of each year, would have the same value as the payments of $1/p$ during the year accumulated to that time. This payment may be found algebraically, or by general reasoning as follows:

The accumulated amounts paid during the year are

$$\frac{1}{p}\{(1+i)^{1-1/p} + (1+i)^{1-2/p} + \dots + 1\}$$

$$= \frac{1}{p}\left\{\frac{(1+i)-1}{(1+i)^{1/p}-1}\right\}$$

$$= \frac{i}{p\{(1+i)^{1/p}-1\}}$$

$$= \frac{i}{i^{(p)}}.$$

Alternatively, if a unit be invested at rate i it is immaterial whether i is paid at the end of the year, or $i^{(p)}/p$ at $p$thly intervals during the year. Hence as the series of payments of $i^{(p)}/p$ during the year is equivalent to a payment of i at the end of the year, the equivalent payment at the end of the year to a series of payments of $1/p$ during the year is, by proportion, $i/i^{(p)}$. The annuity therefore is equivalent to one of $i/i^{(p)}$ at the end of each year for n years certain, and its value is therefore

$$a^{(p)}_{\overline{n}|} = \frac{i}{i^{(p)}} a_{\overline{n}|}. \tag{4·3}$$

This is a more convenient form since $a_{\overline{n}|}$ is available from interest tables, and as $i/i^{(p)}$ does not involve the variable n, tables can readily be constructed for its value for the common values of i and p. In the special case when $p \to \infty$

$$\bar{a}_{\overline{n}|} = \int_0^n v^t\,dt = \frac{v^n - 1}{\log_e v} = \frac{1 - v^n}{\delta},$$

or in the alternative form

$$\bar{a}_{\overline{n}|} = \frac{i}{\delta} a_{\overline{n}|}. \tag{4·4}$$

This principle of making the time intervals for the annuity payments and the interest coincide is of great practical importance, for, although other formulae can easily be deduced algebraically, the resulting expressions are generally not in a form which enables tabular values from interest tables to be used in their evaluation. They are therefore usually more cumbersome to apply arithmetically.

4·7. The principle of choosing a form which involves tabular values is further exemplified in the consideration of the annuity-due. It is true that

$$\ddot{a}^{(p)}_{\overline{n}|} = \frac{1}{p} + a^{(p)}_{\overline{n-1/p}|},$$

but except when $p = 1$ and the formula gives $\ddot{a}_{\overline{n}|} = 1 + a_{\overline{n-1}|}$, this form is inconvenient, as the value of $a^{(p)}_{\overline{n-1/p}|}$ cannot readily be found from interest tables. It is therefore better to proceed on the line of substituting an equivalent payment made at the end of the year for the series of payments during the year. By the same argument as before, a series of payments of $d^{(p)}/p$ payable in advance during a year has the same value at the end of the year as a payment of i

made then. Hence, by proportion, the equivalent payment at the end of a year, to a series of payments of $1/p$ payable in advance during the year is $i/d^{(p)}$ and the value of the series represented by $\ddot{a}_{\overline{n|}}^{(p)}$ is identical with the value of a series of payments of $i/d^{(p)}$ in arrear for n years. Hence

$$\ddot{a}_{\overline{n|}}^{(p)} = \frac{i}{d^{(p)}} a_{\overline{n|}}, \tag{4·5}$$

and if tables of the values of $i/d^{(p)}$ are constructed on the same lines as tables of $i/i^{(p)}$ the evaluation of $\ddot{a}_{\overline{n|}}^{(p)}$ is much simplified.

Even if tables of $i/d^{(p)}$ are not available it is still possible to deduce a more convenient form than $1/p + a_{\overline{n-1/p|}}^{(p)}$, since

$$\begin{aligned}\ddot{a}_{\overline{n|}}^{(p)} &= (1+i)^{1/p} a_{\overline{n|}}^{(p)} \\ &= \left(1 + \frac{i^{(p)}}{p}\right)\left(\frac{i}{i^{(p)}}\right) a_{\overline{n|}} \\ &= \left(\frac{i}{i^{(p)}} + \frac{i}{p}\right) a_{\overline{n|}}.\end{aligned}$$

If tables of $i/i^{(p)}$ are available it is therefore not strictly necessary to have tables of $i/d^{(p)}$ as well.

4·8. Accumulations of the annuity

By a similar process expressions for the amount of an annuity may be deduced as follows:

$$\begin{aligned}s_{\overline{n|}} &= (1+i)^{n-1} + (1+i)^{n-2} + \dots + 1 \\ &= \frac{(1+i)^n - 1}{i}.\end{aligned} \tag{4·6}$$

Similarly

$$s_{\overline{n|}}^{(p)} = \frac{(1+i)^n - 1}{p[(1+i)^{1/p} - 1]} = \frac{i}{i^{(p)}} s_{\overline{n|}}, \tag{4·7}$$

and

$$\ddot{s}_{\overline{n|}}^{(p)} = \frac{i}{d^{(p)}} s_{\overline{n|}} = \left(\frac{i}{i^{(p)}} + \frac{i}{p}\right) s_{\overline{n|}}, \tag{4·8}$$

the appropriate form being used according as tables of $i/d^{(p)}$ are or are not available.

4·9. Nominal rates of interest

By following the principles already set out, little difficulty should be found in evaluating annuities at a given nominal rate of interest. It is necessary only to consider the values of $a_{\overline{n|}}^{(p)}$, as the values of other functions are readily deduced from it. If it is desired to evaluate $a_{\overline{n}|}^{(p)}$ at a nominal rate of interest $i^{(m)}$ per annum, four cases must be distinguished:

(*a*) the case where $m=p$,

(*b*) the case where $m>p$ and m/p is an integer,

(*c*) the case where $m<p$ and p/m is an integer,

(*d*) the case where m/p or p/m is not integral.

4·10. Annuity payable with same frequency as interest convertible ($m=p$)

This is the simplest case. Since $m=p$ the problem becomes one of evaluating a series of payments of $1/p$ per period for n years at an effective rate per period of $i^{(p)}/p$, i.e. of evaluating an annuity of $1/p$ per period for np periods at an effective rate $i^{(p)}/p$ per period. Hence under these conditions

$$a_{\overline{n}|}^{(p)}=\frac{1}{p}a_{\overline{np}|} \quad \text{at rate} \quad \frac{i^{(p)}}{p}.$$

4·11. Annuity payable less frequently than interest is convertible ($m>p$)

The effective rate of interest per period is $i^{(m)}/m$, but the annuity instalments do not fall due at the end of each period. The case which will be considered in this section is the simplest one, namely, where m/p is integral and equal to, say, K. In accordance with the general principles of §4·6 it is desirable to replace the given series of payments with a series which will correspond with the intervals in which the interest is convertible.

If X be the instalment payable at the end of each $(1/m)$th of a year, such that the value of the K payments of X accumulated to the end of each $(1/p)$th of a year is equal to $1/p$, then

$$X\left\{\left(1+\frac{i^{(m)}}{m}\right)^{K-1}+\left(1+\frac{i^{(m)}}{m}\right)^{K-2}+\ldots+1\right\}=\frac{1}{p}$$

or

$$X=\frac{1}{p}\frac{1}{s_{\overline{K}|}} \quad \text{at rate} \quad \frac{i^{(m)}}{m}.$$

Hence the series of payments to be valued is equivalent to a series of payments of $\frac{1}{p}\frac{1}{s_{\overline{K}|}}$ made at the end of each $1/m$th of a year, and the value by § 4·10 is therefore

$$\frac{1}{p}\frac{a_{\overline{mn}|}}{s_{\overline{K}|}} \quad \text{at rate} \quad \frac{i^{(m)}}{m}.$$

4·12. Annuity payable more frequently than interest is convertible ($m<p$)

This is merely a general case of the annuity $a_{\overline{n}|}^{(p)}$ at an effective rate of interest. The obvious time interval is $(1/m)$th of a year, and the effective rate for that period is $i^{(m)}/m$ or say i'. The annuity will be payable p/m times in that interval, or say K times where $K=p/m$. The annuity therefore becomes one of $1/m$ per period for mn periods payable K times per period, and the value by § 4·6 is therefore

$$\frac{1}{m}\frac{i'}{i'^{(K)}}a_{\overline{mn}|} \quad \text{at rate} \quad i'\left(=\frac{i^{(m)}}{m}\right).$$

4·13. Annuity payable with a frequency which does not correspond in any way with the frequency of interest conversion

This case is not often met with in practice, and it can best be dealt with from first principles.

If the corresponding effective rate of interest per annum were i, where $(1+i)=\left(1+\frac{i^{(m)}}{m}\right)^m$, the value of the annuity would be $a_{\overline{n}|}^{(p)}$ at rate i, or $\frac{1-v^n}{p[(1+i)^{1/p}-1]}$. Hence substituting the above value for $(1+i)$

$$a_{\overline{n}|}^{(p)}=\frac{1-\left(1+\frac{i^{(m)}}{m}\right)^{-mn}}{p\left[\left(1+\frac{i^{(m)}}{m}\right)^{m/p}-1\right]},$$

which would probably best be evaluated by logarithmic means.

4·14. Applications to the accumulation of the annuity

Although the formulae of §§4·11–4·13 have been derived for present values only, exactly similar considerations apply to the accumulation of the annuity, and if the same principles are followed, there should be no difficulty in deriving corresponding expressions for amounts of annuities under the same conditions.

4·15. Perpetuities

An annuity of which the payments are to continue for ever is called a perpetuity. The expressions 'immediate perpetuity', 'perpetuity-due', 'deferred perpetuity', and 'continuous perpetuity' are used with the same meanings as for the corresponding descriptions of annuities.

For example, if a loan is floated on the Stock Exchange it may be:

(*a*) redeemable at the end of a stated term of years,
(*b*) redeemable at the end of a stated term of years at the option of the borrower,
or (*c*) not redeemable at all.

In (*a*) the interest payments form an annuity-certain. In (*b*) the term of the loan is not known and the interest payments may form either an annuity-certain or a perpetuity. In (*c*) the payments will continue indefinitely and therefore form a perpetuity.

The value of such a series of payments is readily found. Since an investment of 1 at rate i will produce a series of payments of i per annum payable so long as the unit is invested, the value of a perpetuity of i per annum is 1. Hence, by proportion, the value at rate i of a perpetuity of 1 per annum is $1/i$. Alternatively, as $a_{\overline{n}|} = \frac{1 - v^n}{i}$ the value of the perpetuity is

$$\lim_{n \to \infty} a_{\overline{n}|} = \lim_{n \to \infty} \frac{1 - v^n}{i} = \frac{1}{i} \quad (\text{since } v < 1).$$

The symbol used to denote the present value of an immediate perpetuity is a_{∞}.

4·16. Formulae by general reasoning

It is instructive to derive the formula $a_{\overline{n}|} = \frac{1 - v^n}{i}$ by general reasoning. If a unit be invested at rate i it will provide a series of payments of i per annum for any given time, say n years, and will remain intact at the end of that period. The present value of the sums it will produce is therefore:

(*a*) the value of an annuity of i per annum for n years, i.e. $ia_{\overline{n}|}$,
(*b*) the value of 1 due after n years, i.e. v^n.

$$\therefore\ 1 = ia_{\overline{n}|} + v^n \quad \text{or} \quad a_{\overline{n}|} = \frac{1 - v^n}{i}.$$

The student will find it instructive to derive the formula for $s_{\overline{n}|}$ by similar reasoning.

4·17. Deferred annuities

The values of deferred annuities are readily found, since at the moment when the deferred annuity ${}_{m|}a^{(p)}_{\overline{n}|}$ becomes an immediate annuity its value is $a^{(p)}_{\overline{n}|}$ and it can be evaluated as before. The value at the present time is therefore $v^m a^{(p)}_{\overline{n}|}$. It should be noted that if v^m is calculated at the same rate of interest as $a^{(p)}_{\overline{n}|}$, this expression is the same as $a^{(p)}_{\overline{m+n}|} - a^{(p)}_{\overline{m}|}$ (as on general grounds it must be), and this is a far more convenient form for calculation, involving as it does a subtraction rather than a multiplication.

4·18. Fractional terms

It has been assumed that n is integral. This is not necessarily so, but it should be noted that strictly speaking formula (4·1) for $a_{\overline{n+K}|}$, where k is fractional does not truly represent the value of a series of payments of 1 per annum for n years plus a proportional payment of k after $n+k$ years. If it be assumed that $a_{\overline{n+K}|} = \frac{1 - v^{n+K}}{i}$, where k is fractional, then

$$\begin{aligned} a_{\overline{n+K}|} &= \frac{1 - v^n + v^n - v^{n+K}}{i} \\ &= a_{\overline{n}|} + v^{n+K}\left[\frac{(1+i)^K - 1}{i}\right], \end{aligned}$$

and the final payment, to make the formula true, would have to be $\frac{(1+i)^K-1}{i}$ instead of K. The difference numerically is of course small and in practice would not be of much account. The easiest method of dealing with a numerical example is probably

(a) to value the series of payments for the integral term by the appropriate formula,

(b) to value the remaining payments separately from first principles and add them to the value found in (a).

If this is done there should be no confusion about what payments have actually been valued.

4·19. Varying annuities

The simplest types of varying annuity can readily be valued algebraically. Consider an annuity whose payments begin at P per annum and increase in arithmetic progression with constant difference Q. If X is the value of the annuity then

$$X = Pv + (P+Q)v^2 + \ldots + (P + \overline{n-1}\,Q)v^n,$$

and

$$(1+i)X = P + (P+Q)v + \ldots + (P + \overline{n-1}\,Q)v^{n-1}.$$

$$\therefore\ iX = P + Qv + Qv^2 + \ldots + Qv^{n-1} - Pv^n - \overline{n-1}\,Qv^n$$

$$= P(1-v^n) + Q(v + v^2 + \ldots + v^n) - nQv^n.$$

$$\therefore\ X = P\frac{1-v^n}{i} + Q\frac{a_{\overline{n}|} - nv^n}{i}$$

$$= Pa_{\overline{n}|} + Q\frac{a_{\overline{n}|} - nv^n}{i}. \qquad (4·9)$$

If $P = Q = 1$ the annuity becomes an ordinary increasing annuity and the value is written $(Ia)_{\overline{n}|}$. Hence

$$(Ia)_{\overline{n}|} = a_{\overline{n}|} + \frac{a_{\overline{n}|} - nv^n}{i}$$

$$= \frac{1 - v^n + a_{\overline{n}|} - nv^n}{i}$$

$$= \frac{\ddot{a}_{\overline{n+1}|} - (n+1)v^n}{i} = \frac{\ddot{a}_{\overline{n}|} - nv^n}{i}. \qquad (4·10)$$

The amount of such an annuity is $(Is)_{\overline{n}|}$ and by a similar process it will be found that

$$(Is)_{\overline{n}|} = \frac{\ddot{s}_{\overline{n}|} - n}{i}$$

or

$$= \frac{s_{\overline{n+1}|} - (n+1)}{i},$$

the latter form being preferable for arithmetical work. If $P=n$ and $Q=-1$ the annuity is defined as a 'decreasing annuity' and the value is written $(Da)_{\overline{n}|}$. Hence

$$(Da)_{\overline{n}|} = na_{\overline{n}|} - \frac{a_{\overline{n}|} - nv^n}{i}$$

$$= \frac{n - nv^n - a_{\overline{n}|} + nv^n}{i}$$

$$= \frac{n - a_{\overline{n}|}}{i}. \qquad (4 \cdot 11)$$

If the annuity payments increase in geometric progression with common ratio $(1+K)$ the value of the annuity is

$$v + (1+K)\,v^2 + \ldots + (1+K)^{n-1} v^n$$

$$= v \left[\frac{1 - \left(\frac{1+K}{1+i}\right)^n}{1 - \left(\frac{1+K}{1+i}\right)} \right]$$

$$= \frac{1 - \left(\frac{1+K}{1+i}\right)^n}{i - K},$$

which may be evaluated either by logarithms or by interest tables, depending on the value of $1+K/1+i$.

4·20. Varying annuities—general formulae

More complicated types of varying annuity can be evaluated by methods similar to those of §4·19. By using the methods of the calculus, however, it is possible to deduce results in a more general form.

For example, if it be desired to find the present value at an effective rate of interest of i of the series of payments $u_1, u_2, \ldots, u_n$, and denoting this by the symbol $(va)_{\overline{n}|}$, then

$$\begin{aligned}(va)_{\overline{n}|} &= vu_1 + v^2u_2 + \ldots + v^n u_n \\ &= [v + v^2(1+\Delta) + \ldots + v^n(1+\Delta)^{n-1}]\, u_1 \\ &= \frac{v}{1 - v(1+\Delta)}[1 - v^n(1+\Delta)^n]\, u_1 \\ &= \frac{1}{i-\Delta}(u_1 - v^n u_{n+1}) \\ &= \frac{1}{i}\left[1 + \frac{\Delta}{i} + \frac{\Delta^2}{i^2} + \ldots\right][u_1 - v^n u_{n+1}] \\ &= \frac{u_1 - v^n u_{n+1}}{i} + \frac{\Delta u_1 - v^n \Delta u_{n+1}}{i^2} + \ldots.\end{aligned}$$

Provided that u_t is a function whose differences either diminish rapidly, or vanish after the first few orders, this general expression can readily be evaluated. For example, if u_t is constant and equal to 1, $(va)_{\overline{n}|}$ becomes $a_{\overline{n}|}$ and first and subsequent differences of u_t vanish. The expression then becomes $\frac{1-v^n}{i}$ as in formula (4·1).

Similarly, if $u_t = t$ for all values of t, $(va)_{\overline{n}|}$ becomes $(Ia)_{\overline{n}|}$ and the expression becomes

$$\begin{aligned}\frac{1-(n+1)v^n}{i} + \frac{1-v^n}{i^2} &= \frac{1-(n+1)v^n + a_{\overline{n}|}}{i} \\ &= \frac{\ddot{a}_{\overline{n}|} - nv^n}{i} \quad \text{as in formula (4·10).}\end{aligned}$$

Another method of approach is suggested by the relationship between successive differential coefficients of $a_{\overline{n}|}$. Since

$$a_{\overline{n}|} = v + v^2 + \ldots + v^n \quad \text{and} \quad v = (1+i)^{-1},$$

$$\frac{d}{di} a_{\overline{n}|} = -[v^2 + 2v^3 + \ldots + nv^{n+1}].$$

$$\begin{aligned}\therefore\quad -(1+i)\frac{d}{di} a_{\overline{n}|} &= v + 2v^2 + \ldots + nv^n \\ &= (Ia)_{\overline{n}|}.\end{aligned}$$

Differentiating once again

$$-\frac{d}{di}a_{\overline{n}|}-(1+i)\frac{d^2}{di^2}a_{\overline{n}|}=-[v^2+2^2v^3+3^2v^4+\ldots+n^2v^{n+1}].$$

$$\therefore\ (1+i)^2\frac{d^2}{di^2}a_{\overline{n}|}+(1+i)\frac{d}{di}a_{\overline{n}|}=v+2^2v^2+3^2v^3+\ldots+n^2v^n,$$

and by continuing the process it is clear that a series of expressions may be obtained for several varying annuities. A more general expression may be found as follows. If

$$\begin{aligned}(va)_{\overline{n}|}&=vu_1+v^2u_2+\ldots+v^nu_n\\&=vu_1+v^2(1+\Delta)u_1+\ldots+v^n(1+\Delta)^{n-1}u_1\\&=vu_1+v^2(1+\Delta)u_1+\ldots\\&\qquad+v^n\left[1+(n-1)\Delta+\frac{(n-1)(n-2)}{2!}\Delta^2+\ldots\right]u_1,\end{aligned}$$

the coefficient of $\Delta^t u_1$ will be

$$v^{t+1}+(t+1)v^{t+2}+\frac{(t+1)(t+2)}{1\cdot 2}v^{t+3}+\ldots+\frac{(n-1)!}{(n-t-1)!\,t!}v^n.$$

But $\dfrac{d^t}{di^t}a_{\overline{n-t}|}=(-1)^t\left[t!\,v^{t+1}+\dfrac{(t+1)!}{1!}v^{t+2}+\ldots+\dfrac{(n-1)!}{(n-t-1)!}v^n\right],$

and hence the expression $\dfrac{(-1)^t}{t!}\dfrac{d^t}{di^t}a_{\overline{n-t}|}$ may be substituted for the coefficient of $\Delta^t u_1$ in the expansion.

$$\begin{aligned}\therefore\ (va)_{\overline{n}|}&=a_{\overline{n}|}u_1-\frac{d}{di}a_{\overline{n-1}|}\Delta u_1+\ldots\\&\qquad+\frac{(-1)^t}{t!}\frac{d^t}{di^t}a_{\overline{n-t}|}\Delta^t u_1+\ldots+v^n\Delta^{n-1}u_1.\end{aligned}$$

If u_t is either a polynomial of low order in t, or if the successive differences of u_t are small, this expression will give useful results. Otherwise, as the results of successive differentiation of $a_{\overline{n}|}$ are increasingly complicated, it becomes too cumbersome for practical use.

The method in its first form is, however, of some use in expressing a general relationship between an ordinary and an increasing series of payments. For example, if

$$(va)_{\overline{n}|} = vu_1 + v^2u_2 + \ldots + v^nu_n$$

and
$$(Iva)_{\overline{n}|} = vu_1 + 2v^2u_2 + \ldots + nv^nu_n,$$

then
$$\frac{d}{di}(va)_{\overline{n}|} = -[v^2u_1 + 2v^3u_2 + \ldots + nv^{n+1}u_n]$$

or
$$-(1+i)\frac{d}{di}(va)_{\overline{n}|} = (Iva)_{\overline{n}|}.$$

If values of $(va)_{\overline{n}|}$ at different rates of interest are known the value of $\frac{d}{di}(va)_{\overline{n}|}$ can be found approximately from the relation

$$\frac{d}{di}(va)_{\overline{n}|} = \frac{1}{\Delta i}\left[\Delta (va)_{\overline{n}|} - \frac{\Delta^2}{2}(va)_{\overline{n}|} + \ldots\right].$$

This method is not of great importance in problems which involve only compound interest, but it can be of considerable practical use in assurance problems involving the calculation of the present value of a series of payments depending on the happening of some contingency.

4·21. Application of the calculus

The formulae which have been developed so far have been based in the main on the value at an effective rate of interest of a series of payments made at finite intervals of time. From a practical point of view this is the natural approach, but in considering the theory of this branch of compound interest it is perhaps easier, as was suggested in § 3·6, to consider the evaluation at a given force of interest of a series of payments assumed to be payable continuously. This method of approach will not produce expressions in the most convenient form for practical work, and the formulae so deduced should not be memorized, but it does remove certain theoretical difficulties (for example, the case discussed in § 4·18 dealing with fractional terms).

In the following analysis the only expressions considered are those for the present values of given series. Expressions for the amounts of these series can be deduced on exactly similar lines, and this is left the student as an exercise.

The continuous annuity-certain represents a series of infinitely small payments made at infinitely small intervals of time. If, therefore, the present value of a payment of 1 due at time t is $\phi(t)$, the present value of such an annuity-certain payable for a period of n years (i.e. $\bar{a}_{\overline{n}|}$) must equal $\int_0^n \phi(t)\,dt$. But $\phi(t)$ is known to be $e^{-t\delta}$, where δ is the force of interest at which the discounting operation is carried out and therefore

$$\begin{aligned}\bar{a}_{\overline{n}|} &= \int_0^n e^{-t\delta}\,dt \\ &= -\frac{1}{\delta}[e^{-t\delta}]_0^n \\ &= \frac{1-e^{-n\delta}}{\delta},\end{aligned}$$

and if $(1+i)$ is substituted for e^{δ} this expression may be written as $\frac{1-v^n}{\delta} = \frac{i}{\delta} a_{\overline{n}|}$, as in §4·6. It will be noted that in this approach there is no assumption, implicit or other, that n is an integer.

By similar reasoning if the annuity consists not of a level series of payments but a series of continuously increasing payments, its present value is $(\bar{I}\bar{a})_{\overline{n}|}$, and this is equal to $\int_0^n t\,e^{-t\delta}\,dt$.

$$\begin{aligned}\text{Hence}\qquad (\bar{I}\bar{a})_{\overline{n}|} &= \left[t\int e^{-t\delta}\,dt - \int\left(\int e^{-t\delta}\,dt\right)dt\right]_0^n \\ &= \left[-\frac{t}{\delta}e^{-t\delta} - \frac{1}{\delta^2}e^{-t\delta}\right]_0^n \\ &= \frac{-n\,e^{-n\delta}}{\delta} - \frac{e^{-n\delta}}{\delta^2} + \frac{1}{\delta^2} \\ &= \frac{1}{\delta}\left[\frac{1-e^{-n\delta}}{\delta} - n\,e^{-n\delta}\right] \\ &= \frac{1}{\delta}[\bar{a}_{\overline{n}|} - nv^n],\end{aligned}$$

and the similarity to formula (4·10) will be noted.

This method of approach is of great importance in considering problems involving varying rates of interest, and it will be considered more fully in Chapter 11.

4·22. In this chapter the main emphasis has been on methods of determining the present value or the amount of a given series of future payments. It must not, however, be overlooked that the question may easily arise in the converse form. For example, the present value might be stated and the question asked what future series of payments is equivalent value thereto. Thus if 1 be invested at rate i the uniform series of payments for n years whose present value is 1 is clearly $1/a_{\overline{n}|}$. This aspect of the transaction will be considered in more detail in Chapter 5.

4·23. The following examples illustrate the work done in this chapter.

Example 4·1

Find (*a*) at 3% per annum effective,

(*b*) at 4% per annum convertible quarterly,

(*c*) at $2\frac{1}{2}$% per annum convertible every 2 years,

the present values of the following annuities, and write down formulae in their most practical form for their amounts:

(i) £10 per annum payable yearly for 20 years,

(ii) £20 per annum payable quarterly for 10 years,

(iii) £100 per annum payable every three years for 18 years.

(*a*) *At 3% per annum effective*

(i) The value is clearly $10a_{\overline{20}|}$ at 3% = £148·77.

(ii) The value is clearly $20a^{(4)}_{\overline{10}|}$ at 3%

$$= 20\frac{i}{i^{(4)}}a_{\overline{10}|}$$

$$= 20 \times 1{\cdot}01118 \times 8{\cdot}5302$$

$$= £172{\cdot}51.$$

(iii) The payment made at the end of 3 years is £300. The corresponding annual payment is $\frac{300}{s_{\overline{3}|}}$ at 3%, and the value is therefore

$$\frac{300}{s_{\overline{3}|}}a_{\overline{18}|} \text{ at } 3\%$$

$$= \frac{300 \times 13{\cdot}7535}{3{\cdot}0909}$$

$$= £1334{\cdot}90.$$

Expressions for the amounts would be

$$\text{(i) } 10s_{\overline{20}|}, \quad \text{(ii) } 20\frac{i}{i^{(4)}}s_{\overline{10}|}, \quad \text{and} \quad \text{(iii) } \frac{300s_{\overline{18}|}}{s_{\overline{3}|}}.$$

(*b*) *At* 4% *per annum payable quarterly*

It is convenient to work in quarter years, at an effective rate of 1% per quarter.

(i) The payment here is £10 made at the end of 4 quarter-years. The corresponding payment at the end of each quarter is therefore $\frac{10}{s_{\overline{4}|}}$ at 1%. The present value is therefore $\frac{10}{s_{\overline{4}|}}a_{\overline{80}|}$ at 1%

$$= \frac{548 \cdot 882}{4 \cdot 0604}$$

$$= £135 \cdot 18.$$

(ii) Payments are £5 per quarter for 40 quarter-years. The value is therefore $5a_{\overline{40}|}$ at 1%

$$= £164 \cdot 17.$$

(iii) £300 is paid every twelve quarters. The corresponding quarterly sum is therefore $\frac{300}{s_{\overline{12}|}}$ and the value is

$$300\frac{a_{\overline{72}|}}{s_{\overline{12}|}} \text{ at } 1\%.$$

In the tables at the end of this book the value of $a_{\overline{72}|}$ is not given, but it can readily be calculated as follows:

$$a_{\overline{72}|} = a_{\overline{60}|} + v^{60}a_{\overline{12}|}$$

$$= 44 \cdot 955 + \cdot 55045 \times 11 \cdot 2551$$

$$= 51 \cdot 150.$$

The value is therefore $\frac{15345 \cdot 0}{12 \cdot 6825}$

$$= £1209 \cdot 93.$$

3-2

Expressions for the amounts would be

$$\text{(i)}\ \frac{10s_{\overline{80}|}}{s_{\overline{4}|}},\quad \text{(ii)}\ 5s_{\overline{40}|},\quad \text{and}\quad \text{(iii)}\ \frac{300s_{\overline{72}|}}{s_{\overline{12}|}}.$$

(*c*) *At* $2\frac{1}{2}$% *per annum convertible every 2 years*

It is convenient to work in 2-year periods at an effective rate of 5% per period.

(i) The annuity may be considered as one of £20 per 2 years payable twice every 2 years. The value is therefore $20a_{\overline{10}|}^{(2)}$ at 5%

$$= 20 . \frac{i}{i^{(2)}} . a_{\overline{10}|}$$

$$= 20 \times 1{\cdot}012348 \times 7{\cdot}7217$$

$$= £156{\cdot}34.$$

(ii) This annuity is similarly

$$40a_{\overline{5}|}^{(8)}$$

$$= 40 . \frac{i}{i^{(8)}} \times 4{\cdot}3295.$$

(The value of $i^{(8)}$ must be determined, since values of $i/i^{(8)}$ are not included in the tables at the end of this book.)

Now $$\frac{i^{(8)}}{8} = (1{\cdot}05)^{\frac{1}{8}} - 1$$

$$= \frac{{\cdot}05}{8} - \frac{7}{128}({\cdot}0025) + \frac{105}{3072}({\cdot}000125).$$

$$\therefore\ i^{(8)} = {\cdot}05 - \frac{7}{16}({\cdot}0025) + \frac{105}{384}({\cdot}000125)$$

$$= {\cdot}048940.$$

The value is therefore

$$40 \times \frac{{\cdot}05}{{\cdot}048940} \times 4{\cdot}3295$$

$$= £176{\cdot}93.$$

(iii) There is no convenient method of substitution in this case, and the simplest method is to write down the value from first principles. The value of £300 after 3 years is $300v^{\frac{3}{2}}$ at 5%.

The value of the next payment is $300v^{\frac{6}{2}}$ at 5 %, and so on. The value required is therefore

$$300\{v^{\frac{3}{2}}+v^{\frac{6}{2}}+\dots+v^{\frac{18}{2}}\}$$

$$=300v^{\frac{3}{2}}\left[\frac{1-v^{\frac{18}{2}}}{1-v^{\frac{3}{2}}}\right]$$

$$=300\frac{1-v^9}{(1{\cdot}05)^{\frac{3}{2}}-1}$$

and
$$(1{\cdot}05)^{\frac{3}{2}}=(1{\cdot}05)\left(1+\frac{i^{(2)}}{2}\right) \text{ at } 5\%$$

$$=1{\cdot}05\times 1{\cdot}024695$$

$$=1{\cdot}07593.$$

The value is therefore

$$300\times\frac{{\cdot}35539}{{\cdot}07593}$$

$$=£1404{\cdot}15.$$

The amounts would be

$$\text{(i)}\quad 20.\frac{i}{i^{(2)}}s_{\overline{10}|} \text{ at } 5\%,$$

$$\text{(ii)}\quad 40\frac{i}{i^{(8)}}s_{\overline{5}|} \text{ at } 5\%,$$

$$\text{(iii)}\quad 300\times\frac{(1{\cdot}05)^9-1}{(1{\cdot}05)^{\frac{3}{2}}-1}.$$

Example 4·2

Given only that, when $i={\cdot}05$, $v^{50}={\cdot}08720373$, find to four decimal places the value of

(a) $(Ia)_{\overline{50}|}$,

(b) $(Ia)_{\infty}$.

(a)
$$(Ia)_{\overline{50}|}=\frac{\ddot{a}_{\overline{50}|}-50v^{50}}{i}$$

$$=\frac{(1{\cdot}05)\,a_{\overline{50}|}-50v^{50}}{i},$$

$$a_{\overline{50}|}=\frac{1-v^{50}}{i}=\frac{{\cdot}91279627}{{\cdot}05},$$

$$\therefore\ (Ia)_{\overline{50}|}=\frac{1}{{\cdot}05}\left[\frac{(1{\cdot}05)({\cdot}91279627)}{{\cdot}05}-4{\cdot}3601865\right]$$

$$=20[19{\cdot}1687217-4{\cdot}3601865]$$

$$=296{\cdot}1707.$$

(*b*)
$$\begin{aligned}(Ia)_\infty &= v + 2v^2 + 3v^3 + \dots \\ &= v(1 + 2v + 3v^2 + \dots) \\ &= \frac{v}{(1-v)^2} \\ &= \frac{1+i}{i^2} = \frac{1}{i^2} + \frac{1}{i} \\ &= 420.\end{aligned}$$

Example 4·3

Show that the differential coefficient of $s_{\overline{1}|}^{(p)}$ with respect to i may be expressed either as

$$\frac{1}{i^{(p)}} - \frac{(1+i)^{1/p} d}{[i^{(p)}]^2}$$

or as

$$a_{\overline{1}|}^{(p)} - \frac{\ddot{a}_{\overline{1}|}^{(p)} - v}{i^{(p)}},$$

and prove these expressions equal to one another.

$$s_{\overline{1}|}^{(p)} = i/i^{(p)}.$$

$$\therefore \quad \frac{d}{di} s_{\overline{1}|}^{(p)} = \frac{i^{(p)} - i \dfrac{d}{di} i^{(p)}}{[i^{(p)}]^2},$$

$$\frac{d}{di}[i^{(p)}] = \frac{d}{di} p[(1+i)^{1/p} - 1] = p(1/p)(1+i)^{1/p-1}.$$

$$\therefore \quad \frac{d}{di} s_{\overline{1}|}^{(p)} = \frac{i^{(p)} - i(1+i)^{1/p-1}}{[i^{(p)}]^2}$$

$$= \frac{1}{i^{(p)}} - \frac{(1+i)^{1/p} d}{[i^{(p)}]^2}, \quad \text{since} \quad d = iv.$$

Also, writing

$$s_{\overline{1}|}^{(p)} = \frac{1}{p}[(1+i)^{1-1/p} + (1+i)^{1-2/p} + \dots + 1],$$

$$\frac{ds_{\overline{1}|}^{(p)}}{di} = \frac{1}{p}\left[\left(1 - \frac{1}{p}\right)(1+i)^{-1/p} + \left(1 - \frac{2}{p}\right)(1+i)^{-2/p} + \dots + \left(1 - \frac{p-1}{p}\right)(1+i)^{-(p-1)/p}\right]$$

$$= \frac{1}{p}\left[p a_{\overline{1}|}^{(p)} - \frac{1}{p}(v^{1/p} + 2v^{2/p} + \dots + pv)\right]$$

and $$\frac{1}{p}[v^{1/p}+2v^{2/p}+\dots+pv]=\frac{\ddot{a}_{\overline{1}|}^{(p)}-v}{\dfrac{i^{(p)}}{p}}$$ from formula (4·9).

$$\therefore\ \frac{d}{di}s_{\overline{1}|}^{(p)}=a_{\overline{1}|}^{(p)}-\frac{\ddot{a}_{\overline{1}|}^{(p)}-v}{i^{(p)}}$$

$$=\frac{1-v-\ddot{a}_{\overline{1}|}^{(p)}+v}{i^{(p)}}$$

$$=\frac{1-(1+i)^{1/p}i/i^{(p)}v}{i^{(p)}}$$

$$=\frac{1}{i^{(p)}}-\frac{(1+i)^{1/p}d}{[i^{(p)}]^2}.$$

Example 4·4

Two annuities-certain of 1 per annum are each payable half-yearly for n years. The first payment under one is due at the end of 3 months and under the other at the end of 6 months from now. The total present value of the two annuities is 20·255. The amount of an immediate annuity of 1 per quarter for n years is 47·719. If the same effective rate of interest applies throughout find n and the rate of interest.

The total present value of the two annuities is

$$a_{\overline{n}|}^{(2)}+{}_{\frac{1}{4}|}\ddot{a}_{\overline{n}|}^{(2)}=a_{\overline{n}|}^{(2)}+v^{\frac{1}{4}}\ddot{a}_{\overline{n}|}^{(2)}$$

$$=a_{\overline{n}|}^{(2)}[1+v^{\frac{1}{4}}(1+i)^{\frac{1}{2}}]$$

$$=a_{\overline{n}|}^{(2)}[1+(1+i)^{\frac{1}{4}}]$$

$$=\frac{i}{2[(1+i)^{\frac{1}{2}}-1]}a_{\overline{n}|}[1+(1+i)^{\frac{1}{4}}]$$

$$=2\frac{i}{i^{(4)}}a_{\overline{n}|}$$

(as it is apparent it must be since the combination of the two annuities may be regarded as one quarterly annuity of 2 per annum), and this is equal to 20·255.

But $$4\frac{i}{i^{(4)}}s_{\overline{n}|}=47{\cdot}719.$$

$$\therefore\ \frac{a_{\overline{n}|}}{s_{\overline{n}|}}=v^n=\frac{40{\cdot}510}{47{\cdot}719}$$

$$={\cdot}84893.$$

$$\therefore \quad \frac{1-v^n}{2[(1+i)^{\frac{1}{4}}-1]} = \frac{\cdot 15107}{2[(1+i)^{\frac{1}{4}}-1]} = 20\cdot 255,$$

whence $$(1+i)^{\frac{1}{4}} = 1\cdot 00373$$

and $$(1+i) = 1\cdot 015,$$

and, from an interest table at $1\frac{1}{2}\%$, $n = 11$.

Therefore the effective rate per annum is $1\frac{1}{2}\%$ and the term involved is 11 years.

Example 4·5

A fund is to be set up out of which a payment of £100 will be made to each person who in any year qualifies for membership of a certain profession. Assuming that 10 persons will qualify at the end of 1 year from now, 15 at the end of 2 years, 20 at the end of 3 years, and so on till the number of qualifiers is 50 per annum, when it will remain constant, find at 3% per annum effective what sum must be paid into the fund now so that it may be sufficient to meet the outgo. If instead of paying one sum now it was desired to pay twenty equal quarterly instalments, the first due now, what would the amount of the instalment be?

The payments from the fund are

£1000 at the end of the first year,
£1500 at the end of the second year,
£2000 at the end of the third year,
£5000 at the end of the ninth and subsequent years.

The present value at 3% is therefore

$$1000[v + 1\cdot 5v^2 + 2v^3 + \ldots + 5v^9] + 5000[v^{10} + v^{11} + \ldots]$$

$$= 500a_{\overline{9}|} + 500(Ia)_{\overline{9}|} + 5000v^9 a_{\overline{\infty}|}$$

$$= 500a_{\overline{9}|} + 500\frac{\ddot{a}_{\overline{9}|} - 9v^9}{i} + \frac{5000v^9}{i}$$

$$= 3893\cdot 1 + \frac{500}{\cdot 03}[8\cdot 0197 - 6\cdot 8978 + 7\cdot 6642]$$

$$= £150328.$$

From formula (4·9) the value of the first expression in square brackets could have been written down direct as $1000a_{\overline{9}|} + 500\frac{a_{\overline{9}|} - 9v^9}{i}$, leading to the same numerical result.

If the equivalent level sum be X then

$$4X\ddot{a}_{\overline{5}|}^{(4)} = 150328$$

or
$$X = \frac{37582}{\frac{i}{d^{(4)}} a_{\overline{5}|}}$$

$$= \frac{37582}{4 \cdot 6652}$$

$$= £8056 \text{ per quarter.}$$

Example 4·6

A depositor has an account with a bank and has a credit balance of £5000. He is allowed $2\frac{1}{2}\%$ on credit balances and he may overdraw at 5% while his overdraft is less than £1000 and at 6% if it is £1000 or more, all these rates being effective rates per annum. He has to pay from the account £200 at the end of 1 year, £400 at the end of 2 years and so on up to £3000 at the end of 15 years, the payments then ceasing. For how many years must he pay in £1000 per annum, commencing at the end of 12 months, in order to meet the outgoings? What is the amount of the final payment he must make, so that his account will just balance?

If the first year in which an overdraft occurs is the $(n+1)$th the position at the end of n years is:

$$\text{Accumulated account} = 5000(1 \cdot 025)^n + 1000 s_{\overline{n}|}.$$

$$\text{Accumulated outgoings} = 200(Is)_{\overline{n}|} = 200 \frac{s_{\overline{n+1}|} - (n+1)}{i},$$

where $i = \cdot 025$.

Hence $5000(1 \cdot 025)^n + 1000 s_{\overline{n}|}$ must be $> 8000[s_{\overline{n+1}|} - (n+1)]$.
This inequality can be solved only by trial.
When $n = 14$, the left-hand side is

$$7065 + 16519 = 23584,$$

and the right-hand side is

$$8000(2 \cdot 9319) = 23455.$$

Hence after 14 years the credit balance is £129.

The position is then

Balance at start year 15	129
Interest at $2\frac{1}{2}\%$	3·22
Deposit	1000
	1132·22
Withdrawn	3000
Overdraft at start year 16	1867·78
Interest at 6%	112·07
	1979·85
Deposit	1000
Overdraft at start year 17	979·85
Interest at 5%	48·99
	1028·84
Deposit	1000
Overdraft at start year 18	28·84
Interest at 5%	1·44
	30·28

Hence £1000 must be paid for 17 years with a final payment of £30·28 at the end of 18 years to clear the account.

Example 4·7

A agrees to pay *B* the sum of £1000 at the end of 25 years in return for a yearly payment for 25 years of £24·01, the first payment being due in 12 months. At the end of 8 years *B* cannot continue in full and suggests that

either (*a*) payments by *B* should cease and *A* should be liable to pay only £350 at the end of the original 25 years;

or (*b*) *B* should pay in future only £10 per annum and *A* should pay £600 at the end of the original 25 years;

or (*c*) *A* should pay £180 now and close the transaction.

Which offer, if any, should *A* accept, assuming that the rate of interest upon which the transaction was originally based is still appropriate?

First, to find the original rate of interest,

$$24{\cdot}01 s_{\overline{25}|} = 1000.$$

$$\therefore\ s_{\overline{25}|} = 41{\cdot}649.$$

$$\therefore\ i = {\cdot}04 \quad \text{by inspection of the interest tables.}$$

At the end of 8 years *A* should have in hand $24{\cdot}01 s_{\overline{8}|}$ at 4% = £221·23. The values at this time of the various offers are:

(*a*) The value of £350 at the end of 17 years is

$$350v^{17} = £179{\cdot}68.$$

(*b*) The value of £600 at the end of 17 years less £10 per annum for 17 years is

$$600v^{17} - 10a_{\overline{17}|} = 308{\cdot}02 - 121{\cdot}66$$
$$= £186{\cdot}36.$$

(*c*) The value of £180 payable now is £180.

Hence the position is that the true sum which *A* should pay *B* is £221·23, and the difference between this and the amount he pays is his profit. Clearly therefore (*a*) is very slightly the most favourable option to *A*.

Example 4·8

Find the value of a 25-year annuity under which the annual rent is £100 for the first 5 years, £120 for the next 5, £140 for the next 5 and so on. The annuity is to be paid annually for the first 5 years, half-yearly for the next 10, and quarterly thereafter. Interest is $4\frac{1}{2}\%$ convertible half-yearly for the first $12\frac{1}{2}$ years and 4% convertible half-yearly thereafter.

In order to obtain the value as simply as possible, it is necessary to divide the 25 years into four periods and to find the present value of the payments in each period separately.

First 5 years

The present value of £100 per annum paid yearly

$$= 100 . \frac{a_{\overline{10}|}}{s_{\overline{2}|}} \quad \text{at } 2\tfrac{1}{4}\% \qquad = £438{\cdot}4$$

Years 5–$12\frac{1}{2}$

The present value of £60 paid per half-year for 5 years and of £70 paid per half-year for a further $2\frac{1}{2}$ years

$$= 60(a_{\overline{20}|} - a_{\overline{10}|}) + 70(a_{\overline{25}|} - a_{\overline{20}|}) \quad \text{at } 2\tfrac{1}{4}\% \qquad = £635{\cdot}8$$

Years $12\frac{1}{2}$–15

The present value of £70 paid per half-year for $2\frac{1}{2}$ years

$$= v^{25} \text{ at } 2\tfrac{1}{4}\% \times 70a_{\overline{5}|} \quad \text{at } 2\% \qquad = £189{\cdot}2$$

Years 15–25

The present value of £40 paid per quarter for 5 years and of £45 paid per quarter for a further 5 years

$$= v^{25} \text{ at } 2\tfrac{1}{4}\% \times [80(a_{\overline{15}|} - a_{\overline{5}|}) + 90(a_{\overline{25}|} - a_{\overline{15}|})]\frac{i}{i^{(2)}} \quad \text{at } 2\% \qquad = £721{\cdot}1$$

Total £1984·5

Example 4·9

Under an annuity-certain payable continuously for a term of 10 years payments are made during the first 3 months at the rate of 1 per annum, during the second 3 months at the rate of 2 per annum and so on. What is the amount of the annuity at the end of the term at 5% convertible half-yearly?

Let $$(1+j)^2 = 1{\cdot}025 \quad \text{and} \quad \delta = \log_e(1+j).$$

Then the amount of the payments made in the rth quarter at the end of that quarter

$$= \int_0^1 \frac{r}{4} e^{t\delta}\, dt$$

$$= \frac{r}{4}\frac{1}{\delta}(e^{\delta} - 1)$$

$$= \frac{r}{4} \times \frac{j}{\delta}.$$

The value required $= \frac{1}{4} \times j/\delta\, (Is)_{\overline{40}|}$ at rate j

$$= \frac{1}{4}\frac{s_{\overline{41}|} - 41}{\delta}$$

$$= \frac{1}{4} \times \frac{2}{\delta(\cdot 025)} [(1+j)\, s_{\overline{40}|} - 40],$$

where $\delta(\cdot 025)$ is the force of interest corresponding to an effective rate of $2\frac{1}{2}\%$

$$= \frac{1}{4} \times \frac{2}{\delta(\cdot 025)} \left[(1{\cdot}025)^{\frac{1}{2}} \times 2 \times \frac{i}{i(2)}\, s_{\overline{20}|}^{\cdot 025} - 40 \right]$$

$$= \frac{1}{2\delta} \left[2\left(\frac{i}{i^{(2)}} + \frac{i}{2} \right) s_{\overline{20}|} - 40 \right] \quad \text{at } 2\tfrac{1}{2}\%$$

$$= 243{\cdot}94.$$

Example 4·10

Use the calculus of finite differences to find the present value at 4% per annum of a 20-year annuity of which the successive annual payments are $1^2, 2^2, 3^2, \ldots, 20^2$.

The required value is $vu_1+v^2u_2+\ldots+v^{20}u_{20}$, where

$$u_t=t^2$$

$$=vu_1+v^2(1+\Delta)u_1+\ldots+v^{20}(1+\Delta)^{19}u_1$$

$$=v\left[\frac{1-v^{20}(1+\Delta)^{20}}{1-v(1+\Delta)}\right]u_1$$

$$=\frac{1}{i-\Delta}(u_1-v^{20}u_{21})$$

$$=\frac{1}{i}\left[1+\frac{\Delta}{i}+\frac{\Delta^2}{i^2}+\ldots\right][u_1-v^{20}u_{21}]$$

$$=\frac{u_1-v^{20}u_{21}}{i}+\frac{\Delta u_1-v^{20}\Delta u_{21}}{i^2}+\frac{\Delta^2u_1-v^{20}\Delta^2u_{21}}{i^3},$$

since Δ^3 and higher differences vanish (u_t being a function of the second degree).

Now

$$u_1=1,$$

$$u_{21}=441,$$

$$\Delta u_1=3,$$

$$\Delta u_{21}=43,$$

$$\Delta^2u_1=\Delta^2u_{21}=2.$$

Therefore the required value

$$=\frac{1-441v^{20}}{\cdot 04}+\frac{3-43v^{20}}{\cdot 0016}+\frac{2-2v^{20}}{\cdot 000064}$$

$$=1590\cdot 69.$$

Example 4·11

Calculate the present value at 4% per annum of a continuous annuity for 10 years under which the payment at time t is at the rate of t^2 per annum, and find the equated time of the annuity payments.

The present value

$$=\int_0^{10}t^2e^{-t\delta}\,dt$$

$$\int t^2e^{-t\delta}\,dt=-\frac{t^2e^{-t\delta}}{\delta}+\frac{2}{\delta}\int te^{-t\delta}\,dt$$

$$=-\frac{t^2v^t}{\delta}+\frac{2}{\delta}\left[-\frac{te^{-t\delta}}{\delta}-\frac{e^{-t\delta}}{\delta^2}\right]$$

$$=-\frac{t^2v^t}{\delta}-\frac{2tv^t}{\delta^2}-\frac{2v^t}{\delta^3}.$$

$$\therefore \int_0^{10} t^2 e^{-t\delta}\,dt = -\frac{100v^{10}}{\delta} - \frac{20v^{10}}{\delta^2} - \frac{2v^{10}}{\delta^3} + \frac{2}{\delta^3}$$

$$= 249{\cdot}3.$$

The total payments $\displaystyle\int_0^{10} t^2\,dt = \frac{1000}{3}.$

Therefore if t be the equated time

$$\tfrac{1000}{3}v^t = 249{\cdot}3.$$

$$\therefore\ v^t = {\cdot}7479.$$

$$\therefore\ t = \frac{\log {\cdot}7479}{-\log 1{\cdot}04}$$

$$= 7{\cdot}4 \text{ years.}$$

Example 4·12

Assuming a force of interest of 5% per annum find to the nearest integer the term of a continuous annuity-certain under which the payment at any time is proportional to the time elapsed since the start of the annuity and such that the present value of the annuity is equal to half of the aggregate payments to be made.

The payment at time t is kt.

The present value of 1 due at time t is $e^{-{\cdot}05t}$.

Therefore the present value of the annuity is $\displaystyle k\int_0^n t\,e^{-{\cdot}05t}\,dt.$

Now $$\int t\,e^{-{\cdot}05t}\,dt = -\frac{t}{{\cdot}05}e^{-{\cdot}05t} + \frac{1}{{\cdot}05}\int e^{-{\cdot}05t}\,dt.$$

$$\therefore\ k\int_0^n t\,e^{-{\cdot}05t}\,dt = k\left[-\frac{n\,e^{-{\cdot}05n}}{{\cdot}05} + \frac{1}{{\cdot}05}\bar{a}_{\overline{n}|}\right]$$

$$= k\,\frac{\bar{a}_{\overline{n}|} - nv^n}{{\cdot}05}.$$

The aggregate payments are $\displaystyle\int_0^n kt\,dt = \frac{kn^2}{2}.$

$$\therefore\ k\,\frac{\bar{a}_{\overline{n}|} - nv^n}{{\cdot}05} = \frac{kn^2}{4}.$$

This equation can most readily be solved by trial.

Putting $n=21$,
$$\bar{a}_{\overline{n|}}=\frac{1-e^{--21\delta}}{\delta}$$
$$=\frac{1-e^{-1\cdot05}}{\cdot05}$$
$$=13\cdot001,$$
$$21v^{21}=21e^{-1\cdot05}=\frac{7\cdot350}{5\cdot651}.$$
$$\therefore\quad \frac{\bar{a}_{\overline{n|}}-nv^n}{\delta}=113\cdot02$$
and
$$\frac{n^2}{4}=110\cdot25.$$

Putting $n=22$,
$$\bar{a}_{\overline{n|}}=\frac{1-e^{-1\cdot1}}{\cdot05}$$
$$=13\cdot343$$
$$22v^{22}=22e^{-1\cdot05}=\frac{7\cdot323}{6\cdot020}.$$
$$\therefore\quad \frac{a_{\overline{n|}}-nv^n}{\delta}=120\cdot4$$
and
$$\frac{n^2}{4}=121\cdot0.$$

Hence n lies between 21 and 22 and to the nearer integer $n=22$.

Any attempt to solve the equation
$$\bar{a}_{\overline{n|}}-nv^n=\frac{\delta n^2}{4}$$
by expanding $\bar{a}_{\overline{n|}}$ and ι^n in terms of δ and neglecting terms in δ of the second and higher degrees will fail, because the resultant series converges only slowly. This point will be discussed further in Chapter 11.

EXERCISES 4

4·1 Complete the following table to show the present value of an immediate annuity of 1 per annum payable for 25 years certain at 4%:

Annuity payable	Interest convertible			
	Yearly	Half-yearly	Quarterly	Momently
Yearly				
Half-yearly				
Quarterly				
Momently				

4·2 A series of payments is to be made at the end of each 10 years during the next 100 years, the payment at the end of the tth period being $10t$. What is the present value of the payments at 5 % effective?

4·3 Find at 5 % effective the present value of an annuity-certain payable for 40 years under which the successive payments are 4, 7, 12, 19, etc.

4·4 At an effective rate of interest i the value of an annuity-certain of 1 per annum payable continuously for n years is a, and the value of a corresponding annuity for $2n$ years is b. Find in terms of a and b the value at the same effective rate of interest of $(\bar{I}\bar{a})_{\overline{n}|}$.

4·5 On 1 January 1928 a firm of importers purchased a cask of wine for £200. They shipped it to this country, incurring expenses of £25 in the process, and it remained in cask until 1 January 1952, when it was bottled at a further cost of £40. While the wine was in cask it evaporated in such a way that its volume on 1 January in any year had decreased by $\frac{1}{101}$ of its volume on the preceding 1 January. During the period from 1928 to 1952 it was insured for such a proportion of £225 as its volume at the start of each year bore to its original volume. The premium for this insurance was calculated at the rate of 25p %, payable yearly in advance. Assuming the wine will be sold uniformly throughout the year 1952, what should be the total price the sellers should receive if they wish to earn an effective rate of interest of 5 % per annum on all the money they have invested?

4·6 Members of the staff of a firm contribute to a fund £5 per annum if their salaries are £250 per annum or less, and £10 per annum if their salaries exceed that amount. Members enter the fund at age 20 when their annual salary is £100 per annum, which increases every alternate year by £20 until it reaches £300 and thereafter increases yearly by £15 per annum. On retiring at age 60 the member receives twice the amount of his contributions accumulated at 4 % per annum effective. The funds earn 3 % per annum effective, and the difference between the benefits provided and the accumulation of the members' contributions is met by the firm who pay into the fund a level percentage of each member's salary. If the members' contributions are paid continuously, and the firm's annually in arrear, what should this percentage be?

4·7 A fund accumulates at 4 % per annum effective so long as it is £2000 or more, and at 3 % per annum effective when it falls below that figure. From the fund a series of varying annual payments is to be made for 30 years, the first being due in 1 year. At the end of n years the payment is either 10 % of the fund at the beginning of the year or £ $(100+5n)$, whichever is the greater. If the fund exactly suffices to meet the payments as they fall due what is its initial amount?

CHAPTER 5

ANALYSIS OF THE ANNUITY

5·1. Nature of payments of the annuity

In Chapter 4 the main emphasis was laid on finding the present value of a series of future payments, and when the value was found no further investigation was considered necessary. It is, however, instructive to consider the question from another angle, i.e. given that a purchaser has paid a certain price for a given series of future payments, how should he treat each payment as he receives it?

5·2. Division between principal and interest

The statement that $a_{\overline{n}|}$ at rate i is the present value of a series of payments of 1 per annum for n years means that if a purchaser invests $a_{\overline{n}|}$ he will secure a yield at the rate of i on his capital during the n years. The payment he receives is 1 per annum, and it must be clear that he cannot regard this payment purely as income, or interest, because if he did not reinvest any part of it, then at the end of n years when the annuity ceased he would find that he had none of his original capital left. Hence each payment of 1 must comprise

(*a*) interest on the capital invested,

and (*b*) a portion representing a repayment of part of the capital.

5·3. Elementary examples

Consider the simplest case of a purchase of n payments of 1 per annum at yearly intervals for a sum of $a_{\overline{n}|}$ at rate i. At the end of the first year the interest which the purchaser requires is $ia_{\overline{n}|}$, and the balance of the payment of 1, i.e. $1-ia_{\overline{n}|}$, must represent a repayment of capital. Two courses are now open to the purchaser. He may (*a*) consider $(1-ia_{\overline{n}|})$ of his capital as having been repaid, or (*b*) set aside the payment of $(1-ia_{\overline{n}|})$ to accumulate so that after $(n-1)$ years its accumulated amount, together with the accumulations of future payments to be set aside, will be sufficient to repay the purchase price.

In method (*a*) the amount repaid at the end of the first year is $1-ia_{\overline{n}|}=1-1+v^n=v^n$.

The principal, or purchase price, remaining outstanding is therefore $a_{\overline{n}|}-v^n=a_{\overline{n-1}|}$.

Interest in the next year is $ia_{\overline{n-1}|}$, and the amount of principal repaid in this year is therefore $1-ia_{\overline{n-1}|}=v^{n-1}$. The same arguments can be followed for each year until, in the last year, the interest is $ia_{\overline{1}|}$ and the amount repaid is v, which is equal to the principal then outstanding of $a_{\overline{1}|}$. This may be shown in tabular form:

Payment	Interest in payment	Principal repaid	Principal outstanding after payment
1	$ia_{\overline{n}|}=1-v^n$	v^n	$a_{\overline{n-1}|}$
2	$ia_{\overline{n-1}|}=1-v^{n-1}$	v^{n-1}	$a_{\overline{n-2}|}$
⋮	⋮	⋮	⋮
t	$ia_{\overline{n-t+1}|}=1-v^{n-t+1}$	v^{n-t+1}	$a_{\overline{n-t}|}$
⋮	⋮	⋮	⋮
n	$ia_{\overline{1}|}=1-v$	v	0

The total of the interest payments is therefore $n-a_{\overline{n}|}$, and of the principal payments $a_{\overline{n}|}$ as it should be.

Considering now the alternative method (*b*) above, the amount set aside each year is $1-ia_{\overline{n}|}$ or v^n. If these payments are accumulated at rate i they will amount to $v^n s_{\overline{n}|}=a_{\overline{n}|}$, or, in other words, they will suffice to replace the capital. There is no essential difference between the two methods. They are merely different ways of looking at the same transaction, and it is important that this fact be clearly understood. At first sight it might seem that the second method is more advantageous for the purchaser than the first, since it involves an interest income in each year of $(1-v^n)$, while under the first method the interest income appears to be $(1-v^n)$, $(1-v^{n-1})$, ..., $(1-v)$, i.e. to form a diminishing series. This difference is, however, only apparent and not real, for under the first method v^n of the purchaser's capital is treated as having been repaid in the first year, and this amount is therefore *ex hypothesi* available to be invested at rate i

elsewhere. Hence at the end of the tth year the interest received under method (a) is

from the annual payment of 1 in that year	$1 - v^{n-t+1}$,
from the investment of v^n in year 1	iv^n,
from the investment of v^{n-1} in year 2	iv^{n-1},
....	
from the investment of v^{n-t+2} in year $t-1$	iv^{n-t+2},

i.e., in total,

$$1 - v^{n-t+1} + i(v^n + v^{n-1} + \dots + v^{n-t+2})$$
$$= 1 - v^{n-t+1} + i(a_{\overline{n}|} - a_{\overline{n-t+1}|})$$
$$= ia_{\overline{n}|}$$
$$= 1 - v^n \quad \text{as before.}$$

Provided therefore the same rate of interest is involved in each method the results from the purchaser's point of view are identical.

5·4. Nature of the problem further examined

In the discussion above, the transaction has been considered as the purchase of a given series of payments for a price of $a_{\overline{n}|}$. It would lead to exactly the same result if the transaction were described as a loan of $a_{\overline{n}|}$ to be repaid by n annual instalments of 1. From the point of view of the purchaser, or the lender, as the case may be, the transaction is still the investment of a capital sum of $a_{\overline{n}|}$. From the point of view of the vendor, or borrower, the transaction is in each case an undertaking to provide a series of n annual payments of 1 in return for a cash payment of $a_{\overline{n}|}$ at the outset. For example, if the borrower himself were to invest the amount borrowed at rate i, at the end of the first year he would have $(1+i)a_{\overline{n}|} = 1 + a_{\overline{n-1}|}$, and out of this he could make the payment of 1 and still have $a_{\overline{n-1}|}$ left. At the end of a further year he would have $(1+i)a_{\overline{n-1}|} = 1 + a_{\overline{n-2}|}$, and the process can be repeated till at the end of n years he would have $(1+i)a_{\overline{1}|} = 1$ left which would discharge his debt. It is not of course suggested that anyone would borrow a sum of $a_{\overline{n}|}$ merely to reinvest it at the same rate of interest, but the process has been described to show how the value $a_{\overline{n}|}$ could form a fund, which if invested at rate i would exactly suffice to provide the required payments.

5·5. General expressions

If, instead of a loan of $a_{\overline{n}|}$ at rate i, a loan of A is considered, to be repaid over n years by instalments payable p times yearly, and if the rate of interest involved in the transaction is i, then

$$A = Xa_{\overline{n}|}^{(p)},$$

where X is the payment per annum (payable in p instalments of X/p each) required to repay the loan, i.e.

$$X = \frac{A}{a_{\overline{n}|}^{(p)}}.$$

The interest contained in the first payment is $\frac{i^{(p)}}{p}A$, which can be written in the form $\frac{A}{pa_{\overline{n}|}^{(p)}}(1-v^n)$, and the principal repaid is

$$\begin{aligned}\frac{X}{p} - \frac{i^{(p)}}{p}A &= \frac{1}{p}\left[\frac{A}{a_{\overline{n}|}^{(p)}} - i^{(p)}A\right]\\ &= \frac{A}{p}\left[\frac{1-i^{(p)}a_{\overline{n}|}^{(p)}}{a_{\overline{n}|}^{(p)}}\right]\\ &= \frac{A}{p}\left[\frac{1-1+v^n}{a_{\overline{n}|}^{(p)}}\right]\\ &= \frac{A}{pa_{\overline{n}|}^{(p)}}v^n\\ &= \frac{A}{ps_{\overline{n}|}^{(p)}}.\end{aligned}$$

The principal then outstanding is

$$A - \frac{Av^n}{pa_{\overline{n}|}^{(p)}} = \frac{A}{a_{\overline{n}|}^{(p)}}a_{\overline{n-1/p}|}^{(p)} \quad \text{and so on.}$$

In schedule form as before the results are

Payment	Interest in payment	Principal repaid	Principal outstanding after payment
1	$\frac{A}{pa_{\overline{n}\|}^{(p)}}(1-v^n)$	$\frac{A}{pa_{\overline{n}\|}^{(p)}}v^n$	$\frac{A}{a_{\overline{n}\|}^{(p)}}a_{\overline{n-1/p}\|}^{(p)}$
2	$\frac{A}{pa_{\overline{n}\|}^{(p)}}(1-v^{n-1/p})$	$\frac{A}{pa_{\overline{n}\|}^{(p)}}v^{n-1/p}$	$\frac{A}{a_{\overline{n}\|}^{(p)}}a_{\overline{n-2/p}\|}^{(p)}$
⋮	⋮	⋮	⋮
np	$\frac{A}{pa_{\overline{n}\|}^{(p)}}(1-v^{1/p})$	$\frac{A}{pa_{\overline{n}\|}^{(p)}}v^{1/p}$	—
Totals	$\frac{A}{pa_{\overline{n}\|}^{(p)}}(np-pa_{\overline{n}\|}^{(p)})$	A	—

5·6. Relationship between successive payments

It is apparent from the above that the successive amounts of principal repaid form a geometric progression with common ratio $(1+i)^{1/p}$. It is easy to show on general grounds that this must be so.

Let C_m be the capital repaid in the mth instalment.

The loan outstanding after this instalment is $A - \sum_1^m C_m$.

The interest on this will be $\dfrac{i^{(p)}}{p}\left(A - \sum_1^m C_m\right)$.

The next instalment will be $\dfrac{A}{pa_{\overline{n}|}^{(p)}}$.

$$\therefore\ C_{m+1} = \frac{A}{pa_{\overline{n}|}^{(p)}} - \frac{i^{(p)}}{p}\left(A - \sum_1^m C_m\right).$$

or
$$C_{m+1} - \frac{i^{(p)}}{p}\sum_1^m C_m = \frac{A}{p}\left[\frac{1 - i^{(p)}\,a_{\overline{n}|}^{(p)}}{a_{\overline{n}|}^{(p)}}\right].$$

$$= \frac{A}{ps_{\overline{n}|}^{(p)}}, \quad \text{which is independent of } m.$$

$$\therefore\ C_m - \frac{i^{(p)}}{p}\sum_1^{m-1} C_m = \frac{A}{ps_{\overline{n}|}^{(p)}}.$$

$$\therefore\ C_{m+1} - C_m - \frac{i^{(p)}}{p}C_m = 0.$$

$$\therefore\ C_{m+1} = C_m\left(1 + \frac{i^{(p)}}{p}\right)$$

$$= C_m(1+i)^{1/p}.$$

5·7. Summary

It may be convenient to summarize the results obtained up to this point:

In respect of a loan of A repayable by instalments of $\dfrac{A}{pa_{\overline{n}|}^{(p)}}$ payable p times a year for n years to yield i per annum

(*a*) the *interest* contained in the *t*th payment is

$$\frac{A}{pa_{\overline{n}|}^{(p)}}\left(1 - v^{n-(t-1)/p}\right);$$

(*b*) the *principal* contained in the *t*th payment is

$$\frac{A}{pa_{\overline{n}|}^{(p)}} v^{n-(t-1)/p};$$

(*c*) the *principal outstanding* after the *t*th payment is

$$\frac{A}{a_{\overline{n}|}^{(p)}} a_{\overline{n-t/p}|}^{(p)}.$$

It will be seen that these expressions give the values for any payment, and if it is required to find only one or two isolated values this may be done without constructing a full schedule.

5·8. Practical examples

In practice, examples of loans repayable by terminable annuities occur perhaps most frequently in Building Society transactions, where part of the purchase price of a house is advanced subject to repayment by a level sum, including principal and interest, for a fixed term of years. In addition, such annuities may be met with on the Stock Exchange (for example, Indian Railway Annuities), and in sóme cases (for example loans raised by local authorities on the security of rates) the practice is specially authorized by the legislature, or even prescribed by the relevant Act of Parliament. Loans dealt with on the Stock Exchange will be considered later in this work, but it will be convenient to consider further the building society type of loan.

In Building Society transactions instalments are generally paid monthly over a perid of 20 years or more, and the rate of interest is usually a nominal rate convertible monthly also. A schedule for such a loan would therefore involve 240 sets of entries, and for illustrative purposes the example below considers the simpler case of a loan of £1000 repayable by instalments payable half-yearly over a period of 5 years at 4% per annum convertible half-yearly. There is of course no difference in principle between this and the longer schedules required in practice for Building Society transactions.

If X be the half-yearly instalment then $Xa_{\overline{10}|}$ at 2% = 1000 or

$$X = \frac{1000}{a_{\overline{10}|}} = 111{\cdot}3265.$$

If it is required to construct a schedule showing the division of each payment into principal and interest two types of method are open:

(*a*) to proceed from first principles and calculate the interest on the loan outstanding from time to time and hence to deduce the remainder of the schedule;

(*b*) to calculate the values of one of the other items in the schedule from the appropriate formula and deduce the remainder of the schedule from this.

The choice of method will depend on various factors which will be discussed later in this chapter but the methods are exemplified below.

5·9. Construction of schedule—First method

The half-yearly instalment is 111·3265. The interest required in the first half-year is $\cdot 02 \times 1000 = 20$, and hence the principal considered as repaid is $111\cdot 3265 - 20 = 91\cdot 3265$. The loan outstanding is now $1000 - 91\cdot 3265 = 908\cdot 6735$, and the interest required for the second half-year is $\cdot 02 \times 908\cdot 6735 = 18\cdot 1735$, and the principal considered as repaid is $111\cdot 3265 - 18\cdot 1735 = 93\cdot 1530$. The loan now outstanding is $908\cdot 6735 - 93\cdot 1530 = 815\cdot 5205$, and the process can similarly be continued leading to the following schedule:

Half-year no.	Outstanding principal at beginning of half-year	Interest for half-year	Principal contained in payment for half-year
1	1000·0000	20·0000	91·3265
2	908·6735	18·1735	93·1530
3	815·5205	16·3104	95·0161
4	720·5044	14·4101	96·9164
5	623·5880	12·4718	98·8547
6	524·7333	10·4947	100·8318
7	423·9015	8·4780	102·8485
8	321·0530	6·4211	104·9054
9	216·1476	4·3230	107·0035
10	109·1441	2·1829	109·1436
			999·9995

The total of the last column should be the same as the loan advanced, and the discrepancy in the last decimal place is due to the fact that only four decimal places have been retained in the calculations. It would be necessary to adjust the values in the schedule to correct this small discrepancy, but as in common practice such schedules are expressed in pounds and pence, and as this process will in itself almost certainly involve further minor discrepancies, it is usual to make all the adjustments at one time.

5·10. Construction of schedule—Alternative methods

In certain circumstances (e.g. when calculating machines such as are described in Chapter 12 are available) the schedule may be constructed by other methods more convenient than that of § 5·9. Three such methods are considered below, each of which involves the calculation in the first place of one complete column of the schedule from which the other columns may be obtained by a simple process.

(*a*) *Calculation of principal outstanding after each payment*

The principal outstanding after t instalments is

$$111 \cdot 3265 a_{\overline{n-t}|} = F_t \text{ say.}$$

Then

$$F_{t-1} - F_t = 111 \cdot 3265 (a_{\overline{n-t+1}|} - a_{\overline{n-t}|})$$
$$= 111 \cdot 3265 v^{n-t+1}.$$
$$\therefore \; F_{t-1} = F_t + 111 \cdot 3265 v^{n-t+1}.$$

Hence if a calculating machine is available 111·3265 may be set up as a constant multiplicand. On multiplying by v the value of F_9, i.e. $111 \cdot 3265 v$, appears in the product indicator. Subsequent multiplications by v^2, without clearing the machine, gives F_8 and so on. The advantage of this method is that it is continuous, and if the final value for F_1 so obtained agrees with the value $111 \cdot 3265 a_{\overline{9}|}$ which can be calculated separately, the accuracy of the whole calculation is ensured, apart, of course, from the possibility of error in copying the figures from the machine to the schedule. Once this column is complete the amounts of principal repaid each year are found by differencing the capital outstanding and thus finding the capital repaid in each instalment. Subtraction of this amount from the instalment gives the amount of interest. The accuracy of the whole can be checked by summing the schedule. The total of the principal repaid should be 1000, the total of the principal outstanding should be $111{\cdot}3265 \sum_{1}^{10} a_{\overline{t}|}$ or

$$111{\cdot}3265\left(\frac{10-a_{\overline{10}|}}{{\cdot}02}\right)=\frac{1113{\cdot}265-1000}{{\cdot}02},$$

and the sum of the interest column should be

$$111{\cdot}3265\,(10-a_{\overline{10}|})=1113{\cdot}265-1000.$$

(This latter result follows also from general reasoning, since the total payments made by the borrower are $10 \times 111{\cdot}3265$. The principal repaid is 1000, and the difference between this and the total payments must be the total amount of interest paid by the borrower.)

(*b*) *Construction of principal repaid in any instalment*

This can be done on a calculating machine by multiplying the constant $111{\cdot}3265$ by v^t. This process, however, is not continuous, and the correctness of any one value does not prove or disprove the correctness of any other value. But if ϕ_t be written for the amount of principal repaid in the tth instalment

$$\begin{aligned}\phi_{t+1}&=111{\cdot}3265v^{10-t}\\&=(1{\cdot}02)(111{\cdot}3265)\,v^{11-t}\\&=\phi_t+({\cdot}02\times 111{\cdot}3265)\,v^{11-t}.\end{aligned}$$

Hence if the value of $\phi_1=111{\cdot}3265v^{10}$ is entered in the product indicator and the value of ${\cdot}02 \times 111{\cdot}3265$ set up as a constant and multiplied by v^{10}, v^9, etc., successively without clearing the machine the successive amounts appearing in the product indicator will be values of the capital repaid in the tth year. As the process is continuous the accuracy of the whole process is checked by the correctness of the final value subject to the same qualification as in (*a*) above. The remainder of the schedule may be calculated and checked by summation as before.

(*c*) *Construction of* total *principal repaid after each payment*

The total principal repaid after t payments is

$$111{\cdot}3265\,(v^n+v^{n-1}+\ldots+v^{n-t+1})=111{\cdot}3265v^n s_{\overline{t}|}=\theta_t \text{ say.}$$

Then $\theta_{t+1}=\theta_t+(1+i)^t \times 111{\cdot}3265v^n$.

Thus, starting with the initial value, and using a similar process to that adopted in (*a*), the complete column of *total* principal repaid can be calculated. By differencing this column the amounts of principal repaid in each instalment are obtained and the whole schedule can then be completed as in (*a*).

5·11. Choice of method

The choice of method must depend on the resources available. It is desirable that a continuous process should be followed so that the correctness of any one value checks all the previous work. From this point of view, if no mechanical aids are available, the method of § 5·9 is usually convenient and readily worked. If the schedule is long, however, it is desirable to insert check values at periodic intervals, to avoid carrying on an error made in the early stages. If mechanical aids are available, it will usually be quickest to adopt one of the methods of § 5·10. Method (*b*) is probably the easiest as the relative magnitude of the products is smaller than in methods (*a*) or (*c*). It is therefore unnecessary to retain so many decimal places in the values of v^t employed, and the work is thus reduced. It should also be noted that the methods of § 5·10 tacitly assume that tables of v^t and $(1+i)^t$ are available. If they were not (if, for example, i is not a tabular rate), and if a calculating machine is available, it would probably be easiest to calculate the successive amounts of principal contained in each instalment by successive multiplication by $(1+i)$.

5·12. Further consideration of the methods of § 5·3

It has already been pointed out that the recipient of the annuity payments has two methods of dealing with the instalments. It has also been shown that, for a loan of 1, each instalment can be regarded as either (*a*) $1/a_{\overline{n}|}$, or (*b*) interest at rate i plus the sum which will accumulate after n years to 1, i.e. $1/s_{\overline{n}|}$.

In other words,

$$\frac{1}{a_{\overline{n}|}} = i + \frac{1}{s_{\overline{n}|}}, \tag{5·1}$$

which can readily be established algebraically. The identity, however, depends on the fact that the amounts invested to replace the capital accumulate at rate i. The purchaser, or lender, might perhaps wish to calculate the price or loan he could give in return for a future series of payments assuming that

(*a*) he wished to realize interest at rate i' on his invested capital,

and (*b*) he wished to replace his capital by accumulating at rate i the part of the instalment not required for interest. (In practice, i would be a lower rate than i'.)

Here i' is called the 'remunerative' rate and i the 'reproductive' rate of interest. The part of the instalment not required for interest is often referred to as a 'sinking fund'. This expression is also used in referring (1) to the operation of replacing capital generally or (2) to the actual amount of the accumulated payments. Thus the problem above might be stated as one where the lender wishes to realize interest at rate i' on his invested capital, and to replace his capital by a sinking fund accumulating at rate i.

5·13. Analysis of the annuity at two rates of interest

Let $a_{\overline{n}|}^{i'\&i}$ represent the present value of a series of payments of 1 under the conditions of § 5·12. Then if a loan of 1 be made under these conditions, the annual instalment will be $\dfrac{1}{a_{\overline{n}|}^{i'\&i}}$. But, as before, the instalment must consist of

(*a*) the interest required, i.e. i',

(*b*) the sum required to replace 1 after n years, i.e. $\dfrac{1}{s_{\overline{n}|}}$ at rate i.

$$\therefore \quad \frac{1}{a_{\overline{n}|}^{i'\&i}} = \frac{1}{s_{\overline{n}|}^{i}} + i'$$

$$= \frac{1}{a_{\overline{n}|}^{i}} + (i' - i),$$

or
$$a_{\overline{n}|}^{i'\&i} = \frac{a_{\overline{n}|}^{i}}{1 + (i' - i)\,a_{\overline{n}|}^{i}}. \qquad (5\cdot2)$$

Alternatively, the sum available for sinking fund out of each instalment is $\left(\dfrac{1}{a_{\overline{n}|}^{i'\&i}} - i'\right)$, and this sinking fund will accumulate to $\left(\dfrac{1}{a_{\overline{n}|}^{i'\&i}} - i'\right) s_{\overline{n}|}^{i}$ which must replace the capital invested.

Hence
$$\left(\frac{1}{a_{\overline{n}|}^{i'\&i}}-i'\right)s_{\overline{n}|}^{i}=1,$$

or
$$a_{\overline{n}|}^{i'\&i}=\frac{s_{\overline{n}|}^{i}}{1+i's_{\overline{n}|}^{i}}. \qquad (5\cdot3)$$

It should be noted that if the instalments are payable p times a year the value of $a_{\overline{n}|}^{(p)i'\&i}$ will vary according as the assumption is made that

(*a*) interest per unit after $1/p$th of a year is $\frac{i'^{(p)}}{p}$,

or (*b*) interest per unit after $1/p$th of a year is X, where $Xps_{\overline{1}|}^{(p)}=i'$,

i.e. $X=\frac{i'}{ps_{\overline{1}|}^{(p)}}$ at rate i.

If assumption (*a*) is made it implies that the lender can invest each interest payment as he receives it at a rate such that the total accumulated interest received during the year is i' per unit, and this satisfies the conditions of the problem. On the other hand, it might be felt that since the lender assumes that i is the appropriate rate for the accumulation of the sinking fund portion of each instalment received during the year, the same assumption should be made for the interest portion of each instalment. The resulting expressions for $a_{\overline{n}|}^{(p)i'\&i}$ may be obtained by a process similar to that used in deriving formula 4·3 and are:

$$(a)\qquad \frac{s_{\overline{n}|}^{(p)}}{1+i'^{(p)}s_{\overline{n}|}^{(p)}},$$

$$(b)\qquad \frac{s_{\overline{n}|}^{(p)}}{1+i's_{\overline{n}|}}.$$

where $s_{\overline{n}|}^{(p)}$ and $s_{\overline{n}|}$ are each calculated at rate i.

5·14. Construction of schedules at two rates

From the expression

$$\frac{1}{a_{\overline{n}|}^{i'\&i}}=\frac{1}{a_{\overline{n}|}^{i}}+(i'-i)$$
$$=\frac{1}{s_{\overline{n}|}^{i}}+i',$$

it will be seen that, as in the simpler case of § 5·3, the repayment of the capital of 1 can be considered either from the point of view of the gradual writing down of the capital, or from the point of view of the division of each instalment into fixed proportions of interest and sinking fund. If the first method is used the analysis of each payment into principal and interest will be exactly the same as for a loan of 1 repayable by n instalments of $1/a_{\overline{n}|}^{i}$, except that a constant addition of $(i'-i)$ will be made to the interest portion. Hence any of the methods of §§ 5·9 and 5·10 may be used, and the final schedule will be constructed by adding the constant excess interest to the interest column. For example, if it were desired to calculate the series of payments payable half-yearly to repay a loan of 1000 so that the yield might be 5 % convertible half-yearly and to permit of the capital being replaced at 4% convertible half-yearly, the instalment would be

$$\frac{1000}{a_{\overline{10}|}^{\cdot 025\&\cdot 02}} = \frac{1000}{a_{\overline{10}|}^{\cdot 02}} + (\cdot 025 - \cdot 02)\,1000$$

$$= 116{\cdot}3265.$$

The columns 'principal outstanding' and 'principal repaid' would be the same as in § 5·9, while each entry in the interest column would be increased by 5, the final schedule being as follows:

Half-year no.	Outstanding principal at beginning of half-year	Interest for half-year	Principal contained in payment for half-year
1	1000·0000	25·0000	91·3265
2	908·6735	23·1735	93·1530
3	815·5205	21·3104	95·0161
4	720·5044	19·4101	96·9164
5	623·5880	17·4718	98·8547
6	524·7333	15·4947	100·8318
7	423·9015	13·4780	102·8485
8	321·0530	11·4211	104·9054
9	216·1476	9·3230	107·0035
10	109·1441	7·1829	109·1436
			999·9995

The general expression for the amount of interest in the tth payment may be derived as follows:

Consider a loan of 1 repaid by instalments of $\dfrac{1}{a_{\overline{n}|}^{i'\&i}}$.

The interest contained in the tth payment is

$$\frac{1}{a^{i}_{\overline{n}|}}(1-v^{n-t+1})+(i'-i)=\frac{1-v^{n-t+1}+i'a_{\overline{n}|}-1+v^n}{a_{\overline{n}|}}$$

$$=\frac{i'a_{\overline{n}|}+v^n(1-v^{-t+1})}{a_{\overline{n}|}}$$

$$=i'-i\frac{s_{\overline{t-1}|}}{s_{\overline{n}|}},$$

which is equal to interest at rate i' on the whole loan, less interest at rate i on the amount of loan previously repaid. This is also equivalent to interest at rate i' on the loan outstanding plus interest at rate $(i'-i)$ on the amount of loan previously repaid.

5·15. Transactions at two rates of interest

It will be understood that transactions at two rates of interest such as are discussed above will not usually arise explicitly as such in practice. In the example in § 5·14 the borrower in effect is discharging a debt of £1000 by 10 payments of £116·3265, i.e. from his point of view he would be paying the rate of interest represented by the equation

$$\frac{1}{a_{\overline{10}|}}=\cdot 1163265,$$

which is approximately 2·85 % per half-year or nearly $5\frac{3}{4}$ % per annum. Before he would consider borrowing at this rate or selling a series of payments of £116·3265 for £1000, it would be necessary for the market rate to be not less than this rate, as otherwise he could obtain more advantageous terms elsewhere. The division of the payments into principal and interest as suggested would then to some extent be an artificial one adopted by the purchaser or lender for his own particular purposes, and not really one which would appear as part of the terms of the loan. Such transactions should therefore be regarded more in the nature of a sale and purchase of a given series of payments than as a loan. This aspect of the problem is clearly brought out in considering what would happen if it were desired to close the transaction at some future intermediate point. This would be a matter for negotiation depending on market rates of interest at the time and on which party to the contract wished to close it. It is considered in detail below.

If A purchases a series of n annual payments from B and calculates his price on remunerative and reproductive rates of interest of i' and i respectively, and if after t years

(a) A wishes to obtain the immediate use of his capital and to forgo the future instalments,

or (b) B wishes to pay a lump sum in lieu of the future instalments,

or (c) both A and B desire to close the transaction,

what price should be paid? It will be assumed that no material change in the rates of interest ruling in the market has taken place.

(a) If A wishes to close the transaction it is fair that he should credit B with the whole of the capital assumed to be repaid according to his schedule, i.e. for an original price of $a_{\overline{n}|}^{i'\&i}$ he should credit B with $\dfrac{a_{\overline{n}|}^{i'\&i}}{s_{\overline{n}|}^{i}} \times s_{\overline{t}|}^{i}$, and should therefore accept

$$a_{\overline{n}|}^{i'\&i}\left[1-\frac{s_{\overline{t}|}}{s_{\overline{n}|}}\right].$$

(b) If B wishes to close the transaction he should pay A enough to buy an annuity of 1 per annum for $(n-t)$ years, i.e. $a_{\overline{n-t}|}$ at rate i, assuming, as is reasonable, that this is the market rate of interest at the time.

(c) If both parties wish to close the transaction a reasonable basis would be $a_{\overline{n-t}|}^{i'\&i}$, i.e. A should sell the remaining instalments on the same basis as he purchased them.

If these prices be P_1, P_2 and P_3, it is instructive to consider the relationship between them from first principles. Under the existing arrangement A expects to receive a series of payments which will provide interest of $\left(i'-i\dfrac{s_{\overline{t}|}}{s_{\overline{n}|}}\right)$ per unit of his capital in the $(t+1)$th year, plus a payment towards the replacement of his capital (§ 5·14). If the arrangement under (a) above is adopted he treats the transaction as if it had been carried out at rate i throughout, and therefore as if in future he expected to receive interest payments of $i\left(1-\dfrac{s_{\overline{t}|}}{s_{\overline{n}|}}\right)$ per unit of his original capital. If the arrangement under (*b*) above is adopted he receives a sum which is sufficient to provide the same future series as before, and he can therefore subdivide the payments as originally. Under the arrangement in (*c*) above, if he invests the price at rate i (by hypothesis the market rate) he will receive i per unit of capital invested instead of i' as under the original transaction. Hence the difference between P_2 and P_1 should be the value of $\left(i' - \frac{is_{\overline{t}|}}{s_{\overline{n}|}}\right) - i\left(1 - \frac{s_{\overline{t}|}}{s_{\overline{n}|}}\right)$ per unit of original capital for the remaining term, i.e.

$$P_2 = P_1 + (i' - i)\, a^{i'\&i}_{\overline{n}|}\, a^{i}_{\overline{n-t}|}.$$

The difference between P_3 and P_2 should be the value of $(i' - i)$ per unit of price now accepted for the remaining term, i.e.

$$P_2 = P_3 + (i' - i)\, P_3 a^{i}_{\overline{n-t}|}.$$

These results may be confirmed from the expressions already found:

$$\begin{aligned} P_1 + (i' - i)\, a^{i'\&i}_{\overline{n}|}\, a^{i}_{\overline{n-t}|} &= a^{i'\&i}_{\overline{n}|}\left[1 - \frac{s_{\overline{t}|}}{s_{\overline{n}|}}\right] + (i' - i)\, a^{i'\&i}_{\overline{n}|}\, a^{i}_{\overline{n-t}|} \\ &= a^{i'\&i}_{\overline{n}|}\left[1 - \frac{s_{\overline{t}|}}{s_{\overline{n}|}} + (i' - i)\, a_{\overline{n-t}|}\right] \\ &= a^{i'\&i}_{\overline{n}|}\, a_{\overline{n-t}|}\left[\frac{1}{a_{\overline{n}|}} + (i' - i)\right] \\ &= a_{\overline{n-t}|} \\ &= P_2 \end{aligned}$$

as it should.

Also $$\begin{aligned} P_3 + (i' - i)\, P_3 a^{i}_{\overline{n-t}|} &= a^{i'\&i}_{\overline{n-t}|}\left[1 + (i' - i)\, a^{i}_{\overline{n-t}|}\right] \\ &= \frac{a_{\overline{n-t}|}}{1 + (i' - i)\, a_{\overline{n-t}|}}\left[1 + (i' - i)\, a_{\overline{n-t}|}\right] \\ &= a_{\overline{n-t}|} \\ &= P_2, \end{aligned}$$

as it should.

In practice the price would be fixed by negotiation, but P_1 and P_2 represent probable minimum and maximum values respectively.

5·16. Varying series of payments

Exactly similar arguments can be adopted even if the series of payments varies. For example, if it be desired to find the value of the series of payments of $u_1, u_2, \ldots, u_n$ to yield i per annum, then if X is this value, the amount available for replacing capital in the first year is $(u_1 - iX)$ and in the next year $(u_2 - iX)$ and so on. Hence, as these amounts when accumulated amount to X, the equation of value is

$$(u_1 - iX)(1+i)^{n-1} + (u_2 - iX)(1+i)^{n-2} + \ldots + (u_n - iX) = X,$$

or

$$X = \frac{\sum_1^n u_t (1+i)^{n-t}}{1 + i s_{\overline{n}|}}$$

$$= \frac{\sum_1^n u_t (1+i)^{n-t}}{(1+i)^n}$$

$$= \sum_1^n v^t u_t,$$

a result which is of course apparent from first principles.

If two rates of interest were involved, i' and i as before, the equation would become

$$X = \frac{\sum_1^n u_t (1+i)^{n-t}}{1 + i' s^{i}_{\overline{n}|}}.$$

This method, however, assumes implicitly that none of the terms $(u_t - i'X)$ is negative. If there were a negative term, the position in that year would be that the payment made would not be sufficient to pay the interest required. In such circumstances, the fundamental hypothesis underlying the idea of remunerative and reproductive rates of interest as defined in § 5·12 would be inapplicable except by the introduction of the conception of a 'negative sinking fund'. Such a conception is beyond the scope of this book, but the student who wishes to investigate the matter further is referred to *J.I.A.* vol. 56, pp. 25 et seq., dealing with the valuation of a deferred annuity (which is an extreme case of a 'negative sinking fund'). The student, however, should always be on the look-out for the possibility of a 'negative sinking fund' arising in any question involving the valuation of a varying series of payments at two rates of interest.

5·17. The following examples illustrate the work of this chapter.

Example 5·1

A building society established on 1 May 1927 lent to house purchasers

£10,000 on 1 May 1927,
£20,000 on 1 May 1928,
£30,000 on 1 May 1929,

and so on increasing by £10,000 each year to

£200,000 on 1 May 1946.

Thereafter, the amount lent on 1 May of each year remained constant at £200,000. The loans are subject to level annual repayment, including principal and interest, at the rate of 5% per annum convertible yearly for 20 years from the date of the loan.

Find the amount of capital outstanding on 1 May 1946 (immediately after the loan granted and the repayments due on that date have been made) and the amount of capital outstanding when the Society reaches a stationary condition.

The capital outstanding on 1 May 1946 in respect of a loan of X made in year $1927+t$ is

$$\frac{X}{a_{\overline{20}|}} a_{\overline{20-\overline{19-t}}|} = \frac{X}{a_{\overline{20}|}} a_{\overline{t+1}|},$$

and the amount advanced in year $1927+t$ is

$$10{,}000 + 10{,}000t = 10{,}000(t+1).$$

The capital outstanding on 1 May 1946 is therefore

$$\sum_{0}^{19} \frac{10{,}000(t+1)\,a_{\overline{t+1}|}}{a_{\overline{20}|}} = \frac{10{,}000}{ia_{\overline{20}|}}\left[\sum_{0}^{19}(t+1) - \sum_{0}^{19}(t+1)v^{t+1}\right]$$

$$= \frac{10{,}000}{ia_{\overline{20}|}}\left[\frac{20\times 21}{2} - \frac{\ddot{a}_{\overline{20}|} - 20v^{20}}{i}\right]$$

$$= 200{,}000 \times \cdot 080243\left[210 - \frac{13\cdot 0853 - 7\cdot 5378}{\cdot 05}\right]$$

$$= £1{,}589{,}613.$$

The Society will reach a stationary condition when all the loans of less than £200,000 have been repaid, since after that date the instalments payable under new loans will be the same as the instalments ceasing on loans of the same amount granted 20 years previously. The capital outstanding at this point is therefore

$$\frac{200{,}000}{a_{\overline{20}|}}[a_{\overline{1}|}+a_{\overline{2}|}+\ldots+a_{\overline{20}|}]=\frac{200{,}000}{a_{\overline{20}|}}\left[\frac{20-a_{\overline{20}|}}{\cdot 05}\right]$$

$$=\frac{4{,}000{,}000\times 20}{a_{\overline{20}|}}-4{,}000{,}000$$

$$=£2{,}419{,}440.$$

Example 5·2

A loan of £1000 is to be repaid with interest by an annuity due for 20 years payable half-yearly. Find the amount of principal contained in the 10th half-yearly payment if the lender wishes to obtain an effective rate of interest of $3\frac{1}{2}\%$ per annum on the transaction.

Here, if X is the payment per annum,

$$X\ddot{a}^{(2)}_{\overline{20}|}=1000$$

or

$$X=\frac{1000}{\frac{i}{d^{(2)}}a_{\overline{20}|}}$$

$$=\frac{1000}{1\cdot 02617\times 14\cdot 2124}$$

$$=68\cdot 57.$$

The half-yearly instalment is therefore 34·28.

Immediately after the 9th payment has been made the loan outstanding is

$$\frac{X}{2}[v^{\frac{1}{2}}+v+v^{1\frac{1}{2}}+\ldots+v^{15\frac{1}{2}}]=\frac{X}{2}[2a^{(2)}_{\overline{15}|}+v^{15\frac{1}{2}}]$$

$$=\frac{X}{2}v^{\frac{1}{2}}[2\ddot{a}^{(2)}_{\overline{15}|}+v^{15}]$$

$$=\frac{68\cdot 567}{1+\frac{i^{(2)}}{2}}\left[11\cdot 8188+\frac{\cdot 59689}{2}\right].$$

The interest is $\frac{i^{(2)}}{2}$ per unit of loan outstanding.

$$\therefore\ \text{Interest}=\frac{\cdot 01735}{1\cdot 01735}\times 68\cdot 567\times 12\cdot 1172$$

$$=14\cdot 17.$$

The instalment is 34·28.

Therefore the principal is 20·11

$$=£20·11.$$

Example 5·3

A loan of £1000 is to be repaid over 40 years by equal instalments, to include principal and interest, payable at the end of every second year. Find the amount of the instalment to give the lender an effective rate of 3% per annum on the whole of his invested capital throughout and to enable him to replace his capital by a sinking fund to be invested at an effective rate of 2% per annum.

Let X be the amount of the instalment.

The interest required from this payment is

$$1000\,[(1·03)^2 - 1] = 60·90.$$

The amount available for sinking fund, every second year, is therefore $X - 60·9$.

The accumulation of the sinking fund is therefore

$$(X - 60·9)(1·02)^{38} + (X - 60·9)(1·02)^{36} + \ldots + (X - 60·9)$$

$$= (X - 60·9)\left(\frac{s_{\overline{40}|}}{s_{\overline{2}|}}\right) \text{ at } 2\%,$$

and this must replace the capital invested.

$$\therefore\ (X - 60·9)\frac{s_{\overline{40}|}}{s_{\overline{2}|}} = 1000.$$

$$\therefore\ X - 60·9 = 1000\frac{s_{\overline{2}|}}{s_{\overline{40}|}}$$

$$= \frac{2020}{60·402}$$

$$= 33·44.$$

$$\therefore\ X = 94·34$$

$$= £94·34.$$

Example 5·4

Find the purchase price of an immediate annuity-certain payable annually for 10 years starting at £110 per annum and increasing each year by £10 per annum if the purchaser desires to earn 4% on his investment and to replace his capital by a sinking fund accumulating at $3\frac{1}{2}\%$ during the first 5 years and at 3% during the second 5 years.

Let X be the price.

The amounts available for sinking fund are $110-\cdot 04X$, $120-\cdot 04X$, $130-\cdot 04X$, ..., $200-\cdot 04X$, and these accumulate to

$$(110-\cdot 04X)(1\cdot 035)^4(1\cdot 03)^5+(120-\cdot 04X)(1\cdot 035)^3(1\cdot 03)^5+\dots$$
$$+(200-\cdot 04X),$$

i.e.
$$(1\cdot 03)^5\left[110s_{\overline{5}|}^{\cdot 035}+10\frac{s_{\overline{5}|}^{\cdot 035}-5}{\cdot 035}-\cdot 04Xs_{\overline{5}|}^{\cdot 035}\right]$$
$$+\left[160s_{\overline{5}|}^{\cdot 03}+10\frac{s_{\overline{5}|}^{\cdot 03}-5}{\cdot 03}-\cdot 04Xs_{\overline{5}|}^{\cdot 03}\right],$$

and this must equal X.

$$\therefore\ X=\frac{(1\cdot 03)^5\left[110s_{\overline{5}|}^{\cdot 035}+10\dfrac{s_{\overline{5}|}^{\cdot 035}-5}{\cdot 035}\right]+160s_{\overline{5}|}^{\cdot 03}+10\dfrac{s_{\overline{5}|}^{\cdot 03}-5}{\cdot 03}}{1+\cdot 04s_{\overline{5}|}^{\cdot 03}+(1\cdot 03)^5\times\cdot 04s_{\overline{5}|}^{\cdot 035}}$$
$$=\frac{803\cdot 891+952\cdot 489}{1\cdot 46102}$$
$$=1202\cdot 2,$$

or, say, £1202·20.

Interest on this at 4% is less than the first instalment, therefore no 'negative sinking fund' arises.

Example 5·5

A loan of £1000, granted on 1 January 1947, is to be repaid by six instalments, including principal and interest, at the rate of 2% effective per half-year. The first instalment is due on 15 May 1947, and subsequent instalments will be made at half-yearly intervals until 15 November 1949. Each May instalment is £20 greater than the instalment paid in the following November, and the total annual charge increases by £50 per annum. What is the first instalment?

If $X+20$ is the first instalment the remainder are

$$X,\ X+45,\quad X+25,\quad X+70,\quad X+50.$$

$$\therefore\ X[v^{\frac{3}{4}}+v^{\frac{7}{4}}+v^{\frac{11}{4}}+\dots+v^{\frac{23}{4}}]+20v^{\frac{3}{4}}+45v^{\frac{11}{4}}+\dots+50v^{\frac{23}{4}}=1000.$$

$$\therefore\ X[v+v^2+\dots+v^6]+20v+45v^3+25v^4+70v^5+50v^6=1000v^{\frac{1}{4}}.$$

$$\therefore\ X=\frac{1000v^{\frac{1}{4}}-19\cdot 608-42\cdot 404-23\cdot 096-63\cdot 401-44\cdot 399}{a_{\overline{6}|}}.$$

Now $$v^{\frac{1}{4}} = 1 - \frac{i^{(4)}}{4} \text{ approximately}$$

$$= \cdot 99504.$$

$$\therefore\ X = \frac{802 \cdot 13}{5 \cdot 60143}$$

$$= 143 \cdot 20.$$

The first instalment is therefore £163·20.

(The device of multiplying both sides of the equation by $v^{\frac{1}{4}}$ to avoid calculating fractional powers of v should be noted.)

Example 5·6

A 20-year annuity-certain of £100 per annum payable yearly was purchased by A from B to yield 4% per annum effective on the whole capital and to provide a sinking fund accumulating at 3½% per annum effective. Immediately after the 12th instalment has been paid it is desired to end the transaction. Find the sum which should be paid by B:

(1) if A desires to end the transaction,
or (2) if B desires to end the transaction,
or (3) if both A and B desire to end the transaction.

The price of the annuity is X, where

$$(100 - \cdot 04X)\, s_{\overline{20}|} = X \quad \text{at } 3\tfrac{1}{2}\%,$$

i.e. $$X = \frac{100 s_{\overline{20}|}}{1 + \cdot 04 s_{\overline{20}|}}$$

$$= \frac{100}{\cdot 075361}.$$

(1) If A desires repayment he is requiring B to find cash immediately instead of in the future and he therefore should give B credit for the sinking fund which A has accumulated, i.e. for

$$\frac{X}{s_{\overline{20}|}} s_{\overline{12}|} \quad \text{at } 3\tfrac{1}{2}\%.$$

Therefore the sum to be paid is

$$X\left[1 - \frac{s_{\overline{12}|}}{s_{\overline{20}|}}\right] = \frac{100}{\cdot 075361} \times \frac{13 \cdot 6777}{28 \cdot 2797}$$

$$= £641 \cdot 79.$$

(2) If B desires to repay he is depriving A of the right to £100 per annum for 8 years. He should therefore pay A enough to buy such an

annuity, and this would have to be done at whatever was the current market rate of interest. This cannot be assumed to be more than $3\frac{1}{2}\%$, the reproductive rate, and the answer is therefore

$$100a_{\overline{8}|} \text{ at } 3\tfrac{1}{2}\% = £687{\cdot}40.$$

(3) If both desire to end the transaction the value should in equity be the value of an annuity for 8 years on the same terms as the original one, i.e.

$$\frac{100s_{\overline{8}|}}{1+{\cdot}04s_{\overline{8}|}} \text{ at } 3\tfrac{1}{2}\%, \quad \text{by analogy with the expression for } X \text{ above}$$

$$= \frac{100}{{\cdot}15047}$$

$$= £664{\cdot}55.$$

It will be noted that $\frac{(1)+(2)}{2} = 664{\cdot}6$, which provides a rough check on (3), as it should be about midway between the two.

Example 5·7

A borrower is repaying one debt of £4000 by 30 equal half-yearly instalments of principal and interest calculated at 5% per annum convertible half-yearly of which the 12th has just been paid, and another debt of £1500 by 20 equal half-yearly instalments of principal and interest calculated at 4% per annum convertible half-yearly of which the 8th has just been paid. If the remaining instalments of the two debts are to be replaced by an annuity-certain of 20 half-yearly payments, what rate of interest should be paid on the combined loan so that the total sum to be paid in future by the borrower will not be altered?

The instalments under the two loans are therefore

$$\frac{4000}{a_{\overline{30}|}} \text{ per half-year at } 2\tfrac{1}{2}\%$$

and $$\frac{1500}{a_{\overline{20}|}} \text{ per half-year at } 2\%,$$

i.e. 191·11 and 91·74 respectively.

The loans outstanding are

$$191{\cdot}11a_{\overline{18}|}^{{\cdot}025} + 91{\cdot}74a_{\overline{12}|}^{{\cdot}02} = 191{\cdot}11 \times 14{\cdot}3534 + 91{\cdot}74 \times 10{\cdot}5753$$

$$= 2743{\cdot}08 + 970{\cdot}18$$

$$= £3713{\cdot}26.$$

The total sum to be paid in future by the borrower is to be the same and he must therefore pay

$$\frac{191{\cdot}112 \times 18 + 91{\cdot}735 \times 12}{20} \text{ per annum,}$$

or 227·04 per annum.

Hence

$$227{\cdot}04a_{\overline{20}|} = 3713{\cdot}26$$

or

$$a_{\overline{20}|} = 16{\cdot}355,$$

and by inspection of the interest tables it will be seen that as nearly as may be the value of $a_{\overline{20}|}$ at 2% satisfies this equation.

The new rate of interest is therefore 4% per annum convertible half-yearly.

Example 5·8

Annuities issued to yield an effective rate of 4% per annum are to be consolidated on the basis that the total payments under the consolidated annuity are to be equal to the total remaining payments under the existing annuities. The annuity rents and terms to run are as follows:

Rent (£)	Term to run in years
100	20
150	22
175	24
200	25

Assuming all the annuities are payable annually and that the next payment in all cases is due 1 year hence, find the rent and term of the consolidated annuity so that the effective rate of interest will be unaltered.

The total payments still to be made

$$= 20(100) + 22(150) + 24(175) + 25(200)$$

$$= 14{,}500.$$

The total present values of the annuities are

$$100a_{\overline{20}|} + 150a_{\overline{22}|} + 175a_{\overline{24}|} + 200a_{\overline{25}|}$$

$$= 1359{\cdot}03 + 2167{\cdot}66 + 2668{\cdot}22 + 3124{\cdot}42$$

$$= 9319{\cdot}33.$$

Let the instalments under the consolidated annuity be X per annum for t years with a final reduced payment of Y after $t+1$ years.

Then $$tX + Y = 14{,}500.$$

$$\therefore\ tXv^{t+1} + Yv^{t+1} = 14500v^{t+1}$$

and $$Xa_{\overline{t}|} + Yv^{t+1} = 9319{\cdot}33.$$

$$\therefore\ X[a_{\overline{t}|} - tv^{t+1}] = 9319{\cdot}33 - 14500v^{t+1}$$

or $$X = \frac{9319{\cdot}33(1+i)^{t+1} - 14500}{s_{\overline{t+1}|} - (t+1)}$$

(this form of the expression being chosen to minimize the arithmetical work).

When $t = 23$, which is a first approximation to the average term of the payments, i.e. $\dfrac{14500}{100+150+175+200}$,

$$X = \frac{9388{\cdot}3}{15{\cdot}0826}$$
$$= 622{\cdot}45.$$
$$\therefore\ Y = 14500 - 23 \times 622{\cdot}45$$
$$= 183{\cdot}65.$$

Hence a series of 23 payments of £622·45 followed by one payment after 24 years of £183·65 will have the same present value as the present annuities, and the total instalments will be £14,500 as at present.

It might be that there were other series of payments which would satisfy the conditions, but if t is taken as 22, X will be found to be 622 and Y will be 817, and since Y by hypothesis is less than X this would not be a solution. Equally, if t is taken as 24, X will be found to be 621 and Y would then be negative. It appears, therefore, that the only solution which will meet the conditions is obtained when $t = 23$.

EXERCISES 5

5·1 A loan of £5000 is to be repaid by level annual instalments of principal and interest over a period of 15 years. The rate of interest is 5% effective. Find:

(*a*) the annual instalment,
(*b*) the capital contained in the 10th payment,
(*c*) the interest content of the 12th payment,
(*d*) the principal repaid after 13 instalments have been made.

5·2 If in the loan in question 1 the instalments had been calculated at 7%, the lender replacing his capital by a sinking fund accumulating at 5% effective, what differences would there be in your answers?

5·3 A loan of £5000 is to be repaid by an annuity over a period of 20 years, the payment at the end of the first year being £150, and thereafter such a uniform sum as will secure to the investor an effective rate of interest of 5% per annum on the whole capital of £5000 throughout the term, and permit of replacement of the capital by a sinking fund at an effective rate of 4% per annum. Find:

(*a*) the annual payment to be made at the end of each of the 2nd to the 20th years,

(*b*) the amounts of principal and interest included in the payment made at the end of the 10th year, and the loan outstanding after that payment.

5·4 *A* borrowed from *B* a sum of money which he is to repay in *n* years by level annual instalments, including principal and interest, of £100. *A* calculated that he was borrowing at 5%. *B* expected to earn a certain effective rate on his investment and to replace his capital by a sinking fund accumulating at 4% effective. Had *B* been content to earn an effective rate of 67p% less on his capital, replacing it as before, *A* would only have had to pay an annual instalment of £91·70. Find the amount borrowed, the number of instalments to be paid, and the effective rate of interest involved in *B*'s calculation.

5·5 *A* is entitled to receive a series of payments annually for 20 years, the successive payments being 1, 2, 3, ..., 20. He wishes to borrow as much as possible from *B* and the loan is arranged on the following conditions:

(*a*) *A* will pay interest on the loan at 4% per annum. If in any year the interest so calculated exceeds the instalment then due *B* will advance the difference. These advances will be subject to the same rate of interest and the same terms of repayment as the original loan.

(*b*) If in any year the interest due is less than the instalment *A* will invest the balance in a sinking fund to accumulate at 3% effective.

(*c*) At the end of 20 years the original loan, plus any amounts advanced under (*a*) will be repaid by the accumulated sinking fund.

Find the amount of the loan.

CHAPTER 6

CAPITAL REDEMPTION POLICIES

6·1. Definitions

A 'Capital Redemption Policy' (or 'Capital Redemption Assurance') is a policy which secures the payment of a fixed sum of money at the end of a stated period of time in return for periodic payments to be paid for a fixed period of years, or in return for a single payment made at the time the policy is effected. Such policies, having originally been issued mainly in connexion with the purchase of leases, where the investor was buying a series of payments for a fixed period and wished to replace his purchase price when the income stopped, are frequently known as 'Leasehold Policies', or 'Leasehold Redemption Policies'. They are also sometimes referred to as 'Sinking Fund Policies'. The fixed sum to be paid at the end of the stated time is the 'Sum Assured' and the stated time is the 'term' of the policy. The periodic payments to be made, or the single payment as the case may be, are the premiums. If the term of the policy is n years, and if the sum assured is unity, the symbol used to denote the annual premium which should be paid throughout the duration of the policy to secure the sum assured is $P_{\overline{n}|}$. If premiums are paid m times per annum the symbol used is $P_{\overline{n}|}^{(m)}$. If only one payment of premium is to be made, a 'single premium', the symbol denoting this is $A_{\overline{n}|}$. If the annual premiums are payable for a shorter period than the whole term of the policy the policy is said to be effected by limited payments, and the symbol ${}_tP_{\overline{n}|}$ is used to denote the annual premium payable for t intervals of time to secure a payment of 1 at the end of n intervals of time.

6·2. Rates of premium

If a single premium is to be paid its value is readily found, since it must equal the present value of the sum assured, i.e.

$$A_{\overline{n}|} = v^n = 1 - d\ddot{a}_{\overline{n}|}. \qquad (6·1)$$

If an annual premium payable throughout the whole term of the policy is to be paid its value may be found as follows:

(*a*) The present value of the sum assured is v^n. The present value of the premiums is $P_{\overline{n}|}\ddot{a}_{\overline{n}|}$.

$$\therefore\ P_{\overline{n}|}\ddot{a}_{\overline{n}|}=v^n$$

or
$$P_{\overline{n}|}=\frac{v^n}{\ddot{a}_{\overline{n}|}}=\frac{A_{\overline{n}|}}{\ddot{a}_{\overline{n}|}}=\frac{1}{\ddot{a}_{\overline{n}|}}-d. \tag{6·2}$$

or (*b*) The accumulated value, at the end of the term, of the premiums is $P_{\overline{n}|}\ddot{s}_{\overline{n}|}$. This must equal the sum assured.

$$\therefore\ P_{\overline{n}|}\ddot{s}_{\overline{n}|}=1,$$

or
$$P_{\overline{n}|}=\frac{1}{\ddot{s}_{\overline{n}|}}=\frac{v^n}{\ddot{a}_{\overline{n}|}}\quad\text{as before.}$$

or (*c*) If a unit be invested in the purchase of an annuity-due for n years it will produce a payment of $1/\ddot{a}_{\overline{n}|}$ at the start of each year. The interest payable at the start of each year is d and the balance, i.e. $1/\ddot{a}_{\overline{n}|}-d$, must be the sum which, when accumulated at rate i, will amount to a sum sufficient to replace the purchase price, i.e. to 1. But by definition this is $P_{\overline{n}|}$.

$$\therefore\ P_{\overline{n}|}=\frac{1}{\ddot{a}_{\overline{n}|}}-d\quad\text{as before.}$$

Expressions for the value of ${}_tP_{\overline{n}|}$ may readily be deduced on similar lines.

6·3. Policy values

It is clear that the insurance company issuing a capital redemption policy must accumulate the premiums it receives, in order that at the end of the term it may have in hand enough to meet the sum assured. At any point during the currency of the policy the amount to which the premiums have accumulated is called the 'Reserve Value' of the policy, or the 'Policy Value' and is denoted for a unit policy by the symbol ${}_tV_{\overline{n}|}$, where n is the original term of the policy and t the time that has elapsed since it was issued. The

'Reserve Value' or 'Reserve' may be found by either of two methods:

(*a*) *Retrospectively*, i.e. by accumulating the premiums. First assume that t is an integral number of years. Then the amount to which the premiums have accumulated assuming one to be due and unpaid is

$$P_{\overline{n}|}[(1+i)^t+(1+i)^{t-1}+\ldots+(1+i)]$$

$$=\frac{1}{\ddot{s}_{\overline{n}|}}\ddot{s}_{\overline{t}|}.$$

$$\therefore\ {}_tV_{\overline{n}|}=\frac{s_{\overline{t}|}}{s_{\overline{n}|}}. \tag{6·3}$$

(*b*) *Prospectively*. The insurance company is bound to pay the sum of 1 at the end of $(n-t)$ years, and it is due to receive $P_{\overline{n}|}$ for $(n-t)$ years. The reserve must therefore be such that, when it is added to the present value of future premiums, the total is equal to the present value of the sum assured, i.e.

$${}_tV_{\overline{n}|}+P_{\overline{n}|}\ddot{a}_{\overline{n-t}|}=v^{n-t}.$$

$$\begin{aligned}\therefore\ {}_tV_{\overline{n}|}&=v^{n-t}-P_{\overline{n}|}\ddot{a}_{\overline{n-t}|}\\&=1-(P_{\overline{n}|}+d)\ddot{a}_{\overline{n-t}|}\\&=1-\frac{\ddot{a}_{\overline{n-t}|}}{\ddot{a}_{\overline{n}|}} \qquad (6·4)\\&=1-\frac{a_{\overline{n-t}|}}{a_{\overline{n}|}}\\&=v^{n-t}\frac{a_{\overline{t}|}}{a_{\overline{n}|}}\\&=\frac{s_{\overline{t}|}}{s_{\overline{n}|}}\quad\text{as before.}\end{aligned}$$

6·4. Non-integral value of t

If $t=r+1/p$ (where r is an integral number of years) the reserve ${}_tV_{\overline{n}|}$ may be found as follows:

(*a*) *Retrospectively*: ${}_tV_{\overline{n}|}=({}_rV_{\overline{n}|}+P_{\overline{n}|})(1+i)^{1/p}$, since after r years the policy value is ${}_rV_{\overline{n}|}$. A further payment of $P_{\overline{n}|}$ is made and the total amount then accumulates for a further period of $1/p$ years.

(*b*) *Prospectively.* The value of future premiums is

$$P_{\overline{n}|}.v^{1-1/p}\ddot{a}_{\overline{n-(r+1)}|},$$

and the value of the sum assured is $v^{n-r-1/p}$.

$$\therefore\ {}_tV_{\overline{n}|}+P_{\overline{n}|}\,v^{1-1/p}\ddot{a}_{\overline{n-(r+1)}|}=v^{n-r-1/p}.$$

$$\begin{aligned}\therefore\ {}_tV_{\overline{n}|}&=v^{-1/p}\left[v^{n-r}-P_{\overline{n}|}.v.\ddot{a}_{\overline{n-(r+1)}|}\right]\\&=(1+i)^{1/p}\left[v^{n-r}-P_{\overline{n}|}a_{\overline{n-(r+1)}|}\right]\\&=(1+i)^{1/p}\left[v^{n-r}-P_{\overline{n}|}(\ddot{a}_{\overline{n-r}|}-1)\right]\\&=(1+i)^{1/p}\left[{}_rV_{\overline{n}|}+P_{\overline{n}|}\right]\quad\text{as before.}\end{aligned}$$

(*c*) Since, as is apparent from first principles,

$$({}_tV_{\overline{n}|}+P_{\overline{n}|})(1+i)={}_{t+1}V_{\overline{n}|},$$

the reserve for a policy after a non-integral period can be written either as

$$(1+i)^{1/p}\,({}_rV_{\overline{n}|}+P_{\overline{n}|})$$

or as

$$v^{1-1/p}\,{}_{r+1}V_{\overline{n}|}.$$

6·5. Paid-up policies

After a policy has been in force for some time the insurance company may be asked to quote a reduced sum assured payable at the end of the original term if future premiums be discontinued. This sum is called the 'Paid-up Policy', or 'Free Policy', and in respect of a unit policy is denoted by ${}_tW_{\overline{n}|}$, where n is the original term of the policy and t the time that has elapsed since it was issued. It may be found by either of two methods.

(*a*) The accumulated premiums are equal to ${}_tV_{\overline{n}|}$. If this were applied as a single premium it would secure a sum assured of $\dfrac{{}_tV_{\overline{n}|}}{A_{\overline{n-t}|}}$, and therefore if no future premiums are to be paid this should be the paid-up policy, i.e.

$$\begin{aligned}{}_tW_{\overline{n}|}&=\frac{{}_tV_{\overline{n}|}}{A_{\overline{n-t}|}}\\&=\frac{s_{\overline{t}|}}{s_{\overline{n}|}}\times\frac{1}{v^{n-t}}\\&=\frac{v^ts_{\overline{t}|}}{v^ns_{\overline{n}|}}\\&=\frac{a_{\overline{t}|}}{a_{\overline{n}|}}.\end{aligned}\tag{6·5}$$

(*b*) The future premium for a new assurance of 1 is $P_{\overline{n-t}|}$. Hence future premiums of $P_{\overline{n}|}$ will secure a sum assured of $\dfrac{P_{\overline{n}|}}{P_{\overline{n-t}|}}$. The sum assured already secured must therefore be

$$1-\frac{P_{\overline{n}|}}{P_{\overline{n-t}|}}$$

or

$$\begin{aligned} {}_tW_{\overline{n}|} &= 1-\frac{P_{\overline{n}|}}{P_{\overline{n-t}|}} \\ &= 1-\frac{\ddot{s}_{\overline{n-t}|}}{\ddot{s}_{\overline{n}|}} \\ &= 1-\frac{s_{\overline{n-t}|}}{s_{\overline{n}|}} \\ &= \frac{s_{\overline{n}|}-s_{\overline{n-t}|}}{s_{\overline{n}|}} \\ &= \frac{(1+i)^{n-t}s_{\overline{t}|}}{s_{\overline{n}|}} \\ &= \frac{a_{\overline{t}|}}{a_{\overline{n}|}} \quad \text{as before.} \end{aligned}$$

6·6. Effect of changes in the rate of interest

The effect of a change in the rate of interest used in calculating premiums, reserves and paid-up policies is as follows:

(*a*) *Premiums*. Since $P_{\overline{n}|}=\dfrac{1}{\ddot{s}_{\overline{n}|}}$,

and since $s_{\overline{n}|}$ increases with an increase in i, an increase in the rate of interest reduces the premium, and vice versa.

(*b*) *Policy values*. It is not possible to deduce by general reasoning alone what will be the effect of an alteration in the rate of interest used in calculating policy values. It is assumed that the alteration applies both to the calculation of the premium under the policy and to the operation of accumulating this premium in order to find the policy value. It has been shown that if the rate of interest is increased the premium will be reduced, but this reduced premium will be accumulated at the increased rate of interest, and without further investigation it is not clear whether the result of this accumulation will be greater or less than the policy value found at the original rate of interest.

Since

$$ {}_tV_{\overline{n}|} = \frac{s_{\overline{t}|}}{s_{\overline{n}|}}, $$

$$ {}_1V_{\overline{n}|} = \frac{s_{\overline{1}|}}{s_{\overline{n}|}} = \frac{1}{s_{\overline{n}|}}, $$

and as $s_{\overline{n}|}$ increases with an increase in i it is clear that for a policy of one year's duration an increase in the rate of interest will reduce the policy value. But

$$ {}_tV_{\overline{n}|} = 1 - \frac{a_{\overline{n-t}|}}{a_{\overline{n}|}}. $$

$$ \therefore\ 1 - {}_tV_{\overline{n}|} = \frac{a_{\overline{n-t}|}}{a_{\overline{n}|}} $$

$$ = \frac{a_{\overline{n-t}|}}{a_{\overline{n-t+1}|}} \cdot \frac{a_{\overline{n-t+1}|}}{a_{\overline{n-t+2}|}} \cdots \frac{a_{\overline{n-1}|}}{a_{\overline{n}|}} $$

$$ = (1 - {}_1V_{\overline{n-t+1}|})(1 - {}_1V_{\overline{n-t+2}|}) \cdots (1 - {}_1V_{\overline{n}|}), $$

and if the rate of interest is increased the values of $(1 - {}_1V_{\overline{n-t+k}|})$ are all increased. Hence the value of $1 - {}_tV_{\overline{n}|}$ increases with an increase in the rate of interest; i.e. an increase in the rate of interest decreases the value of ${}_tV_{\overline{n}|}$, and vice versa.

(c) *Paid-up policies.*

Since

$$ {}_tW_{\overline{n}|} = \frac{a_{\overline{t}|}}{a_{\overline{n}|}}, $$

$$ {}_1W_{\overline{n}|} = \frac{1}{\ddot{a}_{\overline{n}|}}, $$

and, as $\ddot{a}_{\overline{n}|}$ decreases with an increase in i, it is clear that for a policy of one year's duration an increase in the rate of interest will increase the paid-up policy value.

Now $1 - {}_tW_{\overline{n}|} = \dfrac{s_{\overline{n-t}|}}{s_{\overline{n}|}}$

$$= \frac{s_{\overline{n-t}|}}{s_{\overline{n-t+1}|}} \frac{s_{\overline{n-t+1}|}}{s_{\overline{n-t+2}|}} \cdots \frac{s_{\overline{n-1}|}}{s_{\overline{n}|}}$$

$$= [1 - {}_1W_{\overline{n-t+1}|}][1 - {}_1W_{\overline{n-t+2}|}] \cdots [1 - {}_1W_{\overline{n}|}].$$

Hence, by similar reasoning to that used for reserves, an increase in the rate of interest increases the value of the paid-up policy value, and vice versa.

6·7. Premiums payable other than yearly

It has been assumed up to the present that premiums are payable annually. If premiums are payable m times per annum, expression for rates of premium, policy values and paid-up policies can be derived as follows:

(*a*) *Rates of premium.* The equation of value here is

$$P_{\overline{n}|}^{(m)} \ddot{s}_{\overline{n}|}^{(m)} = 1.$$

$$\therefore\ P_{\overline{n}|}^{(m)} = \frac{1}{(1+i)^{1/m} s_{\overline{n}|}^{(m)}}$$

$$= \frac{1}{\left(1 + \frac{i^{(m)}}{m}\right)\left(\frac{i}{i^{(m)}}\right) s_{\overline{n}|}}$$

$$= \frac{1}{\left(\frac{i}{i^{(m)}} + \frac{i}{m}\right) s_{\overline{n}|}} \quad \text{or} \quad \frac{1}{\frac{i}{d^{(m)}} s_{\overline{n}|}}, \qquad (6·6)$$

the expression to be used being chosen according as tables of $i/d^{(m)}$ are, or are not, available. Alternatively, prospectively,

$$P_{\overline{n}|}^{(m)} \ddot{a}_{\overline{n}|}^{(m)} = v^n.$$

$$\therefore\ P_{\overline{n}|}^{(m)} = \frac{v^n}{\ddot{a}_{\overline{n}|}^{(m)}}$$

$$= \frac{v^n}{(1+i)^{1/m} a_{\overline{n}|}^{(m)}}$$

$$= \frac{1}{(1+i)^{1/m} s_{\overline{n}|}^{(m)}} \quad \text{as before.}$$

From the foregoing it is also evident that

$$P_{\overline{n}|}^{(m)} = \frac{1 - ia_{\overline{n}|}}{(1+i)^{1/m}\, a_{\overline{n}|}^{(m)}}$$

$$= \frac{1}{\ddot{a}_{\overline{n}|}^{(m)}} - \frac{ia_{\overline{n}|}}{(1+i)^{1/m} \dfrac{i}{i^{(m)}} a_{\overline{n}|}}$$

$$= \frac{1}{\ddot{a}_{\overline{n}|}^{(m)}} - \frac{m[(1+i)^{1/m} - 1]}{(1+i)^{1/m}}$$

$$= \frac{1}{\ddot{a}_{\overline{n}|}^{(m)}} - m(1 - v^{1/m}) = \frac{1}{\ddot{a}_{\overline{n}|}^{(m)}} - d^{(m)}.$$

This corresponds to the expression $P_{\overline{n}|} = \dfrac{1}{\ddot{a}_{\overline{n}|}} - d$, and a verbal explanation of it in this form can be given on precisely the same lines as in § 6·2. If premiums are payable continuously the symbol used is $\bar{P}_{\overline{n}|}$ and it will be seen from the above that $\bar{P}_{\overline{n}|} = 1/\bar{a}_{\overline{n}|} - \delta$.

An alternative expression for $P_{\overline{n}|}^{(m)}$ can be derived by considering the fact that by accepting premiums in instalments throughout the year the insurer earns less interest on them than on the premium paid in one sum at the start of the year. To compensate for this loss of interest the premiums must be correspondingly increased. At the end of a year the annual premium has accumulated to $P_{\overline{n}|}(1+i)$. The *m*thly premiums have accumulated to

$$\frac{1}{m} P_{\overline{n}|}^{(m)} [(1+i) + (1+i)^{1-1/m} + \ldots + (1+i)^{1/m}] = \frac{1}{m} P_{\overline{n}|}^{(m)} (1+i)^{1/m}\, m s_{\overline{1}|}^{(m)}.$$

$$\therefore\ P_{\overline{n}|}^{(m)} = P_{\overline{n}|} \times \frac{1+i}{(1+i)^{1/m}\, s_{\overline{1}|}^{(m)}}$$

$$= \frac{P_{\overline{n}|}}{\ddot{a}_{\overline{1}|}^{(m)}},$$

or $P_{\overline{n}|}^{(m)} \ddot{a}_{\overline{1}|}^{(m)} = P_{\overline{n}|}$, which is obvious from first principles.

(*b*) *Policy values.* If the duration is an integral number of years then the policy value of a policy subject to *m*thly premium must be the same as that of a policy subject to annual premiums, since the accumulated amount of the premiums at the end of any year is the same in either case. This can easily be proved as follows:

$$\begin{aligned}{}_tV^{(m)}_{\overline{n}|} &= v^{n-t} - P^{(m)}_{\overline{n}|}\,\ddot{a}^{(m)}_{\overline{n-t}|}\\ &= v^{n-t} - \frac{P_{\overline{n}|}}{\ddot{a}^{(m)}_{\overline{1}|}}\,\ddot{a}^{(m)}_{\overline{1}|}\,\ddot{a}_{\overline{n-t}|}\\ &= v^{n-t} - P_{\overline{n}|}\,\ddot{a}_{\overline{n-t}|}\\ &= {}_tV_{\overline{n}|}.\end{aligned}$$

If the duration is not integral let $t = r + \frac{l}{m} + \frac{1}{qm}$.

$$\therefore\ {}_tV^{(m)}_{\overline{n}|} = (1+i)^{1/qm}\,P^{(m)}_{\overline{n}|}\,s^{(m)}_{\overline{r+\frac{l+1}{m}}|},$$

since $P^{(m)}_{\overline{n}|}\,s^{(m)}_{\overline{r+\frac{l+1}{m}}|}$ is the value of the policy immediately after payment of the $(l+1)$th instalment of premium due in the $(r+1)$th year.

Alternatively, the value could be found by assuming premiums to be payable annually and deducting from the policy value so found the present value of the unpaid balance of the year's premiums. This leads to a rather complex expression, and in practice the value is best found by a consideration of the problem from first principles.

(*c*) *Paid-up policies.* If the duration is an integral number of years, then, by reasoning similar to that employed in (*b*) above, it may readily be shown that ${}_tW^{(m)}_{\overline{n}|} = {}_tW_{\overline{n}|}$. If the term is not integral the paid-up policy is best determined by calculating the reserve as in (*b*) above and then calculating what sum assured this amount will purchase if applied as a single premium to effect a new policy.

6·8. Premium conversion tables

The formulae

$$\begin{aligned}A_{\overline{n}|} &= 1 - d\ddot{a}_{\overline{n}|}\\ &= 1 - d(1 + a_{\overline{n-1}|})\end{aligned}$$

and

$$P_{\overline{n}|} = \frac{1}{1 + a_{\overline{n-1}|}} - d$$

suggest that it might be convenient to have tabulated the values of $1 - d(1 + X)$ and $\frac{1}{1+X} - d$ for values of X progressing by small differences over a range which will cover the annuity values at practical terms and rates of interest. Such tables are called 'Conversion Tables'. Their main use is in connexion with problems of life annuities, and their scope is discussed more fully in the textbooks dealing with that subject. From the point of view of annuities-certain there is little, if any, advantage in using them, since it is almost as easy to evaluate $P_{\overline{n}|} = \frac{1}{\ddot{s}_{\overline{n}|}} = \frac{1}{s_{\overline{n+1}|} - 1}$ as to enter conversion tables with the value of $a_{\overline{n-1}|}$. It should be noted that as

$$P_{\overline{n}|}^{(m)} = \frac{1}{\ddot{a}_{\overline{n}|}^{(m)}} - d^{(m)},$$

it is not possible to use conversion tables to calculate premiums payable m times per annum. If premiums are payable continuously, however, $\bar{P}_{\overline{n}|} = \frac{1}{\bar{a}_{\overline{n}|}} - \delta$, and continuous conversion tables can be constructed and employed.

6·9. Practical considerations

The foregoing paragraphs have dealt with the theoretical aspects of capital redemption policies. In practice certain variations may be made in applying this theory and these are discussed below.

(*a*) *Interest basis.* Capital redemption policies are guaranteed contracts extending often over very long periods of time. The insurance company issuing the policy may feel that the future course of interest rates cannot be foreseen with certainty and may therefore deem it prudent to assume that rates of interest may fall. As formulae involving an annual decrease in the rate of interest are cumbersome it is more usual, if the assumption of a varying rate of interest is being made, to assume that the changes in the rate of interest take place quinquennially or even at longer intervals. Thus if the rate were i_1 for t_1 years, i_2 for t_2 years and i_3 thereafter, the formula for $P'_{\overline{n}|}$ would be

$$P'_{\overline{n}|}[\ddot{s}_{\overline{t_1}|}^{i_1}(1+i_2)^{t_2}(1+i_3)^{n-t_1-t_2} + \ddot{s}_{\overline{t_2}|}^{i_2}(1+i_3)^{n-t_1-t_2} + \ddot{s}_{\overline{n-t_1-t_2}|}^{i_3}] = 1.$$

(*b*) *Office premiums.* The expenses incurred by an office in the issue of capital redemption policies may be met either by adding a 'loading' to the premium, or by calculating the premium at a lower rate of interest than the office expects to earn. The only point to be noted is that the loading is frequently expressed as a percentage of what is known as the *office* or gross premium. If the net premium is π and the loading is expressed as being $k\%$ of the office premium, the office premium P is found from the equation

$$P = \pi + \cdot 01kP$$

or

$$P = \frac{\pi}{1 - \cdot 01k}.$$

(*c*) *Surrender values.* If a policy is discontinued during its currency the insurance company will generally make some return. The full theoretical return would be the reserve value of the policy as it stands in the company's books. In practice, however, the company will usually make a smaller return to allow for the expenses which have been incurred. Possible methods of allowing for these are by accumulating the premium at a lower rate of interest than that used in calculating the reserve, or by taking a percentage of the reserve value, or by making some other deduction—for example, the office might give an accumulation of all premiums paid except the first. Some adjustment may be necessary in the last few years of the term if the surrender value on such a basis compares very unfavourably with the face value of the policy.

(*d*) *Paid-up policies.* Again in practice it is not usual for an office to give the full theoretical paid-up policy value. One method would be to allow a proportionate policy of t/n per unit sum assured, where t equals the number of premiums paid and n equals the number of premiums payable. This is less than the theoretical value of ${}_tW_{\overline{n}|}$, for as

$$a_{\overline{t}|} = v + v^2 + \ldots + v^t$$

and

$$a_{\overline{n}|} = v + v^2 + \ldots + v^n,$$

and as v^t decreases with an increase in t, $\dfrac{v+v^2+\dots+v^t}{t}$ (i.e. the average of the first t terms) must be greater than

$$\frac{v+v^2+\dots+v^n}{n}.$$

$$\therefore\quad \frac{a_{\overline{t}|}}{t} > \frac{a_{\overline{n}|}}{n}$$

or

$$\frac{a_{\overline{t}|}}{a_{\overline{n}|}} > \frac{t}{n}.$$

Another method would be to relate the paid-up policy to the surrender value so that the surrender value of the policy before and after alteration remains the same.

6·10. The following examples illustrate the points discussed above:

Example 6·1

Calculate at an effective rate of interest of 3% per annum the net annual premium, payable quarterly from 25 December 1933 to 25 September 1946 inclusive to secure £100 on 12 January, 12 May and 12 September in each of the five years 1947–51.

Let P be the annual premium.

The value of premiums accumulated to 12 January 1947

$$= Ps^{(4)}_{\overline{1}|}\, s_{\overline{13}|}\,(1+i)^{1/4+\frac{18}{365}}.$$

The value of the sum assured at the same date

$$= 300 s^{(3)}_{\overline{1}|}\, a_{\overline{5}|}\,(1+i)^{1/3}.$$

$$\therefore\quad P = \frac{300 s^{(3)}_{\overline{1}|}\, a_{\overline{5}|}(1+i)^{1/3}}{s_{\overline{13}|} s^{(4)}_{\overline{1}|}(1+i)^{1/4+\frac{18}{365}}}$$

$$= \frac{300 i^{(4)} a_{\overline{5}|}\,(1+i)^{12/365}}{i^{(3)} s_{\overline{13}|}}.$$

By calculation from the binomial expansion $i^{(3)} = \cdot029705$ and $(1\cdot03)^{\frac{12}{365}}$ is approximately $1\cdot001$.

$$\therefore\quad P = \frac{300 \times 1\cdot001 \times 4\cdot5797 \times \cdot029668}{15\cdot6178 \times \cdot029705}$$

$$= 87\cdot95$$

$$= £87\cdot95.$$

Example 6·2

If $\sum_{1}^{30} \log_{10}(P_{\overline{t|}}+1)=1\cdot31388$, find i.

$$P_{\overline{t|}}+1=\frac{1}{\ddot{a}_{\overline{t|}}}+1-d$$

$$=\frac{1+v\ddot{a}_{\overline{t|}}}{\ddot{a}_{\overline{t|}}}$$

$$=\frac{\ddot{a}_{\overline{t+1|}}}{\ddot{a}_{\overline{t|}}}.$$

$$\therefore\ \log(P_{\overline{t|}}+1)=\log\ddot{a}_{\overline{t+1|}}-\log\ddot{a}_{\overline{t|}}.$$

$$\therefore\ \sum_{1}^{30}\log(P_{\overline{t|}}+1)=\log\ddot{a}_{\overline{31|}}-\log\ddot{a}_{\overline{1|}}.$$

$$=\log\ddot{a}_{\overline{31|}}.$$

$$\therefore\ \log_{10}(1+a_{\overline{30|}})=1\cdot31388$$

or

$$a_{\overline{30|}}=20\cdot601-1$$

$$=19\cdot601,$$

and from inspection of the tables

$$i=\cdot03.$$

Example 6·3

(This question is designed to illustrate the use to which sinking fund policies were originally put.)

A buys a ground rent of £100 per annum which is payable for 30 years and then ceases. The first payment is due one year hence. To replace the capital invested he effects a sinking fund policy at a premium calculated on a net $2\frac{1}{2}\%$ basis. He calculates that he will earn 5% on his investment. What price can he pay if

(*a*) a 30-year policy is effected now by single premium;
(*b*) a 30-year policy is effected now by annual premiums;
(*c*) a 31-year policy is effected now by annual premiums;
(*d*) a 29-year policy is to be effected one year hence by annual premiums;
(*e*) a 30-year policy is to be effected one year hence by annual premiums?

Let the price paid and the sum assured be denoted in each case by A and S respectively.

(*a*) The premium is Sv^{30} at $2\frac{1}{2}\%$, and the total outlay is $A+Sv^{30}$. At the end of 30 years the purchaser receives $S+100$, and this must pay interest at 5% on his outlay, and repay the outlay, i.e.

$$S+100=\cdot 05\,[A+Sv^{30}]+A+Sv^{30}.$$

Also each payment of 100 must provide one year's interest at 5% on the outlay, i.e.

$$100=\cdot 05\,[A+Sv^{30}].$$

From these equations it will be seen that

$$A=S(1-v^{30}).$$

$$\therefore\quad 100=\cdot 05\left[A+\frac{Av^{30}}{1-v^{30}}\right].$$

$$\therefore\quad 2000(1-v^{30})=A.$$

$$\therefore\quad A=1046.$$

(*b*) The outlay is now $A+SP_{\overline{30}|}$. At the end of 30 years the payments received are $S+100$, and these must pay interest at 5% on the outlay, and repay the outlay, i.e.

$$S+100=\cdot 05\,[A+SP_{\overline{30}|}]+[A+SP_{\overline{30}|}].$$

Also each payment of 100 must provide 5% on the outlay and pay the annual premium due, i.e.

$$\begin{aligned}100&=\cdot 05\,[A+SP_{\overline{30}|}]+SP_{\overline{30}|}\\&=S+100-A-SP_{\overline{30}|}+SP_{\overline{30}|}.\end{aligned}$$

$$\therefore\quad S=A.$$

$$\begin{aligned}\therefore\quad A&=\frac{100}{P_{\overline{30}|}+\cdot 05\,[1+P_{\overline{30}|}]}\\&=\frac{100}{\cdot 02222+\cdot 05\times 1\cdot 0222}\\&=1363\cdot 6.\end{aligned}$$

(*c*) The outlay in this case is $A+SP_{\overline{31}|}$. At the end of the 31st year the only payment made is S, the income having ceased one year before, and this must repay the outlay with one year's interest.

$$\therefore S = 1{\cdot}05\,[A + SP_{\overline{31}|}].$$

Also $\quad 100 = {\cdot}05\,[A + SP_{\overline{31}|}] + SP_{\overline{31}|}$

$$= S - A - SP_{\overline{31}|} + SP_{\overline{31}|}.$$

$$\therefore S = A + 100.$$

$$\therefore\ A + 100 = 1{\cdot}05\,[A + (A + 100)\,P_{\overline{31}|}].$$

$$\therefore\ A = 100\left[\frac{1 - 1{\cdot}05P_{\overline{31}|}}{1{\cdot}05P_{\overline{31}|} + {\cdot}05}\right]$$

$$= 100\left[\frac{1}{P_{\overline{31}|} + \underset{\cdot 05}{d}} - 1\right]$$ (this form saves arithmetic).

Now $\quad P_{\overline{31}|} = \dfrac{1}{47{\cdot}15} = {\cdot}021209.$

$$\therefore\ A = 100\left[\frac{1}{{\cdot}068828} - 1\right]$$

$$= 1352{\cdot}9.$$

(*d*) In this case the outlay is A. At the end of year 30 the income is $S + 100$. $\quad \therefore\ S + 100 = 1{\cdot}05A.$

In each of the first 29 years the income of 100 must provide 5% on the outlay and pay the premium then due, i.e.

$$100 = {\cdot}05A + SP_{\overline{29}|}$$

$$= S + 100 - A + SP_{\overline{29}|}.$$

$$\therefore\ S = A - SP_{\overline{29}|}.$$

$$\therefore\ \frac{A}{1 + P_{\overline{29}|}} + 100 = 1{\cdot}05A.$$

$$\therefore\ A = \frac{100}{1{\cdot}05 - \dfrac{1}{1 + P_{\overline{29}|}}}$$

$$= \frac{100}{1{\cdot}05 - \dfrac{1}{1{\cdot}023308}}$$

$$= 1374{\cdot}1.$$

(*e*) In this case the outlay is A. At the end of year 31 the income is S.

$$\therefore \quad S = 1{\cdot}05A.$$

During each of the first 30 years the income of 100 must provide 5% on the outlay and pay the premium then due, i.e.

$$100 = {\cdot}05A + SP_{\overline{30}|}$$

$$= {\cdot}05A + P_{\overline{30}|}(1{\cdot}05)A.$$

$$\therefore \quad A = \frac{100}{{\cdot}05 + 1{\cdot}05P_{\overline{30}|}}$$

$$= 1363{\cdot}6 \quad \text{as before.}$$

The particular points to note in this problem are (*a*) the sum assured is not necessarily the same as the price paid, and (*b*) as the outlay is repaid in full, each year's transaction can be considered by itself, i.e. in (*b*) for example it is possible to write

$$100 = {\cdot}05\,[A + SP_{\overline{30}|}] + SP_{\overline{30}|}.$$

This is a more direct form than the equation of value

$$SP_{\overline{30}|}\,\ddot{a}_{\overline{30}|} + A = 100a_{\overline{30}|} + Sv^{30}$$

(where all functions except $P_{\overline{30}|}$ are calculated at 5%), which of course can be reduced to the same form.

Example 6·4

A sinking fund policy for £10,000 payable on 1 July 1999 was effected on 1 January 1920 at a quarterly premium limited to 200 payments, calculated at a net rate of interest per annum of 3% effective. It was desired to alter the contract starting with the premium payment due on 1 April 1935. The sum assured was to become £8000, and the future premiums were to be reduced in proportion. How many premiums should be paid if the office made the conversion using a net rate of interest of 3% per annum effective throughout.

Let the reserve held by the office on 31 March 1935 be V. Then, since the whole transaction is carried out at 3% effective, the reserve which the office should hold after the alteration is ${\cdot}8V$. The difference of ${\cdot}2V$ must therefore be equal to the value of the premium which the office is not now to receive.

Let X be the original quarterly premium and let the new premium of $\cdot 8X$ be payable for n years.

$$\therefore \quad \cdot 2V = 4 \times \cdot 8X[\ddot{a}^{(4)}_{\overline{34\frac{3}{4}}|} - \ddot{a}^{(4)}_{\overline{n}|}]$$

and

$$V = 4X[s^{(4)}_{\overline{15}|}(1+i)^{\frac{1}{4}} + \tfrac{1}{4}(1+i)^{\frac{1}{4}}].$$

$$\therefore \quad X[s^{(4)}_{\overline{15}|}(1+i)^{\frac{1}{4}} + \tfrac{1}{4}(1+i)^{\frac{1}{4}}] = 4X[\ddot{a}^{(4)}_{\overline{34\frac{3}{4}}|} - \ddot{a}^{(4)}_{\overline{n}|}].$$

$$\therefore \quad a_{\overline{34\frac{3}{4}}|} - a_{\overline{n}|} = \frac{1}{4}\left[s_{\overline{15}|}(1+i)^{\frac{1}{4}} + \frac{i^{(4)}}{4i}\right].$$

$$\therefore \quad a_{\overline{n}|} = a_{\overline{35}|} - \tfrac{1}{4}v^{35} - \frac{1}{4}\left[s_{\overline{15}|}\left(1 + \frac{i^{(4)}}{4}\right) + \frac{i^{(4)}}{4i}\right].$$
$$= 16 \cdot 654.$$

Therefore by interpolation in the tables

$$n = 23 + \frac{210}{492}$$
$$= 23 \cdot 42 \text{ years,}$$

i.e. the quarterly premium will have to be paid for a further 23¼ years, and at the end of 23½ years a reduced premium will be payable.

Example 6·5

A 20-year leasehold policy for £1000 was effected on 1 January 1929 at an annual premium of £37·50. On 31 December 1938 it was converted to a paid-up policy on a 4% net premium reserve basis, and on 1 January 1946 was surrendered for its prospective value on a 4½% basis. If the office earned 4% per annum on its funds up to 31 December 1934 and 4½% thereafter, ascertain the profit on the whole transaction assuming initial expenses of £1% calculated on the sum assured and renewal expenses equivalent to 5% of each premium paid after the first.

The statement that the policy was converted on a 4% net premium basis means that the calculations were carried out as if the policy had been issued with a net premium calculated at 4% and as if the reserves held by the office for the policy were also calculated at 4%. The paid-up policy is therefore $1000\,{}_{10}W_{\overline{20}|}$ at 4%

$$= 1000 \frac{a_{\overline{10}|}}{a_{\overline{20}|}}$$
$$= 596 \cdot 81.$$

The surrender value 7 years later is $596 \cdot 81 v^3$ at 4½%

$$= 522 \cdot 98.$$

The amount the company has in hand is

(*a*) Up to 31 December 1934 the accumulation of premiums less expenses at 4%, i.e.

$$27{\cdot}5\,(1{\cdot}04)^6 + {\cdot}95 \times 37{\cdot}5\,(s_{\overline{6}|} - 1)$$
$$= 34{\cdot}796 + 200{\cdot}676$$
$$= 235{\cdot}472.$$

(*b*) Up to 31 December 1938 the accumulation of the sum in (*a*) plus the accumulation of premiums less expenses at $4\frac{1}{2}$%, i.e.

$$235{\cdot}472\,(1{\cdot}045)^4 + {\cdot}95 \times 37{\cdot}5\,(s_{\overline{5}|} - 1)$$
$$= 280{\cdot}805 + 159{\cdot}269$$
$$= 440{\cdot}074.$$

(*c*) Up to 31 December 1945 the amount in (*b*) will accumulate at $4\frac{1}{2}$%, i.e.

$$440{\cdot}074\,(1{\cdot}045)^7 = 598{\cdot}879.$$

The amount paid is 522·98. Therefore the profit is

$$75{\cdot}90$$

say £75·90.

Example 6·6

An assurance company calculates its rates of premium for leasehold policies on the assumption that it will earn an effective rate of interest of 3% net per annum and incur expenses of 21% of the premium in the first year and 1% in each year thereafter. What sum assured can it grant under a 20-year policy for a premium of £1 per month? If after $10\frac{1}{2}$ years, before the premium then due is paid, the assured wishes to alter the policy to a paid-up policy under which the sum assured at maturity will be payable in nine half-yearly instalments, what will the amount of the instalment be?

In 20 years premiums of £1 per month less expenses will accumulate to

$$12\,(1+i)^{\frac{1}{12}} s^{(12)}_{\overline{20}|} - 12 s^{(12)}_{\overline{1}|}\,(1+i)^{\frac{1}{12}} \times {\cdot}21 \times (1+i)^{19} - 12\,(1+i)^{\frac{1}{12}} s^{(12)}_{\overline{19}|} \times {\cdot}01$$
$$= 12\,(1+i)^{\frac{1}{12}} s^{(12)}_{\overline{1}|}\,[s_{\overline{20}|} - {\cdot}21\,(1+i)^{19} - {\cdot}01 s_{\overline{19}|}]$$
$$= 12\left[\frac{i}{i^{(12)}} + \frac{i}{12}\right][{\cdot}99 s_{\overline{20}|} - {\cdot}2\,(1+i)^{19}]$$
$$= 12 \times 1{\cdot}01613 \times (26{\cdot}6017 - {\cdot}3507)$$
$$= 320{\cdot}093$$

or say £320.

After $10\frac{1}{2}$ years the premiums, less expenses, will have accumulated at 3 % to

$$12s_{\overline{1}|}^{(12)}(1+i)^{\frac{1}{2}}[\cdot 99(1+i)^{\frac{1}{12}}s_{\overline{10}|}-(1+i)^{\frac{1}{12}}\times\cdot 2(1+i)^{9}]$$
$$+\cdot 99[(1+i)^{\frac{1}{2}}+(1+i)^{\frac{5}{12}}+\ldots+(1+i)^{\frac{1}{12}}],$$

and in $9\frac{1}{2}$ years time this amount will give a sum assured of

$$12s_{\overline{1}|}^{(12)}(1+i)^{10}(1+i)^{\frac{1}{12}}[\cdot 99s_{\overline{10}|}-\cdot 2(1+i)^{9}]$$
$$+\cdot 99[(1+i)^{10}+(1+i)^{9\frac{11}{12}}+\ldots+(1+i)^{9\frac{7}{12}}]$$
$$=12\times 1\cdot 01613[\cdot 99(s_{\overline{20}|}-s_{\overline{10}|})-\cdot 2(1+i)^{19}]$$
$$+\cdot 99(1+i)^{9}\left(1+\frac{i^{(2)}}{2}\right)\left(1+\frac{i^{(12)}}{12}\right)\times 6\frac{i^{(2)}}{i^{(12)}}$$
$$=181\cdot 68+7\cdot 977$$
$$=189\cdot 66.$$

Hence if X is the instalment

$$X[1+v^{\frac{1}{2}}+\ldots+v^{4}]=189\cdot 66 \text{ at } 3\%.$$

Now
$$1+v^{\frac{1}{2}}+\ldots+v^{4}=\frac{1-v^{4\frac{1}{2}}}{1-v^{\frac{1}{2}}}$$
$$=\frac{1+\dfrac{i^{(2)}}{2}-v^{4}}{1+\dfrac{i^{(2)}}{2}-1}.$$

$$\therefore\ X=\frac{189\cdot 66\times\dfrac{i^{(2)}}{2}}{1+\dfrac{i^{(2)}}{2}-v^{4}}=\frac{189\cdot 66\times\cdot 01489}{\cdot 12640}=22\cdot 343$$

or say £22·34.

Alternatively, the sum assured which can be granted at maturity is the original sum assured less the accumulation of the unpaid premiums, i.e. $320\cdot 093-\cdot 99\times 12s_{\overline{9\frac{1}{2}}|}^{(12)}$, and it might be assumed for ease of calculation that $s_{\overline{9\frac{1}{2}}|}=\frac{1}{2}(s_{\overline{9}|}+s_{\overline{10}|})$. This method is perhaps simpler and the numerical result is the same.

Example 6·7

In return for a loan granted at the present time a borrower is prepared to make 20 yearly payments each of £100, the first payment falling due at the end of 6 years. The lender intends to effect a leasehold policy of

£1000, maturing in 25 years time by annual premiums. The first six premiums and interest for the first 5 years will be treated by the lender as additions to the original loan. Thereafter the interest and premium will be paid out of the £100 payment each year, and the balance accumulated as a sinking fund which, with the proceeds of the leasehold policy, will extinguish the loan.

The premium is calculated on a 3% basis, with a loading of $2\frac{1}{2}$% of the gross premium. The sinking fund will accumulate at $3\frac{1}{2}$% per annum effective. The lender wishes to realize 4% per annum effective on his investment. What amount can he lend?

The net premium is $\dfrac{1}{s_{\overline{26}|}-1}$ at 3% = ·02663 per unit sum assured.

Therefore the office premium is $\dfrac{\cdot 02663}{\cdot 975} = \cdot 02731$ per unit sum assured.

Let the amount of the loan be X. During the first 5 years the premiums and interest accumulate at 4%.

Therefore at the start of year 6 the amount of debt is

$$X(1\cdot 04)^5 + 27\cdot 31 s_{\overline{6}|} \text{ at } 4\%.$$

The interest at the end of year 6 is therefore

$$\cdot 04X(1\cdot 04)^5 + \cdot 04 \times 27\cdot 31 s_{\overline{6}|}.$$

The premium then due is 27·31. Therefore the amount available for sinking fund is

$$100 - \{\cdot 04X(1\cdot 04)^5 + \cdot 04 \times 27\cdot 31 s_{\overline{6}|} + 27\cdot 31\} = Y \text{ say.}$$

In the last year the amount available will be $Y+P$, as no premium is due at the end of that year, therefore

$$Y.s_{\overline{20}|}^{\cdot 035} + 27\cdot 31 + 1000 = X(1\cdot 04)^5 + 27\cdot 31 s_{\overline{6}|}^{\cdot 04},$$

since the sinking fund plus the sum assured must repay the amount of accumulated loan.

By eliminating Y between the latter two equations it will be found that

$$X = £1040.$$

Example 6·8

A borrows from *B* a sum of money to be repaid partly by 20 annual instalments of £50 each, the first being due at the end of one year from the date of loan. The remainder of the loan is to be repaid by a 20-year leasehold policy, the yearly premium for which is to be calculated on a 4% effective basis for 10 years and $3\frac{1}{2}$% effective thereafter, with a loading of 2% of the gross premium. *B* will realize an effective rate of interest of $4\frac{1}{2}\%$ on his investment, while A calculates that, taking the transaction as a whole, he is borrowing at 5%. What is the sum borrowed?

Let X be the sum borrowed.

The accumulated loan, with interest at $4\frac{1}{2}\%$, less the accumulation of £50 per annum paid during the 20 years, will amount to

$$X(1\cdot045)^{20} - 50s_{\overline{20}|},$$

and this must be the sum for which the policy is effected. If this amount be S the premium is

$$\frac{S}{\cdot98\,[(\ddot{s}_{\overline{10}|}^{\,\cdot04})(1\cdot035)^{10} + \ddot{s}_{\overline{10}|}^{\,\cdot035}]} = \frac{S}{29\cdot16}.$$

From A's point of view he is discharging a debt of X by making payments as follows:

(1) £50 per annum in arrear for 20 years.

(2) $£\dfrac{S}{29\cdot16}$ per annum in advance for 20 years.

Since he calculates that he is borrowing at 5% the present value at that rate of the payments he is to make must equal the sum of money which he borrows at present, i.e.

$$X = 50a_{\overline{20}|} + \frac{S}{29\cdot16}\ddot{a}_{\overline{20}|},$$

and substituting for S its value, $X(1\cdot045)^{20} - 50s_{\overline{20}|}^{\,\cdot045}$ it is seen that

$$X = 50a_{\overline{20}|}^{\,\cdot05} + \frac{X(1\cdot045)^{20} - 50s_{\overline{20}|}^{\,\cdot045}}{29\cdot16}\ddot{a}_{\overline{20}|}^{\,\cdot05},$$

i.e.

$$X = 50\,\frac{\left[a_{\overline{20}|}^{\,\cdot05} - \dfrac{s_{\overline{20}|}^{\,\cdot045}}{29\cdot16}\ddot{a}_{\overline{20}|}^{\,\cdot05}\right]}{1 - \dfrac{(1\cdot045)^{20}}{29\cdot16}\ddot{a}_{\overline{20}|}^{\,\cdot05}}$$

$$= £982.$$

The reason that A pays a higher rate of interest than B realizes is that A is in effect repaying part of the loan by a sinking fund accumulating at less than the rate which B desires to earn.

Example 6·9

A company has issued every year since 1910, 1000 leasehold policies by annual premiums for each of the terms 10, 20 and 30 years, the sum assured under each policy being £100. The policies are issued uniformly over the year and the premiums are calculated on a 3% basis, with a loading of 5% of the gross premium. A 3% net premium valuation is made on 1 January in each year, allowance being made for the exact interval between the due date of premium and the valuation date. Assuming that the funds on 1 January 1953 were exactly equal to the valuation reserves on that date, that during 1953 the office expenses were 6% of the premiums received, and that the ratio between the interest earned in 1953 and the average funds in that year was 5%, what were the interest receipts for 1953?

The first step is to calculate the net and office premiums as follows:

	Term n		
	10	20	30
$\ddot{s}_{\overline{n}\vert}$	11·808	27·677	49·003
$\dfrac{100}{\ddot{s}_{\overline{n}\vert}}=\pi$	8·469	3·613	2·041
$\cdot 95\ddot{s}_{\overline{n}\vert}$	11·218	26·293	46·553
$\dfrac{100}{\cdot 95\ddot{s}_{\overline{n}\vert}}=P$	8·915	3·803	2·148

Now as the longest term for which a policy is issued is for 30-years, and as the same number of policies has been issued each year for over 30 years, it will be seen that the company has reached a stationary condition. The number of policies in force will be

10-year term	10,000
20-year term	20,000
30-year term	30,000

The 1000 policies of each class which mature during each year will be replaced by the 1000 new policies of each class issued during that year. The distribution of the policies by durations will also be identical at the beginning and end of each year, and hence the reserves required on 1 January in each year for the policies then in force will not vary.

The reserves can be calculated either by general reasoning or directly. Since the reserves are the same in two consecutive years the following equation must hold good:

$$\text{Reserves at start of year} + \text{net premiums received} + \text{interest received}$$
$$= \text{claims paid} + \text{reserves at end of year},$$

i.e. $$\text{interest received} = \text{claims paid} - \text{net premiums received}.$$

The interest received will, however, be $\delta\times$ reserves at start of year, since the mean amount invested during the year $=\frac{1}{2}$ (reserves at start of year + reserves at end of year).

$\therefore$ reserves at start of year

$$=\frac{1}{\delta}[300{,}000-10{,}000(8\cdot469)-20{,}000(3\cdot613)-30{,}000(2\cdot041)]$$

$$=\frac{81820}{\cdot029559}$$

$$=2{,}768{,}023.$$

This method of approach is possible only because the net premiums and the valuation are calculated on the same interest basis, as will be seen from the development of the expression for the total reserves from first principles as follows.

The premiums may be considered as being received continuously throughout the year, and the reserves on a 3% basis at the start of any year are therefore

$$8469\sum_1^{10}\bar{s}_{\overline{n}|}+3613\sum_1^{20}\bar{s}_{\overline{n}|}+2041\sum_1^{30}\bar{s}_{\overline{n}|}.$$

Now $$\sum_1^{t}\bar{s}_{\overline{n}|}=\frac{i}{\delta}\sum_1^{t}\frac{(1+i)^n-1}{i}=\frac{1}{\delta}[s_{\overline{t+1}|}-(t+1)].$$

$$\therefore\ \sum_1^{10}\bar{s}_{\overline{n}|}=\frac{1}{\delta}[s_{\overline{11}|}-11].$$

Similarly $$\sum_1^{20}\bar{s}_{\overline{n}|}=\frac{1}{\delta}[s_{\overline{21}|}-21]$$

and $$\sum_1^{30}\bar{s}_{\overline{n}|}=\frac{1}{\delta}[s_{\overline{31}|}-31].$$

$$\therefore\ \text{reserves}=\frac{1}{\delta}[8469\times1\cdot8078+3613\times7\cdot6767+2041\times19\cdot0027]$$

$$=£2{,}768{,}387.$$

The identity of this expression with the one previously derived follows from the fact that, for example, the reserves for the 10-year policies are $\frac{\pi}{\delta}[s_{\overline{11}|}-11]=\frac{\pi}{\delta}[\ddot{s}_{\overline{10}|}-10]$ and if π and $\ddot{s}_{\overline{10}|}$ are calculated at the same rate of interest $\pi\ddot{s}_{\overline{10}|}=100$. The small difference in the final figures is of no significance, and is due to lack of sufficient significant figures in the tables available.

The premiums due in the following year

$$=10\times8915+20\times3803+30\times2148$$
$$=£229{,}650.$$

The claims will be £300,000, since 1000 policies of each class will mature during the year.

The expenses are $\cdot 06 \times 229{,}650 = £13{,}779$.

If I is the interest received, A the fund at the start of the year and B is the fund at the end of the year, we are given that

$$\frac{I}{\dfrac{A+B}{2}} = \cdot 05,$$

and, as discussed above,

$$A + I + 229{,}650 = B + 300{,}000 + 13{,}779$$

and $$A = 2{,}768{,}387.$$

$$\therefore \quad \cdot 05 = \frac{2I}{2{,}768{,}387 + 2{,}684{,}258 + I}.$$

$$\therefore \quad I = \frac{272{,}632}{1\cdot 95}$$
$$= £139{,}811.$$

Example 6·10

On 1 April 1935, A bought for £1023·50 a ground rent payable annually in arrear for 25 years under which the first payment was £30, and subsequent payments increased in arithmetical progression. The purchase price was calculated on a $4\frac{1}{2}\%$ interest basis. At the beginning of the 11th year A sold the annuity to B, who effected a 15-year capital redemption policy to replace his capital. The annual premiums on this policy increase by the annual increase in the ground rent—the first premium being the amount of the ground rent due at the end of the 10th year less $3\frac{1}{2}\%$ on B's investment. The premiums were calculated on a 2% net basis and B earned $3\frac{1}{2}\%$ on his investment. Find (*a*) the annual increase in the ground rent, (*b*) the price B paid.

(*a*) Let the annual increase be X. Then

$$1023\cdot 5 = 30a_{\overline{25}|} + X\sum_{1}^{24} tv^{t+1} \quad \text{at } 4\tfrac{1}{2}\%$$
$$= 30a_{\overline{25}|} + Xv\,(Ia)_{\overline{24}|}$$
$$= 30a_{\overline{25}|} + Xv\frac{\ddot{a}_{\overline{24}|} - 24v^{24}}{\cdot 045}.$$

$$\therefore \quad X = \cdot 045\,\frac{1023\cdot 5 - 30a_{\overline{25}|}}{a_{\overline{24}|} - 24v^{25}}$$
$$= \cdot 045 \times \frac{578\cdot 654}{6\cdot 51}$$
$$= 3\cdot 9999,$$

or say £4 per annum.

(b) The ground rent due at the end of the 10th year

$$=30+9\times4=£66.$$

Let the sum assured under the policy be S, the first premium P and the price B paid be X. At the end of 15 years B receives £126 from the ground rent and S from the policy. This must repay his outlay of $(X+P)$ plus a year's interest, i.e.

$$S+126=(X+P)(1\cdot035).$$

At the end of year n the ground rent yields $66+4n$ and the premium due is $P+4n$, i.e.

$$66+4n=\cdot035(X+P)+P+4n.$$

$$\therefore\ S+126=(X+P)(1\cdot035)$$

and $$66=(X+P)(\cdot035)+P.$$

$$\therefore\ S+60=X$$

and $$P[s_{\overline{16}|}^{02}-1]+4[(1\cdot02)^{14}+2(1\cdot02)^{13}+\ldots+14(1\cdot02)]=S.$$

$$\therefore\ P(s_{\overline{16}|}^{\cdot02}-1)+4[(Is)_{\overline{15}|}-15]=S.$$

$$=X-60.$$

But the first premium is £66 less $3\frac{1}{2}$% on B's investment, i.e.

$$P=66-\cdot035(X+P).$$

$$\therefore\ \cdot035X=66-1\cdot035P$$

$$=66-1\cdot035\,\frac{X-60-4\left(\dfrac{s_{\overline{16}|}-16}{\cdot02}-15\right)}{s_{\overline{16}|}^{\cdot02}-1}.$$

$$\therefore\ X=\frac{66+\dfrac{1\cdot035}{17\cdot639}\times527\cdot86}{\cdot035+\dfrac{1\cdot035}{17\cdot639}}$$

$$=1035\cdot19$$

or $$£1035\cdot19.$$

It is intructive to check this answer.

The sum assured $=£1035\cdot19-60=£975\cdot19$.

Therefore the initial premium $=\dfrac{975\cdot19-467\cdot86}{17\cdot639}=28\cdot76$.

B's investment $=(1035{\cdot}19+28{\cdot}76)$, $3\frac{1}{2}\%$ on which is $37{\cdot}24$. The ground rent due one year after B's purchase is £70. This must pay the interest for the year plus the premium due, i.e. $37{\cdot}24+32{\cdot}76=£70{\cdot}00$ which confirms this part of the working. In the last year B receives $975{\cdot}19+126=1101{\cdot}19$. His investment is $1063{\cdot}95$ and a year's interest is $37{\cdot}24$ so the total is $1101{\cdot}19$ which equals his receipts and confirms this part of the answer.

EXERCISES 6

6·1 Find the annual premium, limited to 50 payments, to secure £100 under a leasehold policy payable at the end of 60 years. The effective rates of interest are $3\frac{1}{2}\%$ for the first 20 years, 3% per annum for the next 20 years and $2\frac{1}{2}\%$ per annum thereafter.

6·2 5 years ago A effected a 25 years leasehold policy for the sum of £10,000. He now wishes to extend the term by 10 years. On the basis of an effective rate of interest of 3% per annum throughout, what will the new annual premium be?

6·3 An immediate annuity of 1 payable for n years is offered for sale. The purchaser wishes to obtain an effective yield of i per annum on his investment and to replace his capital either

(a) by a sinking fund accumulating at rate j ($j>i$),

or (b) by effecting a capital redemption policy for a term of $(n+1)$ years, by annual premiums calculated at rate j.

Obtain expressions for the purchase prices under each method. Explain why they differ and show that if $i=j$ they are identical.

6·4 The following table shows the estimated commitments arising under a certain arrangement:

Years	Commitment
0– 9	Nil
10–19	£100 per annum increasing by £10 each year
20–25	£200 per annum
26–35	£190 per annum decreasing by £10 each year

It is desired to effect a leasehold policy to secure the payment of these sums. The policy is to be subject to a single premium and to 10 annual premiums. The annual premiums decrease each year by 5% of the initial annual premium and the total premiums paid at the outset amount to £1000. Premiums are calculated at 3% per annum effective with loadings on the gross premium of $2\frac{1}{2}\%$ for single premiums and 5% for annual premiums. Find the single premium payable.

6·5 Five years ago an assurance company granted a loan of £1000 at 5% payable half-yearly. The loan is to be repaid by the proceeds of a 25 years leasehold policy subject to half-yearly premiums calculated at $3\frac{1}{2}$% per annum effective. At any time the borrower could close the transaction by repaying the loan and taking either the surrender value of the policy, or a proportionate-paid-up policy. The surrender value is 95% of all premiums paid, excluding the first, accumulated at $2\frac{1}{2}$% per annum effective.

The company will now grant a loan, repayable on the same date, by a leasehold policy, at $4\frac{1}{2}$% per annum payable half-yearly. Find, to the nearest $\frac{1}{4}$% the maximum rate of interest at which it may calculate the half-yearly premiums on the new policy in order to make it unprofitable for the borrower to repay the original loan and take a new loan at the reduced interest rate.

CHAPTER 7

VALUATION OF SECURITIES

7·1. General considerations

From the point of view of a Life Assurance Company perhaps the most important application of compound interest, apart from its application to the calculation of premiums, is in valuing securities quoted on the Stock Exchange. The various types of such securities and the considerations which affect their value are discussed in greater detail in other text-books in this series, but, for the sake of completeness, and to aid in the understanding of the nature of the problem, a brief description of the main types of securities and of certain technical terms used in connexion with them is given in the following sections.

7·2. Stock Exchange securities

When a government, or a local authority, or a business concern, wishes to raise money for some purpose it may do so by floating a loan on the Stock Exchange. Investors are invited to subscribe to the loan at a given price (called the issue price), and the terms of the issue will include the conditions on which the loan may be repaid and the rate of interest which will be payable on the loan. The repayment or redemption terms, and also the rate of interest, will be fixed by quoting them in terms of some convenient unit of the total loan—thus a government might raise a loan by issuing 10,000 bonds of £100 each. The statement that a bond represents £100 does not mean that it represents £100 in cash—it is merely a nominal sum fixing the investor's share in the total loan. The actual value of the bond at any time would depend not on its nominal or face value, but on the series of future payments it represents, and on the value which an investor would place on that series of payments, in the light of conditions prevailing at the time of the valuation. The series of payments it represents will, of course, be determined by:

(*a*) the interest payable on each nominal amount of loan,
(*b*) the period during which that interest will be payable,
(*c*) the sum which is to be paid in respect of each nominal amount of loan when it comes to be repaid.

Thus if a loan were issued in bonds of £100 each, repayable in 25 years at 105 %, and bearing interest at 4 % payable half-yearly, the holder of one bond would be entitled to receive £2 per half-year for 25 years, plus a payment of £105 at the end of that period. The issue price of the loan, i.e. the amount which the borrower receives in respect of each bond of nominal value £100, would be fixed having regard to the current rate of interest ruling in the market and the 'security' of the borrower, i.e. the probability that the promised payments of capital and interest will be made. There is an obvious difference between, say, a loan guaranteed by the British government, where it may reasonably be assumed that the promised payments will be made, and a loan issued to finance an expedition to discover buried treasure in the South Seas, where the remunerative nature of the project is, to say the least of it, speculative. Securities in the first class are called, in financial jargon, 'Gilt Edged', and the fact that they are considered to be absolutely secure induces investors to accept a lower rate of interest on any money they invest in the purchase of such securities than they would demand if they invested their money in a security issued by any other class of borrower. The more element of risk there is in the security behind a loan, the greater will be the rate of interest the investor will require if he is to invest in it. This book, however, is concerned only with the theoretical methods of valuing securities, and not with questions of their intrinsic worth, or of what the appropriate rate of interest to value any particular loan will be, and it will be assumed that the borrower will always meet the obligations he has undertaken.

7·3. Stock Exchange terminology

In order clearly to understand the nature of the problem of valuing Stock Exchange securities, a knowledge of the meaning of certain Stock Exchange terms is necessary, and some of the more common terms are therefore defined below.

(*a*) *Stocks, shares and bonds*

Subscriptions may be invited through the Stock Exchange for (i) a loan or (ii) an issue of capital. In either case it is necessary to divide the nominal amount of the issue into units of a convenient size so that dealings may be facilitated. These units are usually called bonds or debentures in case (i) or units of stock or shares for the preference and ordinary shares involved in case (ii). The technical differences between them are irrelevant for the purposes of this book. What must be clearly understood is that they are all means of defining the nominal amount of the obligations involved towards each investor and hence of defining the future payments which the investor will receive in respect of his investment.

(*b*) *Fixed-interest securities*

These are securities where the rate of interest to be paid by the borrower is fixed by the terms of the issue and include government securities, loans issued by local authorities, debenture stocks, or bonds, of commercial undertakings, and the majority of preference shares and stocks. Preference shares and stocks are dealt with in a separate note. The rate of interest on such securities is always included in the title of the security—for example 4% Funding Loan, Government of Kenya 5% Stock, London Midland Associated Properties $3\frac{1}{4}$% Debenture Stock and so on. This rate denotes the interest or dividend payable in respect of each nominal £100 of loan. The alternative word 'dividend' is often used in Stock Exchange circles.

(*c*) *Preference shares or stocks*

Preference shares or stocks usually bear a fixed rate of interest, but they are more speculative than fixed-interest securities issued by way of loans. The interest payments are met only after the interest due on any debentures has been paid and, if an undertaking does not make a profit in any year out of which the interest on its debentures (or prior charges) can be paid, the preference shareholders may have to accept less than the stated rate of interest, or in an extreme case no interest at all. To meet this objection, preference shares are sometimes issued as 'Cumulative Preference Shares', and this means that if in any year the interest paid on the shares is less than the fixed rate the balance is carried forward and becomes a charge on profits in future years till it has been paid off. For example, if a company issued 5 % cumulative preference shares and in some year could pay only 3 % on them, the holder of 100 shares of £1 each would receive £3 instead of £5. The balance of £2 would be carried forward and paid in some future year when the profits had increased. It should, however, be noted that the arrears do not themselves earn interest—for example, if in the case cited, they were paid off at the end of the third year from the time of underpayment, the holder of the 100 shares would receive £2 and not $£2 \times (1{\cdot}05)^3$.

The interest payment on a preference share or stock is nearly always described as a 'dividend' for although the rate of interest is fixed the ability of the company to pay this rate may depend on the profits it earns.

(*d*) *Ordinary shares and stock*

These securities are issued by commercial undertakings and do not normally carry a fixed rate of interest. They rank after preference shares and stocks, and are entitled to receive the whole of the divisible profits of the undertaking after the interest on any debentures and dividends on any preference shares have beeen paid. The amount received in respect of each share or unit of stock is called the 'dividend', and the rate of dividend may vary from year to year with the profits of the company.

(*e*) *Par*

This is a term denoting the nominal value of an investment. If a loan is issued in bonds of £100 the 'par value' of each bond is £100. If the issue price of the loan is 102 the issue would be said to be made at a price 'above par' or at a premium. The corresponding description for an issue price of 98 would be 'below par' or 'at a discount'.

(*f*) *Redemption terms*

Stocks, shares and bonds may be classified into

(i) Those where the borrower has no right to repay the capital borrowed, i.e. irredeemable securities. These include most preference and all ordinary stocks and shares.

(ii) Those where the borrower must repay the capital borrowed at some definite future date, i.e. securities with a 'fixed redemption date'.

(iii) Those where the borrower has the right to repay the capital borrowed after some stated period without, however, being under a definite obligation to do so, i.e. securities with an 'optional redemption date'.

(*g*) *Ex-dividend*

In Britain it is usual for the purchaser of a Stock Exchange security to be entitled to receive in full the next interest payment which becomes due. For example, the interest on $3\frac{1}{2}\%$ War Loan is paid on 1 June and 1 December each year, and a purchaser of £100 of the loan on 1 October will receive a payment on 1 December of £1·75, even though he has held the security for only two months. As a matter of convenience to the borrower, however, who has to prepare statements of the interest to be paid ready for issue on the next due date, it is usual for a date to be fixed after which the purchaser of the security will not be entitled to receive the next interest payment. The price is then said to be quoted 'ex-dividend'. For example, the price of $3\frac{1}{2}\%$ War Loan on 24 October 1969 was $41\frac{1}{8}$, but on 27 October the price was quoted as $39\frac{5}{8}$ ex-dividend. A purchaser on 27 October at this price will not receive the interest payment of £1·75 due on 1 December 1969 which will be retained by the seller. The difference between the two prices is less than this, first because prices fluctuate daily in accordance with normal laws of supply and demand, and second because the value of the payment of £1·75 to the purchaser will vary according to whether or not he has to pay any taxes on it.

7·4. Elementary considerations

Much confusion of thought will be avoided if it is remembered that the nominal value of any security is merely a means of fixing the payments to which a holder of the security is entitled. In itself it does not truly represent the theoretical value of the security nor, for a redeemable security, need it even represent the amount which will be paid on redemption. The value of the security from an investor's point of view is the value, at the rate of interest he considers appropriate, of the payments that will be made. The value will, of course, vary from time to time, depending on

(*a*) the number and amount of the payments to be made, and
(*b*) the rate of interest at which they are valued.

It is not the function of this book to discuss the merits of different securities or the appropriate rates of interest to be used in valuing them. The problems dealt with here all assume that the contractual obligations will be carried out and resolve themselves basically into the problem of finding either what rate of interest is yielded by an investment in a given security at a particular price, or, conversely, the price at which a given security will yield a particular rate of interest. It is important to distinguish between the so-called 'rate of interest' payable on a security, and calculated on its nominal amount, and the true rate of interest used in valuing the security. To avoid confusion the former will generally be referred to in succeeding sections as the 'rate of dividend', though strictly the term 'dividend' applies only to preference and ordinary shares or stock.

7·5. Irredeemable securities

If a security has no fixed redemption date, and if the rate of dividend payable on each nominal amount of it is known, the problem is very simple. For if the rate of dividend be g per annum, then a purchaser of part of the loan at a price A will obtain a yield of i per annum, where $iA = g$, and hence $i = g/A$ if the price is known and it is required to find the yield or $A = g/i$ if the yield is known and the price has to be determined.

If dividends are payable more frequently than yearly, say p times per annum, the expressions become

$$i^{(p)}=\frac{g}{A}$$

for a nominal yield of $i^{(p)}$ per annum convertible p times a year or

$$A=\frac{g}{i^{(p)}}$$

in the other case. If it is desired to work at an effective rate of interest of i per annum, the expressions would be

$$i=\frac{gs_{\overline{1|}}^{(p)}}{A} \quad \text{and} \quad A=\frac{gs_{\overline{1|}}^{(p)}}{i}$$

respectively, $s_{\overline{1|}}^{(p)}$ being calculated at rate i.

The payment in each year can be considered by itself, and it must suffice to pay interest at the desired rate on the capital invested.

7·6. Redeemable securities

If a security has a fixed redemption date the formulae of §7·5 no longer apply, since at some future time the purchaser of the security will receive a redemption price normally differing from the price paid for the security, and the profit or loss involved must be brought into account. For example, if a security redeemable at 100 in ten years time and bearing interest of 4% payable annually stands at a price of 108·53, it would not be correct to take the yield as $\frac{4}{108\cdot53}$ or 3·69%. A purchaser of £100 of loan at this price would receive £4 at the end of each year, but after 10 years he would receive only £100 back, instead of his invested capital of £108·53. Hence, a portion of each interest payment of £4 must represent a part return of his capital and the yield must be less than 3·69%. Similarly, if the price were 92·28% the yield would be more than $\frac{4}{92\cdot28}$ or 4·33%, for on redemption a profit of 7·72 would be made and credit for this should be taken. The true rate of interest in either case is the rate which satisfies the equation

$$A=100v^{10}+4a_{\overline{10|}},$$

where A is the purchase price per cent, since the payments to be received are the repayment of the nominal capital of £100 at the end of 10 years, plus interest at 4% on the nominal capital for 10 years.

7·7. Redeemable securities (valuation)

Consider the general case where the amount to be repaid after n years is C, and the dividend is gC per annum payable p times per annum. (It will be noted that these definitions do not depend on the *nominal* amount of the bond. Thus in the particular case of a loan bearing interest at $5\frac{1}{4}$% which is repayable at 105, $C=105$, $g=\cdot 05$, since $g\times 105=5\frac{1}{4}$.) If A is the value of the security to yield an effective rate of i per annum

$$A=Cv^n+gCa_{\overline{n}|}^{(p)}$$

$$=\text{value of capital plus value of interest.} \qquad (7\cdot 1)$$

If the symbol K be used for the present value of the capital (i.e. Cv^n) equation (7·1) can be written as

$$A=Cv^n+\frac{gC}{i^{(p)}}(1-v^n)$$

$$=K+\frac{g}{i^{(p)}}(C-K). \qquad (7\cdot 2)$$

This form is known as Makeham's formula, and its importance will become apparent in later and more complicated examples. It expresses in symbolic form the two facts

(*a*) that the value of the security is the value of the capital, plus the value of the interest,

(*b*) that in certain circumstances the value of the interest can be deduced from the value of the capital instead of having to be calculated independently.

This can readily be deduced by general reasoning as follows:

Suppose that the dividend on the stock calculated on the redemption price, instead of being at rate g were at rate $i^{(p)}$ per annum. The value of the security to yield an effective rate of i would be C, since the dividend would pay interest at the desired rate during the term of the investment, and the purchase price would be repaid in whole at the end of the term. Also, if there were no dividend at all the value of the security to yield i would be simply the value of the capital, i.e. K. Hence

Value at an effective rate i of capital plus value of dividends of $i^{(p)}C$ paid p times per annum $=C$.

Value at an effective rate i of capital $=K$.

Therefore value of dividends of $i^{(p)}C$ paid p times per annum $=C-K$.

Hence by proportion, the value of the dividends of gC paid p times per annum $=\frac{g}{i^{(p)}}(C-K)$.

Therefore the whole value of the security is $K+\frac{g}{i^{(p)}}(C-K)$.

If it were desired to value the security at a nominal rate of interest, say $i^{(m)}$, equation (7·1) would become

$$A=Cv^{mn}+gCa_{\overline{n}|}^{(p)},$$

where v^{mn} is calculated at rate $i^{(m)}/m$ and $a_{\overline{n}|}^{(p)}$ would be evaluated as in Chapter 3.

Similarly, A could be found from equation (7·2)

$$A=K+\frac{g}{i^{(p)}}(C-K),$$

where $$K=Cv^{mn} \text{ at rate } i^{(m)}/m,$$

and $$\left(1+\frac{i^{(p)}}{p}\right)^p=\left(1+\frac{i^{(m)}}{m}\right)^m.$$

7·8. More complicated examples

The following are some of the complications which may arise in practice:

(*a*) the security may be bought at a date intermediate between two dividend payments,

(*b*) the security may be redeemable not at some fixed time, but at the option of the borrower,

(*c*) the security may be redeemable not at one fixed date, but by instalments over a period of years,

(*d*) the redemption price may vary,

(*e*) the rate of dividend may vary.

In the remainder of this chapter and in the next chapter it is proposed to consider these in turn.

7·9. Valuation at a date between two interest dates

It will be the rule, rather than the exception, for a security to be purchased at a time other than immediately after a dividend payment has been made. Apart from the complication of purchasing a security 'ex dividend' there is no real difficulty in arriving at its value, for if its value to yield i immediately after a dividend payment is A, its value $1/m$ of a year later is $A(1+i)^{1/m}$. Alternatively, if its value to yield i immediately before the next interest payment is A', its value $(1-1/m)$ of a year before that date is $A'(v^{1-1/m})$, and these may readily be shown to be identical. If the security is bought 'ex dividend', allowance must be made in calculating A that the purchaser will not receive the next dividend payment to be made. In practice it is usual to adopt the form $A(1+i)^{1/m}$, and to use, as a convenient approximation, $A+\frac{iA}{m}$, i.e. to use a first difference interpolation between A and A'. An exactly similar argument may be applied to securities where the interest is paid p times per annum.

7·10. Optional redemption dates

A security is sometimes issued which may be repaid by the borrower at his option

(*a*) after some date specified at the time of issue

or (*b*) at any time between two specified dates.

Examples of these are $2\frac{1}{2}\%$ Consols and 3% Transport (1978–88) respectively. When $2\frac{1}{2}\%$ Consols were issued the government reserved the right to repay this stock at par in 1923, or at any later date. It may therefore now be repaid at any time if the government so desire. The redemption dates of the Transport Stock under discussion are 1978–88, and this means that in 1978 the government may, if they wish, redeem this loan. If the government does not redeem the loan in 1978, there remains the option to redeem it in any year up to 1988, when it must be redeemed if the option to redeem it earlier has not been exercised.

The purchaser of such securities naturally cannot know what the borrower's intentions are, and in valuing them he must therefore make assumptions which will ensure that, however the options may be exercised, he will realize at least the yield he desires. It is clear that the options are unlikely to be exercised unless it pays the borrower to do so, and the prospective purchaser should therefore assume that they will be exercised to his disadvantage. The effect of this will perhaps be more clearly shown by considering the two securities mentioned above.

At the present time (October 1969) the price of $2\frac{1}{2}\%$ Consols is about 28. If the government decided to redeem the stock they would have to pay the holders £100 for each £100 nominal of stock held, whereas the market value is £28. It is clear that this transaction would not be to the borrower's advantage, and it is therefore safe to assume that the yield on $2\frac{1}{2}\%$ Consols bought at a price of £28 may be calculated as if they were irredeemable. If by any chance they were redeemed the purchaser would secure a higher yield because he would be paid £72 more than his purchase price and his calculations did not make any allowance for this hypothetical profit.

The present price of 3% Transport Stock (1978–88) is about 50, and the yield on it is clearly more than 3%, no matter when it may be repaid. Now if present conditions continue, and if the yield on government securities in 1978 is still more than 3%, it will obviously not pay the government to issue a new loan at this increased rate of interest and to use the proceeds to repay the Transport Stock. In finding the yield on this security at the present time, at a price of 50, it should therefore be assumed that the loan will be repaid in 1988. If it is repaid at some earlier date, the yield to the purchaser will be higher than he expected because his calculations allow for a profit of £50% on redemption, and if the date at which he makes that profit is advanced it must obviously be to his advantage. On the other hand, if it were desired to find the price at which the Transport Stock would yield $2\frac{1}{2}\%$ it would no longer be safe to assume redemption in 1988, for if $2\frac{1}{2}\%$ were the rate of interest at which the government could borrow in 1978 it would clearly be advantageous to repay a loan on which 3% was being paid. In this case it would be prudent to assume that the loan would be repaid at the earliest possible moment, i.e. in 1978.

A consideration of these particular cases leads to the general rule which is adopted in valuing a security with optional redemption dates:

(*a*) *Assume redemption will take place at the latest possible date* when valuing the security at an effective rate of interest greater than the rate of dividend on the loan per unit of redemption price (i.e. in the notation of §7·7 if $i > g$).

(*b*) *Assume redemption will take place at the earliest possible date* when valuing the security at an effective rate of interest less than the rate of dividend on the loan per unit of redemption price (i.e. in the notation of §7·7 if $i < g$).

7·11. Securities redeemable by instalments

A loan may be issued which is redeemable, not in one lump sum, but by a series of payments extending over a period of years. For example, a loan of £1,000,000 might be issued in 10,000 bonds of £100 each, the bonds to be redeemed at the rate of 500 per annum for each of the next 20 years. In such a case the bonds would probably be numbered, and the bonds to be redeemed each year would be selected by drawing 500 numbers, as in a lottery. It is clear, therefore, that it is impossible to value any individual bond, since its redemption date may be anything from 1 to 20 years hence. But the value of the whole loan can be found and it is usual to assume that, provided a reasonably large proportion of the loan is bought, the number of bonds of this holding redeemed in any year will be in proportion to the number drawn for the whole loan; in other words, that if N bonds are purchased the number of bonds drawn in any year will be $N/20$. This is, of course, only a convenient assumption, and for present purposes it will be assumed that the problem is to find the value of the whole loan, a process which permits of an exact solution.

7·12. Securities repayable by instalments (continued)

Assume that a loan of C bearing interest at g per annum per unit of C, payable p times per annum, is repayable by instalments as follows:

$$C_1 \text{ in } n_1 \text{ years,}$$
$$C_2 \text{ in } n_2 \text{ years,}$$
$$\cdots\cdots\cdots\cdots\cdots\cdots$$
$$C_t \text{ in } n_t \text{ years,}$$

where
$$\sum_1^t C_m = C.$$

Then if A_m be the value of the portion C_m redeemable in n_m years

$$A_m = C_m v^{n_m} + gC_m a_{\overline{n_m}|}^{(p)}$$
$$= K_m + \frac{g}{i^{(p)}}(C_m - K_m),$$

using the notation of §7·7. Also if A is the value of the whole loan

$$A = \sum_1^t A_m$$
$$= \sum_1^t K_m + \frac{g}{i^{(p)}}\left[\sum_1^t C_m - \sum_1^t K_m\right]$$
$$= K + \frac{g}{i^{(p)}}(C - K),$$

as in §7·7.

This result follows also from the general reasoning set out in the latter portion of §7·7, as in that reasoning it was not assumed that the capital was repayable in one sum. The only assumption which has been made is that g does not vary. This is of the greatest importance, and while it will be shown in Chapter 8 that the formula can be adapted to the case where either g or C varies the limitations of the present simple formula must be realized. Makeham's formula itself is of the greatest importance; indeed, it is not going too far to say that it is the most potent instrument available for the solution of the more complicated problems involving redeemable securities. The value of such securities can always be written down from first principles, but this will usually involve a separate valuation of the capital and interest payments. The beauty of Makeham's formula is that it enables the value of the interest payments to be found from the value of the capital payments without further calculation, and its use will usually save much numerical work.

7·13. Determination of yields

The problem of finding the price of a security to yield a particular rate of interest is relatively simple. The reverse process of finding the yield corresponding to a particular price is less easy. The methods which may be adopted may be classified roughly as follows:

(*a*) by first difference interpolation between two trial rates of interest,

(*b*) by analytical means involving the solution of an equation of the type $a_{\overline{n}|}=X$ by expansion of $a_{\overline{n}|}$ in powers of i,

(*c*) by further analytical means, depending upon approximate expressions for $a_{\overline{n}|}$ or $\dfrac{1}{a_{\overline{n}|}}$.

Of these (*a*) is by far the most generally used. Methods (*b*) and (*c*) will be discussed more fully in Chapter 11, but it is safe to say they are of greater theoretical interest than practical use. In the remainder of this chapter method (*a*) will be considered in relation to the following problem:

> Given a security redeemable at the end of n years at a price C and bearing interest at rate gC per annum, and given that the price of the security is A, what is the yield on a purchase at this price?

7·14. Determination of yields by interpolation

This method consists of finding the price, A_1 and A_2 say, to yield known rates i_1 and i_2, where $A_1 > A > A_2$. It is assumed that i, the desired yield, is a first difference function of A, i.e. that

$$i=i_1+\frac{A_1-A}{A_1-A_2}(i_2-i_1).$$

This is the method used most frequently in practice. Provided that i_1 and i_2 are fairly close, very accurate results can be obtained. For this reason special tables are sometimes prepared called tables of 'Bond Values', which show for different rates of interest and terms the prices to give known yields advancing by, say, ·1 %. The following is an extract from such a set of tables:

Term to run 10 *years*

Yield %	Rate of interest (%) 3	$3\frac{1}{2}$	4	$4\frac{1}{2}$
	Price			
2·90	100·86	105·18	109·49	113·80
3·00	100	104·29	108·58	112·88
3·10	99·15	103·42	107·69	111·96
3·20	98·30	102·55	106·80	111·05
3·30	97·46	101·69	105·92	110·15
3·40	96·63	100·84	105·05	109·26

This is really a set of tables of values of A_t corresponding to a known rate of interest i_t, and it enables the method described above to be applied with very little labour.

A device which may save work, if the price A is not greatly different from C, is to use g as one of the trial rates and to write

$$i = i_1 + \frac{A_1 - A}{A_1 - C}(g - i_1),$$

and this involves only the calculation of A_1. This method will, however, give reasonably accurate results only if g and i_1 are not widely different.

For example, if the only interest tables available were at $2\frac{1}{2}$ and $3\frac{1}{2}$ %, and if it were desired to find the yield on a security bearing interest at 4 % payable yearly and redeemable at par in 10 years time which is bought at a price of 108·53, the method would be

$$A = 100v^{10} + 4a_{\overline{10}|},$$

$$\text{at } 2\tfrac{1}{2}\% \quad A_1 = 113{\cdot}128,$$

$$\text{and at } 3\tfrac{1}{2}\% \quad A_2 = 104{\cdot}158.$$

Therefore if $A = 108{\cdot}53$, the yield i will be found from

$$i = {\cdot}025 + \frac{113{\cdot}128 - 108{\cdot}53}{113{\cdot}128 - 104{\cdot}158} \times {\cdot}01$$

$$= 3{\cdot}013\ \%.$$

If interest tables at 3% had been available it would have been found that 3% satisfies the equation exactly and this is therefore the true value of i.

If the value $A_2 = 100$ at 4% were used the expression would be

$$i = \cdot 025 + \frac{4 \cdot 598}{13 \cdot 128} \times \cdot 015$$

$$= 3 \cdot 025\%,$$

and clearly the wider the interval between the trial rates the less accurate will be the answer.

In practice it is desirable that the interval between the trial rates should not be more than a quarter or an eighth of 1%, and if interest tables are available to enable this to be done very accurate answers can be obtained.

7·15. The following examples illustrate the work of this chapter.

Example 7·1

A loan bears interest at 5% payable yearly and is redeemable at any time after 1948 at the option of the borrower. The loan is to be repaid and the following options are available:

(*a*) The holder may accept repayment at par.

(*b*) The holder may convert his holding to a new loan under which the rate of interest will be

5%	for the first 5 years,
$4\frac{3}{4}$%	for the next 5 years,
$4\frac{1}{2}$%	for the next 10 years,
4%	thereafter.

This loan will be repaid at 105% at the end of 40 years.

(*c*) The holder may convert to a new loan under which the rate of interest will be

$4\frac{3}{4}$%	for the first 20 years,
$4\frac{1}{4}$%	thereafter.

This loan will be repaid at 98% at the end of 40 years.

If the effective yield secured on similar types of securities is $4\frac{1}{2}$%, which option should the lender accept?

Under option (*a*) the lender will receive £100 for each £100 of loan. This will be more or less favourable than options (*b*) and (*c*), according as the values at $4\frac{1}{2}$% of the payments to be made under these options are less or more than £100.

Under option (*b*) the value of the payments is

$$5a_{\overline{5}|}+4\cdot75\,(a_{\overline{10}|}-a_{\overline{5}|})+4\cdot5\,(a_{\overline{20}|}-a_{\overline{10}|})+4\,(a_{\overline{40}|}-a_{\overline{20}|})+105v^{40}$$
$$=\cdot25\,(a_{\overline{5}|}+a_{\overline{10}|})+\cdot5a_{\overline{20}|}+4a_{\overline{40}|}+105v^{10}$$
$$=83\cdot1861+18\cdot0526$$
$$=101\cdot24.$$

Under option (*c*) the value of the payments is

$$4\cdot75a_{\overline{20}|}+4\cdot25\,(a_{\overline{40}|}-a_{\overline{20}|})+98v^{40}$$
$$=4\cdot25a_{\overline{40}|}+\cdot5a_{\overline{20}|}+98v^{40}$$
$$=84\cdot7107+16\cdot8492$$
$$=101\cdot56.$$

Hence, as the value at $4\frac{1}{2}\%$ of the payments under the three options is greatest under option (*c*), this is the one which should be accepted.

Example 7·2

Find the value to yield 4% per annum effective of a loan of £100,000 redeemable at 110% by quinquennial payments. The cash amount of the first repayment is £10,000 payable at the end of 15 years, the cash amount of each successive repayment being £6000 more than the previous payment. Interest on the loan is payable quarterly at the rate of 5% per annum, the first payment being made in 3 months' time.

The term of the loan is given by the equation

$$\frac{n}{2}[20{,}000+6000\,(n-1)]=110{,}000,$$

where n is the number of quinquennial payments, since the total amount of capital repaid must be £110,000.

$$\therefore\quad 3000n^2+7000n-110{,}000=0$$

or
$$3n^2+7n-110=0$$

or
$$(n-5)\,(3n+22)=0,$$

i.e., as a practical solution, $n=5$. Therefore the value of the capital repayments is

$$10{,}000v^{15}+16{,}000v^{20}+22{,}000v^{25}+28{,}000v^{30}+34{,}000v^{35}$$
$$=10{,}000\,(v^{15}+v^{20}+\ldots+v^{35})+6000\,(v^{20}+2v^{25}+\ldots+4v^{35})$$
$$=38{,}357.$$

C in this case is 110,000 and g is $\frac{5}{110}$. For ease of calculation $\frac{g}{i^{(p)}}$ is best written as $\frac{g}{i} s_{\overline{1}|}^{(p)}$, and hence

$$A = 38{,}357 + \frac{5}{110} \times \frac{1}{\cdot 04} \times 1{\cdot}01488\,(110{,}000 - 38{,}357)$$
$$= 38{,}357 + 82{,}624$$
$$= 120{,}981.$$

Example 7·3

A company issues a loan of £1,000,000 bearing interest at 4% per annum, payable yearly, and repayable by drawings at par at the rate of £10,000 per annum for the first 10 years, £20,000 per annum for the next 10 years, and so on until the whole issue is redeemed. What is the actual effective rate of interest at which the company is borrowing if the issue price is 96¼%?

Here

$$K = 10{,}000\,[a_{\overline{10}|} + 2\,(a_{\overline{20}|} - a_{\overline{10}|}) + 3\,(a_{\overline{30}|} - a_{\overline{20}|}) + 4\,(a_{\overline{40}|} - a_{\overline{30}|})]$$
$$= 10{,}000\,[4a_{\overline{40}|} - a_{\overline{30}|} - a_{\overline{20}|} - a_{\overline{10}|}].$$

At 4½% the value of K is

$$10{,}000\,[73{\cdot}6064 - 16{\cdot}2889 - 13{\cdot}0079 - 7{\cdot}9127] = 363{,}969.$$

Therefore the price of the whole loan to yield 4½% effective is

$$363{,}969 + \frac{\cdot 04}{\cdot 045}(1{,}000{,}000 - 363{,}969) = 929{,}330.$$

The price of the whole loan to yield 4% effective is of course 1,000,000. Hence if the price per cent is 96·25 the rate of interest yielded is approximately

$$4 + \frac{3{\cdot}75}{7{\cdot}067} \times {\cdot}5,$$

or, say, £4·27.

In practice it would be desirable to value the loan at 4½% and, say, 4⅜% in order to narrow the interval between the two trial rates and so to obtain a more accurate answer.

Example 7·4

Given $(5v^{30} + 6v^{40} + 7v^{50} + 8v^{60})$ at 2½% = 8·4732, find without using tables the price to yield 5% convertible half-yearly of an issue of 100 debentures of £100, each bearing interest at 3% per annum payable half-yearly. The issue is redeemable as follows:

25 bonds at the end of 15 years at £110,
25 bonds at the end of 20 years at £120,
25 bonds at the end of 25 years at £130,
25 bonds at the end of 30 years at £140.

Give a verbal explanation of the method used.

Consider each 25 bonds separately.

The value of the first 25 bonds,

$$A_1 \text{ say, is } 25\,[1{\cdot}5a_{\overline{30}|} + 110v^{30}] \text{ at } 2\tfrac{1}{2}\%$$

$$= 25\left[1{\cdot}5\frac{(1-v^{30})}{{\cdot}025} + 110v^{30}\right]$$

Similarly,

$$A_2 = 25\left[1{\cdot}5\frac{(1-v^{40})}{{\cdot}025} + 120v^{40}\right]$$

$$A_3 = 25\left[1{\cdot}5\frac{(1-v^{50})}{{\cdot}025} + 130v^{50}\right]$$

$$A_4 = 25\left[1{\cdot}5\frac{(1-v^{60})}{{\cdot}025} + 140v^{60}\right]$$

Therefore the total value is

$$25\left[\frac{6}{{\cdot}025} - \frac{1{\cdot}5}{{\cdot}025}(v^{30}+v^{40}+v^{50}+v^{60}) + 110v^{30} + 120v^{40} + 130v^{50} + 140v^{60}\right]$$

$$= 25\,[240 + 50v^{30} + 60v^{40} + 70v^{50} + 80v^{60}]$$

$$= 25\,[240 + 84{\cdot}372]$$

$$= 25 \times 324{\cdot}732$$

$$= 8118{\cdot}3.$$

The above result might have been deduced more simply as follows.

The loan can be considered as consisting of debentures of £60 each on which interest of £3 is paid. These debentures are redeemable as stated in the question, but, in addition, bonuses are paid on redemption of £50 for bonds drawn after 15 years, £60 for bonds drawn after 20 years and so on. In effect therefore they may be valued as 5% debentures of £60 each with bonuses payable on redemption. The value of such debentures at 5% is clearly 60 plus the value of the bonuses, and the value of the bonuses must be $\frac{1}{4} \times 84{\cdot}732$ from the information given.

The value of one debenture is therefore $60 + 21{\cdot}183 = 81{\cdot}183$ as before. If this method is adopted no further verbal explanation is required.

Example 7·5

A loan of £100,000 is issued in bonds of £100 each bearing interest at $3\frac{1}{2}\%$ per annum payable half-yearly and redeemable at par in 30 years by annual drawings as follows:

10 bonds at the end of each of the first 5 years,
20 bonds at the end of each of the second 5 years,
30 bonds at the end of each of the third 5 years,
30 bonds at the end of each of the fourth 5 years,
50 bonds at the end of each of the fifth 5 years,
60 bonds at the end of each of the last 5 years.

The price of issue is such as to yield on the average an effective rate of $4\frac{1}{2}\%$. What is the chance that a person who purchased one bond at the date of issue will obtain a higher effective yield than 5% per annum on his purchase?

Here $C = 100{,}000$

and
$$K = 100[10a_{\overline{5}|} + 20(a_{\overline{10}|} - a_{\overline{5}|}) + 30(a_{\overline{15}|} - a_{\overline{10}|}) + 30(a_{\overline{20}|} - a_{\overline{15}|}) + 50(a_{\overline{25}|} - a_{\overline{20}|}) + 60(a_{\overline{30}|} - a_{\overline{25}|})] \quad \text{at } 4\tfrac{1}{2}\%,$$
$$= 1000[6a_{\overline{30}|} - a_{\overline{25}|} - 2a_{\overline{20}|} - a_{\overline{10}|} - a_{\overline{5}|}]$$
$$= 1000[97\cdot7334 - 14\cdot8282 - 26\cdot0158 - 7\cdot9127 - 4\cdot3900]$$
$$= 44{,}587.$$

Therefore the issue price of the whole loan is

$$44{,}587 + \frac{\cdot035}{\cdot045} \times s_{\overline{1}|}^{(2)}(100{,}000 - 44{,}587) = 44{,}587 + 43{,}578$$
$$= 88{,}165.$$

The purchaser of one bond buys at a price of 88·165. If he is to obtain a yield of at least 5% his bond must be redeemed in not more than n years, where

$$88\cdot165 = 100v^n + 3\cdot5a_{\overline{n}|}^{(2)} \quad \text{at } 5\%$$
$$= 100v^n + 3\cdot5s_{\overline{1}|}^{(2)}a_{\overline{n}|}$$
$$= 100v^n + 3\cdot5432\frac{(1 - v^n)}{\cdot05},$$

or
$$v^n = \frac{88\cdot165 \times \cdot05 - 3\cdot5432}{5 - 3\cdot5432}$$
$$= \frac{\cdot8650}{1\cdot4568}$$
$$= \cdot5938,$$

and by inspection of the tables it will be seen that $10 < n < 11$. Hence if the purchaser is to obtain a yield of at least 5% the bond must be redeemed in not more than 10 years, since the sooner the bond is redeemed the greater is the yield.

The number of bonds redeemed in 10 or less years is

$$5 \times 10 + 5 \times 20 = 150,$$

and as there are 1000 bonds in all, the required chance is ·15.

Example 7·6

A debenture stock bearing interest at 5% per annum payable half-yearly and redeemable at par in 25 years was bought at a price to yield $3\frac{1}{2}$% per annum convertible half-yearly after effecting a leasehold policy to replace the loss of capital on redemption under which half-yearly premiums are calculated on the basis of interest at 3% effective with a loading of 5% of the gross premium. After 20 years it is decided to sell the stock which is then quoted in the market at a price to yield a purchaser 4% convertible half-yearly, and to surrender the leasehold policy for an amount equal to the premiums paid accumulated at $2\frac{3}{4}$% effective. What nominal rate of interest convertible half-yearly is yielded by the transaction?

Let the original price be X per £100 stock.

The leasehold policy must therefore secure $X - 100$.

The net half-yearly premium is $\frac{1}{2}P_{\overline{25}|}^{(2)}$ per unit $= \dfrac{1}{2\ddot{s}_{\overline{25}|}^{(2)}}$

$$= \frac{1}{74\cdot 555}.$$

The gross half-yearly premium per unit is therefore

$$\frac{1}{\cdot 95 \times 74\cdot 555} = \frac{1}{70\cdot 827}.$$

The total initial outlay on the purchase is therefore $X + \dfrac{X-100}{70\cdot 827}$.

The half-yearly interest payment must provide interest at $1\frac{3}{4}$% on the total initial outlay plus the half-yearly premium payable under the policy, i.e.

$$\cdot 0175\left[X + \frac{X-100}{70\cdot 827}\right] + \frac{X-100}{70\cdot 827} = 2\cdot 5.$$

$$\therefore\ X\left[\cdot 0175 + \frac{1\cdot 0175}{70\cdot 827}\right] = 2\cdot 5 + \frac{101\cdot 75}{70\cdot 827}.$$

$$\therefore\ X = \frac{278\cdot 82}{2\cdot 257}$$

$$= 123\cdot 54.$$

The half-yearly premium is therefore $\frac{23{\cdot}54}{70{\cdot}827} = {\cdot}3326$ or, say 33p per half-year.

At the end of 20 years the price of the stock in the market is

$$2{\cdot}5a_{\overline{10}|} + 100v^{10} \text{ at } 2\% = 104{\cdot}49.$$

The surrender value of the policy is

$$2 \times {\cdot}33 \times \ddot{s}^{(2)}_{\overline{20}|} = \tfrac{2}{3}\,(i/i^{(2)} + i/2)\, s_{\overline{20}|} \quad \text{at } 2\tfrac{3}{4}\%$$
$$= 17{\cdot}82.$$

Therefore the proceeds of the sale and the surrender are

$$104{\cdot}49 + 17{\cdot}82 = 122{\cdot}31.$$

The position therefore is that at the outset the purchaser pays 123·54. He pays the premiums under the policy as they fall due and receives the half-yearly interest payments and the sum of 122·31 at the end of 20 years. Therefore the rate of interest earned per half-year is given by the equation

$$123{\cdot}54 + {\cdot}33\ddot{a}_{\overline{40}|} = 2{\cdot}5a_{\overline{40}|} + 123{\cdot}31v^{40},$$

i.e. $$123{\cdot}54 + {\cdot}33\,(1 + a_{\overline{40}|} - v^{40}) = 2{\cdot}5a_{\overline{40}|} + 122{\cdot}31v^{40}$$

or $$123{\cdot}87 = 2{\cdot}17a_{\overline{40}|} + 122{\cdot}64v^{40}.$$

At $1\frac{3}{4}\%$ the right-hand side is 123·32.
At $1\frac{1}{2}\%$ the right-hand side is 132·52.

Therefore the yield per cent is $1{\cdot}75 - \frac{{\cdot}55}{9{\cdot}20} \times {\cdot}25$ or, say, 1·735 per half-year = 3·47% per annum convertible half-yearly.

In this problem the points to note are:

(1) The method of determining X by considering one half-year by itself. This is possible only because the capital is being replaced intact (cf. Example 3 in Chapter 6).

(2) Once this has been done it is necessary to calculate what the purchaser will receive after 20 years so that the equation of value may be written down.

(3) As the purchase price is not replaced intact after 20 years, the yield must be slightly less than $3\frac{1}{2}\%$ per annum, convertible half-yearly.

Example 7·7

A loan of £500,000 is issued in bonds of £100 bearing interest at 4% per annum and redeemable by 50 annual drawings, the first drawing taking place at the end of 10 years. The first 20 annual drawings are made at par, thereafter the redemption price is £105 per bond. The number of bonds drawn is given in the following schedule:

30 bonds at each of the first 5 annual drawings,
50 bonds at each of the second 5 annual drawings,
70 bonds at each of the second 10 annual drawings,
100 bonds at each of the third 10 annual drawings,
130 bonds at each of the fourth 10 annual drawings,
160 bonds at each of the fifth 10 annual drawings.

The average effective yield at the issue price is $4\frac{1}{2}\%$. What yield is obtained by a purchaser of one bond at this price if his bond is drawn 32 years after the date of issue?

If the redemption price were 100 throughout the value of the capital payments would be, per £500 of loan,

$$\begin{aligned}&3(a_{\overline{14}|}-a_{\overline{9}|})+5(a_{\overline{19}|}-a_{\overline{14}|})+7(a_{\overline{29}|}-a_{\overline{19}|})\\&\qquad+10(a_{\overline{39}|}-a_{\overline{29}|})+13(a_{\overline{49}|}-a_{\overline{39}|})+16(a_{\overline{59}|}-a_{\overline{49}|})\\&=16a_{\overline{59}|}-3(a_{\overline{49}|}+a_{\overline{39}|}+a_{\overline{29}|}+a_{\overline{9}|})-2(a_{\overline{19}|}+a_{\overline{14}|})\\&=99\cdot92052.\end{aligned}$$

Therefore if the redemption price were constant the value of the loan would be

$$99\cdot92052+\frac{\cdot04}{\cdot045}(500-99\cdot92052).$$

The value of the additional amounts payable during the last 30 years of the loan are

$$\begin{aligned}\cdot05\,[10(a_{\overline{39}|}-a_{\overline{29}|})+13(a_{\overline{49}|}-a_{\overline{39}|})+16(a_{\overline{59}|}-a_{\overline{49}|})]\\=2\cdot7633.\end{aligned}$$

Therefore the value of the whole loan is

$$\begin{aligned}99\cdot92052+\frac{\cdot04}{\cdot045}(400\cdot07948)+2\cdot7633\\=458\cdot32.\end{aligned}$$

Therefore the issue price per cent is 91·66. Hence the required yield is i where, at rate i,

$$91\cdot66=4a_{\overline{32}|}+105v^{32}=f(i)\text{ say.}$$

At $4\frac{1}{2}\%$ $f(i)=92\cdot83$.
At 5% $f(i)=85\cdot25$.

Therefore the yield is $\cdot045+\cdot005\dfrac{1\cdot17}{7\cdot58}$

$$=\cdot0458.$$

EXERCISES 7

7·1 A loan is redeemable at 105 at the end of 25 years. Interest is payable half-yearly at the rate of 4% per annum. What price should be paid to obtain an effective yield of 4% per annum?

7·2 A loan of £10,000 is repayable as follows:

£94 at the end of 1 year,
£102 at the end of 2 years,
£110 at the end of 3 years,

and so on till the whole loan is repaid. The loan bears interest at the rate of 3% per annum payable yearly. What is its value to yield a purchaser 5%?

7·3 A loan of £27,000 is to be repaid at 125 by level annual instalments of principal of £1000 starting at the end of 4 years. Interest is payable yearly at the rate of 6% per annum. The amount received by the borrowers from the flotation of the loan was £33,000. At what effective rate are they borrowing?

7·4 Two loans are each repayable at the end of n years at par. Interest on one is payable quarterly at the rate of 4% per annum, and on the other half-yearly at the rate of 3% per annum. The prices at which the loans are quoted are such as secure for a purchaser of either loan an effective yield of $3\frac{1}{2}$% per annum, and the difference between the prices is £14·58. What is the value of n?

7·5 A loan bearing interest at the rate of 4% per annum payable half-yearly is redeemable as follows:

(*a*) at the end of 30 years at par, if not redeemed earlier,
or (*b*) at the end of 20 years or at any time thereafter at 105.

What price should be paid to secure an effective yield of

(*a*) 3%,
(*b*) 4%?

CHAPTER 8

VALUATION OF SECURITIES—CONTINUED

8·1. Makeham's formula, when *g* is variable

In Chapter 7 it was pointed out that the Makeham formula

$$A = K + \frac{g s_{\overline{1}|}^{(p)}}{i}(C - K)$$

was applicable only when g, the rate of dividend per unit of capital to be repaid, was a constant. In practice the rate of dividend payable on a security may vary, or the price at which it is to be redeemed may not always be the same. In these circumstances g as defined above is no longer constant, and it is necessary either to work from first principles or to consider whether the Makeham formula can be adapted to this type of problem. In practice it will be found that the necessary modifications can be made without great difficulty, and that a method which uses a modified form of the Makeham formula is usually simpler and less liable to error than a method involving a direct valuation of the capital and interest payments separately.

8·2. Securities redeemable by instalments and bearing varying interest rates

Consider a loan of C repayable by instalments at a fixed redemption price as follows:

C_1 at the end of n_1 years,
C_2 at the end of n_2 years,
C_t at the end of n_t years,

let it be assumed that the rate of dividend payable on the loan is g_1 for n_1 years, g_2 for the next $(n_2 - n_1)$ years, and so on. Let the present values of the capital instalments at the valuation rate of interest be K_1, K_2, etc., where $K_t = v^{n_t} C_t$. Then, writing K for

$\sum_1^t K_t$ and C for $\sum_1^t C_t$, if the rate of dividend were constant at g_1 during the whole term the value of the security would be

$$A = K + \frac{g_1}{i}(C - K).$$

This value, however, allows for dividends at the rate of g_1 throughout. This is correct for the first n_1 years, but the dividends for the next $(n_2 - n_1)$ years should be $g_2(C - C_1)$ per annum and not $g_1(C - C_1)$ per annum as the formula assumes. Similarly, after n_2 years the actual dividends are $g_3(C - C_1 - C_2)$, whereas the formula includes dividends of $g_1(C - C_1 - C_2)$ and so on. Hence to find the value of the security under the given conditions the difference in the value of the dividends must be added to the value found above, and therefore

$$\begin{aligned} A = K + \frac{g_1}{i}(C - K) &+ (g_2 - g_1)(C - C_1)(a_{\overline{n_2}|} - a_{\overline{n_1}|}) \\ &+ (g_3 - g_1)(C - C_1 - C_2)(a_{\overline{n_3}|} - a_{\overline{n_2}|}) \\ &+ \dots + (g_t - g_1)\, C_t(a_{\overline{n_t}|} - a_{\overline{n_{t-1}}|}). \end{aligned}$$

This expression looks cumbersome, but in actual arithmetical work it will be found quite simple to apply.

8·3. Securities redeemable by instalments with varying redemption prices

Consider a loan of nominal amount P repayable by instalments of P_1 at the end of n_1 years, P_2 at the end of n_2 years and so on up to P_t at the end of n_t years, so that

$$\sum_1^t P_t = P.$$

Let the rate of dividend per nominal amount of capital be g' throughout, and assume that the instalment redeemed at the end of n_r years is redeemed at a price of $(1 + \lambda_r)$ per unit, i.e. that the cash payable is

$$P_r(1 + \lambda_r) = C_r \text{ (say)}.$$

In this case g, the rate of dividend per unit of capital repaid, has the successive values

$$\frac{g'}{1+\lambda_1}, \quad \frac{g'}{1+\lambda_2}, \quad \ldots, \quad \frac{g'}{1+\lambda_t},$$

and therefore the Makeham formula is not directly applicable. If, however, it were assumed that redemption was at the price of $(1+\lambda_1)$ throughout, the value of the loan to yield i per annum would be

$$A = K + \frac{g}{i}(C-K),$$

where
$$K = \sum_1^t P_r(1+\lambda_1)\, v^{n_r} \text{ at rate } i,$$

$$g = \frac{g'}{1+\lambda_1},$$

and
$$C = \sum P_r(1+\lambda_1).$$

This value is correct so far as the dividends are concerned, but the value of the capital payments is incorrect, since the payment after n_r years is assumed to be $P_r(1+\lambda_1)$ instead of $P_r(1+\lambda_r)$. Hence to find the true value it is necessary to add the present value of these differences, i.e.

$$A = K + \frac{g}{i}(C-K) + P_2(\lambda_2-\lambda_1)\, v^{n_2} + \ldots + P_t(\lambda_t-\lambda_1)\, v^{n_t}.$$

Numerical examples of this process are given in §8·12, from which it will be seen that in practice it is relatively easy to apply, and is simpler than the direct valuation of the capital and interest payments separately.

8·4. Profit or loss on redemption of securities

In §7·6 it was pointed out that in calculating the yield on a redeemable security at a particular price it is necessary to take into account any profit or loss on redemption as well as the nominal rate of dividend per unit of redemption price. It is instructive to consider how the purchaser should treat the periodical payments of interest which he receives on his stock. Consider first the simple case of a loan of C bearing interest payable yearly at the rate of g per unit of C, purchased at a price of A to give a yield of i and redeemable at par at the end of n years. Expressed symbolically this statement means that

$$A = Cv^n + gCa_{\overline{n}|} \text{ at rate } i$$
$$= C(1 - ia_{\overline{n}|}) + gCa_{\overline{n}|}$$
$$= C + (g-i)\,Ca_{\overline{n}|},$$

i.e. $$A - C = (g-i)\,Ca_{\overline{n}|} \quad \text{if} \quad g > i \tag{8·1}$$

or $$C - A = (i-g)\,Ca_{\overline{n}|} \quad \text{if} \quad i > g. \tag{8·2}$$

This expression might have been deduced from general considerations. If $g > i$ the purchase price will be greater than the redemption price and the loan may be considered as being divided into two parts,

(*a*) a loan of C bearing interest of iC per annum and redeemable at C,

(*b*) a loan of an additional amount of $A - C$ which can only be repaid out of the excess interest per annum of $gC - iC$, i.e. the value at rate i of an annuity of $(gC - iC)$ for n years must be $A - C$ whence $A - C = (g-i)\,Ca_{\overline{n}|}$.

8·5. Redeemable securities—'Writing down'

The expression $A - C = (g-i)\,Ca_{\overline{n}|}$ suggests the method which should be adopted for the treatment of the periodical interest payments, since by the methods of Chapter 5 the periodical payment of gC can be analysed into

(*a*) an amount of iC to pay i on the capital of C to be repaid,

(*b*) the amount of interest contained in the balance of $(g-i)\,C$ to pay interest at rate i on $A - C$,

(*c*) the amount of capital contained in the balance of $(g-i)\,C$ to repay the amount invested in excess of the redemption price, i.e. $A - C$.

A numerical example will make this clear. Consider a loan of 100, bearing interest at 4% payable yearly and redeemable at par in 10 years' time which is standing at a price of 108·53. The yield at this price is found from the equation

$$108{\cdot}53 = 100v^{10} + 4a_{\overline{10}|},$$

and by trial it will be found that 3% satisfies this equation. The periodical payment of 4 should therefore be used

(*a*) to pay interest at 3% on 100 = 3,
(*b*) to pay interest at 3% on 8·53 = ·256,
(*c*) the balance of ·744 should be set aside to accumulate at 3% to repay the 8·53 which would otherwise be lost when the loan is redeemed.

Alternatively, which amounts to the same thing, the periodical payment of 4 may be used to pay interest at 3% on the capital outstanding from time to time and the balance may be applied to write down the value of the security so that at the end of the term the capital outstanding will be the same as the redemption price. This process of 'writing down' is quite commonly applied in practice to redeemable securities. It involves the construction of a schedule dividing the periodical payments into capital and interest on similar lines to the analysis of the annuity in Chapter 5. In the example given the schedule would be:

Year	Dividend received	Capital outstanding at start of each year	Interest at 3% on capital outstanding	Balance of dividend to write down value of capital
1	4	108·53	3·256	·744
2	4	107·786	3·233	·767
3	4	107·019	3·211	·789
4	4	106·230	3·187	·813
5	4	105·417	3·163	·837
6	4	104·580	3·137	·863
7	4	103·717	3·111	·889
8	4	102·828	3·086	·914
9	4	101·914	3·057	·943
10	4	100·971	3·029	·971

This schedule shows that at the beginning of the tenth year the value of the security as it stands in the purchaser's books would be 100·971. The redemption price received one year later plus the capital portion of the dividend payment then made would exactly suffice to meet this sum.

8·6. Redeemable securities—'Writing up'

Similar considerations apply if the security is bought at a price below the redemption price, i.e. if $i>g$. The periodical payment of g will not suffice to pay interest at rate i on the investment of A, and the balance must therefore be made up by taking credit each year for part of the profit on redemption of $(C-A)$. If, for example, the security discussed in § 8·5 were bought at 92·28 the yield would be given by the equation

$$92{\cdot}28 = 100v^{10} + 4a_{\overline{10}|},$$

and by trial it will be found that 5 % satisfies this equation. If a schedule were now constructed as before it would have to be on the following lines:

Year	Dividend received	Capital outstanding at start of each year	Interest at 5 % on capital outstanding	Deficiency of dividend received to be added to capital outstanding
1	4	92·280	4·614	·614
2	4	92·894	4·644	·644
3	4	93·538	4·677	·677
4	4	94·215	4·710	·710
5	4	94·925	4·746	·746
6	4	95·671	4·783	·783
7	4	96·454	4·823	·823
8	4	97·277	4·864	·864
9	4	98·141	4·907	·907
10	4	99·048	4·952	·952

and at the end of the 10th year the capital shown as outstanding in the purchaser's books would be 100, which would be repaid by the return of the capital then due. This process may be described as 'writing up' the value of the security so that when it is repaid the value in the purchaser's books corresponds exactly to the redemption price. In practice, however, it is less common to write up the value of a security bought at a price below the redemption price than to write down the value of a security bought at a price higher than the redemption price.

8·7. Purchase of a redeemable security allowing for replacement of the capital at a rate of interest other than the yield

The problem discussed in §8·5 may also be considered on the same lines as that discussed in Chapter 5 in considering the analysis of the annuity at two rates of interest. A purchaser of a security might wish to obtain a yield i' on his investment, but to replace his loss of capital on redemption by accumulating the excess of the interest at a different rate, i. In theory this rate might be greater than the rate i' yielded by the purchase of the security, but in practice this is most unlikely. If it were possible to accumulate the excess of the interest payments over the yield required, at a rate higher than that yield, it would imply that the original capital could also have been invested at this higher rate, and that the purchase of the investment to yield only i' would have been ill-advised. In the paragraphs which follow, therefore, only the case when $i<i'$ is considered.

Considering a security of C, redeemable at the end of n years, on which annual interest of g per annum is paid, the price A to yield i' when the capital loss on redemption is to be replaced by accumulation at rate i may readily be found from first principles.

The interest required each year is $i'A$, and the balance of the dividend payment, i.e. $(gC-i'A)$, is available to accumulate at rate i. These accumulations must amount to $(A-C)$ to replace the capital lost on redemption. Hence

$$(gC-i'A)\,s_{\overline{n}|}=A-C \text{ at rate } i$$

or

$$A=\frac{C(1+gs_{\overline{n}|})}{1+i's_{\overline{n}|}} \text{ at rate } i. \tag{8·3}$$

An important point to notice in dealing with the valuation of securities under these conditions is that, if the valuation is made at other than an interest date, it is not possible to proceed on the lines of §7·9. Thus the value of a security under the conditions discussed above, $1/m$ of a year after an interest date would *not* be

$$A(1+i')^{1/m}.$$

The reason is that if the purchase price be A' the amount of interest required at the end of the first year is

$$A'\{(1+i')^{1-1/m}-1\},$$

and therefore the amount available for sinking fund that year is

$$gC-A'\{(1+i')^{1-1/m}-1\}.$$

Hence the equation of value is

$$[gC-A'\{(1+i')^{1-1/m}-1\}](1+i)^{n-1}+(gC-i'A')s_{\overline{n-1}|}=A'-C$$

or

$$A'=\frac{C[1+gs^{i}_{\overline{n}|}]}{1+i's^{i}_{\overline{n-1}|}+\{(1+i')^{1-1/m}-1\}(1+i)^{n-1}}.$$

In this case it is necessary to consider the problem from first principles, as otherwise the working of the sinking fund will be upset.

8·8. Alterations in conditions of existing loans

Unless there is a definite option to the borrower to repay the loan at some intermediate point in its currency, the question of an alteration in the terms of a loan should arise only

(*a*) as a matter of mutual convenience to the borrower and the lender whereby neither party should gain or lose by the transaction,

(*b*) as a result of the borrower's inability to meet the original terms in which case it may be necessary for the lender to accept some loss.

In theory, however, the principle should generally be that, at the time of the alteration, the present value of the future payments under the old arrangement should be the same as the present value of the future payments under the new. These principles are most readily illustrated by numerical examples (cf. Examples 6 and 8 of Chapter 5).

8·9. Consolidation of loans

The following is an example of what may be described as an alteration to suit the mutual convenience of the borrower and of the lender. Let it be assumed that loans have been granted for the following sums repayable by level annuities at the rates of interest shown, and that the borrower subsequently wishes to consolidate them into one loan:

Amount of loan	Original term of loan in years	No. of half-yearly instalments now outstanding	Rate of interest (convertible half-yearly)
£3000	30	15	6 %
£1000	10	5	$5\frac{1}{2}$ %
£2000	20	10	5 %

Assuming it is desired to consolidate these payments into a level half-yearly payment for 10 years, what should this payment be?

The half-yearly payments are, respectively,

$$\frac{3000}{a_{\overline{60}|}} \text{ at } 3\,\%, \quad \frac{1000}{a_{\overline{20}|}} \text{ at } 2\tfrac{3}{4}\,\% \quad \text{and} \quad \frac{2000}{a_{\overline{40}|}} \text{ at } 2\tfrac{1}{2}\,\%,$$

i.e. 108·399, 65·672 and 79·672. Hence the total present value of the future payments outstanding is

$$108{\cdot}399a_{\overline{15}|} + 65{\cdot}672a_{\overline{5}|} + 79{\cdot}672a_{\overline{10}|},$$

and this must be equal to $Xa_{\overline{20}|}$, where X is the new instalment. As, however, the rate of interest at which the transaction is to be carried out must be fixed before X can be determined, this is an indeterminate equation. Since the borrower has no powers to compel the lender to vary the conditions of the loan, the transaction should be carried out at the current market rate of interest. The lender could presumably sell his rights under the three loans for their value at that rate of interest, and if he accepted less from the borrower he would be suffering a loss. If for purposes of illustration it be assumed that this rate is 5 % per annum convertible half-yearly the equation would be

$$X = \frac{108{\cdot}399a_{\overline{15}|} + 65{\cdot}672a_{\overline{5}|} + 79{\cdot}672a_{\overline{10}|}}{a_{\overline{20}|}} \quad \text{at } 2\tfrac{1}{2}\,\%$$

$$= 2344{\cdot}5 \times {\cdot}064147,$$

whence $X = £150{\cdot}39.$

This question might have been put in another way. Assuming that the conditions are as before, if the borrower wishes to repay the three loans at once, what compensation should he pay?

The amounts nominally outstanding under the three loans are

$$108{\cdot}399 a_{\overline{15}|}^{\cdot 03} + 65{\cdot}672 a_{\overline{5}|}^{\cdot 0275} + 79{\cdot}692 a_{\overline{10}|}^{\cdot 025}$$
$$= £2297{\cdot}2.$$

The value of the outstanding instalments is, as before,

$$£2344{\cdot}4.$$

Hence the compensation to be paid is $£2344{\cdot}4 - 2297{\cdot}2$
$$= £47{\cdot}2.$$

8·10. Consolidation of annuities (local authority loans)

The question of consolidation of loans sometimes arises in connexion with loans issued by local authorities, but the methods adopted in such cases are determined by legislation and may not follow the principles illustrated in §8·9. Suppose there are r annuities of amounts per annum $X_1, X_2, \ldots, X_r$ payable for $n_1, n_2, \ldots, n_r$ years, and they are to be replaced by one annuity of X payable for n years, the equation of value is

$$X a_{\overline{n}|} = \sum_1^r X_t a_{\overline{n_t}|},$$

and this equation is indeterminate if both X and n are variables. It is understood that the method adopted in local government practice is to fix n first and to take it as being

$$\frac{\sum_1^r n_t X_t a_{\overline{n_t}|}}{\sum_1^r X_t a_{\overline{n_t}|}},$$

i.e. to find the 'equated time' of the amounts outstanding under each loan. Having thus fixed n, X may readily be found from the equation above.

Other methods which might be employed are

(*a*) to fix X as being say $\sum_1^r X_t$ and hence to determine n, or (*b*) to provide that the total payments under the consolidated loan should equal the total payments under the original loans, i.e. to fix the relationship $nX = \sum_{1}^{r} n_t X_t$.

No difficulty arises in the first case, but in the second the values of n and X are interrelated and the resulting equations

$$nX = \Sigma n_t X_t$$

and

$$Xa_{\overline{n}|} = \Sigma X_t a_{\overline{n_t}|}$$

can be solved only by trial and error. If the equations are rearranged as

$$\frac{a_{\overline{n}|}}{n} = \frac{\Sigma X_t a_{\overline{n_t}|}}{\Sigma X_t n_t},$$

the value of n can readily be found by inspection of a table of $a_{\overline{n}|}$ at the appropriate rate of interest.

8·11. Alterations in the terms of loans other than by mutual consent

It must, of course, be realized that the principle that the lender should not be penalized by the alteration holds good only when the alteration is being carried out at the request of both parties. The other possible cases

(*a*) where the borrower has an option to redeem the security in question,

and (*b*) where the borrower cannot meet his obligations and the lender may feel it expedient to agree to some adjustment in the terms,

are distinct from the cases considered above and can be dealt with only on their own merits. As an example of the first case if a 4% loan was issued repayable at par in 1966, or at 105 at any time after 1956, and if interest rates in 1956 for comparable securities were 3%, the borrower would repay the loan at 105. If there were no such option, i.e. if the loan were repayable only at par in 1966, the value to yield 3% would be

$$100v^{10} + 4a_{\overline{10}|} = 108·53.$$

It would therefore be to the borrower's advantage to repay the loan at 105, since in effect he would be buying a series of payments worth 108·53 for 105. The lender would lose by the transaction, but if the option existed he would be unable to prevent it. The second case of a borrower being unable to meet his obligations does unfortunately arise in practice, but no rules can be laid down for dealing with it. It is usually a matter of the borrower proposing a scheme which the lenders will accept if they feel it is the best arrangement which the borrower will be able to implement.

8·12. The following examples illustrate further the work of Chapter 7 and of this chapter.

Example 8·1

A loan bears interest at 6% per annum payable yearly on 1 January and is redeemable at a premium of 2% on 1 January 1954. Find the price paid on 1 April 1947 by a purchaser to realize an effective yield of 5% per annum on his whole purchase price throughout the term, after providing for the loss of capital on redemption by a sinking fund invested to accumulate at 4% effective. If instead of accumulating a separate sinking fund at 4% the purchaser decided to write down the value of the security in his books to the redemption price, construct a schedule showing how this would be done.

Let X be the price.

The sinking fund accumulates to

$$\{6 - X[(1{\cdot}05)^{\frac{3}{4}} - 1]\}(1{\cdot}04)^6 + (6 - {\cdot}05X)s_{\overline{6|}}^{{\cdot}04},$$

and this must equal $\qquad X - 102.$

$$\therefore\; X = \frac{102 + 6s_{\overline{6|}} + 6(1{\cdot}04)^6}{1 + {\cdot}05s_{\overline{6|}} + (1{\cdot}04)^6[(1{\cdot}05)^{\frac{3}{4}} - 1]}.$$

The value of $(1{\cdot}05)^{\frac{3}{4}}$ may be found by logs or taken as

$$\left(1 + \frac{i^{(4)}}{4}\right)\left(1 + \frac{i^{(2)}}{2}\right) = 1{\cdot}0373,$$

whence $X = 108{\cdot}347$.

The schedule is constructed after the first year exactly on the same lines as a schedule at two rates of interest for an annuity. The process is as follows:

After 1 year the interest required is $108{\cdot}347 \times {\cdot}0373 = 4{\cdot}038$, and hence the amount available for writing down is 1·962. Thereafter the interest required is 4% on the capital outstanding at the start of the year, plus 1 % of 108·347 to make up the total interest required at 5 % on the whole purchase price. The schedule is as follows:

Year	Capital at start of year	Interest for year at 4 %	Constant extra interest	Total interest for year	Dividend payment	Amount of capital written down during year
1	108·347	—	—	4·038	6	1·962
2	106·385	4·256	1·083	5·339	6	·661
3	105·724	4·229	1·083	5·312	6	·688
4	105·036	4·202	1·083	5·285	6	·715
5	104·321	4·173	1·083	5·256	6	·744
6	103·577	4·144	1·083	5·227	6	·773
7	102·804	4·113	1·083	5·196	6	·804
8	102	—	—	—	—	—

(*Note.* The figures in the last decimal place have been adjusted to agree with the final redemption price.)

Example 8·2

A loan of £20,000 is issued in bonds of £1000 bearing interest at $5\frac{1}{2}$ % payable yearly. One bond is redeemed at the end of each year after the 20th, the redemption price R_n being given by the formula

$$R_n = 1100 + 10\left(1 - \tfrac{1}{106}\right)^{n-20},$$

where n is the year of redemption. Find the price at which the loan was issued if the borrowers reckon they are borrowing at 5 % effective.

If the redemption price of each bond were 1100, the total issue price would be 22,000, since $g = \dfrac{5\cdot 5}{110} = \cdot 05$. This neglects payments of $10\left(\dfrac{1\cdot 05}{1\cdot 06}\right)^{n-20}$ made in years 21–40.

The value of these payments is

$$10\sum_{21}^{40} v_{\cdot 05}^{n}\frac{(1\cdot 05)^{n-20}}{(1\cdot 06)^{n-20}} = 10v_{\cdot 05}^{20}a_{\overline{20}|}^{\cdot 06}$$

$$= 43 \quad \text{approximately.}$$

The price is therefore 22,000 + 43 = 22,043, or £1102·15 per bond.

This method is an application of the principles underlying Makeham's formula. The problem could be solved directly as follows, but it will be seen that the direct method involves more work and it is not recommended.

During the first 20 years interest only is payable and the value of these payments is $1100a_{\overline{20}|}$ at 5 %. Consider the value, at the end of the 20th year, of a bond redeemed in year $20 + t$.

The value of the interest is $55a_{\overline{t}|}$.
The value of the capital is

$$v^t\left[1100+10\left(1-\frac{1}{106}\right)^t\right]=v^t\left[1100+10\frac{(1\cdot05)^t}{(1\cdot06)^t}\right] \quad \text{at } 5\%$$

$$=1100v^t_{\cdot05}+10v^t_{\cdot06}.$$

The value of this bond is therefore

$$55a^{\cdot05}_{\overline{t}|}+1100v^t_{\cdot05}+10v^t_{\cdot06}.$$

Hence the value of the twenty bonds is

$$\sum_1^{20}(55a^{\cdot05}_{\overline{t}|}+1100v^t_{\cdot05}+10v^t_{\cdot06})=\frac{55}{\cdot05}(20-a^{\cdot05}_{\overline{20}|})+1100a^{\cdot05}_{\overline{20}|}+10a^{\cdot06}_{\overline{20}|}$$

$$=22000+10a^{\cdot06}_{\overline{20}|}$$

$$=22114\cdot7.$$

Therefore the value of the whole loan now is

$$1100a_{\overline{20}|}+22114\cdot7v^{20} \quad \text{at } 5\%$$

$$=£22{,}043 \quad \text{as before.}$$

Example 8·3

A bond of £1250 is redeemable at 105% by 25 equal annual instalments of capital, the first due 6 years hence. Interest, which is payable half-yearly, is at $4\frac{1}{2}\%$ in the first year after purchase, and thereafter decreases by $\frac{1}{40}\%$ each year. What price should be paid to yield 4% per annum convertible half-yearly?

Working per £25 nominal of loan, the value of the capital payments would be

$$K=1\cdot05(v^{12}+v^{14}+\ldots+v^{60})$$

$$=1\cdot05v^{10}\frac{a_{\overline{50}|}}{s_{\overline{2}|}} \quad \text{at } 2\%$$

$$=13\cdot3996.$$

Therefore if interest were constant the value of the loan would be

$$13\cdot3996+\frac{\cdot0225}{1\cdot05}\cdot\frac{1}{\cdot02}(25\times1\cdot05-13\cdot3996)=27\cdot1678.$$

This value is too large, as it includes interest at $4\frac{1}{2}\%$ instead of at a reducing rate. The amounts to be deducted are (*a*) interest at $\frac{1}{80}\%$

increasing every half-year by $\frac{1}{80}\%$ on £25, less (*b*) interest at the above rates on the amounts of loan repaid, i.e.

$$\tfrac{25}{8000}\left[v^3+v^4+2(v^5+v^6)+\ldots+29(v^{59}+v^{60})\right]$$
$$-\tfrac{1}{8000}\left[6(v^{13}+v^{14}+\ldots+v^{60})+8(v^{15}+v^{16}+\ldots+v^{60})\right.$$
$$\left.+10(v^{17}+v^{18}+\ldots+v^{60})+\ldots+52(v^{59}+v^{60})\right]$$
$$=\tfrac{25}{8000}[S]-\tfrac{1}{8000}\left[6(a_{\overline{60}|}-a_{\overline{12}|})+8(a_{\overline{60}|}-a_{\overline{14}|})+\ldots+52(a_{\overline{60}|}-a_{\overline{58}|})\right]$$
$$=\tfrac{25}{8000}[S]-\tfrac{1}{8000}\left[696a_{\overline{60}|}-\frac{1}{i}(696-6v^{12}-8v^{14}-\ldots-52v^{58})\right].$$

Now
$$S=v^3+v^4+2(v^5+v^6)+\ldots+29(v^{59}+v^{60})$$
$$=a_{\overline{2}|}\left[v^2+2v^4+\ldots+29v^{58}\right].$$
$$\therefore\ v^2S=a_{\overline{2}|}\left[v^4+2v^6+\ldots+29v^{60}\right].$$
$$\therefore\ S(1-v^2)=a_{\overline{2}|}\left[v^2+v^4+\ldots+v^{58}-29v^{60}\right]$$
$$=a_{\overline{2}|}\left[\frac{a_{\overline{58}|}}{s_{\overline{2}|}}-29v^{60}\right].$$
$$\therefore\ S=\frac{1}{\cdot 02}\left[\frac{a_{\overline{58}|}}{s_{\overline{2}|}}-29v^{60}\right]$$
$$=403{\cdot}291.$$

Let
$$S'=6v^2+8v^4+\ldots+52v^{48}.$$
$$\therefore\ v^2S'=6v^4+8v^6+\ldots+52v^{50}.$$
$$\therefore\ S'(1-v^2)=6v^2+2v^4+2v^6+\ldots+2v^{48}-52v^{50}$$
$$=2.\frac{a_{\overline{48}|}}{s_{\overline{2}|}}+(4v^2-52v^{50}).$$
$$\therefore\ S'=\frac{1}{1-v^2}\left[2\frac{a_{\overline{48}|}}{s_{\overline{2}|}}+4v^2-52v^{50}\right]$$
$$=383{\cdot}59.$$

Therefore the value of the excess interest

$$=\tfrac{25}{8000}(403{\cdot}291)-\tfrac{1}{8000}\left[696a_{\overline{60}|}-\frac{1}{\cdot 02}(696-383{\cdot}59v^{10})\right]$$
$$=\cdot 6193.$$

The value of the loan is therefore $27{\cdot}1678 - {\cdot}6193 = 26{\cdot}5485$ per £25 nominal or £1327·42 for the whole loan.

Example 8·4

A company issues a loan of £100,000 in bonds redeemable at par in four equal amounts at the end of 10, 12, 14 and 16 years and bearing interest at 7% per annum payable half-yearly. The terms of issue provide that at the end of each half-year a level sum shall be paid into a reserve account and that the sums in this account shall be applied in the first place to pay interest on the loan outstanding, any balances being credited with interest at 5% per annum convertible half-yearly and applied to redeem the bonds as they fall due.

How much should be paid into the account each half-year?

The present value at 5% convertible half-yearly of all the payments to be made from the account is A, where

$$A = K + \frac{{\cdot}035}{{\cdot}025}(100{,}000 - K)$$

and

$$K = 25{,}000(v^{20} + v^{24} + v^{28} + v^{32}) \quad \text{at } 2\tfrac{1}{2}\%$$

$$= 52{,}945.$$

$$\therefore\ A = 52{,}945 + 65{,}877$$

$$= 118{,}822.$$

This must be the same as the present value of the level sum X, i.e.

$$Xa_{\overline{32}|} \text{ at } 2\tfrac{1}{2}\% = 118{,}822.$$

$$\therefore\ X = £5438{\cdot}2.$$

Alternatively, if all the payments are accumulated at $2\frac{1}{2}\%$ to the end of the term

$$Xs_{\overline{32}|} = 875\,[4s_{\overline{32}|} - s_{\overline{12}|} - s_{\overline{8}|} - s_{\overline{4}|}]$$
$$+ 25{,}000\,[(1{\cdot}025)^{12} + (1{\cdot}025)^{8} + (1{\cdot}025)^{4} + 1],$$

whence

$$X = £5438{\cdot}3.$$

Example 8·5

30,000 bonds of £100 each were issued on 1 July 1947. The issue carried interest for the first 15 years at 3·2% per annum and for the second

15 years at 4% per annum. Interest is paid half-yearly and bonds will be redeemed on 1 July in each year as follows:

Year	No. redeemed	Redemption price
1954	100	100
1955	200	100
1956	300	100
⋮		
1962	900	100
1963	1000	105
1964	1100	105
⋮		
1977	2400	105

At what price was the loan issued if the yield secured by taking up the whole loan was 4% effective?

The value of the bonds redeemed in the first 15 years is

$$10{,}000\,(v^7 + 2v^8 + \ldots + 9v^{15}) = 10{,}000\,v^6\left[\frac{\ddot{a}_{\overline{9}|} - 9v^9}{i}\right]$$

$$= \frac{10{,}000}{i}(a_{\overline{14}|} - a_{\overline{5}|} - 9v^{15})$$

$$= 278{,}500.$$

The nominal amount of these bonds is $\dfrac{9 \times 10}{2} \times 10{,}000 = 450{,}000.$ Therefore the value of this portion of the loan is

$$278{,}500 + \frac{3{\cdot}2}{4} s^{(2)}_{\overline{1}|}(450{,}000 - 278{,}500) = 417{,}000.$$

The value of bonds redeemed in the second 15 years, excluding the premium on redemption, is

$$10{,}000\,[10v^{16} + 11v^{17} + \ldots + 24v^{30}] = 10{,}000v^{15}\left[10a_{\overline{15}|} + \frac{a_{\overline{15}|} - 15v^{15}}{i}\right]$$

$$= 1{,}004{,}560.$$

The nominal amount is $\dfrac{15 \times 34}{2} \times 10{,}000 = 2{,}550{,}000.$ Therefore the value of these bonds, excluding the premium on redemption and assuming that interest is paid at 4% throughout, is

$$1{,}004{,}560 + s^{(2)}_{\overline{1}|}(2{,}550{,}000 - 1{,}004{,}560) = 2{,}565{,}300.$$

To this must be added the value of the premium, i.e.

$$\cdot 05 \times 1{,}004{,}560 = 50{,}228.$$

From it must be subtracted the value of interest at ·8% for the first 15 years, since the method assumes interest to be payable at 4% throughout instead of at 3·2% during the first 15 years. The value of this is

$$2{,}550{,}000 \times {\cdot}008 a^{(2)}_{\overline{15}|} = 229{,}000.$$

The total value of the loan is, to the nearest £100,

$$417{,}000 + 2{,}565{,}300 + 50{,}200 - 229{,}000 = 2{,}803{,}500,$$

or, say, £93·45 per £100 bond.

EXERCISES 8

8·1 A loan of £10,000 bearing interest at 6% per annum payable half-yearly is redeemable in four equal instalments at the end of 5, 10, 15 and 20 years at 102, 104, 106 and 108 respectively. Find the issue price to yield 8% convertible half-yearly.

8·2 Twenty years ago an investment trust borrowed £100,000 from an assurance company at 5%, the loan being repayable by 30 equal instalments of principal and interest. The trust is now considering the issue of a 3% debenture stock at a price of 80. This stock is repayable at par in 41 years' time. The trust offers to allot the assurance company £66,000 nominal of the stock in settlement of its obligations under the existing loan. Should this offer be accepted?

8·3 An investor bought debentures bearing interest at 3·2% at a price of 90; they were redeemable at par in 10 years. On maturity he applied the proceeds to purchase a 4% preference stock at 95, and after a further 5 years he sold this stock at 101. Interest on both the securities is payable half-yearly, and both the purchases and the sale were made immediately after a payment of interest had been made. What rate of interest did he earn on the transaction?

8·4 A bond for £1000 was issued on 1 July 1950 bearing interest of 3¼% payable half-yearly. It was redeemable by 10 equal instalments payable at the end of 11, 13, 15, ..., 29 years. The redemption price of the first five instalments was 105, and of the second five £100. Find the price of the loan on 1 October 1950 to yield 2½% effective per annum.

8·5 A loan, on which interest is payable half-yearly, was issued on 1 January 1949. The loan was to be redeemed in accordance with the following schedule:

Date	Amount redeemed in each year	Redemption price
1 January 1959 to 1 January 1968 (inclusive)	10,000	105%
1 January 1969 to 1 January 1978 (inclusive)	5,000	101%
1 January 1985	50,000	Par

Interest is payable at the rate of 5% per annum until the payment on 1 July 1970 has been made and thereafter at 3% per annum. What was the issue price if a purchaser of the whole loan secured a yield of 4% convertible half-yearly on his investment?

8·6 An issue was made 15 years ago of bonds of £100 bearing interest at 5% per annum payable half-yearly and redeemable at par at the end of 25 years. A purchaser of one bond effected a leasehold policy by half-yearly premiums to replace his loss of capital on redemption. The leasehold premiums were calculated on a net 3% basis, and the purchaser expected to earn a nominal yield of $4\frac{1}{2}$% convertible half-yearly on his investment. Under an option the bonds have just been repaid at 102%, and the investor has just surrendered the policy, the value allowed being the accumulation of all premiums paid at $2\frac{1}{4}$% effective.

Find (*a*) the original price at which he purchased his bond,

(*b*) the altered yield as a result of the repayment of the loan.

CHAPTER 9

CUMULATIVE SINKING FUNDS

9·1. Definitions

(*a*) A loan is said to be repayable by a cumulative (or accumulative) sinking fund when a fixed sum is applied periodically:

(i) To pay interest at a stated rate on the loan outstanding at the start of the period. This interest may be paid in one sum at the end of the period or in equal sums at stated intervals throughout the period.

(ii) To redeem part of the loan at a stated price at the end of each period, the amount applied towards redemption being the balance of the fixed sum after paying interest as in (i). The amount available for this purpose increases from year to year as more and more of the loan is redeemed and the actual amount required for interest diminishes.

The portion of the loan redeemed in any period is normally selected by lot, the loan usually being issued as a series of numbered bonds or units of stock from which drawings are made periodically.

(*b*) The fixed periodical sum is called the 'service' of the loan.

9·2. General considerations

The redemption date of any individual part of the loan is a matter of chance and therefore the value of an individual part of the loan cannot be calculated precisely. On the other hand, if an investor buys the whole loan an accurate valuation can be made, as the position as a whole is known, and it is immaterial when any individual part of the loan is redeemed. It is unlikely that any single investor will ever hold the whole of a loan, but it may reasonably be assumed that if a substantial part of the whole loan is held, the experience of that part will not deviate markedly from the experience of the whole loan. It is on this assumption that the following paragraphs are written and it must be remembered that some such assumption is implicit in any attempt to value a loan redeemable by a cumulative sinking fund.

9·3. Nature of the problem

In the following sections the symbols used have the same meanings as in § 7·7. The cash sum payable at redemption is denoted by C, and the annual rate of dividend per unit of the cash sum payable at redemption is denoted by g, so that the actual dividend received in the first year is gC. The annual amount applied to redeem the loan is denoted by z, where z is such that the cash sum applied at the outset is zC. The total cash applied towards the service of the loan each year is therefore $(g+z)C$. For example, if a loan is issued in bonds of £100, redeemable at 105 %, bearing interest at $5\frac{1}{4}$ % per annum and redeemable by a cumulative sinking fund of 1 % per annum, the rates of interest and of sinking fund as expressed in this statement are in effect 'nominal' rates only. They express the fact that each year a total cash sum of £6. 5*s.* for each £100 bond will be applied to the service of the loan. Each holder of a bond which has not been redeemed will receive £5. 5*s.* and the balance of £1 per bond originally issued will be applied each year to redeem part of the loan at a price of 105. The real measure of the borrower's indebtedness is 105, and the rate of interest on the loan per unit of that indebtedness (i.e. g) is $\frac{5\cdot25}{105}$, or 5 %. Similarly, the initial rate of sinking fund per unit of that indebtedness (i.e. z) is $\frac{1}{105}$.

Much confusion of thought will be avoided if the following principles are grasped at the outset:

(*a*) the value of the loan at any time should always be calculated for the whole of the loan outstanding at that time, and no attempt should be made to value an individual part of the loan,

(*b*) the value of the loan at any time is the value of an annuity of the cash sum applied towards the service of the loan each year,

(c) the actual indebtedness of the borrower is determined by the redemption price, and the stated rates of interest and sinking fund should always be expressed per unit of such redemption price before any calculations are made.

In general, the main problem will be either to determine the term of the loan given the amount of the service and redemption price, or to find the service of the loan given the term and redemption price. The same principles apply to both processes, and as the first problem is probably the more common it is considered in detail in the following sections.

9·4. Determination of the term of the loan

Since the total actual indebtedness of the borrower is C, which is to be extinguished by an annual payment of $(g+z)C$ for a term of n years where n is unknown, then at rate g

$$(g+z)\,Ca_{\overline{n}|}=C, \tag{9·1}$$

or

$$\frac{1}{a_{\overline{n}|}}=g+z, \tag{9·2}$$

or

$$\frac{1}{s_{\overline{n}|}}=z. \tag{9·3}$$

From these three equations it is clear that if any two of the three factors g, z and n are known the value of the third may be deduced. For example, if a loan of £100,000 were issued consisting of 1000 bonds of £100 nominal value each to be repaid at £125 per bond by means of a cumulative sinking fund of $2\frac{1}{2}$ % per annum operating by yearly drawings, interest being paid yearly at the rate of 5 % per annum, the term could be found as follows.

The actual indebtedness is £125,000 and the service is £7500 per annum. The rate of interest, per unit of redemption price, is $\frac{5}{125}=4\%$, and hence, from equation (9·1),

$$7500a_{\overline{n}|}=125{,}000 \quad \text{at } 4\%.$$

$$\therefore\ a_{\overline{n}|}=16{\cdot}667,$$

and, from interest tables at 4 %, n is seen to be almost exactly 28.

Alternatively, the rate of sinking fund, per unit of redemption price, is $\frac{2 \cdot 5}{125} = 2\%$, and hence from equation (9·3)

$$\frac{1}{s_{\overline{n}|}} = \cdot 02 \quad \text{at } 4\%,$$

or

$$s_{\overline{n}|} = 50 \quad \text{at } 4\%,$$

leading to $n = 28$ as before.

If g were not a tabular rate of interest, or if interest tables were not available, the value of n could be found directly from an extension of equation (9·3). Since

$$\frac{1}{s_{\overline{n}|}} = z \quad \text{at rate } g,$$

and since

$$\frac{1}{s_{\overline{n}|}} = \frac{g}{(1+g)^n - 1},$$

$$(1+g)^n - 1 = \frac{g}{z},$$

or

$$(1+g)^n = \frac{g+z}{z}, \tag{9·4}$$

and the value of n could be determined by using logarithms.

The direct method of approach can always be used in the simple conditions discussed above. A more general method can, however, be developed which may usefully serve to focus attention on the method of operation of a cumulative sinking fund. It depends on the following four identities which are true no matter what complications are introduced:

(*a*) the nominal amount of loan outstanding at the end of any year is the nominal amount outstanding at the start of that year less the nominal amount repaid by the sinking fund in that year,

(*b*) the nominal amount repaid in any year multiplied by the redemption price (per £1 nominal of loan), plus interest on the nominal amount outstanding at the start of the year must equal the service of the loan,

(*c*) the nominal amount of loan repaid in the first year multiplied by the redemption price (per £1 nominal of loan) must equal the annual amount of cumulative sinking fund, (*d*) if the term of the loan is integral the nominal amount repaid in the last year must equal the nominal amount outstanding at the start of the last year.

From equations (*a*) and (*b*) the relationship between the successive amounts of capital repaid can be determined, and from this relationship and either (*c*) or (*d*) the amount of capital repaid in any year can be found. For example, in the simple case already discussed in this section let $F(t)$ be the nominal amount of loan outstanding at the end of the tth year, and let $f(t)$ be the nominal amount of loan repaid during that year. Then

$$F(t)=F(t-1)-f(t)$$

and $$f(t)\times C+gC\times F(t-1)=(g+z)C,$$

also $$f(t-1)\times C+gC\times F(t-2)=(g+z)C.$$

Hence, by subtraction,

$$C[f(t)-f(t-1)]+gC[F(t-1)-F(t-2)]=0,$$

i.e. $$C[f(t)-f(t-1)]-gCf(t-1)=0,$$

or $$f(t)=(1+g)f(t-1).$$

Hence in this case the successive amounts of capital repaid form a geometric progression with common ratio $(1+g)$. The first term of this series is $f(1)$, and as $f(1)\times C=zC$ it follows that

$$\begin{aligned}f(t)&=(1+g)^{t-1}f(1)\\&=z(1+g)^{t-1}.\end{aligned}$$

The nominal amount of loan repaid in n years is

$$=zs_{\overline{n|}} \quad \text{at rate } g.$$

$$\therefore\ zs_{\overline{n|}}=1 \quad \text{at rate } g \text{ as in equation (9·3).}$$

Using the principles of this method equation (9·4) may be explained verbally as follows. The cash sum available in the final year for redemption of capital is, as shown above, $zC(1+g)^{n-1}$. This must be the amount of loan outstanding at the start of the year and the interest due for the year is therefore $gzC(1+g)^{n-1}$. The total cash applied to the service in the nth year is therefore $zC(1+g)^{n-1}(1+g)$, and this by definition is also $(g+z)C$. Hence $z(1+g)^n=(g+z)$ as in equation (9·4).

The principles underlying the method are of fundamental importance to an understanding of the problem, and the student should be sure that he has a clear mental picture of the operation involved before going further.

9·5. Example of the working of a cumulative sinking fund

The following numerical example may assist in the understanding of the problem. A loan of £1000 bearing interest at 5 % per annum payable yearly is issued in bonds of £10 and is redeemable by the operation of a cumulative sinking fund of 18·1% operating by annual drawings at par. Find the term of the loan, and draw up a schedule showing the number of bonds redeemed in each year.

Here $g = \cdot 05, \quad z = \cdot 181.$

$$\therefore \frac{1}{s_{\overline{n}|}} \text{ at } 5\% = \cdot 181,$$

whence $n = 5.$

The schedule is drawn up as follows:

End of year	Loan outstanding	Service	Interest at 5 % on loan outstanding	Balance of service	No. of bonds drawn	Balance of service	Balance of service plus interest at 5 %
1	£1000	231	50	181	18	1·00	1·05
2	£820	232·05	41	191·05	19	1·05	1·10
3	£630	232·10	31·5	200·60	20	·60	·63
4	£430	231·63	21·5	210·13	21	·13	·14
5	£220	231·14	11·0	220·14	22	·14	—

This shows how the loan will be repaid in 5 years. The small error of ·14 or 14p is due to the work having been carried out to two decimal places, and for practical purposes it can be disregarded. It must be noted that as each bond is redeemed at £10 and it is not possible to repay a portion of a bond, there is a small balance of the service over each year. It is assumed that this balance is accumulated at 5 % and added to the next year's sinking fund. This arrangement is unlikely to be made in practice, but it is implicit in the equation $zCs_{\overline{n}|} = C$. The possible error so introduced is so small as to be negligible.

9·6. Fractional term

Up to this point it has tacitly been assumed that the solution of the equation for n, $$zCs_{\overline{n}|} \text{ at rate } g = C,$$ will be integral. In practice this will not usually be true, and the position where the term is not integral must be examined. If the equation $$zCs_{\overline{n}|} = C$$ yields a non-integral result for n, say $n+f$, where n is an integer and f a fraction, it means that the sinking fund operates normally for n periods, but that in the next period the sum required to repay the balance of the loan then outstanding with interest is less than the service for a full period. In theory this balance might be repaid a fraction of a period later, but in practice it is always repaid when the next amount of sinking fund would normally fall due, i.e. after $(n+1)$ periods. From the investor's point of view he is buying an annuity of $(g+z)C$ per period for n periods plus a payment of $(C - zCs_{\overline{n}|})(1+g)$ at the end of $(n+1)$ periods, since $C - zCs_{\overline{n}|}$ is the loan outstanding after n periods, and this is repaid, with interest at rate g, at the next date on which the sinking fund would normally operate.

9·7. Valuation of loans

Since a loan repayable by a cumulative sinking fund represents an annuity of the service of the loan, the value of the loan at a given rate of interest is merely the value of this annuity. As will be seen later, this value needs adjustment if the interest and sinking fund do not operate with the same frequency, i.e. if the whole of the service is not applied in one sum each year, but the principle remains the same, and for the present only the simpler case will be considered. The first step in valuing the annuity will of course be to find the number of years for which it will be payable, and this will be done by one of the methods of §9·4.

Using the same meanings for z, g and C as before, the value of the loan to yield i per annum is $(g+z)\,Ca_{\overline{n}|}$ at rate i if n is integral, or

$$(g+z)\,Ca^{i}_{\overline{n}|} + (C - zCs^{g}_{\overline{n}|})(1+g)\,v_i^{n+1}, \qquad (9\cdot5)$$

if $$s_{\overline{n}|} < \frac{1}{z} < s_{\overline{n+1}|} \quad \text{at rate } g.$$

The same principle applies for finding the value of the loan at any time during its term. If t years have elapsed since the sinking fund began to operate, the value of the loan for the balance of the term would be

$$(g+z)\,Ca_{\overline{n-t}|}^{i}+(C-zCs_{\overline{n}|}^{g})(1+g)\,v_i^{n-t+1}. \qquad (9{\cdot}6)$$

9·8. Variation in g, z or C

The simple problem so far considered may be complicated by variation in the rate of interest payable on the loan, the amounts to be applied towards the sinking fund or the redemption price of the loan. The methods of dealing with such complications are illustrated by Examples 4–6 at the end of this chapter, which show the processes involved more clearly than is possible in an analysis of the general problem. The student should give these examples careful attention and should concentrate on the principles involved. It may be convenient here to summarize certain of the points brought out in these examples.

(*a*) *Variations in g or z*

If either g or z vary it should be noted that the amount of the service is calculated with reference to the *original* loan and not to the loan outstanding when the change is made. This is to some extent conventional, but it is generally understood in commercial practice that, for example, the service of a loan of £100,000 redeemable by a cumulative sinking fund of 1% per annum, interest being at 4% for 10 years and 5% thereafter, would be £5000 per annum for 10 years and £6000 per annum subsequently.

(*b*) *Variations in C*

At first sight it might appear that a variation in C should have the same effect as a variation in g, but this is not so. If g varies the amount applied to the service of the loan will also vary, whereas a variation in C affects only the nominal amount of loan repaid in any year and not the actual service of the loan in that year.

(*c*) *Determination of the term*

This is generally the most difficult part of the solution of any problem involving a cumulative sinking fund. It was shown in § 9·4 that, generally, the amounts available for redemption of the loan in any year form a geometric series. This series may be a simple one with a common ratio of $(1+g)$, or, if g varies, it may be more complicated, but if it is borne in mind that such a geometric series exists and that it can always be summed algebraically without reference to interest tables, it should always be possible to find the term of the loan without undue difficulty whatever complications may be introduced.

(*d*) *Valuation*

Once the term has been found, the value of the loan is simply the value of an annuity of the service of the loan for that term.

9·9. Cumulative sinking fund operating with different frequency from interest payments

Hitherto it has been assumed that the sinking fund operates with the same frequency as interest is payable. In practice it is more usual for drawings to be made annually while interest is often paid more than once a year.

Consider a loan of C repayable by an annual service of $(g+z)C$, where drawings are made yearly but interest is paid p times a year. It is first necessary to determine how this affects the capital repayments. After 1 year the loan outstanding is $C-zC$. The total interest on this for the next year is $gC-gzC$, payable by p instalments. But the fact that this interest is payable by instalments throughout the year does not affect the total sum which the borrower has to find by way of interest in the year. The cash available from the service is still $(g+z)C$, so the amount left for sinking fund is still $zC+gzC=zC(1+g)$ in the year in question. The frequency with which interest is payable has therefore no effect on the accumulation of the sinking fund, and the term of such a loan is identical with that of a loan where both interest and sinking fund are annual.

9·10. Valuation problems

It is clear from §9·9 that the methods already discussed for finding the *term* of a loan apply irrespective of the frequency of interest payments. The only remaining problem is to find the adjustment to the *value* of the security to allow for the fact that interest is paid in instalments throughout the year. The value of the loan is still the present value of the service of $(g+z)C$ for the appropriate term, but allowance must be made for the fact that the interest portion of the service is paid by instalments. *Since the capital repayments form the same series, however frequently the interest is payable, the following general method will always be successful:*

(*a*) The security can first be valued assuming interest is payable yearly.

(*b*) The value of the capital can be found either directly by valuing the geometric series of capital payments, or in certain cases indirectly as discussed in §9·12.

(*c*) The difference between (*a*) and (*b*) will be the value of the interest if it were paid in one sum at the end of each year. If payments are made p times a year the value is by proportion $[(a)-(b)]\, s_{\overline{1}|}^{(p)}$ at the valuation rate of interest, and hence the value of the security is the value of the capital as found in (*b*) plus the adjusted value of the interest as found in (*c*).

It may not always be necessary to follow this method in its entirety—for example, if g is constant the security can be valued by the same method as any security redeemable by instalments, and once the value of the capital is known it can be inserted in Makeham's formula to find the value of the loan without going through the process in (*a*) above. The method is illustrated in the examples at the end of this chapter, and in the following sections only the straightforward case where g, z and C are constant is considered in detail.

9·11. Direct valuation of capital

Let C, g and z have the same meanings as before, but let z operate annually and g be payable p times a year.

As before, $zCs_{\overline{n+f}|}=C$, where n is integral and f fractional, and $s_{\overline{n+f}|}$ is calculated at the *effective* rate g (see § 9·9).

Let $X=C-zCs^{g}_{\overline{n}|}$, i.e. let X be the amount of capital outstanding after n years. The capital repaid in each year is

$$zC, \quad zC(1+g), \quad zC(1+g)^2, \quad \ldots,$$

and so on.

Therefore the present value at rate i of capital repaid (say K) is

$$vzC+v^2zC(1+g)+v^3zC(1+g)^2+\ldots+v^nzC(1+g)^{n-1}+Xv^{n+1}.$$

$$\therefore \quad K=vzC\frac{1-v^n(1+g)^n}{1-v(1+g)}+Xv^{n+1}$$

$$=zC\frac{1-v^n(1+g)^n}{i-g}+Xv^{n+1}.$$

The value of the security, if interest were payable yearly, would be

$$(g+z)\,Ca_{\overline{n}|}+v^{n+1}(1+g)\,X.$$

If therefore the value of the capital, as found above, is subtracted from this the result is the value of interest, assuming it is paid yearly. If this value is multiplied by $s^{(p)}_{\overline{1}|}$ at the valuation rate of interest and added to the value of the capital already found, the result will be the value of the whole loan.

In this case, however, it is not necessary to go to the labour of evaluating $(g+z)\,Ca_{\overline{n}|}+v^{n+1}(1+g)X$, since, if the value of K is found, as above, it can be used directly in Makeham's formula to find the value of the loan.

Alternative expressions for the value of K may be found as follows.

By putting

$$\frac{1+g}{1+i}=1+i' \quad \text{if} \quad g>i \quad \text{or} \quad \frac{1+i}{1+g}=1+i'' \quad \text{if} \quad i>g,$$

i.e.

$$i'=\frac{g-i}{1+i} \quad \text{or} \quad i''=\frac{i-g}{1+g}$$

according as $g >$ or $< i$, the value of the capital payments might be written as

$$\frac{zC}{1+i} s_{\overline{n}|}^{i'} + Xv_i^{n+1}$$

or

$$\frac{zC}{1+g} a_{\overline{n}|}^{i''} + Xv_i^{n+1}.$$

In practice, however, these formulae are of little if any, value, as the rates of interest i' or i'' will rarely correspond to any tabular rates.

It should also be noted that if the equation $zCs_{\overline{n}|} = C$ has an integral solution for n then, since $(1+g)^n = \frac{g+z}{z}$, the value of capital can be written as

$$zC\frac{1-v^n\left(\frac{g+z}{z}\right)}{i-g} = C\frac{z-(g+z)v^n}{i-g}.$$

This is perhaps the form which involves least numerical work in calculation. None of these formulae, however, need be memorized if the principles of §9·10 are clearly grasped.

9·12. Indirect valuation of the capital

This method is usually easier to apply in arithmetical work than the direct method of §9·11. It is more limited in its scope, since it makes use of the same methods as the Makeham formula

$$A = K + \frac{g}{i}(C-K),$$

and it can be used therefore only in the conditions in which that formula would apply, i.e. where g is constant. The method depends on the three principles:

(a) the value of the capital payments is the same whether or not interest is payable with the same frequency as the sinking fund operates,

(b) if interest and sinking fund operate with the same frequency the capital payments and the interest payments together can readily be valued as an annuity of the service, (*c*) from the value found in (*b*) the value of the interest payments or of the capital payments can be deduced without direct calculation as shown below.

Method 1

If the sinking fund and interest were paid yearly the value of the loan would be $(g+z)\,Ca_{\overline{n}|}$ at rate i.

If instead of interest of g per annum, interest on the loan were paid at rate i, the value of the loan to yield i would be C, which is equal to $(g+z)\,Ca_{\overline{n}|}$ at rate g.

Therefore as the value of the capital is the same in either case $(g+z)\,C\,[a^g_{\overline{n}|}-a^i_{\overline{n}|}]$ must be the value of dividends of $(i-g)$ per annum paid yearly.

Now $(g+z)\,Ca^i_{\overline{n}|}$ includes dividends at the rate of g per annum instead of $gs^{(p)}_{\overline{1}|}$, i.e. to find the true value we must add the value of dividends of $(gs^{(p)}_{\overline{1}|}-g)$.

But by simple proportion this is $g\dfrac{s^{(p)}_{\overline{1}|}-1}{i-g}(g+z)\,C\,(a^g_{\overline{n}|}-a^i_{\overline{n}|})$.

Substituting $\dfrac{C}{a^g_{\overline{n}|}}$ for $(g+z)\,C$ the value of the whole loan is

therefore
$$C\frac{a^i_{\overline{n}|}}{a^g_{\overline{n}|}}+gC\frac{s^{(p)}_{\overline{1}|}-1}{i-g}\left(1-\frac{a^i_{\overline{n}|}}{a^g_{\overline{n}|}}\right).$$

Method 2

If the sinking fund and dividends were paid yearly the value of the loan would be $(g+z)\,Ca^i_{\overline{n}|}$ or $C\dfrac{a^i_{\overline{n}|}}{a^g_{\overline{n}|}}$.

Its value, however, is also $K+\dfrac{g}{i}(C-K)$, where K is the value of the capital repayments.

$$\therefore\ K+\frac{g}{i}(C-K)=C\frac{a^i_{\overline{n}|}}{a^g_{\overline{n}|}}.$$

$$\therefore\ K\left[1-\frac{g}{i}\right]=C\left[\frac{a^i_{\overline{n}|}}{a^g_{\overline{n}|}}-\frac{g}{i}\right]$$

$$=C\frac{(v^n_g-v^n_i)}{ia^g_{\overline{n}|}}.$$

$$\therefore\ K=\frac{C}{i-g}\left(\frac{v^n_g-v^n_i}{a^g_{\overline{n}|}}\right).$$

Having found K the value of the loan with interest payable p times a year is found either as in §9·11 or from the Makeham formula

$$A = K + \frac{g s_{\overline{1}|}^{(p)}}{i}(C - K).$$

It will be noted that the expression deduced above for K is equivalent to

$$\frac{C}{i-g}\left[\frac{v_g^n - v_i^n}{v_g^n\, s_{\overline{n}|}^g}\right] = Cz\frac{1 - v_i^n(1+g)^n}{i-g}, \quad \text{since} \quad \frac{1}{s_{\overline{n}|}^g} = z,$$

as in §9·11.

In this analysis it has been assumed that n is integral. If it is not, the methods may still be used and in actual arithmetical work will be found equally simple.

9·13. Limitations on above methods

It must be noted that the methods of §§ 9·11 and 9·12 can be used only if Makeham's formula is applicable. They cannot be applied if there are varying dividends or redemption prices. In such cases the direct method of § 9·11 must be used, as also in the case where $i = g$ and the methods of § 9·12 yield indeterminate results.

9·14. Further note on fractional terms

As explained above, there is no great difficulty in dealing with a fractional term if the problem is tackled from first principles. It may be of interest, however, to consider how the formulae of § 9·12 could be modified. In practice there is no saving of work in so doing, and the methods described below are of greater theoretical interest than practical use. They are included for the sake of completeness, and it is not intended that they should be used in favour of the direct approach from first principles, which will always be less confusing.

Method 1

Let g, z and C have the same meanings as before and let

$$zCs_{\overline{n}|} < C < zCs_{\overline{n+1}|} \quad \text{at rate } g.$$

The formula $\quad C\dfrac{a_{\overline{n}|}^i}{a_{\overline{n}|}^g} + gC\dfrac{s_{\overline{1}|}^{(p)} - 1}{i-g}\left(1 - \dfrac{a_{\overline{n}|}^i}{a_{\overline{n}|}^g}\right)$

will not necessarily apply. It could be made to apply, however, by treating the loan in two portions

(*a*) a loan of $zCs_{\overline{n}|}$ ($=C_1$ say) at rate g, repaid by a cumulative sinking fund for n years,

(*b*) a loan of $(C-zCs_{\overline{n}|}^{g})$ with interest at rate g, repaid at the end of $n+1$ years.

It must, however, be noted that if this method is followed the service available for (*a*) is not $(g+z)C$ but

$$(g+z)C-g(C-C_1), \quad =gC_1+zC,$$

since there is a constant requirement of $g(C-C_1)$ for the interest on the portion in (*b*). Similarly, the loan is one of C_1, and the values of g and z must be modified to relate to the loan of C_1 and no longer to the original loan of C. The complications so involved make this method certainly no easier than the direct one.

Method 2

It may be asked whether any appreciable error is involved, if the term be taken as $(n+f)$, where f is fractional and the value of the loan taken as

$$C\frac{a_{\overline{n+f}|}^{i}}{a_{\overline{n+f}|}^{g}}+gC\frac{s_{\overline{1}|}^{(p)}-1}{i-g}\left[1-\frac{a_{\overline{n+f}|}^{i}}{a_{\overline{n+f}|}^{g}}\right]$$

(the values of $a_{\overline{n+f}|}$ being found by ordinary first difference interpolation). It may be demonstrated that provided f is found by first difference interpolation from the equation

$$(g+z)Ca_{\overline{n+f}|}^{g}=C,$$

that is to say, if
$$f=\frac{\dfrac{1}{g+z}-a_{\overline{n}|}^{g}}{a_{\overline{n+1}|}^{g}-a_{\overline{n}|}^{g}},$$

the formula is absolutely accurate. The proof is included in the examples at the end of the chapter.

This method, however, is not recommended. The direct method entails little, if any, more work, and is applicable in all cases where other complications may be introduced which would cause this formula to break down.

9·15. Approximate formulae

For a further discussion on cumulative sinking funds the reader is referred to *J.I.A.* vol. 49, pp. 290–5, where approximate formulae are deduced. These, however, are beyond the scope of this book, and the student coming to the subject for the first time need not trouble to refer to this discussion at the present stage.

9·16. Valuation of securities with options to purchase in the market

The terms on which loans repayable by cumulative sinking funds are issued sometimes provide that the sinking fund may be applied either to repay bonds drawn by lot at a certain price, or to purchase bonds in the market below that price, the purchased bonds being cancelled. If the market price is below the fixed redemption price the option is important, as the borrowers will clearly find it to their advantage to exercise it. The effect will of course be to speed up the redemption process, since for the same sum of money more bonds can be bought at the market price and cancelled than can be drawn by lot and redeemed at the fixed redemption price.

In the strict theory of the valuation of securities repayable by a cumulative sinking fund such an option has no effect, for, as was mentioned in §9·2, such securities can be valued accurately only if the valuer purchases the whole amount of loan. In this case, however, the option could not be exercised, since if the whole amount is held by one person he would be unlikely to agree to sell the bonds in the market below the redemption price. If, however, a substantial portion of the loan is held, and if there is a free market in the remainder of the loan the effect of the option will have to be considered.

The difficulty which arises immediately is that the amount of the loan purchased in any year, and hence the rate at which the sinking fund accumulates, depends on the market price of the bonds in that year, and before the loan can be valued some assumption as to that price must be made. The most reasonable assumption is probably that current conditions will continue, and that if it is appropriate to value the loan at rate i at the present time it will equally be appropriate to use the same rate in future years.

Consider a loan in which the bonds are redeemable at C, or below C by purchases in the market, and let the annual service of the loan be $(g+z)C$ as in § 9·3. Then if it is desired to value the loan at rate i, where $i>g$, the price will be below C and the option will be exercised. Assuming that the loan is repaid in n years, where n is at present unknown, the value per bond of the whole loan is A, where

$$A=(g+z)Ca_{\overline{n}|} \quad \text{at rate } i.$$

Now if an individual holds one bond he cannot be compelled to sell it, and if he holds it to the end of the term, when it will be drawn and repaid at C, its value will be given by the equation

$$A=gCa_{\overline{n}|}+Cv^n \quad \text{at rate } i,$$

where C is the redemption price of one bond.

Since these equations are satisfied by the same value of i, it must follow that

$$(g+z)Ca_{\overline{n}|}=gCa_{\overline{n}|}+Cv^n \quad \text{at rate } i.$$

$$\therefore \; za_{\overline{n}|}=v^n.$$

$$\therefore \; z=\frac{1}{s_{\overline{n}|}} \quad \text{at rate } i.$$

From this equation the value of n may be found and hence the value of A, either by the use of interest tables or as follows:

$$\begin{aligned} A&=(g+z)Ca_{\overline{n}|} \\ &=(g+z)Cv^n s_{\overline{n}|} \\ &=\frac{(g+z)C}{z(1+i)^n} \\ &=\frac{(g+z)C}{z(1+is_{\overline{n}|})} \\ &=\frac{(g+z)C}{z\left(1+\frac{i}{z}\right)} \\ &=\frac{g+z}{i+z}C. \end{aligned}$$

It should be noted that the desired yield will be obtained only if the price of the bonds in the market follows the assumptions made.

If the prices in the market in two successive years are A and A', and if the assumed relationship holds good, then

$$A = gCa_{\overline{n}|} + Cv^n$$

and $$A' = gCa_{\overline{n-1}|} + Cv^{n-1}.$$

If the holder of one bond which he purchased for A decided to sell it in the following year at a price A', the yield he would obtain would be given by the equation

$$\begin{aligned} A &= v_1 A' + v_1 gC \quad \text{at rate } i' \text{ where } v_1 = \frac{1}{1+i'} \\ &= v_1 [gCa_{\overline{n-1}|} + Cv^{n-1} + gC] \\ &= v_1 [gC\ddot{a}_{\overline{n}|} + Cv^{n-1}] \\ &= v_1 (1+i) A. \end{aligned}$$

$$\therefore \quad 1 + i' = 1 + i$$

or $$i' = i.$$

By equating A and $v_1^t A_t + gCa'_{\overline{t}|}$ when A_t is the price after t years it will be found that the same relationship holds, and it is therefore immaterial whether the holder of one bond retains it to the end of the n years, or sells it at any intermediate point *provided the prices follow the basic assumptions above.* If the prices in subsequent years fall below the assumed prices the holder of one bond need not sell. The only result will be that the redemption of the loan is accelerated and therefore if he retains his bond till it is redeemed at the fixed redemption price he will receive a capital profit on redemption at an earlier date than he expected. His investment will therefore give a higher yield than he calculated. If, however, the prices rise above the assumed prices the redemption of the loan will be retarded and hence, if the holder of one bond retains it to the end of the term, his yield would be less than the expected yield. The remedy, however, is in his own hands, for he can always sell his bonds at the market price. Since a sale at a price of A_t will give the desired yield, a sale at a higher price than A_t will give a higher yield, and the investor is therefore certain to receive at least the desired yield whatever course prices actually follow. But if such a security is held it is obviously desirable to construct a table showing the theoretical expected prices from year to year and to compare the actual prices with this table, so that if the actual price exceeds the theoretical price it may be considered whether it is not advantageous to sell the holding instead of retaining it.

9·17. Valuation of securities with options to purchase, interest and sinking fund operating with different frequency

In this case the problem is more complicated. The value of the whole loan is now

$$(g+z)\,Ca_{\overline{n}|} + \text{an adjustment to allow for interest being paid } p \text{ times a year.}$$

The equation $zs_{\overline{n}|}=1$ at rate i would hold good only if

$$(gs_{\overline{1}|}^{(p)}+z)\,Ca_{\overline{n}|}=gCa_{\overline{n}|}^{(p)}+Cv^n.$$

This is not so, because while the right-hand side correctly represents the value to the individual bond holder, the left-hand side is not the correct expression for the value to the bond holders as a whole. To obtain the correct value it would be necessary to ascertain what portion of the total source of $(g+z)\,C$ represents interest in any particular year. This amount, which is payable p times a year, will vary from year to year and will not be constant as is tacitly assumed in the expression on the left-hand side. Hence the method of § 9·16 is not strictly applicable. In practice, however, as the loan can only be valued by making some assumption as to future prices, and as the value so determined is necessarily only an approximation, this would probably be disregarded and the value of n as determined from the equation $zs_{\overline{n}|}=1$ at rate i would be used as a guide and the price would be taken as

$$A=gCa_{\overline{n}|}^{(p)}+Cv^n \quad \text{at rate } i.$$

9·18. The following examples are designed to illustrate numerically the methods of this chapter:

Example 9·1. (*The simplest case where interest and sinking fund operate with the same frequency.*)

A loan bears interest at 5% payable half-yearly and is redeemable at par by a cumulative sinking fund of 1% per annum operating half-yearly. The amount of loan outstanding is 72% of the original amount and the market price is 87½%.

Another loan bears interest at 6% payable half-yearly and is redeemable at 105 by a cumulative sinking fund of 2% per annum operating half-yearly. 80% of this loan is outstanding and the price is 96%.

Which of these loans offers the better yield?

The service of the first loan each year is (5+1) per 100 of original capital. Interest at 5% on the 72% outstanding absorbs 3·6, therefore the sinking fund in the current year is 2·4 per annum, or 1·2 per half-year. Therefore if the term be n half-years

$$1 \cdot 2 s_{\overline{n}|} \text{ at } 2\tfrac{1}{2}\% = 72$$

or

$$s_{\overline{n}|} = 60.$$

Whence the term is 38 half-years, the last payment being a fractional one.

The amount redeemed in 37 half-years is $1 \cdot 2 s_{\overline{37}|} = 71 \cdot 68$.

The balance to be repaid with a half-year's interest after 38 half-years is ·32.

The value of the loan to yield i per half-year is therefore

$$3a_{\overline{37}|} + \cdot 32\,(1 \cdot 025)\,v^{38}.$$

At 3% this value is 66·603.

At $3\tfrac{1}{2}$% this value is 61·800.

Note that these are not the values of each £100 of loan now outstanding, but the values per £100 original of loan of which the outstanding amount is now £72. The value per £100 of the loan now outstanding is

$$\frac{66 \cdot 603}{\cdot 72}.$$

The price is 87·5 per 100 of loan now outstanding $= 87 \cdot 5 \times \cdot 72$ per 100 of the original loan $= 63$.

The yield per cent is therefore $3 + \dfrac{3 \cdot 603}{4 \cdot 803} \times \cdot 5$ per half-year $= 3 \cdot 375\%$ per half-year.

Under the other loan the total service per cent is (6+2) per annum, and interest will absorb $6 \times \cdot 8 = 4 \cdot 8$ per annum in the current year. The sinking fund in the current year is therefore 3·2 per annum or 1·6 per half-year.

$$\therefore \quad 1 \cdot 6 s_{\overline{n}|} = 80.(1 \cdot 05), \text{ at rate } g, \text{ where } g = \frac{3}{105} = 2 \cdot 86\%.$$

$$\therefore \quad s_{\overline{n}|} = 52 \cdot 5.$$

By first difference interpolation between $s_{\overline{n}|}$ at $2\tfrac{1}{2}$% and $s_{\overline{n}|}$ at 3%:

$$s_{\overline{33}|} \text{ at } 2 \cdot 86\% = 53 \cdot 75,$$

$$s_{\overline{32}|} \text{ at } 2 \cdot 86\% = 51 \cdot 28.$$

Therefore the term of this loan is 33 half-years. The balance of the loan to be repaid after 33 half-years is $80(1 \cdot 05) - 1 \cdot 6 \times 51 \cdot 28$, i.e. 1·95.

The value of the loan is therefore $4a_{\overline{32}|} + 1{\cdot}95\,(1{\cdot}0286)\,v^{33}$.

At $3\frac{1}{2}\%$ this is 76·82, which is sufficiently close to the market price of $96 \times {\cdot}8$ ($=76{\cdot}8$) to show that the yield on the second loan is almost exactly $3\frac{1}{2}\%$, and is therefore more attractive than the first.

The following points in the above solution should be noted:

(1) The fact that in the second loan the redemption price is 105 means that the outstanding loan represents an indebtedness of $80 \times 1{\cdot}05$ and not 80. Similarly, the sinking fund accumulates at rate $\dfrac{3}{105}$ and not 3%.

(2) The treatment of the fractional term.

(3) The fact that the values brought out are the cash values of the whole loan outstanding and not the price per cent of a bond nominally worth £100.

Example 9·2. (*Sinking fund annual, interest half-yearly.*)

A loan bears interest at $5\frac{1}{4}\%$ per annum payable half-yearly and is redeemable at 105 by a cumulative sinking fund operating by yearly drawings over a period of 50 years. What price should a purchaser pay to obtain an effective yield of 6% per annum?

Here $C=105$, $g=\dfrac{5{\cdot}25}{105}={\cdot}05$ and $n=50$.

Therefore if z is the sinking fund per unit of C

$$zCs_{\overline{50}|} = C \quad \text{at } 5\%,$$

i.e.

$$z=\frac{1}{s_{\overline{50}|}},$$

i.e.

$$z={\cdot}004777.$$

It is now proposed to solve the question by each of the methods of §§ 9·11 and 9·12.

(*a*) The capital repayments form the series

$$zC,\quad zC(1{\cdot}05),\quad \ldots,\quad zC(1{\cdot}05)^{49}.$$

Therefore their value at 6%

$$=vzC+v^2zC(1{\cdot}05)+\ldots+v^{50}zC(1{\cdot}05)^{49}$$

$$=vzC\,\frac{1-v^{50}(1{\cdot}05)^{50}}{1-v(1{\cdot}05)}$$

$$=105\times{\cdot}004777\times\frac{1-{\cdot}05429\times 11{\cdot}4674}{{\cdot}01}$$

$$=18{\cdot}931.$$

If interest were payable yearly the value of the loan to yield 6% per annum would be $(\cdot054777)(105)a_{\overline{50}|}=90\cdot656$. The value of interest payments is therefore $90\cdot656-18\cdot931=71\cdot725$, and their value payable half-yearly is $1\cdot01478\times71\cdot725=72\cdot782$. The value of the loan is therefore

$$18\cdot931+72\cdot782$$
$$=91\cdot713.$$

In this case, however, it is not necessary to value the loan assuming interest paid yearly as the value of K already found can be used in the Makeham formula and the value of the loan written down as

$$18\cdot931+\frac{\cdot05}{\cdot06}\times1\cdot01478(105-18\cdot931)$$
$$=91\cdot715.$$

(*b*) If interest were payable yearly the value of the loan to yield 6% per annum would be $(\cdot054777)\,105a_{\overline{50}|}$ at 6%

$$=90\cdot656.$$

If interest were payable yearly at 6% on 105 the value of the loan to yield 6% would be 105. Therefore, by subtraction,

The value of dividends of 1% per annum is

$$105-90\cdot656=14\cdot344.$$

The value of dividends of $\cdot05\,(s_{\overline{1}|}^{(2)}-1)$ must therefore be

$$\frac{\cdot05\times\cdot01478\times14\cdot344}{\cdot01}=1\cdot060.$$

Therefore the value of the whole loan $=90\cdot656+1\cdot060=91\cdot716$.

(*c*) If interest were payable yearly the value as in (*b*) would be 90·656.

$$\therefore\ K+\frac{\cdot05}{\cdot06}(105-K)=90\cdot656.$$

$$\therefore\ K=\frac{\cdot06\times90\cdot656-\cdot05\times105}{\cdot01}$$
$$=18\cdot936.$$

Therefore the value of yearly dividends

$$=90\cdot656-18\cdot936$$
$$=71\cdot720.$$

Therefore the value of half-yearly dividends

$$=71\cdot720\times s_{\overline{1}|}^{(2)} \text{ at } 6\%$$

$$=72\cdot780.$$

Therefore the value of the whole security is

$$72\cdot780+18\cdot936$$

$$=91\cdot716.$$

It will be noted that due to the inaccuracies of using five-figure logarithms the values found by the different methods differ in the third decimal place, but this is of no practical account.

Example 9·3. (*Sinking fund annually, interest half-yearly but with extra payments to sinking fund also operating.*)

A loan of £1,000,000 issued in bonds of £100 is redeemable at par

(1) by a cumulative sinking fund of 1% per annum operating annually.

(2) by the following sums allotted to the service of the loan at the end of every second year:

End of year	Amount
2	£1000
4	£2000
6	£3000

and so on, increasing by £1000 every 2nd year till the loan is repaid.

Interest is at 5% per annum payable half-yearly. At the outset a purchaser buys the whole loan to yield 4% effective. What is the probability that a single bond will realize at least this yield?

Here $C=100$, $g=\cdot05$, and $z=\cdot01$.

The additional amounts will also accumulate at rate g as may be seen by considering the amount available for sinking fund in any year (i.e. the difference between the service and the amount required for interest).

Therefore if $2n$ years be the term of the loan

$$1{,}000{,}000\times\cdot01 s_{\overline{2n}|}+(1000)(1\cdot05)^{2n-2}+2000(1\cdot05)^{2n-4}+\ldots+(1000n)$$

$$=1{,}000{,}000.$$

Let $$S=(1\cdot05)^{2n-2}+2(1\cdot05)^{2n-4}+\ldots+n.$$

$$\therefore\ (1\cdot05)^2 S=(1\cdot05)^{2n}+2(1\cdot05)^{2n-2}+\ldots+n(1\cdot05)^2.$$

$$\therefore\ S[(1\cdot05)^2-1]=(1\cdot05)^{2n}+(1\cdot05)^{2n-2}+\ldots+(1\cdot05)^2+1-(n+1).$$

$$=\frac{(1\cdot05)^{2n+2}-1}{(1\cdot05)^2-1}-(n+1)$$

$$=(1\cdot05)^2.\frac{(1\cdot05)^{2n}-1}{(1\cdot05)^2-1}-n$$

$$=(1\cdot05)^2\frac{s_{\overline{2n}|}}{s_{\overline{2}|}}-n.$$

$$\therefore\ S=\frac{1}{(1\cdot05)^2-1}\left[\frac{s_{\overline{2n}|}}{a_{\overline{2}|}}-n\right]=\frac{s_{\overline{2n}|}}{s_{\overline{2}|}-a_{\overline{2}|}}-\frac{20n}{s_{\overline{2}|}},$$

$$\therefore\ 10{,}000s_{\overline{2n}|}+\frac{1000s_{\overline{2n}|}}{s_{\overline{2}|}-a_{\overline{2}|}}-9756\cdot1n=1{,}000{,}000.$$

Try $n=16$, then the left-hand side is

$$752{,}988+\frac{75298\cdot8}{\cdot1906}-9756\cdot1\times16$$

$$=752{,}988+395{,}057-156{,}097$$

$$=991{,}948.$$

Therefore as the normal sinking fund is greater than 10,000 the loan will be repaid at the end of the 33rd year, the payment being 8052 plus a year's interest.

If interest were paid annually the purchaser would receive:

(*a*) an annuity of the normal service, £60,000 for 32 years,
(*b*) a payment of £8052 (1·05) at the end of 33 years,
(*c*) a series of payments £1000 after 2 years, £2000 after 4 years and so on, up to £16,000 after 32 years.

The value of the loan would then be

$$60{,}000a_{\overline{32}|}+8052(1\cdot05)v^{33}+1000\left[\frac{a_{\overline{32}|}}{s_{\overline{2}|}-a_{\overline{2}|}}-\frac{16v^{32}}{(1+i)^2-1}\right]$$

$$=1{,}072{,}416+2323+60{,}241\quad\text{at }4\%$$

$$=1{,}134{,}980.$$

$$\therefore\ K+\frac{\cdot05}{\cdot04}(1{,}000{,}000-K)=1{,}134{,}980.$$

$$\therefore\ \frac{K}{4}=115{,}020$$

or $$K=460{,}080.$$

Therefore the value of the interest payable yearly is 1,134,980 − 460,080

$$=674{,}900.$$

Therefore the value of the interest payable half-yearly

$$=674{,}900 s_{\overline{1}|}^{(2)} \quad \text{at } 4\%.$$

Therefore issue price

$$=460{,}080+674{,}900 s_{\overline{1}|}^{(2)}$$

$$=1{,}141{,}655.$$

or say 114·17 per £100 bond.

If a bond is to yield 4%, then

$$114{\cdot}17=100v^n+5a_{\overline{n}|}^{(2)} \quad \text{at } 4\%,$$

where n is the time before it is redeemed. As the bond is standing over par the longer the term the higher will be the yield.

Now if $n=20$, $100v^{20}+5a_{\overline{20}|}^{(2)}=114{\cdot}27$ so for practical purposes if the bond is *not* redeemed by the beginning of the 20th year, the desired yield will be obtained.

Now in the first 19 years the total loan redeemed will be

$$10{,}000 s_{\overline{19}|}+1{,}000\left[\frac{s_{\overline{18}|}}{s_{\overline{2}|}-a_{\overline{2}|}}-9\times 9{\cdot}7561\right](1{\cdot}05) \quad \text{all at } 5\%$$

$$=305{,}390+(147{,}597-87{,}805)(1{\cdot}05)$$

$$=368{,}172$$

or, say, 3682 bonds.

Therefore 6318 bonds will yield at least 4% as they will be redeemed after 20 or more years.

The required probability is therefore ·632.

It will be noted that in examples of this type the term cannot be found except by a method of trial and error.

Example 9·4. (*Varying rate of z.*)

A loan is to be issued bearing interest at $3\frac{1}{4}\%$ per annum payable half-yearly and redeemable by means of a cumulative sinking fund of 1% per annum, increasing after 10 years to $1\frac{1}{2}\%$ per annum operating by yearly drawings at £108·33. Find (*a*) the term of the loan, (*b*) the price to yield 3% per annum effective.

Here $C=108\frac{1}{3}$, $g=\dfrac{3{\cdot}25}{108\frac{1}{3}}={\cdot}03$ and z varies.

After 10 years the loan outstanding is

$$108{\cdot}33 - s_{\overline{10}|}^{\cdot 03}$$
$$= 96{\cdot}869.$$

The new service is $(3\frac{1}{4} + 1\frac{1}{2}) = 4{\cdot}75$ per annum.

The interest is $\cdot 03 \times 96{\cdot}869 = 2{\cdot}9061$ per annum.

Therefore the new rate of sinking fund is 1·8439 per annum.

Therefore if the term of the loan is n years from the date of increase of the sinking fund

$$1{\cdot}8439 s_{\overline{n}|} \text{ at } 3\% = 96{\cdot}869,$$

whence $32 < n < 33$.

After 32 years the amount repaid

$$= 1{\cdot}8439 s_{\overline{32}|}$$
$$= 96{\cdot}81.$$

Therefore the amount of capital to be repaid after 33 years $= \cdot 059$.

The total term is therefore 43 years.

To value the loan, as $g = i$, it is not possible to use any of the indirect methods of finding the value of the capital and it must be valued from first principles. The capital payments form the series 1, (1·03), (1·03)^2, ..., (1·03)^9, 1·8439, (1·8439)(1·03), ..., (1·8439)(1·03)^{31}, with a final payment of ·059.

$$\therefore\ K = v + (1{\cdot}03)v^2 + (1{\cdot}03)^2 v^3 + \ldots + (1{\cdot}03)^9 v^{10}$$
$$+ 1{\cdot}8439 v^{11}[1 + v(1{\cdot}03) + v^2(1{\cdot}03)^2 + \ldots + v^{31}(1{\cdot}03)^{31}]$$
$$+ \cdot 059 v^{43} \quad \text{at } 3\%$$
$$= 10v + 1{\cdot}8439 v^{11} \times 32 + \cdot 059 v^{43}$$
$$= 52{\cdot}352.$$

Therefore the value of the security, by Makeham's formula, is

$$52{\cdot}352 + \frac{\cdot 03}{\cdot 03} s_{\overline{1}|}^{(2)} (108{\cdot}333 - 52{\cdot}352)$$
$$= 108{\cdot}75.$$

Example 9·5. (*Varying rate of g.*)

A loan of £100,000 is redeemable by annual drawings at 110, by means of a cumulative sinking fund of 2% per annum. The loan bears interest payable yearly as follows:

$5\frac{1}{2}\%$ for the first 5 years,
5% for the next 5 years,
4·4% thereafter.

Find (*a*) the term of the loan, (*b*) the price of the loan at issue to yield 6% effective.

In accordance with the usual practice it is assumed that the service of this loan is £7500 for 5 years, £7000 for the next 5 and £6400 thereafter.

Here $C=110{,}000,\quad g_1=\frac{5\cdot5}{110},\quad g_2=\frac{5}{110},\quad g_3=\frac{4\cdot4}{110}.$

In the first 5 years the amount redeemed

$$=2000s_{\overline{5}|}\quad\text{at } 5\%$$

$$=11{,}051.$$

Therefore loan outstanding $=110{,}000-11{,}051=98{,}949.$

Interest on this in the 6th year is $98{,}949\times g_2$

$$=4497\cdot7.$$

Service available $=7000.$

Therefore the amount of sinking fund in 6th year $=2502\cdot3.$

Amount redeemed in second 5 years

$$=2502\cdot3s_{\overline{5}|}\quad\text{at } g_2$$

$$=2502\cdot3\times5\cdot4756\quad\text{(by interpolation)}$$

$$=13{,}702.$$

Loan outstanding $=98{,}949-13{,}702=85{,}247.$

Interest in 11th year is $85{,}247\times g_3$

$$=3409\cdot9.$$

Service available $=6400.$

Therefore sinking fund $=2990\cdot1.$

Therefore the loan is redeemed in a further n years, where

$$2990\cdot1s_{\overline{n}|}\ \text{at rate } g_3=85{,}247,$$

i.e.

$$s_{\overline{n}|}=\frac{85{,}236}{2990\cdot6}\quad\text{at } 4\%$$

$$=28\cdot51.$$

It is apparent from the tables of $s_{\overline{n}|}$ at 4% that $19<n<20$.

Amount redeemed in 19 years by the sinking fund of 2990·1 is

$$2990\cdot1\times27\cdot6712$$

$$=82{,}740.$$

Therefore amount outstanding

$$=85{,}247-82{,}740$$
$$=2507,$$

which will be repaid with interest at the end of 20 years.

Therefore the total term of the loan is 30 years.

The value to yield 6% is

$$7500a_{\overline{5}|}+7000(a_{\overline{10}|}-a_{\overline{5}|})+6400(a_{\overline{29}|}-a_{\overline{10}|})+2507(1+g_3)v^{30}$$
$$=93{,}956.$$

Note. If interest had been payable other than annually the calculations up to this point would have been identical. It would then have been possible to value the capital payments which form the series:

$$2000,\quad 2000(1+g_1),\quad \ldots,\quad 2000(1+g_1)^4,\quad 2502\cdot3,\quad 2502\cdot3(1+g_2),$$
$$\ldots,\quad 2502\cdot3(1+g_2)^4,\quad 2990\cdot1,\quad 2990\cdot1(1+g_3),\quad \ldots,\quad 2990\cdot1(1+g_3)^{19},$$

and a final payment of 2507 at the end of 30 years.

If K is the value so found the value of the loan to yield 6% per annum with interest payable p times a year would then be

$$K+s^{(p)}_{\overline{1}|}(93{,}956-K),\quad \text{as described in § 9·11.}$$

Example 9·6. (*Varying rate of C.*)

A loan of £500,000 is issued bearing interest at 5% per annum payable half-yearly and is redeemable by a cumulative sinking fund applied by half-yearly drawings over 45 years at the following prices:

During first 5 years	115%.
During next 10 years	110%.
During next 30 years	par.

Find (*a*) the amount applied each year to the service of the loan, and (*b*) the yield secured by the purchase of the whole loan at 105.

The amount applied to the service may be found either from first principles, or by general reasoning. Both methods will be demonstrated. It will be noted that the second is less laborious.

Method 1

Since sinking fund and interest are each payable half-yearly all rates can be expressed in terms of half-years.

Let the cash service of the loan be $(12{,}500+X)$ per half-year.

During the first 5 years $g_1=\dfrac{2\cdot5}{1\cdot15}\%=2\cdot174\%$.

The *nominal* amount redeemed in the first 5 years

$$= \frac{X}{1 \cdot 15} s_{\overline{10}|} \quad \text{at rate } g_1$$

$$= \frac{X}{1 \cdot 15} \times 11 \cdot 0374$$

$$= 9 \cdot 598X.$$

Therefore the nominal amount of loan outstanding

$$= 500{,}000 - 9 \cdot 598X.$$

The interest for the 11th half-year is $12{,}500 - \cdot 025 \times 9 \cdot 598X$.
The service is $12{,}500 + X$.
Therefore the new sinking fund is

$$X(1 + \cdot 025 \times 9 \cdot 598)$$
$$= 1 \cdot 24X,$$

which will redeem a *nominal* amount of loan of $\frac{1 \cdot 24X}{1 \cdot 1}$ and will accumulate at g_2 where $g_2 = \frac{2 \cdot 5}{1 \cdot 1} = 2 \cdot 273\,\%$.

Therefore the nominal amount redeemed in the next 10 years

$$= \frac{1 \cdot 24X}{1 \cdot 1} s_{\overline{20}|} \quad \text{at } g_2$$

$$= \frac{1 \cdot 24X}{1 \cdot 1} \times 24 \cdot 9698$$

$$= 28 \cdot 16X.$$

Therefore the nominal loan now outstanding is

$$500{,}000 - 9 \cdot 598X - 28 \cdot 16X = 500{,}000 - 37 \cdot 758X.$$

The interest is $12{,}500 - \cdot 025(37 \cdot 758)X$.

Therefore the new sinking fund is

$$X(1 + \cdot 025 \times 37 \cdot 758) = 1 \cdot 9438X.$$

As this must repay the loan in a further 60 half-years

$$1 \cdot 9438XS_{\overline{60}|} \text{ at } 2\tfrac{1}{2}\,\% = 500{,}000 - 37 \cdot 758X.$$

$$\therefore\ X = \frac{500{,}000}{264 \cdot 36 + 37 \cdot 758}$$

$$= 1655.$$

Therefore the service of the loan is £28,310 per annum.

Method 2

If X is the sinking fund for the first half-year the sinking fund payment at the end of the last half-year must be

$$X(1+g_1)^{10}(1+g_2)^{20}(1\cdot025)^{59}$$

as X accumulates at rate g_1 for 10 half-years, g_2 for 20 half-years and ·025 for the remainder, where g_1 and g_2 have the same meanings as in Method 1.

As this is the last amount of sinking fund it must be the same as the capital outstanding at the beginning of the last half-year. But this amount of capital, plus a half-year's interest, is repaid by a payment of $12{,}500+X$ i.e.

$$1\cdot025\,[X(1+g_1)^{10}(1+g_2)^{20}(1\cdot025)^{59}] = 12{,}500+X$$

or

$$X = \frac{12{,}500}{1\cdot239\times1\cdot568\times4\cdot4-1}$$

$$=1656.$$

The service is £28,312 per annum, which agrees as nearly as the accuracy of the tables permits with the previous answer.

To find the yield. The loan in effect consists of an annuity of £14,155 for 90 half-years.

Therefore $14{,}155a_{\overline{90}|} = 525{,}000$, if the price per cent is 105, or

$$\frac{1}{a_{\overline{90}|}} = \cdot026962$$

at $2\frac{1}{4}\%$

$$\frac{1}{a_{\overline{90}|}} = \cdot026011$$

at $2\frac{1}{2}\%$

$$\frac{1}{a_{\overline{90}|}} = \cdot028038.$$

$$\therefore\ i = 2\tfrac{1}{4} + \frac{951}{2027}\times\cdot25$$

$$=2\cdot367.$$

The yield is 4·73% per annum convertible half-yearly.

Example 9·7. (*A complicated case with g and C both varying.*)

A loan of £500,000 is subject to the following conditions:

(*a*) Dividends are to be 5% per annum for 15 years and 4% thereafter, payable half-yearly.

(*b*) The sum of £30,000 is to be applied to the service of the loan each year, any balance after paying interest to be applied annually to redeem the loan by drawings.

(*c*) The price of redemption is to be 100 for the first 10 years, $111\frac{1}{9}$ for the next 5 years and $114\frac{2}{7}$ for the balance of the term. Find the price of issue to yield 5% per annum effective.

Here we have

$$g_1 \text{ for the first 10 years} = \cdot 05,$$

$$g_2 \text{ for the next 5 years } \frac{5}{111\frac{1}{9}} = \cdot 045,$$

$$g_3 \text{ thereafter} = \frac{4}{114\frac{2}{7}} = \cdot 035.$$

It is probably most convenient to work in *nominal* amounts of loan throughout.

The original sinking fund is $30{,}000 - \cdot 05\,(500{,}000) = 5000$.

Therefore the amount repaid in first 10 years $= 5000 s_{\overline{10}|}$ at 5%

$$= 62889 \cdot 5.$$

Therefore the nominal amount outstanding at the end of 10 years

$$= 437110 \cdot 5.$$

Interest at 5% thereon

$$= 21{,}855 \cdot 5.$$

Therefore the new sinking fund

$$= 8144 \cdot 5.$$

Cash applied to redemption in years 11–15

$$= 8144 \cdot 5 s_{\overline{5}|} \quad \text{at } 4\tfrac{1}{2}\%.$$

Therefore the nominal amount redeemed in these years

$$= \frac{8144 \cdot 5}{111\frac{1}{9}} \times 100 \times s_{\overline{5}|}$$

$$= 40{,}100 \cdot 4.$$

Therefore the nominal amount outstanding at the end of 15 years

$$= 397{,}010 \cdot 1.$$

Interest on this at 4% $= 15{,}880 \cdot 4$.

Therefore the new sinking fund $= 14{,}119 \cdot 6$.

Therefore the cash applied to redemption in years 16 onwards is $14{,}119{\cdot}6 s_{\overline{n}|}$ which will redeem $\dfrac{14119{\cdot}6 \times 100 s_{\overline{n}|}}{114\frac{2}{7}}$ nominal of loan, i.e. at $3\frac{1}{2}\%$

$$12354{\cdot}6 s_{\overline{n}|} = 397{,}010{\cdot}1,$$

whence $21 < n < 22$.

The amount redeemed in 21 years is $12354{\cdot}6 s_{\overline{21}|} = 373{,}969{\cdot}1$.

Therefore the nominal amount of loan to be repaid at the end of 37 years from the outset $= 23{,}041$.

Therefore the cash payment at the end of 37 years, if dividends were yearly,

$$= 23{,}041 \times \frac{114\frac{2}{7}}{100} \times 1{\cdot}035$$

$$= 27{,}254{\cdot}2.$$

If dividends were yearly the value of the loan would be

$$30{,}000 a_{\overline{36}|} + 27{,}254{\cdot}2 v^{37} \quad \text{at } 5\%$$

$$= 500{,}889.$$

The value of the capital payments alone is

$$5000\,(v + 1{\cdot}05 v^2 + \ldots + (1{\cdot}05)^9 v^{10})$$
$$+ 8144{\cdot}5 v^{11}\,(1 + 1{\cdot}045 v + \ldots + (1{\cdot}045)^4 v^4)$$
$$+ 14{,}119{\cdot}6 v^{16}\,(1 + 1{\cdot}035 v + \ldots + (1{\cdot}035)^{20} v^{20})$$
$$+ 23{,}041 \times \frac{114\frac{2}{7}}{100} v^{37} \quad \text{at } 5\%.$$

$$= 193{,}610$$

(by summing the geometric progressions).

The value of the interest if paid yearly is therefore

$$500{,}889 - 193{,}610 = 307{,}279.$$

The value of the loan, with half-yearly dividends, is therefore

$$193{,}610 + 307{,}279 s_{\overline{1}|}^{(2)}$$

$$= 504{,}684$$

or £100·93 per £100 bond.

Example 9·8

Show that if $a_{\overline{n+f}|}$ be taken as equal to $a_{\overline{n}|}+f(a_{\overline{n+1}|}-a_{\overline{n}|})$ where n is integral, the value of a loan repayable over $n+f$ years by a cumulative sinking fund, with a service of $(g+z)C$ per annum, interest being paid p times a year and sinking fund operating yearly, is accurately stated as

$$C\frac{a^i_{\overline{n+f}|}}{a^g_{\overline{n+f}|}}+g\frac{s^{(p)}_{\overline{1}|}-1}{i-g}C\left(1-\frac{a^i_{\overline{n+f}|}}{a^g_{\overline{n+f}|}}\right).$$

From considerations similar to those in § 9·12 it will be seen that this is equivalent to showing that the value of the loan, if interest were paid yearly is

$$C\frac{a^i_{\overline{n+f}|}}{a^g_{\overline{n+f}|}},$$

i.e. $(g+z)Ca_{\overline{n+f}|}$ at rate i.

Now
$$\begin{aligned}a_{\overline{n+f}|}&=a_{\overline{n}|}+f(a_{\overline{n+1}|}-a_{\overline{n}|})\\&=a_{\overline{n}|}+f.v^{n+1},\end{aligned}$$

and, as f is found from the equation $a^g_{\overline{n+f}|}=\dfrac{1}{g+z}$,

$$\begin{aligned}f&=\frac{\dfrac{1}{g+z}-a^g_{\overline{n}|}}{a^g_{\overline{n+1}|}-a^g_{\overline{n}|}}\\&=(1+g)^{n+1}\left[\frac{1}{g+z}-a^g_{\overline{n}|}\right]\\&=\frac{(1+g)^{n+1}}{g+z}-(1+g)s^g_{\overline{n}|}.\end{aligned}$$

$$\begin{aligned}\therefore\ (g+z)Ca^i_{\overline{n+f}|}&=(g+z)Ca^i_{\overline{n}|}+\left[\frac{(1+g)^{n+1}}{g+z}-(1+g)s^g_{\overline{n}|}\right](g+z)Cv^{n+1}\\&=(g+z)Ca^i_{\overline{n}|}+Cv^{n+1}[(1+g)^{n+1}-(1+g)(g+z)s^g_{\overline{n}|}]\\&=(g+z)Ca^i_{\overline{n}|}+Cv^{n+1}(1+g)[(1+g)^n-(g+z)s^g_{\overline{n}|}]\\&=(g+z)Ca^i_{\overline{n}|}+Cv^{n+1}(1+g)[1-zs^g_{\overline{n}|}]\end{aligned}$$

since
$$(1+g)^n-gs^g_{\overline{n}|}=1.$$

Now the loan outstanding after n years is $C-zCs^g_{\overline{n}|}$, and this is repaid at the end of $(n+1)$ years with a year's interest.

Therefore the true value is $(g+z)Ca^i_{\overline{n}|}+C(1-zs^g_{\overline{n}|})(1+g)v^{n+1}$ as above.

The formula therefore gives an accurate answer.

The next two examples are included to show the applications of the principles of the cumulative sinking fund to problems other than the direct valuation of securities.

Example 9.9

An insurance company issues a policy insuring the return of the excess of price paid over the redemption price in respect of an issue of bonds redeemable by half-yearly drawings at par by means of a cumulative sinking fund. The bonds bear interest at $4\frac{1}{2}\%$ per annum payable half-yearly and are redeemable over a total period of 40 years. What is the net level annual premium payable half-yearly and calculated at a nominal rate of interest of 4% convertible half-yearly which should be paid by an investor who, 22 years after the loan is issued, purchases a bond for £1000 at a price of $102\frac{1}{2}\%$?

The amount applied each half-year to the service of each 100 of the loan $=\dfrac{100}{a_{\overline{80}|}}$ at $2\frac{1}{4}\% = 2{\cdot}7064$.

After 22 years the capital outstanding is

$$\frac{100}{a_{\overline{80}|}} \times a_{\overline{36}|} \text{ at } 2\tfrac{1}{4}\% = 66{\cdot}2925.$$

Interest on this at $2\frac{1}{4}\% = 1{\cdot}4916$.

Therefore the amount applied to sinking fund in the first half of the 23rd year is $2{\cdot}7064 - 1{\cdot}4916 = 1{\cdot}2148$.

The amounts of capital repaid in each successive half-year are therefore

$$1{\cdot}2148, \quad 1{\cdot}2148(1+g), \quad \ldots, \quad 1{\cdot}2148(1+g)^{35}.$$

Therefore the chance that a bond is drawn in any given half-year is

$$\frac{1{\cdot}2148}{66{\cdot}2925}, \quad \frac{1{\cdot}2148}{66{\cdot}2925}(1+g), \quad \ldots, \quad \frac{1{\cdot}2148}{66{\cdot}2925}(1+g)^{35}.$$

Therefore writing $X = \dfrac{1{\cdot}2148}{66{\cdot}2925}$ the single premium to secure a payment of 1 on a bond's being redeemed in any half-year is

$$A = Xv + X(1+g)v^2 + \ldots + X(1+g)^{35}v^{36}$$

$$= Xv\,\frac{1-(1+g)^{36}v^{36}}{1-(1+g)v}$$

$$= \frac{1{\cdot}2148}{66{\cdot}2925} \times \frac{1-(1+g)^{36}v^{36}}{{\cdot}02 - {\cdot}0225}$$

$$= {\cdot}6752.$$

Now from the general relation

$$A = 1 - d\ddot{a}$$

and

$$P = \frac{A}{\ddot{a}},$$

where P is the level half-yearly premium corresponding to A

$$P = \frac{dA}{1-A} = \frac{\cdot 6752 \times \cdot 019608}{\cdot 3248},$$

$$= \cdot 04076.$$

Therefore the premium to insure the excess of the purchase price over the redemption value, i.e. £25 = 1·019 = £1·02 per half-year, or £2·04 per annum.

Note. A slightly neater form for A can be found by writing

$$\frac{66\cdot 2925}{s^{g}_{\overline{36}|}} \quad \text{for} \quad 1\cdot 2148.$$

The expression for A then becomes

$$\frac{1}{s^{g}_{\overline{36}|}} \times \frac{1-(1+g)^{36}v^{36}}{i-g}$$

$$= \frac{1}{a^{g}_{\overline{36}|}} \times \frac{v^{36}_{g} - v^{36}_{i}}{i-g},$$

and the numerical calculations are simpler.

The device of using the value of A to find the value of P without the necessity for finding the value of $\ddot{a}$ should be specially noted.

Example 9·10

An issue of bonds of £100 each is made at par. £6·80% of the total nominal issue is to be applied at the end of each year as follows:

(*a*) interest at 2% per annum, is paid on bonds outstanding

(*b*) one-quarter of the balance remaining is applied in payment of a bonus to outstanding bonds chosen at random, such bonds being still eligible for redemption in that or any subsequent year,

(*c*) the remaining three-quarters of the balance is applied to redeem bonds at 150.

A and B have each held 1000 bonds for 10 years, and immediately after the 10th drawing A wishes to give up his right to interest and bonuses on his holding, in exchange for a share in the redemption prices of *B*'s holding. On the basis of interest at 5% what proportion of the amounts he will receive under heading (*c*) should *B* give up in return for *A*'s rights under (*a*) and (*b*)?

Consider the position at the end of the first year for each £100 of loan.

Amount available after interest is paid $=4\cdot8$.
Amount available for bonuses $=1\cdot2$.
Amount available for redemption $=3\cdot6$ which will redeem $\dfrac{3\cdot6}{1\cdot5}$
$=2\cdot4$.

Next year the loan outstanding $=(100-2\cdot4)$.
Interest $=\cdot02(100-2\cdot4)$.
Therefore the amount available for bonuses and redemption

$$\begin{aligned}&=6\cdot8-\cdot02(100-2\cdot4)\\&=4\cdot8+\cdot02(2\cdot4)\\&=4\cdot8(1+\cdot01).\end{aligned}$$

The amount available for bonuses $=1\cdot2(1+\cdot01)$.
The amount available for redemption $=3\cdot6(1\cdot01)$.

It is clear therefore that the amounts available for bonuses and for redemption increase each year in geometric progression with a common ratio of $1\cdot01$.

Therefore the amount of loan redeemed in n years, per £100 original loan

$$=2\cdot4s_{\overline{n}|}\quad\text{at } 1\%,$$

i.e. $$s_{\overline{n}|}\text{ at }1\%=\frac{1}{\cdot024},\text{ whence } n=35.$$

Amount available for bonuses $=1\cdot2(1\cdot01)^{n-1}$ in year n.
Amount available for redemption $=3\cdot6(1\cdot01)^{n-1}$.
Nominal amount of loan outstanding at beginning of year n

$$=100-2\cdot4s_{\overline{n-1}|}.$$

The position immediately after the 10th drawing is as follows:
The value of the capital payments is

$$\begin{aligned}&\sum_{11}^{35}3\cdot6(1\cdot01)^{n-1}v^{n-10}\quad\text{at } 5\%\\&=3\cdot6\times\frac{(1\cdot01)^{10}}{(1\cdot05)^{25}}\times\frac{(1\cdot05)^{25}-(1\cdot01)^{25}}{1\cdot05-1\cdot01}\\&=61\cdot77.\end{aligned}$$

The value of the whole loan at 5% is $6\cdot8a_{\overline{25}|}=95\cdot84$.
Therefore the value of interest and bonuses is $95\cdot84-61\cdot77=34\cdot07$.

Therefore B should give up $\frac{34\cdot07}{61\cdot77}$ of his rights on redemption in exchange for A's interest payments and bonuses, i.e. say 55%.

Note. This is an ingenious question which well demonstrates the principles underlying the treatment of cumulative sinking funds. The essential steps in its solution are:

(1) The realization that the number of bonds redeemed in each year increases in the ratio 1·01 to 1.
(2) Finding the term by summing the resultant geometric progression, i.e. $2\cdot4s_{\overline{n}|} = 100$ at 1%.
(3) Valuing the capital payments, which form a geometric progression, separately.
(4) Finding the value of the whole loan.
(5) Finding the value of interest and bonuses by deducting (3) from (4) which gives the answer with less work than a direct valuation of the interest and bonuses.

This question also illustrates the remarks of §9·2. The proposed exchange would be equitable as between A and B only if the experience of the 1000 bonds each holds is the same as that expected for the whole loan.

EXERCISES 9

9·1 A loan of £2,000,000 was issued $11\frac{1}{2}$ years ago. The loan bears interest at 5% per annum payable half-yearly and is redeemable at 105 by half-yearly drawings by the operation of a cumulative sinking fund. The annual service of the loan is £130,000. Find to the nearest £1000

(*a*) the amount of loan outstanding,
(*b*) its value to yield a purchaser of the whole loan 4% per annum, convertible half-yearly.

9·2 A loan of £1,000,000 is repayable by a cumulative sinking fund of 2% per annum operating by yearly drawings at par. Interest on the loan is payable quarterly at the rate of 3% per annum. Show that the equated time, as found by the usual commercial rule, of the series of capital payments is $\frac{31 - a_{\overline{31}|}}{1 - v^{31}}$ at 3%.

9·3 A stock is issued bearing interest at $4\frac{1}{2}$% per annum payable half-yearly and is redeemable at par by a cumulative sinking fund with annual drawings. The amount applied to the service of the loan in the first year is 6% of the nominal amount of the stock, and increases in each subsequent year by 1% of the original nominal amount of the stock. Find the issue price to yield 5% per annum effective.

9·4 A loan is issued bearing interest at $4\frac{1}{2}\%$ per annum payable half-yearly for the first half of its term, and at 5% per annum payable half-yearly thereafter. It is redeemable at par by a cumulative sinking fund of $1\frac{1}{2}\%$ per annum operating by yearly drawings. Find the price of the loan at issue if a purchaser of the whole loan secures a yield of 4% per annum effective.

9·5 A loan of £500,000 was issued bearing interest payable annually at the rate of 4% per annum and redeemable at par by means of a cumulative sinking fund operating annually of an amount sufficient to repay the loan in 50 years. After 15 years sinking fund payments were discontinued for 10 years, interest only being paid meantime. Sinking fund operations were then resumed, the annual charge being fixed at an amount sufficient to repay the whole loan by the original date. Find the effective yield secured by a company which purchased the whole of the original issue at a price of 70%.

9·6 A company has in force £100,000 redeemable stock in £1 units bearing interest at 5% per annum payable half-yearly on 1 January and 1 July and redeemable with a premium of 5% on 1 January in any year. The company proposes to pay to Trustees the sum of £10,000 on 1 July in each year. From each such payment the half-year's interest due on 1 July on the outstanding stock will be met. The balance will be invested at 2% per annum convertible half-yearly until the following 1 January, when after payment of the half-year's interest then due it will be applied to redeem as much stock as possible. For how many years must the payments of £10,000 be made, and what sum will be required in the following year, to redeem all the stock?

9·7 A loan of £1,000,000 is redeemable by annual instalments over a period of 20 years and bears interest at 4% per annum payable half-yearly, the first payment being due in 6 months. Each year the sum of £X is applied to the service of the loan and is absorbed as follows:

(*a*) payment is made of the interest due in that year;
(*b*) 2% of the nominal amount of loan outstanding at the start of the year is redeemed at a price of 125;
(*c*) any balance of £X remaining is used to redeem as much as possible of the loan at par.

Find the issue price of the loan if a purchaser of the whole loan secured a yield on his investment of 3% effective.

CHAPTER 10

TAXATION

10·1. Nature of the problem

The preceding chapters have dealt with the application of the theory of compound interest to the types of problem which arise in practice, but they have ignored the effect which the incidence of taxation may have on the calculations. This factor introduces no new principles but the methods employed may require adjustment and this chapter is devoted to the changes which may be necessary.

The incidence of taxation varies as between different countries. In some (as was the case in Great Britain before 1965) payments of a capital nature escape tax, which falls only on payments which can be regarded as income (dividends, salaries and wages and the like), and for obvious reasons such a tax is referred to as 'income-tax'. In others (including Great Britain since 1965) tax is levied both on annual income and on any increase in capital values (for example the excess of the value received on the sale or redemption of a security over the price originally paid for it). The latter tax is referred to as 'capital gains tax'.

Fiscal legislation tends to be complicated and in practice there are many different methods by which the tax liability can be assessed. The rates may vary with the total income of the individual, or with the length of time over which a capital gain has accrued to name only two examples and companies are frequently assessed on a different basis from individuals. At this stage it is not necessary to consider how the rates of tax are determined, and in this chapter it will be assumed

(*a*) that the appropriate rates of tax to be used will be defined in the statement of the problem,

(*b*) that it will be made clear whether these rates are to be applied to income receipts only, to capital gains only, or to both.

For examination purposes both income-tax and capital gains tax should always be ignored, unless it is expressly directed to the contrary.

10·2. Net rates of interest

In order to distinguish between a valuation made after allowing for tax, and one in which tax has been ignored it is usual to state that the former has been made at a net rate of interest and the latter at a gross rate. Unfortunately various other expressions to describe the rates of interest are current in financial circles and these expressions sometimes give rise to confusion of thought in the student's mind. This confusion will be avoided if it is remembered that, if a series of payments of stated amounts is valued at any given rate of interest, the value at that rate of interest is the price which a purchaser may offer for the series in order to secure for himself a yield equivalent to the rate of interest employed in the valuation, and this applies whatever terms are used to describe that rate. In practice the purchaser must decide whether his offer is to be based on the gross rate of interest he desires to earn, or whether he wishes to base it on a net rate of interest. In the first case, having fixed an appropriate gross rate, he will make his calculations ignoring tax completely. In the second case he will value only the actual payments which he will receive after tax has been deducted from them.

The following expressions are sometimes used in place of the simple terms 'gross rate' or 'net rate':

(*a*) A rate of interest 'ignoring tax'.
(*b*) A rate of interest 'free of tax'.
(*c*) An 'equivalent gross rate of interest, subject to tax'.

Of these (*a*) and (*b*) are merely different names for a gross and a net rate respectively, and (*c*) is a hypothetical rate of interest which is not used directly in making a valuation. It merely expresses what gross rate of interest corresponds to a given net rate and a given rate of tax. Thus if the 'equivalent gross rate subject to tax' is I, and the rate of tax is t, the corresponding net rate is $I(1-t)$, or if the net rate is i the 'equivalent gross rate subject to tax' corresponding to it is $\frac{i}{1-t}$. For example if income tax were 25 per cent (i.e. if from every pound of income ·25 was deducted as tax) the equivalent gross rate, subject to tax corresponding to a net rate of 3 %, would be stated as 4 %. But if tax were $37\frac{1}{2}$ per cent the equivalent gross rate subject to tax in the same circumstances would be 4·8 %.

This method of stating the rate may give rise to some confusion since it implies that tax is charged on the return earned on the investment and this is not so. Tax is always payable on the actual receipts and must be allowed for directly in the calculations. Thus if at a given price a security yields 4 % ignoring tax one could not deduce that if tax at 25 % were taken into account the yield would be reduced to 3 %. Tax introduces a new set of conditions and the only safe course is to decide whether tax is to be ignored in which case gross receipts must be valued at a gross rate of interest, or whether it is to be taken into account in which case net receipts must be valued at a net rate of interest. The true 'gross' and 'net' yields at a given price are not directly related to one another.

10·3. Application of net rates to various problems

In considering the effect of taxation on the problems which have been dealt with in previous chapters it may be clearer to deal separately with tax on income and tax on capital gains. §§ 10·4 to 10·13 therefore ignore capital gains tax which is discussed in §§ 10·14 to 10·19. The problems discussed may be classified as follows:

(*a*) *Capital redemption assurances*
  (i) Calculation of premiums, reserves, etc.
  (ii) Problems involving the use of Capital Redemption policies to replace the loss of invested capital.

(*b*) *Valuation of redeemable securities*
  (i) Ordinary stock exchange investments.
  (ii) Loans repayable by annuities.
  (iii) As a particular case of (ii) loans repayable by a cumulative sinking fund.

These are considered in the remaining sections of this chapter and particularly in the examples in §10·20. These particular examples illustrate certain practical points more clearly than would solutions of the same type of general problems, and they should therefore be studied in conjunction with the corresponding sections of this chapter.

10·4. Capital redemption assurances—premiums, reserves, etc.

The assurance company granting the contract has to pay income tax on the interest earned by the securities in which the premiums are invested and must therefore use a net rate of interest in calculating its rates of premiums, reserves and paid up policy values.

10·5. Capital redemption assurances as a means of replacing capital

These problems were considered in Chapter 6 ignoring the effect of income tax. The effect of introducing income tax will be that:

(*a*) all rates of interest used should be net rates,

(*b*) income tax should be deducted from all payments of income involved in the equation of value.

The general type of problem may be stated as

> 'What sum should be paid to earn a gross rate of i', subject to income tax at rate t from the purchase of a ground rent of R per annum payable for n years, the capital invested being replaced by a capital redemption policy at a premium of $P_{\overline{n|}}$ per unit?'

and the solution would be as follows:

The net rate required is $i'(1-t)$ or say i. The income each year will be $R(1-t)$ since the whole of the ground rent is considered to be income and as such is subject to tax. If, therefore, the price to be paid is A, and the sum to be assured is S the following will be the equations of value

$$R(1-t)=i(A+SP_{\overline{n}|})+SP_{\overline{n}|}$$

$$S+R(1-t)=(1+i)(A+SP_{\overline{n}|})$$

whence $$S=A$$

and $$A=\frac{R(1-t)}{i(1+P_{\overline{n}|})+P_{\overline{n}|}}.$$

10·6. Redeemable securities

In the case of a security of C redeemable in n years and bearing interest of gC per annum payable p times per annum, the value to yield a net rate i assuming income tax at rate t, will be

$$A=Cv^n+g(1-t)s_{\overline{1}|}^{(p)}Ca_{\overline{n}|}$$

since the capital payment of C is not subject to income tax, and the periodical payments of gC are reduced by the tax of tgC per annum.

This expression may be transformed into the Makeham form

$$A=K+\frac{g(1-t)}{i}s_{\overline{1}|}^{(p)}(C-K)$$

and this of course is only to be expected since the value of the capital at rate i is K whether the rate of interest is gross or net. The value of dividends of i per annum is, by the same reasoning as in §7·7, $(C-K)$. If the actual dividends are at the rate of $g(1-t)s_{\overline{1}|}^{(p)}$ per annum their value must be $\frac{g(1-t)}{i}.s_{\overline{1}|}^{(p)}.(C-K)$ and the total value of the security is therefore

$$K+\frac{g(1-t)}{i}s_{\overline{1}|}^{(p)}(C-K).$$

So long as the basic principle is remembered, that if income tax is to be taken into account, net receipts must be valued at a net rate of interest, no great difficulty should be encountered in dealing with this type of security.

It is worth noting that, if the rate of income tax varies during the valuation period, $g(1-t)$ will also vary and if Makeham's formula is to be used the methods of §8·2 must be adopted.

10·7 Loans repayable by annuities—amount of tax charged

In the case of a loan of $a_{\overline{n}|}$ repayable by n instalments of 1 per annum the income tax authorities recognize the fact that, as was shown in Chapter 5, part of each instalment of 1 represents a return of capital. Hence tax is charged only on the portion of each instalment which represents interest, according to a schedule drawn up at the rate of interest involved in the equation $A = a_{\overline{n}|}$ where A is the amount of the loan. That is to say, the amount on which tax is charged in the rth year after the issue of the loan is $ga_{\overline{n-r+1}|}$ where g is the rate of interest at which the loan was originally issued. The net amount received in the rth year is therefore $1 - tga_{\overline{n-r+1}|}$, and not $(1-t)$, as it would be if tax were charged on the whole instalment.

Before such a loan can be valued allowing for income tax it is therefore necessary to know the rate of interest originally involved in the transaction, in order to be able to ascertain the net amounts due to be received.

10·8. Loans repayable by annuities—practical examples.

Until they were repaid (the last in 1959) two types of security quoted on the Stock Exchange furnished practical examples of loans repayable by annuities, and such investments might once again become available. Example 9 at the end of this chapter is based on the 'Indian Railway Annuity' which is the type of security referred to above. These annuities took two forms. One was an example of a loan repayable by a terminable annuity which could be valued by the methods of § 10·7, the other introduced the concept of a loan repayable by an annuity-certain where the borrowers would make specific provision for the repayment of the capital invested (instead of the lender as in the normal example of a loan repaid by an annuity-certain.) In this type a fixed sum was deducted from each annuity payment and accumulated in a sinking fund invested under the control of the borrower. When the final payment of annuity was made the accumulated sinking fund was divided *pro rata* amongst the holders of the annuities. To value such an annuity, allowing for income tax it was necessary (*a*) to value the net amount of each annuity payment after deduction of income tax at a net rate of interest, as in § 10·7,

(*b*) to value the deductions to the sinking fund at the same net rate and to reduce the amount in (*a*) by this sum,

(*c*) to estimate the sum to which the sinking fund would accumulate per £1 of annuity and to add the discounted value of this sum to the net value found in (*b*) above.

The valuations would of course be made at a net rate of interest. A practical example of this type of problem will make the method clear and one will be found in Example 10·9.

10·9. Loans repayable by annuities—direct valuation

As explained in § 10·7 the problem is to value a varying series of net payments at a net rate of interest. In respect of a loan repayable by an annuity of 1 for n years in which the original rate of interest involved was g, the payment which will be received in the rth year is $1 - tga_{\overline{n-r+1}|}$ at rate g where t is the rate of tax. If it is desired to secure a net yield of i per annum then the value of these payments per nominal amount of loan of $a^g_{\overline{n}|}$ originally granted is $\sum_1^n v^r(1 - tga^g_{\overline{n-r+1}|})$ at the net rate i.

$$\text{Now} \quad \sum_1^n v^r(1 - tga^g_{\overline{n-r+1}|}) = a^i_{\overline{n}|} - tg\sum_1^n v^r_i \frac{(1 - v_g^{n-r+1})}{g}$$

$$= a^i_{\overline{n}|} - t\left[a^i_{\overline{n}|} - \sum_1^n v^r_i v_g^{n-r+1}\right]$$

$$= a^i_{\overline{n}|}(1 - t) + tv^n_g \,.\, v_i \frac{1 - \dfrac{v^n_i}{v^n_g}}{1 - \dfrac{v_i}{v_g}}$$

$$= a^i_{\overline{n}|}(1 - t) + t\frac{v^n_g - v^n_i}{i - g}.$$

The method by which this result has been derived is the general method which could be applied to find the value of any redeemable security allowing for tax. It is not, in the special circumstances of this type of loan, the most convenient one and there are easier indirect methods of approach which are discussed in the following sections. For simplicity the expressions have been deduced for the value of the loan at the outset. Similar methods would apply if it were desired to value it during its currency.

10·10. Loans repayable by annuities—use of Makeham's formula

Makeham's formula may be used in either of two ways, directly or by inference. If the formula is used directly the problem is to find the present value at rate i of a given series of capital payments of $V^n, V^{n-1}, \ldots, V$, where $V=\frac{1}{1+g}$. If $v=\frac{1}{1+i}$ then

$$K=V^n v+V^{n-1}v^2+\ldots+Vv^n$$

$$=\frac{V^n v\left[1-\frac{v^n}{V^n}\right]}{1-\frac{v}{V}}$$

$$=\frac{V^n-v^n}{i-g}.$$

Now C, the capital outstanding is $a_{\overline{n}|}$ at rate g and hence by Makeham's formula, the value of the outstanding instalments at rate i per annum after allowing for income tax at rate t is

$$\frac{V^n-v^n}{i-g}+\frac{g(1-t)}{i}\left[a^g_{\overline{n}|}-\frac{V^n-v^n}{i-g}\right].$$

A still simpler method is, however, available.

If no tax were deducted from the instalments their value at rate i would be $a^i_{\overline{n}|}$. The value at rate i of the capital instalments is not affected by the deduction of tax from the interest portion of each instalment and the value of the capital instalments, K, may therefore be found from the equation

$$K+\frac{g}{i}(a_{\overline{n}|}^{g}-K)=a_{\overline{n}|}^{i},$$

i.e.

$$K=\frac{ia_{\overline{n}|}^{i}-ga_{\overline{n}|}^{g}}{i-g}$$

$$=\frac{v_g^n-v_i^n}{i-g}$$

(which agrees with the value previously found). Hence K may be readily determined and once it is known its value may be inserted in the formula

$$K+\frac{g(1-t)}{i}(C-K)$$

to value the loan.

It is, however, unnecessary to evaluate K and the following extension of the method is even simpler to apply.

If the loan were valued at a rate of interest i and if no tax were payable the value would be $a_{\overline{n}|}$ at rate i. If the loan were valued at rate i and if dividends were payable at rate i instead of at rate g per annum the value of the loan would be the same as the nominal amount outstanding, i.e. $a_{\overline{n}|}$ at rate g. Since in either case the value of the capital payments is the same, the difference, i.e. $a_{\overline{n}|}^{g}-a_{\overline{n}|}^{i}$ must be the value of dividends of $i-g$ per annum. The value of a dividend of 1 per annum is therefore $\dfrac{a_{\overline{n}|}^{g}-a_{\overline{n}|}^{i}}{i-g}$. Now the dividends included in the value $a_{\overline{n}|}^{i}$ were at the rate of g per annum, instead of at the rate $g(1-t)$, i.e. they included an excess dividend of tg per annum. The value of the excess is, by proportion,

$$\frac{tg}{i-g}(a_{\overline{n}|}^{g}-a_{\overline{n}|}^{i}),$$

and hence the value of the whole loan is

$$a_{\overline{n}|}^{i}-\frac{tg}{i-g}(a_{\overline{n}|}^{g}-a_{\overline{n}|}^{i}).$$

10·11. Loans repayable by annuities, summary

It must be emphasized that the methods of §§10·9 and 10·10 will give identical numerical results and it is purely a matter of convenience which of them is adopted. The formulae themselves are of no importance; it is far more important that the student should be familiar with the principles leading up to them, than that he should attempt to memorize them. It is none the less a useful exercise for him to show algebraically that the formulae of §10·10 can be expressed in the same form as those of §10·9.

10.12. Cumulative sinking funds—preliminary considerations

Loans repayable by a cumulative sinking fund are a particular case of loans repayable by an annuity and methods similar to those of §§10·9 and 10·10 may be used. It is first necessary, however, to consider how the incidence of income tax will affect the amounts of loan repaid in each successive year. The balance of the annual service, after providing for the *gross* interest, is available to redeem capital. The fact that the borrower will only pay the net interest to the lender does not affect this part of the problem since he is retaining the tax only as an agent of the Inland Revenue authorities to whom he must eventually account for it. In the notation of Chapter 9 the amounts repaid in successive years are still

$$zC, \quad zC(1+g), \quad \ldots, \quad zC(1+g)^{n-1}$$

and in determining the term of the loan income tax may be ignored. The question of allowing for income tax arises only when it is required to value the loan at a given net rate of interest.

10.13. Cumulative sinking funds—methods of valuation allowing for income tax

Two cases arise:

(*a*) where interest and sinking fund operate with the same frequency,

(*b*) where interest is payable more frequently than the sinking fund operates.

The first case is exactly on a par with a loan repayable by an annuity such as has been discussed in §§10·9 and 10·10 above and the methods there adopted will apply without alteration to the present problem. The other case is slightly more complicated, but the principles of §9·10 apply equally here. Basically they are:

(*a*) if interest were payable with the same frequency as the sinking fund and there were no income tax the value of the loan would be simply the value, at the given rate of interest, of an annuity of the service of the loan, the term of the annuity being calculated ignoring income tax,

(*b*) the value of the capital payments at the given rate of interest can generally be found either by summing the geometric progression whose rth term is $zC(1+g)^{r-1}v^r$ or by the indirect use of Makeham's formula as in §10·10,

(*c*) the difference between (*a*) and (*b*) is therefore the value of the gross interest payments, assuming them to be made yearly. If this is denoted by I the value of the interest payments subject to tax at rate t and payable p times a year is $I(1-t)s_{\overline{1}|}^{(p)}$ at rate i,

(*d*) by adding the adjusted value of the interest payments found as in (*c*) to the value of the capital payments found as in (*b*), the total value of the loan under the required conditions is readily ascertained.

Numerical examples of these processes are given in Examples 10·10 to 10·13. If there is an option to purchase in the market the process of valuing the loan becomes very difficult and the methods of §9·16 cannot be applied. In practice approximate methods would be used and a full discussion of these will be found in *J.I.A.* vol. 52, pp. 70–72.

10·14. Capital gains tax

This tax is normally levied on the difference between the price paid for an investment and the amount received when it is sold or redeemed. If a capital loss is made (for example if the purchase price exceeds the redemption price) there is of course no gain to be taxed. If gains have been made on other investments the capital loss can be used to reduce the amount of tax due on them, otherwise it is of no immediate value and in what follows we shall consider only the questions involved when a gain arises bringing with it a definite liability to tax.

10·15. Capital redemption assurances

Sums payable under these policies are not normally subject to capital gains tax as such. It will however affect the net rate of interest earned by the investment of the premiums and the assurance company granting the contract will have to allow for this in fixing the basis of its rates of premium, reserves, etc.

10·16. Redeemable securities

If the rate of income tax is t and of capital gains tax is t' then the value A, of a security of C redeemable in n years, and bearing interest of gC per annum payable p times per annum to yield a net rate of i will be found from the relationship

$$A = Cv^n + g(1-t)\, s_{\overline{1}|}^{(p)}\, Ca_{\overline{n}|} - t'(C-A)\, v^n.$$

The periodical payments of gC are reduced by the tax of tgC per annum, and on redemption there is a liability to pay tax at rate t' on the excess of the redemption price C over the price paid A.

The equation above may be transformed into the Makeham form

$$A(1-t'v^n) = K(1-t') + \frac{g(1-t)}{i} s_{\overline{1}|}^{(p)} (C-K)$$

which is perhaps better written as

$$A\left(1-\frac{t'K}{C}\right) = K(1-t') + \frac{g(1-t)}{i} s_{\overline{1}|}^{(p)} (C-K).$$

This could have been derived by general reasoning. If all capital payments were subject to tax the value of the security would be the sum of the values of the net capital payments, i.e. $K(1-t')$ plus the value of the net interest,

$$\text{i.e.}\quad \frac{g}{i}(1-t)\, s_{\overline{1}|}^{(p)} (C-K).$$

But in fact the part of the capital representing the original investment of A is free from capital gains tax, so we must add the value of tax at rate t' on this amount. Now the value of tax on C is, by definition $t'K$ and hence by proportion the value of tax on A is

$$\frac{t'K}{C}.A.$$

Hence $$A = K(1-t') + \frac{g(1-t)}{i} s_{\overline{1}|}^{(p)} (C-K) + \frac{t'KA}{C}.$$

The method of valuing a redeemable security under these conditions therefore involves little more work than if capital gains tax were ignored. If the redemption price is constant and g is variable the methods of §8·2 can be applied to find the value of the additional net payments of dividends. If the redemption price varies the value of the security can be calculated as in §8·3 first on the basis of a constant redemption price and then adjusted to allow for the net value of the premiums paid on redemption. A numerical illustration of the process is given in Example 10·16.

10·17. Redeemable securities—writing up

In the notation of §8·4 the price A to yield i after allowing for gains tax at rate t' is found from

$$A = Cv^n + gCa_{\overline{n}|} - t'(C-A)v^n,$$

i.e. $$(1+i)^n A = C(1-t') + gCs_{\overline{n}|} + t'A,$$

i.e. $$A + iAs_{\overline{n}|} = C(1-t') + gCs_{\overline{n}|} + t'A,$$

i.e. $$iA = \frac{(C-A)(1-t')}{s_{\overline{n}|}} + gC.$$

It would therefore be possible to treat the security as discussed in §8·6 either by writing it up to a final redemption price of C, in which case a separate fund would have to be accumulated setting aside $\frac{t'(C-A)}{s_{\overline{n}|}}$ per annum which would meet the liability for the gains tax which would arise on redemption, or alternatively to write it up to the final net redemption price, i.e. to $C-t'(C-A)$. As explained in §8·6 this process of 'writing up' is not very common and if a capital gains tax is operating it produces results which are somewhat artificial. The actual progress of the second method is best followed from a numerical example. In this example

$$C = 100,$$
$$g = \cdot 04,$$
$$t = \cdot 375,$$
$$t' = \cdot 3,$$
$$i = \cdot 0375.$$

The price A will be found to be 87·045 and the schedule would be

Year	Net dividend	Capital outstanding at start of each year	Interest at $3\frac{3}{4}$% on capital outstanding	Deficiency to be added to capital
1	2·5	87·045	3·264	·764
2	2·5	87·809	3·293	·793
3	2·5	88·602	3·323	·823
4	2·5	89·425	3·353	·853
5	2·5	90·278	3·385	·885
6	2·5	91·163	3·419	·919
7	2·5	92·082	3·453	·953
8	2·5	93·035	3·489	·989
9	2·5	94·024	3·526	1·026
10	2·5	95·050	3·564	1·064

The final 'capital outstanding' would be 96·114 and the net proceeds on redemption would be $100 - \cdot 3(100 - 87\cdot 045) = 96\cdot 114$.

The reason for describing this process as somewhat artificial is that the value of the security as shown in the books would not equal its market value, assuming no change in the valuation rate of interest. In the Schedule in §8·6 (page 155) the figures in the column 'Capital Outstanding' are also the prices at which the security would stand in the market if interest rates remained unchanged (for example after 5 years the market value would be $100v^5 + 4a_{\overline{5}|}$ at 5%, i.e. 95·671 which is the value shown in the table at the beginning of the sixth year.) If the successive market prices of the security discussed in this section are calculated allowing for gains tax they will be found to be

Term to run (n)	Market price of security A_n
10	87·045
9	88·018
8	89·050
7	90·142
6	91·301
5	92·532
4	93·841
3	95·235
2	96·719
1	98·305

and the differences between these and the 'written up' values in successive years are at once apparent.

10·18. Redeemable securities 'writing up' (*cont.*)

It is instructive to analyse the reasons why the introduction of capital gains tax should affect the relationships which have previously been established between the prices in successive years of a redeemable security valued at a given rate of interest. In Chapters 8 and 9 tax was ignored, and in the earlier part of this chapter the amount of income tax taken into account was independent of the date on which the security was sold or redeemed. Under these conditions if the valuation rate of interest remains unchanged the yield obtained is not affected whether the security is held to redemption or sold at some intermediate point. For example if A_n is the price to yield an effective rate i of a security redeemable at C at the end of n years bearing dividends of gC per annum subject to income tax at rate t we have

$$A_n = Cv^n + g(1-t)\,Ca_{\overline{n}|}.$$

The price, after k years will be

$$A_{n-k} = Cv^{n-k} + g(1-t)\, Ca_{\overline{n-k}|}$$
$$= (1+i)^k\, [Cv^n + g(1-t)\, Ca_{\overline{n}|} - g(1-t)\, Ca_{\overline{k}|}].$$

Hence $\quad A_n = v^k A_{n-k} + g(1-t)\, Ca_{\overline{k}|}$

and the same yield will be obtained by selling the security at a price of A_{n-k} after k years as by holding it to redemption.

If however allowance is made for capital gains tax this identity no longer holds good. In determining the price A_n under these conditions it is assumed that a liability to tax on $C - A_n$ will arise at the end of n years. This could be split into two portions, tax on $(C - A_{n-k})$ due after n years, and tax on $(A_{n-k} - A_n)$ due at the same time. In calculating A_{n-k} we allow for tax on $C - A_{n-k}$ due in $(n-k)$ years and the value of this tax k years previously (that is at the outset) is the same as the value of the tax on $(C - A_{n-k})$ allowed for in calculating A_n. The extra tax on $(A_{n-k} - A_n)$ however was assumed (when A_n was calculated) to be due after n years whereas if the security was sold after k years at a price of A_{n-k} this amount of tax would become due at once and hence would reduce the yield obtained.

Symbolically we have

$$A_n = Cv^n + g(1-t)\, Ca_{\overline{n}|} - t'(C - A_n)\, v^n,$$
$$A_{n-k} = Cv^{n-k} + g(1-t)\, Ca_{\overline{n-k}|} - t'(C - A_{n-k})\, v^{n-k}$$
$$= (1+i)^k\, [A_n - g(1-t)\, Ca_{\overline{k}|}] - t'(C - A_{n-k}) v^{n-k}$$
$$= (1+i)^k\, [A_n - g(1-t)\, Ca_{\overline{k}|}] + t'v^n (A_{n-k} - A_n).$$

Hence $\quad A_n = v^k A_{n-k} + g(1-t)\, Ca_{\overline{k}|} - t'v^n (A_{n-k} - A_n).$

The yield obtained by selling the investment after k years would be found from the equation

$$A_n = v^k A_{n-k} + g(1-t)\, Ca_{\overline{k}|} - t'v^k (A_{n-k} - A_n)$$

and since the final deductive term in this equation exceeds

$$t'v^n (A_{n-k} - A_n)$$

the yield must be less than the original rate i.

Reverting to the figures in §10·17 we see that the difference between the written up value and the market price is the value, at the date of sale, of the vendor's tax due at that date but valued as if due at maturity of the security.

For example, when there are 7 years of the term to run

$$v^7(90{\cdot}142-87{\cdot}045)\times 0{\cdot}3 = 0{\cdot}773-3{\cdot}097\times 0{\cdot}3 = 0{\cdot}717$$

and

$$90{\cdot}142-89{\cdot}425 = 0{\cdot}717.$$

10·19. Loans repayable by instalments (including cumulative sinking funds)

The reasoning in §10·16 applies equally whether the security is repayable in one sum, or by instalments. It follows therefore that if the redemption price C is uniform throughout the term of a loan the value of the loan allowing for capital gains tax can be found very simply once the gross value of the capital payments has been calculated. The gross value is not affected by the incidence of capital gains tax and therefore the methods for valuing loans repayable by annuities, including loans repayable by cumulative sinking funds described in §§10·8 to 10·13 can still be applied. The method may be summarised:

(*a*) calculate the term of the loan ignoring all taxes, and value the service for the appropriate term, assuming interest and sinking fund payments operate with the same frequency;

(*b*) calculate the value K of the capital payments either directly or indirectly as described in §10·11;

(*c*) the difference between (*a*) and (*b*) is the value of gross interest at the frequency of the sinking fund payments. This value can readily be adjusted to allow for income tax and actual frequency of payment;

(*d*) the value of the security is now the value of the net capital payments (i.e. the value of K calculated above, less capital gains tax) plus the value of net interest from (*c*) plus the value of capital gains tax on the purchase price A which by proportion is $\frac{KA}{C}$ multiplied by the appropriate rate of gains tax.

10·20 The following examples illustrate the work of this chapter.

Example 10·1

A capital redemption policy for £1000 to run for 50 years was issued on 1 June 1925, subject to annual premiums calculated on a net 3% basis. The following table shows the gross rate at which the office was, or expects to be, able to invest new money, and the rates of tax:

Due dates	Gross rate of interest at which new money invested	Rate of income tax
1 June 1925–34 inclusive	5%	20%
1935–44 inclusive	$4\frac{1}{2}$%	25%
1945 onwards	4%	$37\frac{1}{2}$%

Find the annual premium and derive a formula for the estimated profit or loss at maturity assuming the policy is then in force. Assume

(*a*) all investments are made at par and are repayable at par on 1 June 1975,
(*b*) all premiums are received and invested on the due dates,
(*c*) interest is received annually on 1 June and is immediately invested.

The premium charged is $1000P_{\overline{50|}} = \dfrac{1000}{\ddot{s}_{\overline{50|}}}$ at 3%

$$= 1000v\left[\frac{1}{a_{\overline{50|}}} - \cdot 03\right]$$
$$= 8\cdot 865v$$
$$= 8\cdot 607,$$

or say £8·61.

The estimated profit or loss at maturity will be the difference between the sum assured and the amount to which the premiums accumulate. Consider the accumulation of the premiums in three stages.

(*a*) 1925–34 *inclusive*

The premiums, and interest on them, will be invested at 5%. The interest at the rate of 5% less income tax will be received until 1975. The actual interest received up to 1934 will therefore be 4% after deduction of tax at 20%.

On 1 June 1934 therefore the premiums of say P paid up to and including that date will have amounted to $Ps_{\overline{10|}}$ at 4%, and in every subsequent year the gross interest on this will be $\cdot 05Ps_{\overline{10|}}^{\cdot 04}$.

(*b*) 1935–44 *inclusive*

The gross interest received on 1 June 1935 will be $\cdot05Ps_{\overline{10}|}^{\cdot04}$, and after deduction of tax this will be reduced to $\cdot05Ps_{\overline{10}|}^{\cdot04}\times\frac{3}{4}=\cdot0375Ps_{\overline{10}|}^{\cdot04}$.

The total sums received in each year from 1935 to 1944 will therefore be $\cdot0375Ps_{\overline{10}|}^{\cdot04}+P=P(1+\cdot0375s_{\overline{10}|}^{\cdot04})$, and these will accumulate at $4\frac{1}{2}\%$ gross or $4\frac{1}{2}\times\frac{3}{4}=3\cdot375\%$ net. The accumulation on 1 June 1944 will therefore be

$$P(1+\cdot0375s_{\overline{10}|}^{\cdot04})(s_{\overline{10}|}^{\cdot03375}),$$

and in every subsequent year the gross interest on this sum will be

$$\cdot045P(1+\cdot0375s_{\overline{10}|}^{\cdot04})(s_{\overline{10}|}^{\cdot03375}).$$

(*c*) 1945–75 *inclusive*

The gross interest received on 1 June 1945 on the investments made up to 1944 will be

$$\cdot05Ps_{\overline{10}|}^{\cdot04}+\cdot045P(1+\cdot0375s_{\overline{10}|}^{\cdot04})(s_{\overline{10}|}^{\cdot03375})$$

and after deduction of tax the net sums received will be

$$\cdot03125Ps_{\overline{10}|}^{\cdot04}+\cdot028125P(1+\cdot0375s_{\overline{10}|}^{\cdot04})(s_{\overline{10}|}^{\cdot03375})=X \quad \text{(say)}.$$

The total sums received in each year up to 1 June 1974 will therefore be $X+P$, and they will be invested at $4\times\frac{5}{8}=2\frac{1}{2}\%$. On 1 June 1975 the accumulated total of these sums will be $(X+P)\ddot{s}_{\overline{30}|}$ at $2\frac{1}{2}\%$.

The position on 1 June 1975 therefore will be that the total investments held will be:

From (*a*) above $Ps_{\overline{10}|}^{\cdot04}$.
From (*b*) above $P(1+\cdot0375s_{\overline{10}|}^{\cdot04})(s_{\overline{10}|}^{\cdot03375})$.
From (*c*) above $P[(1+\cdot03125s_{\overline{10}|}^{\cdot04})$

$$+\cdot028125(1+\cdot0375s_{\overline{10}|}^{\cdot04})s_{\overline{10}|}^{\cdot03375}]\ddot{s}_{\overline{30}|}^{\cdot025},$$

where $P=$ £8·61, and the total of these three amounts, less £1000, will be the profit, or if negative the loss, at maturity.

Example 10·2

A loan issued on 1 March 1913 is repayable by an annuity certain payable half-yearly for 50 years from that date and calculated on a basis of $2\frac{1}{2}\%$ per annum convertible half-yearly. Income tax is payable only upon the interest portion of the instalments. What price should be paid on 2 March 1947 for each £1 annuity by an investor who wishes to realize on his whole investment 2% per half-year free of income tax, and to replace his capital by a leasehold policy securing the purchase price at the end of 16 years? The office premiums will be payable half-yearly and calculated on a net 3% per annum effective basis. Assume income tax to be at the rate of $22\frac{1}{2}\%$.

The number of instalments outstanding on 2 March 1947 is 32.

Therefore if income tax were ignored the value of these instalments would be

$$\tfrac{1}{2}a_{\overline{32}|} \quad \text{at } 2\%.$$

Therefore if K be the value of the capital contained in these instalments

$$K+\frac{\cdot 0125}{\cdot 02}\left(\tfrac{1}{2}a_{\overline{32}|}^{\cdot 0125}-K\right)=\tfrac{1}{2}a_{\overline{32}|}^{\cdot 02},$$

whence

$$K=9\cdot 424.$$

The present value of the net payments after deduction of tax will be

$$K+\frac{\cdot 0125}{\cdot 02}\times \cdot 775\left(\tfrac{1}{2}a_{\overline{32}|}^{0125}-K\right)=11\cdot 214.$$

Now if the price paid on 2 March 1947 per £1 of annuity is X, the purchaser will have to pay $\frac{1}{2}P_{\overline{16}|}^{(2)}X$ (at 3%) at the beginning of each of the next 32 half-years and will receive the net payments under the loan (already valued as 11·214) plus the sum of X from the leasehold policy at the end of 16 years. The equation of value is therefore

$$X=11\cdot 214-\frac{X}{2}P_{\overline{16}|}^{(2)}\ddot{a}_{\overline{32}|}+Xv^{32} \quad \text{at } 2\%.$$

$$\therefore X=\frac{11\cdot 214}{1-v^{32}+\dfrac{1\cdot 02}{2}P_{\overline{16}|}^{(2)}a_{\overline{32}|}}$$

$$\therefore\; X=\frac{11\cdot 214}{a_{\overline{32}|}\left(\cdot 02+1\cdot 02\,.\,\tfrac{1}{2}P_{\overline{16}|}^{(2)}\right)}$$

and

$$P_{\overline{16}|}^{(2)}=\frac{1}{\ddot{s}_{\overline{16}|}^{(2)}} \quad \text{at } 3\%$$

$$=\cdot 048522.$$

$$\therefore\; X=£10\cdot 68.$$

Example 10·3

A owns a capital redemption policy effected 15 years ago for £5000. The original term was 46 years and a yearly premium of £50 is now due.

In addition, he is entitled to a ground rent of £1000 per annum for the next 30 years, the first payment of which is due in 1 year's time. He offers for sale the policy plus the instalments of the ground rent payable in years 11–30 inclusive, having reserved the first ten instalments to himself. What price can a purchaser pay if he wishes to earn 4% per annum net, allowing for income tax at 25%, assuming that he effects an additional policy with a term of 31 years to replace his capital, the annual premium under which will be calculated on a net basis of 1% for the first year, and 3% thereafter?

Let A be the price to be paid and let S be the sum assured under the new policy.

The new premium per unit is P, where

$$P[(1\cdot01)(1\cdot03)^{30}+\ddot{s}^{\cdot03}_{\overline{30}|}]=1,$$

or

$$P=\cdot01943 \text{ per unit.}$$

For the next 10 years the purchaser will receive no interest and therefore must accumulate his invested capital and the premiums at 4%. At the end of 10 years the capital invested is therefore

$$A(1\cdot04)^{10}+(50+SP)\ddot{s}^{\cdot04}_{\overline{10}|}=X, \quad \text{say,}$$

and a year's premiums are then due, making a total outlay of $X+50+SP$. At the end of years 11–30 each year's net income must provide interest at 4% on the total outlay plus the premiums due, i.e.

$$1000(\tfrac{3}{4})=\cdot04(X+50+SP)+(50+SP).$$

Also at the end of the 31st year the leasehold policies must repay the outlay with a year's interest, i.e.

$$5000+S=1\cdot04(X+50+SP).$$

Hence

$$750=\frac{\cdot04}{1\cdot04}(5000+S)+50+\cdot01943S,$$

whence

$$S=8770$$

and

$$SP=170\cdot4.$$

$$\therefore\ X=\frac{750-50-170\cdot4}{\cdot04}-50-170\cdot4$$

$$=13{,}019\cdot6.$$

$$\therefore\ A=13{,}019\cdot6v^{10}-220\cdot4\ddot{a}_{\overline{10}|}$$

$$=£6936.$$

Example 10·4

A security is redeemable at the end of n years at a price of C. Interest is payable yearly at $5\frac{1}{2}\%$ on the nominal amount. The value of the security to yield 4% gross is 124·95%, and the value to yield 4% net after allowing for income tax at 25% is 106·26. Find the value of C without using interest tables.

From the data given the value of the security to yield 4% is 124·95. If, instead of dividends at the rate of $\frac{5\cdot5}{C}$, dividends were paid at 4% of the redemption price, the value to yield 4% would be C. Hence the value of dividends of $\left(\frac{5\cdot5}{C}-\cdot04\right)$ per annum is $124\cdot95-C$. The value of tax on dividends of $\frac{5\cdot5}{C}$ is therefore by proportion

$$\frac{\frac{1}{4}\left(\frac{5\cdot5}{C}\right)}{\frac{5\cdot5}{C}-\cdot04}[124\cdot95-C].$$

But the only difference between the value to yield 4%, ignoring tax, and the value to yield 4% after allowing for tax is the value of tax on the dividends, i.e.

$$\frac{\frac{1}{4}\left(\frac{5\cdot5}{C}\right)}{\frac{5\cdot5}{C}-\cdot04}\times(124\cdot95-C)=124\cdot95-106\cdot26.$$

$$\therefore\quad \frac{5\cdot5\times124\cdot95}{4C}-\frac{5\cdot5}{4}=(18\cdot69)\left(\frac{5\cdot5}{C}-\cdot04\right),$$

whence

$$C=\frac{5\cdot5\times12\cdot5475}{\cdot6274}$$

$$=110.$$

Example 10·5

A stock bears interest at 5% per annum payable half-yearly on 1 June and 1 December and is redeemable at 105 on 1 June 1962. If it is quoted at 102 on 1 April 1947, what is the net effective yield to a purchaser at that price if income tax is $37\frac{1}{2}\%$ throughout?

If the price to yield i net on 1 June 1947 is A, the price on 1 April 1947 will be $A(1+i)^{-\frac{1}{6}}$.

But $$A = 105v^{15} + 5 \times \cdot 625\,(\tfrac{1}{2} + a^{(2)}_{\overline{15}|})$$
$$= 105v^{15} + 3\cdot 125 \times \frac{i}{i^{(2)}}\, a_{\overline{15}|} + 1\cdot 5625.$$

At 3% $\quad A = 106\cdot 54.$

The value to yield 3% on 1 April is

$$106\cdot 54\left(1 - \frac{i}{6}\right) \text{ approximately} = 106\cdot 01.$$

At $3\frac{1}{2}$% $\quad A = 100\cdot 54.$

The value to yield $3\frac{1}{2}$% on 1 April is

$$100\cdot 54\left(1 - \frac{i}{6}\right) \text{ approximately} = 99\cdot 95.$$

The yield at a price of 102 is therefore

$$\cdot 03 + \frac{4\cdot 01}{6\cdot 06} \times (\cdot 005) = \cdot 0333$$

or say £3·33 %.

Example 10·6

A loan bears interest at 5% per annum payable half-yearly on 1 January and 1 July. It is redeemable by ten equal instalments of nominal capital on 1 January 1958, 1960, 1962, 1964 and 1966 at 105 and on 1 January 1968, 1970, 1972, 1974 and 1976 at par. Find the price on 1 April 1947 to yield $2\frac{1}{2}$% net effective assuming income tax at $37\frac{1}{2}$%. the pound.

At 1 January 1947 the value of the capital payments per £100 loan, ignoring the premium of 5% up to 1966, is

$$10(v^{11} + v^{13} + \ldots + v^{29}) = 10\frac{a_{\overline{31}|} - a_{\overline{11}|}}{a_{\overline{2}|}} \quad \text{at } 2\tfrac{1}{2}\%$$
$$= 61\cdot 643.$$

The value of the loan to yield $2\frac{1}{2}$%, ignoring the premium, is therefore

$$61\cdot 643 + \frac{\cdot 05 \times \cdot 625}{\cdot 025}\, s^{(2)}_{\overline{1}|}\,(100 - 61\cdot 643) = 109\cdot 887.$$

The value of the premiums is $\cdot 05 \times 10\left(\dfrac{a_{\overline{21}|} - a_{\overline{11}|}}{a_{\overline{2}|}}\right) = 1\cdot 731.$

Therefore the total price on 1 January 1947

$$=109\cdot887+1\cdot731$$
$$=111\cdot618.$$

Therefore the price on 1 April 1947

$$=111\cdot618(1\cdot025)^{\frac{1}{4}}$$
$$=111\cdot618\left(1+\frac{\cdot025}{4}\right)\quad\text{approximately}$$
$$=112\cdot31.$$

Example 10·7

A loan of £1,000,000 bearing interest at 4% payable yearly is repayable in 24 years by annual instalments, the first of which is due at the end of 10 years, as follows:

Years	Nominal amount repaid	Redemption price (%)
10–14	£50,000 per annum	110
15–19	£70,000 per annum	105
20–24	£80,000 per annum	105

What price can be paid for the whole loan to earn 2% net per annum convertible half-yearly after allowing for tax at 45% in the first year, 40% in the second year, $37\frac{1}{2}$% for the next 6 years and 30% thereafter?

The simplest method of dealing with this problem is to make assumptions which will enable Makeham's formula to be used, and then to adjust the answer.

If tax were at 30% throughout, and if the redemption price were 105%

$$C=1,050,000,$$

$$(1-t)g=\frac{\cdot04\times\cdot7}{1\cdot05},$$

$$K=\frac{105}{s_{\overline{2}|}}\{500v^{18}a_{\overline{10}|}+700v^{28}a_{\overline{10}|}+800v^{38}a_{\overline{10}|}\}\quad\text{at }1\%$$

$$=\frac{10,500}{s_{\overline{2}|}}\{8a_{\overline{48}|}-a_{\overline{38}|}-2a_{\overline{28}|}-5a_{\overline{18}|}\}$$

$$=740,131.$$

$$\therefore\ A = 740{,}131 + \frac{\cdot 04\times\cdot 7}{1\cdot 05}\times\frac{1}{\cdot 01}\times\frac{1}{s_{\overline{2}|}}(1{,}050{,}000 - 740{,}131)$$

$$= 1{,}151{,}229.$$

This ignores the additional 5% payable on redemption in years 10–14, i.e.

$$\frac{5}{s_{\overline{2}|}}(500)(a_{\overline{28}|} - a_{\overline{18}|}) = 9849,$$

and it allows too much net interest in the first 8 years. Interest is £40,000 per annum payable yearly, and the additional tax which must be allowed for is 15% in the first year, 10%, and $7\frac{1}{2}$% in the next 6 years, i.e.

$$6000v^2 + 4000v^4 + \frac{3000}{s_{\overline{2}|}}(a_{\overline{16}|} - a_{\overline{4}|}) = 25{,}869.$$

The total value is therefore

$$1{,}151{,}229 + 9849 - 25{,}869 = 1{,}135{,}209$$

or say 113·52%.

Example 10·8

In certain circumstances a borrower is allowed to deduct and retain for his own use income tax on all interest payments made by him. Show that from his point of view the following two methods of repaying a loan subject to interest at rate i gross per annum are equivalent if the rate of income tax is constant at t:

(*a*) by a uniform annual payment including principal and interest at the end of each year for n years,

(*b*) by a leasehold policy for n years where the premiums are calculated at rate $i(1-t)$, interest at rate i being payable on the full loan at the end of each year.

Consider a loan of 1 and let $i(1-t) = i'$.

In the first method the present value at rate i' of all the sums the borrower has to pay must be 1 since the actual interest he pays is $i(1-t)$ per unit of capital outstanding, i.e. at rate i'.

In the second method he pays $P_{\overline{n}|}$ in advance and $i(1-t)$ in arrear for n years.

The present value at rate i' is

$$P_{\overline{n}|}\ddot{a}_{\overline{n}|} + i(1-t)\,a_{\overline{n}|} \quad \text{at rate } i',$$

and, since $P_{\overline{n}|}$ is calculated at rate i', this is equal to

$$v^n + i' a_{\overline{n}|} = 1.$$

Hence the two methods are identical.

Example 10·9

The following is an example of the type of security discussed in § 10·8, and of the valuation of an annuity-certain allowing for income tax.

A loan was raised 20 years ago by the issue of terminable annuities of £100,000 per annum payable for 32 years. Income tax is deducted only from the portion of each instalment which, according to the schedule drawn up when the loan was granted, represents interest. In addition, from each £1 of annuity a sum of 41p is deducted. Of this amount 1p is retained to cover expenses and 40p is paid to trustees to be invested and accumulated in a separate fund. At the end of 32 years the monies in this fund will be divided *pro rata* amongst the holders of the annuities. Given the following information, find the price per £100 of annuity to yield 3 % net, assuming income tax at 27½ % in the pound:

(*a*) Accumulated sinking fund to date is £1,074,815.
(*b*) The sinking fund will accumulate for the next 7 years at the same average net rate as it has up to date, and thereafter at ½ % per annum less.
(*c*) The income tax due to be deducted from an annuity payment of £100 due one year from now is £10·32.

To value this security it is necessary

(*a*) to find the accumulated amount of the sinking fund at the date when it will be distributed,
(*b*) to ascertain the rate of interest involved in the original transaction from the borrower's point of view, and hence the rate at which the schedule was calculated for income tax purposes.

The sinking fund to date is

$$100{,}000 \times \cdot 4 s_{\overline{20}|} \text{ at rate } i = 1{,}074{,}815.$$

$$\therefore \quad s_{\overline{20}|} = 26\cdot 8703,$$

whence

$$i = \cdot 03.$$

The accumulated amount of the sinking fund at the end of the term will therefore be

$$40{,}000 s_{\overline{7}|}^{\cdot 03} (1\cdot 025)^5 + 40{,}000 s_{\overline{5}|}^{\cdot 025} + 1{,}074{,}815 (1\cdot 03)^7 (1\cdot 025)^5$$
$$= 2{,}052{,}619$$
$$= 20\cdot 5262 \text{ per £1 of annuity.}$$

From the borrower's point of view the loan now outstanding is $a_{\overline{12}|}$ at rate g, per unit of annuity. The interest due one year hence is therefore $1-v^{12}$ at rate g, and the tax on it is $\cdot 275(1-v^{12})$.

$$\therefore \quad \cdot 275(1-v^{12}) = \cdot 1032,$$

i.e.
$$v^{12} = \cdot 6247,$$

whence
$$g = \cdot 04.$$

The value of the loan is therefore

(*a*) the present value of the annuity payments, subject to income tax,

less (*b*) the present value of the constant deduction for sinking-fund and expenses,

plus (*c*) the present value of the amount which will be received in 12 years' time from the accumulated sinking fund.

The value of (*a*) may be found by the method of § 10·10 as follows:

If no deduction of tax were made from the interest payments (calculated at 4% per annum) the value per unit annuity to yield 3% would be $a_{\overline{12}|}$ at 3%. If the interest payments were calculated at 3% per annum the value per unit annuity to yield 3% would be the amount of loan outstanding, i.e. $a_{\overline{12}|}$ at 4%. The value of the capital is the same in either case, and hence the difference must be the value of interest payments calculated at 1% per annum. The value of gross interest payments of 4% per annum is therefore $4(a_{\overline{12}|}^{\cdot 03} - a_{\overline{12}|}^{\cdot 04})$, and the value of the income tax to be deducted is therefore $\cdot 275 \times 4(a_{\overline{12}|}^{\cdot 03} - a_{\overline{12}|}^{\cdot 04})$. Hence

$$\text{the value of } (a) \text{ is } a_{\overline{12}|}^{\cdot 03} - \cdot 275 \times 4(a_{\overline{12}|}^{\cdot 03} - a_{\overline{12}|}^{\cdot 04}) = 9\cdot 3282$$

$$\text{the value of } (b) \text{ is } \cdot 41 a_{\overline{12}|} \text{ at } 3\% = 4\cdot 0811$$

$$\text{the value of } (c) \text{ is } 20\cdot 5262 v^{12} \text{ at } 3\% = 14\cdot 3967$$

and hence the value per £100 annuity is 1964·38 or say £1964·38.

Example 10·10

A loan of £1,000,000 bears interest at $5\frac{1}{2}$% per annum payable half-yearly and is repayable by annual drawings at 110. The service of the loan is £70,000 per annum, and after payment of the interest due and placing £5000 to a reserve account, the balance is applied to the redemption of the loan as above. Six years after the issue of the loan an additional sum of £12,100 was paid into the reserve account. The loan will be finally redeemed as soon as the reserve account exceeds the amount required to redeem the balance of loan outstanding. The reserve account accumulates at 4% net. Find the price of the loan 7 years after issue to yield 4% net allowing for income tax at 25%.

The amount available for drawings in the first year is

$$70{,}000 - 55{,}000 - 5000 = £10{,}000.$$

At the end of n years the loan outstanding is

$$1{,}100{,}000\left(1 - \tfrac{1}{110}s_{\overline{n}|}\right) \text{ at rate } g = \frac{5{\cdot}5}{110} \text{ or } 5\%.$$

The reserve fund is then

$$5000s_{\overline{n}|} + 12{,}100(1+i)^{n-6} \quad \text{at } 4\%.$$

When $n = 32$ it will be found that the loan outstanding is 347,012 and the reserve fund is 347,054, and hence the loan is repaid 32 years from the issue date, i.e. 25 years from the valuation date.

The loan outstanding at the valuation date is $1{,}100{,}000 - 10{,}000s_{\overline{7}|}$ at 5%, i.e. 1,018,580. This would be the value to yield 4% if dividends were 4% payable yearly. If dividends were 5% payable yearly the value to yield 4% would be

$$65{,}000a_{\overline{25}|} + 347{,}012v^{25} \text{ at } 4\% = 1{,}145{,}608.$$

Therefore the value of a dividend of 1% payable yearly

$$= 127{,}028.$$

Therefore the value of the dividends of 5% payable yearly

$$= 127{,}028 \times 5$$
$$= 635{,}140.$$

Therefore the value of the capital payments

$$= 1{,}145{,}608 - 635{,}140$$
$$= 510{,}468.$$

Therefore the value of the whole loan, when dividends are half-yearly and subject to tax, is

$$510{,}468 + 635{,}140 \times {\cdot}75 \times s^{(2)}_{\overline{1}|} \text{ at } 4\% = 991{,}538$$

or, say, £99·15 per £100 bond.

Example 10·11

A loan is to be issued bearing interest at $3\frac{1}{4}\%$ per annum payable half-yearly and redeemable by means of a cumulative sinking fund of 1% per annum, increasing after 10 years to $1\frac{1}{2}\%$ per annum operating by yearly drawings at £108·33. Find the price to allow a net effective yield of 3% per annum, allowing for income tax at 22½% throughout.

Here

$$g=\frac{\cdot 0325}{1\cdot 0833}=\cdot 05.$$

At the end of 10 years the amount outstanding is

$$108\cdot 33-s_{\overline{10}|}\text{ at }3\%=96\cdot 8661.$$

The amount now available for sinking fund is

$$4\cdot 75-\cdot 03\,(96\cdot 8661)=1\cdot 8440.$$

The loan will be redeemed in a further n years, where

$$1\cdot 8440s_{\overline{n}|}^{\cdot 03}=96\cdot 8661.$$

Now

$$1\cdot 8440s_{\overline{32}|}=96\cdot 815.$$

The loan is therefore repaid in a further 33 years, the final capital payment being ·051.

The value at 3% of the capital payments is

$$v+1\cdot 03v^2+\ldots+1\cdot 03^9v^{10}+1\cdot 8440(v^{11}+1\cdot 03v^{12}+\ldots+1\cdot 03^{31}v^{42})+\cdot 051v^{43}$$

$$=10v+1\cdot 8440v^{11}\times 32+\cdot 0143$$

$$=52\cdot 352.$$

The value of the loan plus interest at 3% yearly to yield 3% is 108·33.

Therefore the value of yearly interest at 3% is 55·978.

Therefore the value of the loan with interest half-yearly and subject to tax is

$$52\cdot 352+55\cdot 978\,(\cdot 775)\,s_{\overline{1}|}^{(2)}=96\cdot 059$$

say £96·06

Example 10·12

A loan of £5,000,000 was raised on 1 July 1940 by issuing bonds at par carrying interest at 4½% per annum payable quarterly, the bonds being redeemable by annual drawings on 1 July in each year at 112½% by means of a cumulative sinking fund of £25,000 per annum.

On 2 October 1951 special legislation was announced which had the effect of cancelling the January and July interest coupons for the next five years, the amounts available for repayment of capital being unaffected by the alteration. Assuming that it is appropriate to value the bonds both immediately before and immediately after the announcement at an effective rate of interest of 4% per annum, find the total depreciation suffered by a holder of £100,000 of the loan on 2 October

1951 allowing for income tax at $37\frac{1}{2}\%$.

Here

$$g=\frac{4\cdot 5}{112\cdot 5}=\cdot 04.$$

On 1 July 1951 the loan outstanding was

$$5{,}000{,}000\times 1\cdot 125-25{,}000 s_{\overline{11}|} \text{ at } 4\%$$
$$=5{,}287{,}840.$$

The value of capital and interest payments for the next 5 years, if interest were paid annually, is

$$250{,}000\, a_{\overline{5}|} \text{ at } 4\%$$
$$=1{,}112{,}950.$$

The value of the capital repayments included in this figure is

$$25{,}000\,[(1\cdot 04)^{11}\,v+(1\cdot 04)^{12}\,v^2+\ldots(1\cdot 04)^{15}\,v^5]$$
$$=125{,}000\,(1\cdot 04)^{10}$$
$$=185{,}030.$$

The value on 1 July of the interest, if it were paid yearly, would therefore be

$$1{,}112{,}950-185{,}030=927{,}920.$$

The value of half the interest, paid half-yearly on 1 January and 1 July would therefore be $463{,}960 s_{\overline{1}|}^{(2)}$, at 4%, i.e. 468,553.

The value of this interest on 2 October, subject to income tax at $37\frac{1}{2}\%$, is therefore

$$468{,}553\times 0\cdot 625\times(1\cdot 04)^{\frac{1}{4}}=295{,}731.$$

The depreciation per £100,000 nominal is therefore

$$\frac{295{,}731\times 1125}{52{,}878\cdot 4}=£6{,}292.$$

Example 10·13

A loan of £1,000,000 is to be issued on which interest will be payable half-yearly at the rate of $5\frac{1}{2}\%$ per annum. The loan will be repaid by annual drawings over a period of 20 years by a cumulative sinking fund. A fixed annual sum is to be applied to the service of the loan and in addition two special payments are to be made at the end of 10 and 20 years respectively. Normal annual drawings are to be made at 110 and the special payments are to be applied to redeem bonds at 120. The amount of each special payment is to be such sum as will suffice to repay a nominal amount of loan equal to the total nominal amount already repaid at the end of 10 and 20 years respectively (including the amounts due to be repaid at the end of these years by the normal application of the service). Find the annual service of the loan and the issue price to yield 4% effective allowing for income tax at 25%.

Let X be the nominal amount repaid in the first 10 years by the normal sinking fund, and let Y be the corresponding amount repaid in the second 10 years.

The special payment at the end of 20 years will therefore repay a nominal amount of $(2X+Y)$ and this must equal half the nominal amount of the loan.

$$\therefore\ 2X+Y=500{,}000.$$

If S is the normal annual service

$$X=\frac{S-55{,}000}{1\cdot 1}\, s_{\overline{10}|} \text{ at } 5\%.$$

and

$$\begin{aligned} Y&=\frac{S-\cdot 055\,(1{,}000{,}000-2X)}{1\cdot 1}\, s_{\overline{10}|} \text{ at } 5\% \\ &=\frac{S-55{,}000}{1\cdot 1}\, s_{\overline{10}|}+\cdot 05\,(2X)\, s_{\overline{10}|}. \\ &=X\,[1+2\,(1\cdot 05)^{10}-2] \\ &=X[2\,(1\cdot 05)^{10}-1]. \end{aligned}$$

$$\begin{aligned} \therefore\ X&=\frac{500{,}000}{2\,(1\cdot 05)^{10}+1} \\ &=117{,}432 \end{aligned}$$

$$\begin{aligned} \therefore\ S&=\frac{129{,}175}{s_{\overline{10}|}}+55{,}000 \\ &=65{,}270. \end{aligned}$$

From the point of view of a holder of the whole loan, therefore, he will receive

(*a*) an annuity of £65,270 for 20 years.

(*b*) the special payments of $1\cdot 2X$ and $1\cdot 2\,(2X+Y)$ at the end of 10 and 20 years respectively.

If interest were paid yearly without deduction of tax the value would therefore be

$$65{,}270\,a_{\overline{20}|}+117{,}432\times 1{\cdot}2\,[v^{10}+4{\cdot}25778\,v^{20}] \text{ at } 4\%.$$
$$=887{,}039+369{,}032$$
$$=1{,}256{,}071.$$

The value of the capital repayments included in this figure may be found as follows:

The sum available for redemption in the first year is $65{,}270-55{,}000$, i.e. 10,270. After 10 years the loan outstanding is $1{,}000{,}000-2X$, i.e. 765,136, interest on which at $5\frac{1}{2}\%$ absorbs 42,082 leaving 23,188 available for redeeming the loan. The value of the normal capital repayments is therefore

$$10{,}270\,[v+(1{\cdot}05)\,v^2+\ldots+(1{\cdot}05)^9 v^{10}]$$
$$+23{,}188\,[v^{11}+(1{\cdot}05)\,v^{12}+\ldots+(1{\cdot}05)^9 v^{20}] \text{ at } 4\%$$
$$=1{,}027{,}000\,[(1{\cdot}05)^{10}\,v^{10}-1]+2{,}318{,}800\,v^{10}\,[(1{\cdot}05)^{10}\,v^{10}-1]$$
$$=2{,}593{,}489\times 0{\cdot}100413$$
$$=260{,}420.$$

The value of the special payments is 369,032 and therefore the total value of the capital repayments is 629,452. The value of the interest is therefore $1{,}256{,}071-629{,}452$, i.e. 626,619, assuming it to be paid yearly without deduction of income tax. If it is paid half-yearly and subject to income tax at 25 % its value will be $626{,}619\times 0{\cdot}75\times s^{(2)}_{\overline{1}|}=474{,}617$. The total value is therefore £1,104,069 or say £110·41 per £100 bond.

Example 10·14

A loan is repayable over a period of 30 years by annuities, the annual payment under each annuity being £1. From each £1 of annual payment 30p is deducted and paid to trustees, while the remaining 70p is regarded as interest, and is subject to income tax at $23\frac{3}{4}\%$. At the end of each of the first 29 years the trustees invest 20 % of their cash receipts to accumulate at 3 % net effective interest, and apply the remaining 80 % in purchasing their own annuities on the market at £142·33 per £10 of annuity. The total payments under the annuities purchased by the trustees are made direct to them and they deal with these payments in the same manner as with their receipts from unpurchased annuities. At the end of 30 years the total sum then held by the trustees is divided among the holders of unpurchased annuities *pro rata*. Find the issue price if the net effective yield under an unpurchased annuity is 4%.

This question is closely analagous to a cumulative sinking fund. The first step in its solution must be to find how the number of annuities purchased progresses from year to year, and it will be convenient to work in terms of each £1 of annuity originally issued.

Let the total annuities purchased up to the end of year t be F_t. The cash receipts of the trustees at the end of year $(t+1)$ are, therefore

30p from the deductions from all annuities purchased or unpurchased.
70p less tax at $23\frac{3}{4}$% from the purchased annuities held at the beginning of the year, i.e.

$$\cdot 3 + \cdot 7 \times \cdot 7625 F_t.$$

Hence the annuities purchased at the end of year $(t+1)$

$$= \cdot 8\left[\frac{\cdot 3 + \cdot 7 \times \cdot 7625 F_t}{14\cdot 233}\right].$$

$$\therefore \; F_{t+1} = F_t + \cdot 8\left[\frac{\cdot 3 + \cdot 7 \times \cdot 7625 F_t}{14\cdot 233}\right]$$

$$= F_t\left[1 + \frac{\cdot 8 \times \cdot 7 \times \cdot 7625}{14\cdot 233}\right] + \frac{\cdot 3 \times \cdot 8}{14\cdot 233}$$

$$= 1\cdot 03 F_t + \frac{\cdot 8 \times \cdot 3}{14\cdot 233}.$$

Now $$F_1 = \frac{\cdot 8 \times \cdot 3}{14\cdot 233}.$$

$$\therefore \; F_2 = 1\cdot 03 F_1 + F_1 = F_1 s_{\overline{2}|}$$

$$F_3 = 1\cdot 03 F_2 + F_1 = F_1 s_{\overline{3}|}$$

and so on, hence $$F_{t+1} = \frac{\cdot 8 \times \cdot 3}{14\cdot 233} s_{\overline{t+1}|}^{\cdot 03}.$$

At the end of 29 years the total annuities purchased will be

$$\frac{\cdot 8 \times \cdot 3}{14\cdot 233} s_{\overline{29}|} \text{ at } 3\% = \cdot 76249$$

Hence the unpurchased annuities will be ·23751

Consider now the sum which the trustees will have in the sinking fund. It will consist of

(a) the accumulation of 20% of the deduction of 30p from all annuities, i.e. $\cdot 2 \times \cdot 3 \ddot{s}_{\overline{29}|}^{03} = 2\cdot 7945$.

(b) the accumulation of 20% of the interest receipts in each year from purchased annuities.

The amount received at the end of year t from the latter source is

$$\cdot 7\times\cdot 7625\times\cdot 2F_{t-1}=\frac{\cdot 7\times\cdot 7625\times\cdot 2\times\cdot 8\times\cdot 3}{14\cdot 233}s_{\overline{t-1}|}$$

$$=\cdot 3\times\cdot 2\times\cdot 03s_{\overline{t-1}|}$$

$$=\cdot 06\,[(1\cdot 03)^{t-1}-1],$$

and this amount is invested at 3%. Hence it will amount, at the end of $30-t$ years to $\cdot 06\,[(1\cdot 03)^{30-t}(1\cdot 03)^{t-1}-(1\cdot 03)^{30-t}]$.

Hence the total receipts will be

$$\cdot 06\sum_{1}^{29}[(1\cdot 03)^{29}-(1\cdot 03)^{30-t}]=\cdot 06[29\times(1\cdot 03)^{29}-\ddot{s}_{\overline{29}|}]$$

$$=1\cdot 3059.$$

Hence the total sum which the trustees will have available in the sinking fund for distribution at the end of the 30 years will be

$$2\cdot 7945+1\cdot 3059=4\cdot 1004.$$

In addition to this the trustees will have in hand the deduction of 30p from all annuities plus the year's interest received at the end of the 30th year in respect of the total amount of annuities purchased by them. This is equal to $\cdot 3+\cdot 7\times\cdot 7625F_{29}$, i.e. to

$$\cdot 3+\frac{\cdot 7\times\cdot 7625\times\cdot 8\times\cdot 3}{14\cdot 233}s^{\cdot 03}_{\overline{29}|}=\cdot 3+\cdot 03\times\cdot 3\times 45\cdot 2189=\cdot 7070.$$

Therefore the total sum to be divided is 4·8074.

Therefore the sum per £1 of unpurchased annuity

$$=\frac{4\cdot 8074}{\cdot 23751}$$

$$=20\cdot 241.$$

The value to yield 4% net is

$$\cdot 7\times\cdot 7625a_{\overline{30}|}+20\cdot 241v^{30}\text{ at }4\%=15\cdot 470$$

or, say, £15·47 per £1 annuity.

Example 10·15

A security is purchased at a price A to yield an effective rate of interest of i per annum. The security is redeemable at a price C in n years and carries dividends of gC per annum payable yearly. Assuming that all dividends are subject to income tax at rate t, and that the same rate of tax is payable at maturity on the excess of C over A show that the net rate of interest secured by the purchase is greater than $i(1-t)$.

The loan can be split into two parts.

(1) A loan of A which is to be repaid after n years at par.
(2) A further payment of $C-A$, due in n years, which must have the same present value as if it were replaced by a series of annual payments of $\dfrac{C-A}{s_{\overline{n|}}}$ at rate i.

From this point of view we should have an investment of A to be repaid at par and yielding an annual income of $gC+\dfrac{C-A}{s_{\overline{n|}}}$. The yield i is therefore determined by

$$iA=gC+\frac{C-A}{s_{\overline{n|}}}$$

or

$$i=\frac{gC}{A}+\frac{C-A}{As_{\overline{n|}}}.$$

If the income is subject to tax at rate t and if tax at the same rate is deducted from the gain $(C-A)$ at the end of n years the yield i' will, by similar reasoning, be defined by

$$i'=\frac{gC(1-t)}{A}+\frac{(C-A)(1-t)}{As_{\overline{n|}}} \quad \text{at rate } i'.$$

But since i' is less than i, $s_{\overline{n|}}$ at rate i' is less than $s_{\overline{n|}}$ at rate i and hence i' is greater than $i(1-t)$.

Example 10·16

A loan bears interest at 5% per annum payable half-yearly on 1 January and 1 July. It is redeemable by ten equal instalments of nominal capital on 1 January 1977, 1979, 1981, 1983 and 1985 at 105 and on 1 January 1987, 1989, 1991, 1993 and 1995 at par. Find the price on 1 January 1966 to yield $3\frac{1}{2}$% net effective assuming income tax at $37\frac{1}{2}$% and gains tax on the excess of amounts paid on redemption over the initial purchase price at the rate of 30%.

At 1 January 1966 the value of the capital payments per £100 loan ignoring the premium of 5% up to 1985 is

$$10\,(v^{11}+v^{13}+\dots v^{29}) = 10\,\frac{a_{\overline{31|}}-a_{\overline{11|}}}{a_{\overline{2|}}} \quad \text{at } 3\tfrac{1}{2}\,\%$$

$$=51{\cdot}244.$$

The net value of the net interest is therefore

$$\frac{\cdot05\times\cdot625}{\cdot035}\,s_{\overline{1}|}^{(2)}\,(100-51\cdot244)=43\cdot910.$$

Ignoring the premium on redemption the value of gains tax, per unit of purchase price, is $\cdot3\times\cdot51244$. The value of the premium is

$$\cdot05\times10\,\frac{a_{\overline{21}|}-a_{\overline{11}|}}{a_{\overline{2}|}}$$

before gains tax, and only 70% of this will be received after tax. The value is therefore $\frac{\cdot35\times5\cdot6964}{1\cdot8997}=1\cdot050$. Hence if A is the price

$$A(1-\cdot3\times51\cdot244)=\cdot7\times51\cdot244+43\cdot910+1\cdot050.$$

Therefore $$A=\frac{80\cdot831}{\cdot84627}$$

$$=95\cdot51$$

Example 10·17

A loan is to be issued bearing interest at $3\frac{1}{4}$% per annum payable half-yearly and redeemable by a cumulative sinking fund of 1% per annum increasing after 10 years to $1\frac{1}{2}$% per annum operating by yearly drawings at £108·33. Find the price to yield 4% per annum net, allowing for income tax at 40% and gains tax at 35% on the excess of amounts paid on redemption over the purchase price.

(This is the same security as in Example 10·11 and the initial calculations to find the term of the loan, 43 years, and the final capital payment, ·051, are identical.)

If interest were yearly, and tax were ignored, the value of the loan to yield 4% net would be

$$4\cdot75a_{\overline{42}|}-\cdot5a_{\overline{10}|}+\cdot051\,(1\cdot03)\,v^{43}=91\cdot838.$$

If the value of the capital repayments is K we have

$$K+\frac{\cdot03}{\cdot04}\,(108\cdot33-K)=91\cdot838,$$

whence $$K=42\cdot362.$$

The value of the interest payable yearly before tax is therefore

$$91\cdot838-42\cdot362=49\cdot476.$$

Net interest, payable half-yearly is therefore $49\cdot476\times\cdot6s_{\overline{1}|}^{(2)}=29\cdot980.$

Hence, if A is the price we have

A = value of capital, less tax, plus value of net interest, plus value of tax on A.

i.e. $$A = 42{\cdot}362 \times {\cdot}65 + 29{\cdot}980 + {\cdot}35 \frac{(42{\cdot}362)}{108{\cdot}33} A.$$

Whence $$A = \frac{57{\cdot}515}{{\cdot}86313}$$
$$= 66{\cdot}64.$$

Example 10·18

A loan is issued bearing interest payable half-yearly at 5% per annum for 15 years, reducing to $4\frac{1}{2}$% thereafter. The loan is to be redeemed by drawings at par by a cumulative sinking fund of $1\frac{1}{2}$% operating yearly. Find the price of the loan to yield 4% effective allowing for income tax at 40% and capital gains tax at 35% on the excess of amounts paid on redemption over the purchase price.

The sinking fund payments accumulate at 5% for 15 years, and the loan then outstanding is $100 - 1{\cdot}5 s_{\overline{15|}}$ at 5%, i.e. 67·632. In the 16th year the total service is 6 and the interest is $\cdot 045 \times 67{\cdot}632 = 3{\cdot}0434$. The amount available for sinking fund is therefore 2·9566, and this accumulates at $4\frac{1}{2}$%. Hence

$$2{\cdot}9566 s_{\overline{n|}} = 67{\cdot}632,$$

whence $$n = 16,$$

and there is a final payment of ·460 due after 32 years. The value at 4% of the capital payments is

$$1{\cdot}5\,[v + v^2 (1{\cdot}05) + \dots + v^{15} (1{\cdot}05)^{14}]$$
$$+ 2{\cdot}9566 v^{15}\,[v + v^2 (1{\cdot}045) + \dots + v^{16} (1{\cdot}045)^{15}] + {\cdot}460 v^{32}$$

$$= \frac{1{\cdot}5}{{\cdot}05 - {\cdot}04} [(1{\cdot}05)^{15} v^{15} - 1] + \frac{2{\cdot}9566 v^{15}}{{\cdot}045 - {\cdot}04} [(1{\cdot}045)^{16} v^{16} - 1] + {\cdot}460 v^{32}$$

$$= 49{\cdot}474.$$

The value of the loan, if interest were payable yearly and taxation were ignored would be

$$6{\cdot}5 a_{\overline{15|}} + 6\,(a_{\overline{31|}} - a_{\overline{15|}}) + {\cdot}460\,(1{\cdot}045)\, v^{32} = 111{\cdot}227.$$

The value of half-yearly interest less tax at 40% is therefore

$${\cdot}6\,[111{\cdot}227 - 49{\cdot}474]\, s^{(2)}_{\overline{1|}} = 37{\cdot}419.$$

The value of the capital, less tax at 35 % is

$$\cdot 65 \times 49\cdot 474 = 32\cdot 158.$$

The value of the tax on the purchase price is

$$\cdot 35 \times \cdot 49474 \text{ per unit} = \cdot 17316.$$

Hence $$A\,(\cdot 82684) = 69\cdot 577$$

and $$A = 84\cdot 15.$$

Example 10·19

A loan is issued bearing interest at $4\frac{1}{2}$ % per annum, payable half-yearly. It is to be redeemed in 25 years by a cumulative sinking fund operating by yearly drawings. The redemption price in the first 10 years is 90 and thereafter is 100. Find the value to yield 5 % net allowing for a tax of 25 % on all interest payments and at the same rate on the excess of the amounts received at redemption over the purchase price.

Per 100 nominal of loan, if the annual service is $4\cdot 5 + X$ the amount available for sinking fund in the first year is X, and this accumulates for 10 years at 5 % and for 15 at $4\frac{1}{2}$ %. The final payment of capital and interest is therefore $X\,(1\cdot 05)^{10}\,(1\cdot 045)^{15}$ and this must equal the service

$$\therefore\ 3\cdot 1524X = 4\cdot 5 + X,$$

whence $$X = 2\cdot 091.$$

The value of the loan to yield 5 % ignoring tax is therefore $6\cdot 591 a_{\overline{25}|}$ assuming interest is payable yearly, i.e. 92·893. The value at 5 % of the capital payments is

$$2\cdot 091\,[v + v^2\,(1\cdot 05) + v^3\,(1\cdot 05)^2 + \ldots + v^{10}\,(1\cdot 05)^9]$$

$$+ 2\cdot 091\,(1\cdot 05)^{10}\,[v^{11} + v^{12}\,(1\cdot 045) + v^{13}\,(1\cdot 045)^2 + \ldots\ v^{25}\,(1\cdot 045)^{14}]$$

$$= 20\cdot 91v + 2\cdot 091v\,\frac{1-(1\cdot 045)^{15}\,(1\cdot 05)^{-15}}{1-(1\cdot 045)\,(1\cdot 05)^{-1}}$$

$$= 19\cdot 914 + 28\cdot 893$$

$$= 48\cdot 807.$$

The value of the gross interest payable yearly is therefore $92\cdot 893 - 48\cdot 807$, i.e. 44·086 and the value of the net interest, payable half-yearly is therefore $\cdot 75 s_{\overline{1}|}^{(2)} \times 44\cdot 086 = 33\cdot 473$. Since the redemption price varies the value of the tax on capital must be calculated in two parts.

Years 1–10

The cash payment at the end of t years is $2{\cdot}091\ (1{\cdot}05)^{t-1}$. The nominal amount of loan repaid is $\dfrac{2{\cdot}091}{{\cdot}9}\ (1{\cdot}05)^{t-1}$ and if A is the price per 100 of nominal loan tax is due on the difference between the cash received and the nominal cost, i.e. on

$$2{\cdot}091\ (1{\cdot}05)^{t-1} - \frac{2{\cdot}091}{{\cdot}9}\ (1{\cdot}05)^{t-1}\frac{A}{100}.$$

The value at 5 % of this series is, as already calculated, $19{\cdot}914 - {\cdot}22127A$.

Years 11–25

The cash payment at the end of t years is $2{\cdot}091\ (1{\cdot}05)^{10}\ (1{\cdot}045)^{t-1}$ and this is also the nominal amount of loan repaid. Tax is therefore due on

$$2{\cdot}091\ (1{\cdot}05)^{10}\ (1{\cdot}045)^{t-1}\left[1 - \frac{A}{100}\right].$$

The value at 5 % of this series is, as already calculated $28{\cdot}893 - {\cdot}28893A$.

Hence $\qquad A = 48{\cdot}807 \times {\cdot}75 + 33{\cdot}473 - {\cdot}25\ ({\cdot}5102A)$,

whence $\qquad A = \mathbf{80{\cdot}32}$.

EXERCISES 10

10·1 A loan is redeemable at 110 per £100 nominal over a period of years. Interest is paid yearly at the rate of $5\frac{1}{2}$%. The price of the loan to yield 4 % effective is £A per £100 bond and the price of one bond to yield 4 % effective allowing for income tax at $37\frac{1}{2}$ % is £ $(A-14)$. If a man buys one bond at a price of £A, how many years must elapse before the bond is drawn in order that he may earn at least 4 % on his investment, ignoring income tax?

10·2 A debenture of £40,000 bearing interest at 4% per annum payable half-yearly on 1 April and 1 October is redeemable in 4 equal instalments on 1 April 1956, 1957, 1958 and 1959 at premiums of 4, 3, 2 and 1% respectively. Find the price on 1 June 1952 to yield $2\frac{1}{2}$% per annum convertible half-yearly allowing for income tax at $47\frac{1}{2}$ % to 1 April 1953 and 50 % thereafter.

10·3 A loan of £100,000 in bonds of £100 each is to be redeemed by 20 annual drawings each of 50 bonds, the first drawing taking place in 1 year. The redemption price of a bond drawn after n years is

$$£\ [100 + ({\cdot}99515)^{-n}].$$

Interest on the loan is payable half-yearly at 4 % per annum and the loan is issued at a price to yield on the average 3 % effective, allowing for income tax at 25 %. What is the probability that the holder of one bond purchased at the issue price will secure at least this yield?

10·4 An assurance company has a substantial holding of a loan of nominal value £90,000 which is redeemable as follows:

Date	No. of bonds of £100 redeemable	Redemption price (%)
1 October 1954	200	105
1 October 1959	200	106
1 October 1964	300	108
1 October 1974	200	110

Interest on the loan is paid half-yearly at the rate of 4 % per annum. The market price of the loan on 1 October 1949 was £105·05 %. Under a scheme of reorganization the borrowers wished to alter the terms of the loan and made the following offers to each holder of one bond:

(i) to repay the bond on 1 November 1949 at 106,

or (ii) to issue a terminable annuity of £6·70 payable half-yearly for 25 years from 1 October 1949. For income tax purposes the schedule of principal and interest for these annuities will be drawn up at 4 % per annum convertible half-yearly,

or (iii) to allot £105 of a loan which will be repayable at par on 1 October in any of the years 1964–74 inclusive at the borrower's option. Interest will be paid half-yearly at the rate of 4 % per annum.

Which offer is most advantageous to the assurance company if it is liable to income tax at $37\frac{1}{2}$ % and if other comparable securities giving the same net yield as the present loan are readily available?

10·5 Find the price of the security in Exercise 9·4 to yield 4 % effective allowing for income tax at the rate of $27\frac{1}{2}$ %.

10·6 On 1 January 1930 a loan of £1,000,000 was issued, redeemable by a cumulative sinking fund of $1\frac{1}{2}$ % of the original nominal loan, operating by yearly drawings at 110. Interest, which is paid yearly, is calculated at $5\frac{1}{2}$ %. On 2 January 1950, X purchased a small holding of the loan at the average price A per bond, which would have secured for a purchaser of the whole loan then outstanding, a net yield of 3 % per annum effective, after allowing for income tax at 25 %. To safeguard himself against the early redemption of his bond X proposed to Y that he would pay him a fixed proportion of each net interest payment received on any individual bond, if Y would pay him the sum of £ $(A-110)$ when that bond was redeemed. What net yields will X secure on his investment, allowing for income tax at 25 %, if Y makes his calculations

(*a*) on the basis of 3% effective,
and (*b*) on the basis of 4% effective

and ignores any question of income tax in his calculations?

CHAPTER 11

VARYING RATES OF INTEREST. DETERMINATION OF YIELDS

11·1. Varying rates of interest

The fundamental relationship which has formed the basis of the whole of the theory of compound interest as discussed in this book is expressed in the equation:

$$\delta_t = \frac{1}{f(t)} \frac{d}{dt} f(t)$$

where δ_t is the force of interest at time t, and $f(t)$ is the amount at time t of a unit accumulating at compound interest. In practice, of course, it is rare to find any transaction which is based directly on a force of interest, which varies from moment to moment. As the main part of this book has been devoted to the practical application of the theory of compound interest, the major emphasis has naturally been on the *effect* of the operation of a force of interest and most of the work has been based on the tacit assumption either that δ_t does not vary, or varies only at the end of fixed intervals of time. While this is a convenient practical assumption there are points of considerable theoretical interest in considering the problem strictly in terms of a varying force of interest δ_t and as will be shown there are certain types of practical problem which can more readily be solved by this approach. For example, it may be desired in some calculation involving a lengthy future period that some assumption should be made about the probable future course of the rate of interest at which money can be invested, and it will be seen that on certain assumptions as to the method of variation such problems can be solved more readily by considering a variation in δ_t rather than in i_t—the effective *rate* of interest at time t. It may be objected that the conception of a force of interest which varies from moment to moment is artificial but this is not so. For example, the funds of an assurance company may be considered as providing an example of a close approximation to a fund accumulating at a continuously varying force of interest. The assurance company's funds vary from day to day as premiums and interest are received, and claims, surrenders and expenses paid, and the surplus of income over expenditure is invested from day to day at varying rates of interest.

11·2. Methods of variation

There is no theoretical limit to the assumptions which may be made as to the manner in which δ_t varies. If, however, results are to be obtained which are to assist in solving practical problems it is necessary, and reasonable, to make assumptions which will lead to expressions capable of being evaluated analytically and the following suggest themselves for investigation:

(*a*) that the force of interest varies continuously as a linear function,

(*b*) that the force of interest varies continuously as an exponential function,

(*c*) that the force of interest varies continuously but tends towards a finite limiting value.

11·3. Force of interest varying as a linear function

Let $\delta_t = \delta_0 - rt$. Then since

$$\delta_t = \frac{1}{f(t)} \frac{d}{dt} f(t)$$

$$= \frac{d}{dt} \log_e f(t),$$

$$f(t) = e^{\int_0^t \delta_t \, dt}$$

$$= e^{\int_0^t (\delta_0 - rt) \, dt}$$

$$= \exp\left\{\left[t\delta_0 - \frac{rt^2}{2}\right]_0^t\right\}$$

$$= \exp\left\{t\delta_0 - \frac{rt^2}{2}\right\}.$$

If r is positive δ_t gradually decreases and will eventually become negative. It is therefore desirable to postulate a limiting positive value for δ_t, say δ_n, and to assume that for all values of t greater than n the force of interest remains constant. In these conditions

$$\log_e f(t) = \int_0^n (\delta_0 - rt)\,dt + \int_n^t \delta_n\,dt$$

$$= n\delta_0 - \frac{n^2 r}{2} + (t-n)\,\delta_n$$

$$= n\delta_0 - \frac{n}{2}(\delta_0 - \delta_n) + (t-n)\,\delta_n.$$

$$\therefore\ f(t) = e^{\frac{1}{2}n(\delta_0-\delta_n)+t\delta_n}$$

The present value of 1 due at the end of t years is of course $[f(t)]^{-1}$ or $e^{-\frac{1}{2}n(\delta_0-\delta_n)-t\delta_n}$.

It is interesting to consider during the period when δ_t is varying, what the corresponding effective rates of interest would be. If they are $i_1, i_2, \ldots$, etc., then

$$f(1) = (1+i_1)f(0)$$

and generally

$$f(t+1) = (1+i_{t+1})f(t)$$

or

$$(1+i_{t+1}) = \frac{f(t+1)}{f(t)}$$

$$= \exp\left[(t+1)\,\delta_0 - r\frac{(t+1)^2}{2} - t\delta_0 + \frac{rt^2}{2}\right]$$

$$= \exp\left[\delta_0 - \frac{r}{2}(2t+1)\right].$$

$$\therefore\ \frac{1+i_{t+1}}{1+i_t} = e^{-r}$$

$$= \exp\left[-\frac{\delta_0-\delta_n}{n}\right]$$

i.e. $(1+i_1)$, $(1+i_2)$, etc., vary in Geometric Progression.

11·4. Force of interest varying as an exponential function

Let
$$\delta_t = \delta_0 r^t.$$

Then
$$\log_e f(t) = \int_0^t \delta_0 r^t dt$$
$$= \delta_0 \left[\frac{r^t}{\log r}\right]_0^t$$
$$= \frac{\delta_0}{\log r}(r^t - 1).$$
$$\therefore\ f(t) = \exp\left[\frac{\delta_0}{\log r}(r^t - 1)\right].$$

If $i_1, i_2, \ldots$, etc., as before are the corresponding effective rates of interest.

$$1 + i_{t+1} = \frac{f(t+1)}{f(t)}$$
$$= \exp\left\{\frac{\delta_0}{\log r}[r^{t+1} - r^t]\right\}$$
$$= \exp\left[\frac{\delta_0}{\log r} r^t(r - 1)\right]$$
$$= e^{kr^t},$$

where
$$k = \frac{\delta_0}{\log r}(r - 1).$$

In this case there is no constant relationship between successive values of $1 + i_1$, $1 + i_2$, etc.

11·5. Force of interest varying continuously with finite limit

The most obvious method of giving effect to an assumption of this nature would be to assume that the limiting value of the force of interest is, say, a and that $\delta_t = a + br^t$ where r is less than 1. This would give expressions which could be dealt with analytically on lines very similar to those of § 11·4, but it would be subject to the considerable limitations of that section.

An extension of this type of formula was developed at length by C. L. Stoodley in *T.F.A.* vol. 14. Stoodley's formulae were expressed in terms of a varying *rate* of interest and the following is a slight modification of his method to give a corresponding expression for a varying *force* of interest.

Let
$$\delta_t = \frac{a}{a+c^t}\log_e(1+k) + \frac{c^t}{a+c^t}\log_e(1+l),$$

where a, k, and l are constants and $\log_e c = \log_e(1+k) - \log_e(1+l)$. If $c>1$, i.e. if $\log_e(1+k) > \log_e(1+l)$ it will be seen by putting $t=\infty$ that $\delta_\infty = \log_e(1+l)$. Similarly $\delta_{-\infty} = \log_e(1+k)$ and

$$\delta_0 = \frac{a\log_e(1+k)+\log_e(1+l)}{a+1}, \quad \text{whence} \quad a = \frac{\delta_0 - \log_e(1+l)}{\log_e(1+k)-\delta_0}.$$

It follows that the value of δ_t can be determined for any value of t if $\log_e(1+k)$, δ_0 and $\log_e(1+l)$ are known. It is not, however, necessary to know $\log_e(1+k)$, δ_0 and $\log_e(1+l)$ since *any* three values of δ_t are sufficient to fix the general expression for δ_t. Accordingly, to apply the formula, it is necessary to make assumptions only as to the value of the force of interest at any three points of time.

To determine $f(t)$, the amount of 1 at time t it is necessary to evaluate $\int_0^t \delta_t dt$.

$$\begin{aligned}
\log_e f(t) &= \int_0^t \delta_t dt \\
&= \int_0^t \frac{a\log_e(1+k)+c^t\log_e(1+l)}{a+c^t}dt \\
&= \int_0^t \frac{\log_e(1+k)(a+c^t) - c^t[\log_e(1+k)-\log_e(1+l)]}{a+c^t}dt \\
&= \int_0^t \left[\log_e(1+k) - \frac{c^t\log c}{a+c^t}\right]dt \\
&= [t\log_e(1+k) - \log_e(a+c^t)]_0^t \\
&= t\log_e(1+k) - \log_e(a+c^t) + \log_e(a+1).
\end{aligned}$$

If $\delta_{(k)}$ be written for $\log_e(1+k)$

$$\begin{aligned}
\log_e f(t) &= t\delta_{(k)} + \log\frac{a+1}{a+c^t} \\
&= \log_e \frac{e^{t\delta_{(k)}}(a+1)}{a+c^t}.
\end{aligned}$$

$$\therefore\ f(t) = \frac{e^{t\delta_{(k)}}(a+1)}{a+c^t}.$$

If i_t is the effective rate of interest at time t

$$1+i_t=\frac{f(t)}{f(t-1)}=e^{\delta_{(k)}}\frac{a+c^{t-1}}{a+c^t}$$
$$=(1+k)\frac{a+c^{t-1}}{a+c^t}.$$

The present value of 1 due at the end of time t is $[f(t)]^{-1}$

$$=\frac{e^{-t\delta_{(k)}}(a+c^t)}{a+1}$$
$$=\frac{a}{a+1}e^{-t\delta_{(k)}}+\frac{c^t}{a+1}e^{-t\delta_{(k)}}$$

and remembering that $c=\dfrac{1+k}{1+l}$ this may be written as

$$\frac{a}{a+1}(1+k)^{-t}+\frac{1}{a+1}(1+l)^{-t}$$
$$=\frac{a}{a+1}v_k^t+\frac{1}{a+1}v_l^t.$$

Hence the present value of 1 is found as a blend of the present values of 1 at two different rates of interest.

11·6. Expressions for $s_{\overline{n}|}$ and $a_{\overline{n}|}$ at varying rates of interest

In the notation of § 11·1 the amount of an annuity of 1 per annum when the rate of interest varies may be found as follows. Since a unit invested now will amount to $f(t)$ in t years, and to $f(n)$ in n years $(n>t)$ the amount after $(n-t)$ years of a unit invested at time t is clearly $\dfrac{f(n)}{f(t)}$. Hence denoting the amount of an annuity of 1 per annum when the rate of interest varies by $s'_{\overline{n}|}$ it will be seen that

$$s'_{\overline{n}|}=\sum_1^n\left(\frac{f(n)}{f(t)}\right).$$

The present value of a similar annuity, $a'_{\overline{n}|}$ say, is clearly the sum of the present values of the individual payments, i.e.

$$a'_{\overline{n}|}=\sum_1^n\left(\frac{1}{f(t)}\right)$$
$$=\frac{1}{f(n)}s'_{\overline{n}|}$$

as is of course obvious on general grounds.

If the annuities are payable continuously the corresponding expressions would be

$$\bar{s}'_{\overline{n}|} = \int_0^n \frac{f(n)}{f(t)}\,dt$$

and

$$\bar{a}'_{\overline{n}|} = \int_0^n \frac{1}{f(t)}\,dt.$$

It must, however, be emphasized that these expressions will lead to practical results in numerical work only if the function $[f(t)]^{-1}$ is such as can be summed by ordinary algebraic means, or, in the case of the continuous annuity such as can be integrated. This will in fact rarely be the case as may be seen by considering the form the expressions take if the assumptions of §§ 11·3 and 11·4 are made. Since the values of $\bar{s}'_{\overline{n}|}$ can readily be found from those of $\bar{a}'_{\overline{n}|}$, and since the methods of the integral calculus are relatively easier to apply only the function $\bar{a}'_{\overline{n}|}$ will be considered.

Considering first the assumption $\delta_t = \delta_0 - rt$, where $r = \dfrac{\delta_0 - \delta_n}{n}$ and let $t < n$. Then, as in § 11·3

$$f(t) = e^{t\delta_0 - \frac{rt^2}{2}} \quad \text{and} \quad \bar{a}'_{\overline{n}|} = \int_0^n e^{-t\delta_0 + \frac{rt^2}{2}}\,dt.$$

This integral cannot be evaluated by analytical means. It would be possible to expand the series $e^{-t\delta_0 + \frac{rt^2}{2}}$ and integrate each term individually, but although it may be shown that the resultant series is convergent, it converges so slowly that a prohibitively large number of terms would have to be evaluated in order to reach a numerical answer. In practice a suitable formula of approximate integration would probably have to be used.

If it be assumed that $\delta_t = \delta_0 r^t$ the expression for the value of $\bar{a}'_{\overline{n}|}$ would be $\int_0^n e^{-\frac{\delta_0}{\log r}(r^t - 1)}\,dt$ and similar difficulties will arise over its evaluation.

If, however, the assumptions underlying Stoodley's method are made these difficulties vanish. Since

$$\frac{1}{f(t)} = \frac{a}{a+1} v_k^t + \frac{1}{a+1} v_l^t$$

it will be seen at once that

$$\bar{a}'_{\overline{n}|} = \frac{a}{a+1}\int_0^n v_k^t\,dt + \frac{1}{a+1}\int_0^n v_l^t\,dt$$

$$= \frac{a}{a+1}\,\bar{a}^k_{\overline{n}|} + \frac{1}{a+1}\,\bar{a}^l_{\overline{n}|}$$

and that a similar expression holds good for $a_{\overline{n}|}$. The evaluation of these expressions, particularly if k and l are tabular rates of interest is relatively a simple matter. Expressions for $\bar{s}'_{\overline{n}|}$ and $s_{\overline{n}|}$ are readily found from the relationships $\bar{s}'_{\overline{n}|} = f(n)\,\bar{a}_{\overline{n}|}$ and $s_{\overline{n}|} = f(n)\,a_{\overline{n}|}$ where $f(n) = e^{n\delta(k)}.\dfrac{a+1}{a+c^n}$. It will be apparent therefore that Stoodley's method is both simple and powerful in readily giving effect to a varying force of interest.

11·7. Determination of yields

The main emphasis in preceding chapters has been on determining either the present value or the amount of a given series of payments at a specified rate of interest. The cognate problem, that of determining the rate of interest at which a given series of payments will have a specified present value or amount has been discussed briefly in Chapter 7 in the particular case of redeemable securities. In this chapter it is proposed to consider this problem in greater detail. The basic problem is, of course, to solve an equation in which i, the rate of interest, is the only unknown since the algebraic expression for the present value of the given series of payments (or the amount as the case may be) can be equated to the given numerical value. To simplify the equation regard will of course be had to the considerations discussed in Chapter 3 affecting the choice of the time interval on the basis of which the operation of discounting or accumulation is to be performed. The general principles are the same no matter how frequently interest is convertible and in the discussion which follows it will be assumed that the given series of payments is made at yearly intervals and that an annual effective rate of interest is employed.

In general it will be found that an equation of the type

$$f(i) = C$$

is of such a nature that it does not permit of an exact solution and recourse must be had to approximate methods. These may broadly be classified as follows:

(*a*) those, already discussed in Chapter 7 which involve evaluating $f(i)$ at two trial rates of interest, and then determining i by inverse first difference interpolation;

(*b*) those based on an expansion of $f(i)$ in terms of i leading to an equation which can be solved approximately by ordinary algebraic processes.

Method (*a*) is the normal practical method. In simpler cases useful formulae can be developed by method (*b*), but as soon as any complications are introduced the expressions resulting from this method become too involved for practical work. As will be seen it is possible to obtain a greater degree of accuracy (with the tables generally available for use) under method (*b*) than under method (*a*), but the latter gives results which are usually sufficiently accurate for all practical purposes.

11·8. Values of annuities

One of the simplest types of equation to be solved is where the present value of an annuity is known, i.e. where it is required to find the rate of interest which satisfies the equation $a_{\overline{n}|}=C$. As $a_{\overline{n}|}=\frac{1-(1+i)^{-n}}{i}$ the most obvious method of solution would be to expand $a_{\overline{n}|}$ in ascending powers of i, and by neglecting terms of higher degree in i than the first or second to obtain a simple, or a quadratic equation for i which could be solved in the ordinary way. This method is not, however, satisfactory. The series obtained by expanding $\frac{1-(1+i)^{-n}}{i}$ is only slowly convergent and the error involved in neglecting terms of higher degree than the first or second is considerable, particularly if n is large. In practice it will be found that a series which converges more rapidly can be obtained by considering the reciprocal of $a_{\overline{n}|}$, and expanding it in powers of i. Even so, though better results may thus be obtained, the method is still not sufficiently accurate to enable the value of i to be found with reasonable accuracy directly from the annuity value.

The expansion of $(a_{\overline{n}|})^{-1}$ in terms of i is as follows:

$$\frac{1}{a_{\overline{n}|}}=\frac{i}{1-(1+i)^{-n}}$$

$$=\frac{i}{1-\left(1-ni+\frac{n(n+1)}{2!}i^2-\dots\right)}$$

$$=\frac{1}{n\left(1-\frac{n+1}{2!}i+\frac{(n+1)(n+2)}{3!}i^2-\dots\right)}$$

$$=\frac{1}{n}\left[1+\frac{n+1}{2}i+\frac{n^2-1}{12}i^2-\frac{n^2-1}{24}i^3-\dots\right]. \qquad (11\cdot1)$$

If n is large the value of the coefficients is also large, and correspondingly the error in neglecting terms of the second or higher degree is too great to be overlooked. It is necessary therefore to devise some method which will replace i by a smaller quantity, without affecting the value of the coefficients, and thus minimize the error caused by the terms neglected. The method usually adopted is to proceed by successive approximations as follows. If i' is a first approximation to i then i may be written as $(i'+x)$ where x is small in relation to i'. By replacing i in the expansion above by $(i'+x)$ an expression will be obtained which involves values of $a_{\overline{n}|}$ and v^n at the known rate i' and a series in ascending powers of x instead of the previous series in ascending powers of i. Since x is by hypothesis small the error involved in neglecting the later terms in the new series is less than in the old.

Let $$\frac{1}{a^{i}_{\overline{n}|}}=\frac{i'+x}{1-(1+i'+x)^{-n}}$$

$$=\frac{i'+x}{1-v_1^n(1+xv_1)^{-n}} \text{ where } v_1 \text{ is calculated at rate } i'$$

$$=\frac{i'+x}{\left(1-v_1^n(1-nxv_1+\frac{n(n+1)}{2!}x^2v_1^2-\dots\right)}$$

$$=\frac{i'+x}{1-v_1^n+nxv_1^{n+1}-\frac{n(n+1)}{2!}x^2v_1^{n+2}+\dots}.$$

Now $$1-v_1^n=i'a_{\overline{n}|} \quad \text{at rate } i'$$
$$=i'a \quad \text{say.}$$

$$\therefore \quad \frac{1}{a_{\overline{n}|}^{i}}=\frac{i'+x}{i'a+nxv_1^{n+1}-\frac{n(n+1)}{2!}x^2v_1^{n+2}+\dots}$$

$$=\frac{i'\left(1+\frac{x}{i'}\right)}{i'a\left[1+\frac{nxv_1^{n+1}}{i'a}-\dots\right]}$$

$$=\frac{1}{a}\left(1+\frac{x}{i'}\right)\left(1-\frac{nxv_1^{n+1}}{i'a}\right)$$

neglecting terms in $\left(\frac{x}{i'}\right)^2$ and above.

$$\therefore \quad \frac{1}{a_{\overline{n}|}^{i}}=\frac{1}{C}=\frac{1}{a}\left(1-\frac{nxv_1^{n+1}}{i'a}+\frac{x}{i'}\right).$$

$$\therefore \quad \frac{1}{C}-\frac{1}{a}=\frac{x}{i'a}\left(1-\frac{nv_1^{n+1}}{a}\right)$$

or
$$x=\frac{i'\left[\frac{1}{C}-\frac{1}{a}\right]}{\frac{1}{a}-\frac{nv_1^{n+1}}{a^2}}. \tag{11·2}$$

If interest tables are available it is a relatively simple process to determine x from this equation. Once this has been done a closer approximation still can be obtained by putting $i=i'+x+x_1$ and solving a similar equation for x_1, and so on to any degree of accuracy desired. The values of v^n and $a_{\overline{n}|}$ at rate $i'+x$ might of course have to be calculated by logarithms as $i'+x$ would be unlikely to be a rate of interest for which tables are available.

A numerical example will make this clear. If it is given that $a_{\overline{31}|}=19{\cdot}673$ and it is required to find i the following methods are available:

(*a*) *Inverse interpolation.*

From the interest tables

$$a_{\overline{31}|} \text{ at } 3\% = 20{\cdot}000$$

and
$$a_{\overline{31}|} \text{ at } 3\tfrac{1}{2}\% = 18{\cdot}736.$$

If therefore $a_{\overline{31}|}$ were a linear function in i, i would be

$$\cdot 03+\frac{\cdot 327}{1\cdot 264}\times\cdot 005$$
$$=\cdot 03129.$$

Alternatively if the function $1/a_{\overline{n}|}=\cdot 05083$ be considered then

$$\frac{1}{a_{\overline{n}|}} \text{ at } 3\,\% =\cdot 05$$

$$\frac{1}{a_{\overline{n}|}} \text{ at } 3\tfrac{1}{2}\,\% =\cdot 053372,$$

whence $$i=\cdot 03+\frac{\cdot 00083}{\cdot 003372}\times\cdot 005$$
$$=\cdot 03123.$$

(*b*) *Direct expansion of* $a_{\overline{n}|}$

$$a_{\overline{n}|}=n-\frac{n(n+1)}{2!}i+\frac{n(n+1)(n+2)}{3!}i^2-\dots$$

and neglecting terms involving i^2 and higher powers of i a first approximation to i is given by the equation

$$19\cdot 673=31-\frac{31\times 32}{2}i$$

or $$i=\frac{11\cdot 327\times 2}{31\times 32}$$
$$=\cdot 02284.$$

(*c*) *Direct expansion of* $\frac{1}{a_{\overline{n}|}}$

From the expansion

$$\frac{1}{a_{\overline{n}|}}=\frac{1}{n}\left[1+\frac{n+1}{2}i+\frac{n^2-1}{12}i^2-\dots\right]$$

a first approximation to i would be given by the equation

$$\frac{1}{19\cdot 673}=\frac{1}{31}[1+16i],$$

whence $$i=(\cdot 05083-\cdot 03226)\times\frac{31}{16}$$
$$=\cdot 03598.$$

(*d*) *Successive approximation*

A first approximation to i is clearly ·03 since $\frac{1}{a_{\overline{31}|}}$ at 3 % = ·05.

Hence putting $i = \cdot 03 + x$, x will be found from formula (11·2) above as follows:

$$x = \frac{\cdot 03\,(\cdot 05083 - \cdot 05)}{\cdot 05 - 31 \times \cdot 38834 \times \cdot 0025}$$

$$= \frac{\cdot 0000249}{\cdot 05 - \cdot 03010}$$

$$= \cdot 00125.$$

Hence $$i = \cdot 03125.$$

The actual value of i which satisfies the equation is ·03125 and the results of the four methods may be summarized as follows:

(*a*) *Inverse interpolation* gives an error of ·00004 in excess, if the function operated upon is $a_{\overline{n}|}$, or of ·00002 in defect, if the function chosen is $1/a_{\overline{n}|}$.

(*b*) and (*c*) *Direct expansions* give entirely inadequate results, though it will be noted that the result obtained from the expansion of $1/a_{\overline{n}|}$ is the less unsatisfactory.

(*d*) *Successive approximation* gives at the first trial an accurate answer.

In practical work the interval of ½ % between the two trial rates used for the inverse interpolation would be reduced to say ¼ %, and the inaccuracy of the method would thereby be diminished; even with an interval of ½ %, however, the error in the example given is only in the neighbourhood of ½p %, which is sufficient for most practical purposes.

11·9. Redeemable securities

Methods similar to those in § 11·8 can be used for determining the yield on redeemable securities and generally speaking the same considerations will apply. Consider the simplest case of a security redeemable at the end of n years at a price of C, dividends being paid yearly at rate g per unit of C. Then if A is the price of the security the rate of interest yielded by its purchase will be given by the equation

$$A = Cv^n + gCa_{\overline{n}|}$$
$$= C + (g - i)\,Ca_{\overline{n}|}.$$
$$\therefore\ \frac{A-C}{C} = (g-i)\,a_{\overline{n}|}$$

and writing $k = \dfrac{A-C}{C}$ it will be seen that

$$i = g - \frac{k}{a_{\overline{n}|}}.$$

This equation cannot be solved directly, since $a_{\overline{n}|}$ is calculated at rate i and recourse must again be had to approximate methods. Two possible lines of approach suggest themselves:

(*a*) to replace $\dfrac{1}{a_{\overline{n}|}}$ by an approximation developed on the lines of § 11·8,

(*b*) to solve the equation by trial and error.

Since
$$\frac{1}{a_{\overline{n}|}} = \frac{1}{n}\left[1 + \frac{n+1}{2}i + \frac{n^2-1}{12}i^2 - \dots\right]$$

if terms involving i^2 and higher powers of i are neglected the equation may be written

$$i = g - \frac{k}{n}\left(1 + \frac{n+1}{2}i\right) \text{ approximately,}$$

and hence
$$i = \frac{g - \dfrac{k}{n}}{1 + \dfrac{n+1}{2n}k}. \tag{11·3}$$

It is interesting to note that this formula might be derived by general reasoning as follows: The amount by which the security should be written down per unit is $\dfrac{A-C}{C}$ or k. If this is done by equal amounts of k/n per annum the 'free' dividend per unit will be $g - \dfrac{k}{n}$. The amount of capital invested in the first year is A, i.e. $C+Ck$ and in the last year is $C+\frac{Ck}{n}$. Hence as an approximation the average capital invested is

$$\frac{(C+Ck)+\left(C+\frac{Ck}{n}\right)}{2}=C\left[1+\frac{n+1}{2n}k\right].$$

Hence as the 'free' dividend each year is $\left(g-\frac{k}{n}\right)C$ the yield on the average capital is

$$\frac{g-\frac{k}{n}}{1+\frac{n+1}{2n}k}.$$

This of course is not the correct way to treat a redeemable security in the lender's books but it is not very inaccurate unless the term is long, when the formula gives results which are not always reliable.

This method is at best an approximation and as might be expected it is subject to the limitations mentioned in § 11·8 when the direct expansion of $a_{\overline{n}|}$ was discussed. As, however, it is based on the expansion of $1/a_{\overline{n}|}$ it is at least a better approximation than a formula based on an expansion of $a_{\overline{n}|}$ itself would be, and it is often useful as giving a first approximation to the value of i to enable one of the more accurate methods discussed below to be used.

Methods of successive approximation may be employed in just the same way as in the simple case of the annuity value discussed in § 11·8. If, as before, i' is a rate of interest differing from i by a small quantity x the equation

$$(g-i)=\frac{k}{a_{\overline{n}|}} \quad \text{at rate } i$$

may be written as

$$(g-i'-x)=k\left[\frac{1}{a}\right]\left[1-\frac{nxv_1^{n+1}}{i'a}+\frac{x}{i'}\right]$$

if the approximation to the value of $\frac{1}{a_{\overline{n}|}}$ used in § 11·8 is again employed. Hence, as a first approximation

$$x=i'.\frac{g-i'-\dfrac{k}{a}}{i'+k\dfrac{a-nv_1^{n+1}}{a^2}}, \tag{11·4}$$

where $a=a_{\overline{n}|}$ at rate i' and v_1^{n+1} is also calculated at this rate. This formula gives good practical results, and it could of course be used to give any degree of accuracy required by further trials using $(i'+x)+x_1$ as the next approximation to i and determining x_1 on the same lines as above.

The process of inverse interpolation may be applied either to the equation $A=Cv^n+gCa_{\overline{n}|}$ or to its derivative $i=g-\dfrac{k}{a_{\overline{n}|}}$. The first method has already been discussed in Chapter 7. On general grounds one would expect it to give less accurate results than the second, since in the second the variable function in i is $(1/a_{\overline{n}|})$ and it has been seen that this function may more nearly be represented by a linear function of i than $a_{\overline{n}|}$ itself can. The second method, however, cannot be employed in more complicated cases, such as securities with varying dividends, securities redeemable by a cumulative sinking fund, and so on. The first method can be adopted in all such cases and it has been suggested that to increase its accuracy the function to be operated on should be $1/A$ or even $\dfrac{1}{(A)^{\frac{1}{2}}}$ which tend to give better results in practice. These refinements need not however concern the student at this stage of his work.

A numerical example will more clearly illustrate the different methods discussed in this section. Consider a security bought at 114·237 which is redeemable at 100 at the end of 30 years and carries dividends of 4% per annum payable yearly. The yield, i, is the rate of interest which satisfies the equation

$$114{\cdot}237=100v^{30}+4a_{\overline{30}|}.$$

If formula (11·3) be used a first approximation to i would be

$$\frac{{\cdot}04-\dfrac{{\cdot}14237}{30}}{1+\dfrac{31}{60}\times{\cdot}14237}=\frac{{\cdot}035254}{1{\cdot}07356}={\cdot}03284.$$

To obtain a more accurate answer one of the other methods discussed above would have to be used.

For example if i be taken as $\cdot 03+x$ formula (11·4) would give

$$x=\cdot 03\,\frac{\cdot 04-\cdot 03-\dfrac{k}{a_{\overline{30}|}^{\cdot 03}}}{\cdot 03+k\,\dfrac{a_{\overline{30}|}^{\cdot 03}-30v_{.03}^{31}}{(a_{\overline{30}|}^{\cdot 03})^2}}$$

$$=\cdot 03\,\frac{\cdot 01-\dfrac{\cdot 14237}{19\cdot 6004}}{\cdot 03+\cdot 14237\,\dfrac{7\cdot 6007}{(19\cdot 6004)^2}}$$

$$=\cdot 03\times\frac{\cdot 002736}{\cdot 032817}$$

$$=\cdot 002501,$$

whence $$i=\cdot 03250.$$

The method of inverse interpolation may be employed as follows:

(*a*) If $A=100v^{30}+4a_{\overline{30}|}$ then at 3% A will be found to be 119·601 and at $3\frac{1}{2}$% A will be found to be 109·196.

Hence the value of i for which

$$A=114\cdot 237 \text{ is } \cdot 03+\frac{5\cdot 364}{10\cdot 405}\times\cdot 005,$$

i.e. $$\cdot 03258.$$

(*b*) If the same process were applied to $1/A$ the value at 3% would be $\dfrac{1}{119\cdot 601}$, i.e. ·0083686, and at $3\frac{1}{2}$% $\dfrac{1}{109\cdot 196}$, i.e. ·0091578. The value of i at which

$$\frac{1}{A}=\frac{1}{114\cdot 237}=\cdot 0087537$$

is therefore

$$\cdot 03+\frac{\cdot 0003851}{\cdot 0007892}\times\cdot 005=\cdot 03244.$$

(*c*) If the process is applied to the formula $i=g-\dfrac{k}{a_{\overline{n}|}}$, then

If $i=\cdot 03$: $\quad g-\dfrac{k}{a_{\overline{n}|}}=\cdot 04-\dfrac{\cdot 14237}{19\cdot 6004}=\cdot 032736.$

$$\text{If } i = \cdot 035: \quad g - \frac{k}{a_{\overline{n}|}} = \cdot 04 - \frac{\cdot 14237}{18 \cdot 39205} = \cdot 032259.$$

Hence the value of i for which $g - \dfrac{k}{a_{\overline{n}|}} = i$ will be

$$\cdot 03 + \frac{\cdot 005\,[\cdot 032736 - \cdot 03]}{\cdot 005 + (\cdot 032736 - \cdot 032259)} = \cdot 03250.$$

The actual value of i is ·0325 and the results obtained by the various methods may be summarized as follows:

(1) By use of formula (11·3): error in excess ·00033.
(2) By use of formula (11·4): no error.
(3) By inverse interpolation: (*a*) error in excess ·00008,
(*b*) error in defect ·00006,
(*c*) no error.

These results are in accordance with the general trends discussed above. It is fair to say that the result in 3 above would have been more accurate had an interval of interpolation of less than $\frac{1}{2}$% been used.

11·10. Determination of net yields

Bearing in mind the principles of Chapter 10, that net payments should always be valued at a net rate of interest, it should be apparent that there is no real difficulty in determining a yield when allowance has to be made for income tax. If the ordinary method of inverse first difference interpolation is used then the trial rates to be employed will be net rates, and provided the net payments are valued the result will follow as in § 11·9. If the formula $i = \dfrac{g - \frac{k}{n}}{1 + \frac{n+1}{2n} k}$, or one of its extensions is used it will be necessary to replace g by $g(1-t)$ if t is the rate of tax. It should, however, be noted that this method will not apply to the valuation of an annuity-certain subject to income tax on the interest portion of each instalment. The reason is that the payments are no longer uniform, since the amount of tax deducted from each instalment decreases as the interest portion of the instalment decreases and the basic equation can no longer be written as $a_{\overline{n}|}=C$ as in § 11·8. In this case, as in all other similar cases, the simple method of inverse interpolation will usually give a sufficiently accurate answer more readily than any of the other methods.

11·11. Running yields and redemption yields

The term 'running yield' is used in financial parlance to denote the rate of interest which the dividend represents in relation to the price paid, i.e. the yield without making any allowance for the profit or loss on redemption. The term 'flat yield' is also used with the same meaning. The 'redemption yield' is the true yield, due allowance for profit or loss on redemption being made.

It has been shown in § 11·9 that the yield on a security redeemable at the end of n years, and bought at a premium of k per unit of redemption price is given by the equation

$$i=g-\frac{k}{a_{\overline{n}|}}$$

and bearing in mind that $\frac{1}{a_{\overline{n}|}}=\frac{1}{s_{\overline{n}|}}+i$ this may be written

$$i=g-k\left[\frac{1}{s_{\overline{n}|}}+i\right],$$

i.e.

$$i=\frac{g-\frac{k}{s_{\overline{n}|}}}{1+k}$$

or

$$i=\frac{g}{1+k}-\frac{\frac{k}{1+k}}{s_{\overline{n}|}},$$

where $s_{\overline{n}|}$ is calculated at rate i. Since $(1+k)$ is the price paid $\frac{g}{1+k}$ is the running yield and $\frac{\frac{k}{1+k}}{s_{\overline{n}|}}$ is the annual sinking fund per unit of purchase price which, if accumulated at rate i will replace the loss of capital on redemption. Hence redemption yield = running yield − sinking fund. This suggests that approximately the redemption yield can be found by deducting from the running yield the sinking fund calculated at a rate of interest approximating to the required yield. Using the method of successive approximation a very close estimate of the true yield can generally be obtained in this way. For example in the case discussed in § 11·9, $k = 14{\cdot}237$ and the running yield is $\frac{4}{114{\cdot}237} = {\cdot}03502$. It is clear from the application of formula (11·3) that i is in the neighbourhood of ·0325, and using this as a first approximation and the yield would be given by

$$i = {\cdot}03502 - \frac{14{\cdot}237}{114{\cdot}237} \times \frac{1}{s_{\overline{30}|}} \text{ at } 3\tfrac{1}{4}\%$$

$$= {\cdot}03251$$

which is sufficiently close to the assumed yield of ·0325 to require no further investigation.

If allowance is made for income tax at rate t, the net yield i' is given by the equation

$$i' = g(1-t) - \frac{k}{a_{\overline{n}|}}$$

which can be expressed in the form

$$i' = \frac{g(1-t)}{1+k} - \frac{\frac{k}{1+k}}{s_{\overline{n}|}},$$

where $s_{\overline{n}|}$ is calculated at rate i'.

Hence net redemption yield

= net running yield − sinking fund (at net rate).

A similar process of successive approximation to the net yield can be used as in the case of the gross yield.

It is important to note that the sinking fund to be deducted from the running yield to arrive at the redemption rate is calculated at the *gross* redemption yield when dealing with gross yields, and at the *net* redemption yield when dealing with net yields. A common rule for finding the net redemption yield is 'Deduct from the gross redemption yield the tax on the gross running yield'. This is not strictly correct and the fallacy involved will be apparent if the principles set out above are clearly understood. The true net yield may be expressed symbolically as

$$i' = \left(\frac{g}{1+k} - \frac{\dfrac{k}{1+k}}{s'_{\overline{n}|}}\right) - t\frac{g}{1+k},$$

where $s'_{\overline{n}|}$ is calculated at rate i'. In terms of the rule referred to the approximate net yield would be

$$i' = \left(\frac{g}{1+k} - \frac{\dfrac{k}{1+k}}{s_{\overline{n}|}}\right) - t\frac{g}{1+k},$$

where $s_{\overline{n}|}$ is calculated at rate i. In practice, however, it will be found that the rule gives a reasonably close approximation to the true net yield if the term involved is not long, and if the price paid is not greatly different from the redemption price.

11·12. Further approximate methods

Many actuarial notes have been written developing the methods of §§ 11·8 and 11·9 in an effort both to make them applicable to more complicated examples, to improve their accuracy and to simplify them to make them more readily available for use in dealing with the day-to-day problems of an Investment Department. These extensions of the basic formula go beyond the scope of this book, but reference may be made by those interested to the following papers:

(*a*) Extensions of formula (11·3): *J.I.A.* vol. 60, p. 341; *J.I.A.* vol. 72, p. 452.

(*b*) Extensions of formulae based on the methods of § 11·8 applied to redeemable securities, and allowing for income tax: *J.I.A.* vol. 49, p. 366; *J.I.A.* vol. 50, pp. 123 and 247; *J.I.A.* vol. 51, pp. 24 and 144; *J.I.A.* vol. 56, p. 95.

(*c*) Extension of approximate formulae to problems including accumulative sinking funds: *J.I.A.* vol. 60, p. 229; *J.I.A.* vol. 64, p. 350; *J.I.A.* vol. 65, pp. 229 and 356.

Another line of approach which has been suggested in *J.I.A.* vol. 65, p. 49 depends on substituting for $\bar{a}_{\overline{n}|}$ an approximate expression derived from a formula of approximate integration. Since $\bar{a}_{\overline{n}|}=\int_0^n v^t\,dt$, $\bar{a}_{\overline{n}|}$ may approximately be written if Simpson's Rule is applied, as $\frac{n}{6}(1+4v^{n/2}+v^n)$ which gives a quadratic equation in $v^{n/2}$ from which the rate of interest can readily be found. The method can be applied to the non-continuous annuity $a_{\overline{n}|}$ by writing $a_{\overline{n}|}=\bar{a}_{\overline{n}|}-\frac{1}{2}(1-v^n)$ approximately. Such developments are also beyond the scope of this book.

11·14. The following examples illustrate the work done in this chapter:

Example 11·1

Find, in its simplest form, an expression for the amount at the end of 12 years of a continuous annuity certain payable during the first 5 years at the rate of t per annum and during the remainder of the term at double that rate. Interest is at rate i for the first 6 years and at rate j for the second 6 years.

At the end of 5 years the accumulated payments to date will amount to

$$\int_0^5 t(1+i)^{5-t}\,dt=(1+i)^5\int_0^5 te^{-t\delta_1}\,dt,$$

where δ_1 corresponds to an effective rate i.

The payment in the next year will accumulate by the end of that year to

$$\int_5^6 2t(1+i)^{6-t}\,dt=2(1+i)\int_0^1 te^{-t\delta_1}\,dt+10\bar{s}_{\overline{1}|}.$$

The accumlated payments in the next 6 years will amount to

$$\int_6^{12} 2t(1+j)^{12-t}\,dt$$

$$=2(1+j)^6\int_0^6 te^{-t\delta_2}\,dt+12\bar{s}_{\overline{6}|},$$

where δ_2 corresponds to an effective rate j and $\bar{s}_{\overline{6}|}$ is calculated at rate j.

Therefore the required amount

$$=(1+i)^6(1+j)^6\int_0^5 te^{-t\delta_1}dt+2(1+i)(1+j)^6\int_0^1 te^{-t\delta_1}dt$$

$$+10\bar{s}_{\overline{1}|}(1+j)^6+2(1+j)^6\int_0^6 te^{-t\delta_2}dt+12\bar{s}_{\overline{6}|},$$

and since
$$\int_0^n te^{-t\delta}\,dt=(I\bar{a})_{\overline{n}|}=\frac{\bar{a}_{\overline{n}|}-nv^n}{\delta}$$

the amount is

$$(1+i)^6(1+j)^6\left[\frac{\bar{a}_{\overline{5}|}-5v_i^5}{\delta_1}\right]$$

$$+2(1+i)(1+j)^6\left[\frac{\bar{a}_{\overline{1}|}-v_i}{\delta_1}\right]$$

$$+10\frac{i}{\delta_1}(1+j)^6$$

$$+2(1+j)^6\left[\frac{\bar{a}_{\overline{6}|}-6v_j^6}{\delta_2}\right]+12\bar{s}_{\overline{6}|}.$$

$$=(1+j)^6(1+i)\left[\frac{\bar{s}_{\overline{5}|}-5}{\delta_1}\right]$$

$$+2(1+j)^6\left[\frac{\bar{s}_{\overline{1}|}-1}{\delta_1}+5\frac{i}{\delta_1}\right]$$

$$+2\frac{\bar{s}_{\overline{6}|}-6}{\delta_2}+12\bar{s}_{\overline{6}|}$$

where $\delta_1=\log_e(1+1)$ and $\bar{s}_{\overline{1}|}$ and $\bar{s}_{\overline{5}|}$ are calculated at rate i;

$\delta_2=\log_e(1+j)$ and $\bar{s}_{\overline{6}|}$ is calculated at rate j,

and $\bar{s}_{\overline{n}|}=\frac{i}{\delta}s_{\overline{n}|}$.

Example 11·2

Assuming that the force of interest is a linear function and falls continuously from ·04 at present to ·03 at the end of 20 years, find the present value of a continuous annuity payable for 20 years under which the initial payment is at the rate of 80 per annum and subsequent payments decrease continuously at the rate of 1 per annum.

Let δ_t be the force of interest at time t.

Then $$\delta_t = \delta_0 - rt, \quad \text{where} \quad r = \frac{\delta_0 - \delta_{20}}{20}$$

$$= \frac{\cdot 04 - \cdot 03}{20}$$

$$= \cdot 0005.$$

If $f(t)$ is the amount of 1 at time t

$$\log_e f(t) = \int_0^t \delta_t \, dt$$

$$= \int_0^t (\delta_0 - rt) \, dt$$

$$= \left[t\delta_0 - \frac{rt^2}{2} \right]_0^t$$

$$= \cdot 04t - \cdot 00025t^2.$$

$$\therefore \; f(t) = e^{\cdot 04t - \cdot 00025t^2}.$$

The present value of 1 due at time t is $[f(t)]^{-1}$, i.e.

$$e^{-\cdot 04t + \cdot 00025t^2}.$$

The value required is therefore

$$\int_0^{20} (80 - t) \, e^{-\cdot 04t + \cdot 00025t^2} \, dt$$

$$= \int_0^{20} (2000)(\cdot 04 - \cdot 0005t) \, e^{-\cdot 04t + \cdot 00025t^2} \, dt$$

$$= 2000 \int_0^{20} e^{-\cdot 04t + \cdot 00025t^2} \, d(\cdot 04t - \cdot 00025t^2)$$

$$= -2000 \, [e^{-\cdot 04t + \cdot 00025t^2}]_0^{20}$$

$$= -2000 \, (e^{-\cdot 7} - 1)$$

$$= 1006 \cdot 82.$$

The solution of this problem is possible only because $(80 - t)[f(t)]^{-1}$ is an expression which can be integrated. If it were not the remarks in § 11·6 would apply.

Example 11·3

If the force of interest δ_t at time t is ·025 $(1{\cdot}01)^{-t} + \log_e (1{\cdot}01)$, find $\bar{a}_{\overline{50}|}$, given $\log_{10} e = {\cdot}43429$.

If the amount of 1 at time t is $f(t)$ and if v^t and δ are calculated at 1% then

$$f(t) = \exp\left[\int_0^t \delta_t \, dt\right]$$

$$= \exp\left[\int_0^t ({\cdot}025 v^t + \delta)\, dt\right]$$

$$= \exp\,[{\cdot}025 \bar{a}_{\overline{t}|} + t\delta].$$

If therefore we put $\dfrac{{\cdot}025}{\delta} = k$, we have

$$f(t) = e^{k(1-v^t)+t\delta}$$

$$= (1+i)^t \, e^{k(1-v^t)}.$$

Now $$\bar{a}_{\overline{50}|} = \int_0^{50} [f(t)]^{-1}\, dt$$

$$= \int_0^{50} v^t \, e^{-k(1-v^t)}\, dt$$

$$= e^{-k} \int_0^{50} v^t \, e^{kv^t}\, dt.$$

$\therefore$ if $x = v^t$,

$$dx = v^t \log v \; dt$$

$$= -\delta v^t \, dt,$$

$$\therefore \; \bar{a}_{\overline{50}|} = \frac{-e^{-k}}{\delta} \int_1^{v^{50}} e^{kx}\, dx$$

$$= -\frac{e^{-k}}{\delta}\left[\frac{e^{kx}}{k}\right]_1^{v^{50}}$$

$$= \frac{e^{-k}}{{\cdot}025}\,[e^k - e^{kv^{50}}]$$

$$= 40[1 - e^{k(v^{50}-1)}],$$

but $$k(v^{50} - 1) = -{\cdot}025 \bar{a}_{\overline{50}|} \text{ at } 1\%$$

$$\therefore \; \bar{a}_{\overline{50}|} = 40[1 - e^{-{\cdot}025 \bar{a}_{\overline{50}|}}] \text{ at } 1\%.$$

and $$e^{\cdot 025\bar{a}^{\cdot 01}_{\overline{50}|}} = e^{\cdot 025 \times 1\cdot 00499 \times 39\cdot 1961}.$$

$$\therefore\ \log_{10} e^{-\cdot 025\bar{a}^{\cdot 01}_{\overline{50}|}} = -\cdot 025 \times 1\cdot 00499 \times 39\cdot 1961 \times \cdot 43429.$$

$$= -\cdot 4277.$$

$$\therefore\ e^{-\cdot 025\bar{a}^{\cdot 01}_{\overline{50}|}} = \cdot 3735.$$

$$\therefore\ \bar{a}_{\overline{50}|} = 40(1 - \cdot 3735)$$

$$= 25\cdot 060.$$

Example 11·4

A loan is issued which is repayable in 25 years time at 110. Interest is payable half-yearly at $5\frac{1}{2}\%$ and the issue price of the loan is 105. Find without using interest tables the rate of interest convertible half-yearly obtained by taking up part of the loan at the issue price, and by the use of interest tables estimate the error involved.

Here $$g = \frac{5\cdot 5}{110} = \cdot 05 \text{ per annum or } \cdot 025 \text{ per half-year,}$$

$$k = -\frac{5}{110},$$

and $n = 50$ half-years.

Hence, by formula (11·3),

$$i = \frac{\cdot 025 + \frac{1}{50}.\frac{5}{110}}{1 - \frac{51}{100}.\frac{5}{110}}$$

$$= \cdot 026524.$$

Using formula (11·4) and $2\frac{1}{2}\%$ as a first approximation to i

$$x = \cdot 025 \frac{\cdot 025 - \cdot 025 + \frac{5}{110}.\frac{1}{a_{\overline{50}|}}}{\cdot 025 - \frac{5}{110}\,\frac{a_{\overline{50}|} - 50v^{51}}{(a_{\overline{50}|})^2}}$$

$$= \cdot 025 \frac{\frac{1}{22} a_{\overline{50}|}}{\cdot 025\,(a_{\overline{50}|})^2 - \frac{1}{22}(a_{\overline{50}|} - 50v^{51})}$$

$$= \cdot 025 \frac{1\cdot 2892}{19\cdot 4664}$$

$$= \cdot 0016557.$$

Hence a closer approximation to i is ·026656 and it seems that the error is ·000132. If formula (11·4) is applied again using ·026656 as a trial rate instead of ·025 it will be found that ·026656 is the true yield per half-year to 6 decimal places.

Example 11·5

Find the net effective yield obtained by an investor who pays £1150 for a bond for £1000 which is repayable by 20 biennial instalments of £50, the first due at the end of 10 years. Interest on the loan outstanding from time to time is payable quarterly at the rate of 5% per annum. Assume income tax to be at the rate of $22\frac{1}{2}$%.

This example is most readily solved by using Makeham's formula. Allowing for tax at $22\frac{1}{2}$%,

$$g(1-t) = ·05\,(·775),$$

$$K = 50\,(v^{10}+v^{12}+\ldots+v^{48})$$

$$= 50\,\frac{a_{\overline{50}|}-a_{\overline{10}|}}{a_{\overline{2}|}} \quad \text{at the net rate } i,$$

and A, to yield i net is

$$K+\frac{·05\,(·775)}{i}\,s_{\overline{1}|}^{(4)}\,(1000-K).$$

This equation can best be solved by valuing A at two trial rates of interest and interpolating between them. In order to get a rough idea what trial rates should be used it will be noted that the yield must be less than $·05 \times ·775 = 3·875$%, since the difference between the purchase price of £1150 and the redemption price of £1000 must be written off out of net interest. As a first approximation assume that the capital loss of £15 per cent is written off in equal annual instalments. The average term of the loan is $\frac{10+48}{2} = 29$ years and the amount to be applied from each interest payment is therefore approximately $15/a_{\overline{29}|}$ at the valuation rate of interest. Since $a_{\overline{29}|}$ at 3% is approximately 19 and $a_{\overline{29}|}$ at 4% is approximately 17 this suggests that the yield will be in the neighbourhood of 3·875—(say) $\frac{15}{18}$, or just over 3%, i.e. that the trial rates should be 3 and $3\frac{1}{2}$%.

At 3% $\quad A = 449·42 + \dfrac{·03875 \times 1·01118}{·03}\,(1000-449·42)$

$= 1168·54.$

At $3\frac{1}{2}\%$ $A = 398{\cdot}46 + \dfrac{{\cdot}03875 \times 1{\cdot}01303}{{\cdot}035}(1000 - 398{\cdot}46)$

$= 1073{\cdot}13.$

The net yield is therefore ${\cdot}03 + \dfrac{18{\cdot}54}{95{\cdot}41}({\cdot}005)$

$= {\cdot}03097,$

or, say, £3·10%.

Example 11·6

A loan is issued at 105% bearing interest payable half-yearly at 5% per annum for the first 15 years, reducing to $4\frac{1}{2}\%$ per annum thereafter. The loan is redeemable by drawings at par by a cumulative sinking fund of $1\frac{1}{2}\%$ operating yearly. Assuming income tax at 25%, what is the net yield to a purchaser of the whole loan?

To calculate the term it will be noted that the rate at which the sinking fund accumulates is 5% for 15 years, and $4\frac{1}{2}\%$ thereafter, and that income tax has no effect on this. The loan outstanding at the end of 15 years $= 100 - 1{\cdot}5 s_{\overline{15}|}$ at 5%

$= 67{\cdot}632.$

The amount available for sinking fund in the 16th year is

$$6 - {\cdot}045 \times 67{\cdot}632 = 2{\cdot}9566.$$

$$\therefore\ 2{\cdot}9566 s_{\overline{n-15}|} \text{ at } 4\tfrac{1}{2}\% = 67{\cdot}632.$$

Now at $4\frac{1}{2}\%$ $2{\cdot}9566 s_{\overline{16}|} = 67{\cdot}172.$

Therefore the loan is repaid in 32 years, the final payment of capital being ·460%.

The value of the capital repayments at rate i is

$$1{\cdot}5v + 1{\cdot}5(1+g_1)v^2 + \dots + 1{\cdot}5(1+g_1)^{14}v^{15}$$

$$+ 2{\cdot}9566[v^{16} + (1+g_2)v^{17} + \dots + (1+g_2)^{15}v^{31}] + {\cdot}460v^{32}$$

$$= \frac{1{\cdot}5}{i - g_1}[1 - v^{15}(1+g_1)^{15}] + \frac{2{\cdot}9566}{i - g_2}v^{15}[1 - v^{16}(1+g_2)^{16}] + {\cdot}460v^{32},$$

where $g_1 = {\cdot}05$ and $g_2 = {\cdot}045.$

$= K$ say.

To find the net yield it is necessary to value the loan at two rates of interest and to interpolate between them. To obtain an indication of suitable trial rates we note that the average rate of interest payable on the loan is, very roughly, $4\frac{3}{4}\%$. The net rate corresponding to this is slightly over $3\frac{1}{2}\%$ but the yield must be less than this since there is a loss of 5% on redemption to be written off over 32 years. This suggests that the trial rates should be 3 and $3\frac{1}{2}\%$.

Now, at 3%, $K=58{\cdot}186$ and at $3\frac{1}{2}\%$, $K=53{\cdot}591$.

If interest were yearly and not subject to tax, the value of the loan would be

$$6{\cdot}5a_{\overline{15}|}+6(a_{\overline{31}|}-a_{\overline{15}|})+{\cdot}460(1{\cdot}045)v^{32}$$

$$=A \text{ (say).}$$

If $i={\cdot}03$, $A=126{\cdot}158$.

If $i={\cdot}035$, $A=118{\cdot}336$.

But the value of yearly gross interest is $A-K$ and therefore the value of net interest payable half-yearly is $\frac{3}{4}(A-K)s_{\overline{1}|}^{(2)}$.

Therefore the value of the whole loan, allowing for tax, is

$$K+\tfrac{3}{4}(A-K)s_{\overline{1}|}^{(2)}.$$

Hence at 3% the value is

$$58{\cdot}186+\tfrac{3}{4}(126{\cdot}158-58{\cdot}186)s_{\overline{1}|}^{(2)}$$

$$=109{\cdot}55,$$

and at $3\frac{1}{2}\%$ the value is

$$53{\cdot}591+\tfrac{3}{4}(118{\cdot}336-53{\cdot}591)s_{\overline{1}|}^{(2)}$$

$$=102{\cdot}58.$$

The net yield is therefore

$${\cdot}03+\frac{4{\cdot}55}{6{\cdot}97}({\cdot}005)$$

$$={\cdot}0326,$$

say £3·26 %.

Example 11·7

The funds of an insurance company at the start of a year were A. At the end of the year the funds were B and the net interest income received during the year was I. The gross interest income was I'. Show that, approximately, i, the net rate of interest earned, $=\dfrac{2I}{A+B-I'}$, and investigate a similar formula for the gross rate earned.

The excess of income over outgo, ignoring interest, is $B-A-I$. Assume this is received uniformly over the year and that I accrues at the end of the year.

Then $$A(1+i)+(B-A-I)\bar{s}_{\overline{1}|}=B,$$

$$\bar{s}_{\overline{1}|}=\frac{i}{\delta}=\frac{i}{i-\frac{i^2}{2}+\frac{i^3}{3}-\dots}$$

$=1+\frac{1}{2}i$, ignoring powers of i above the first.

$$\therefore\ A(1+i)+(B-A-I)(1+\tfrac{1}{2}i)=B.$$

$$\therefore\ i=\frac{2I}{A+B-I}.$$

An alternative form might be found by considering δ, the force of interest. The value of this at any moment is the ratio of the annual rate at which interest is being received at that moment to the fund at that time. On the average the force of interest for the year may therefore be taken as being approximately equal to the ratio of the total interest to the average fund invested, i.e.

$$\delta=\frac{2I}{A+B}.$$

Now the expression $\dfrac{2I}{A+B-I}$ might be written as

$$\frac{\dfrac{2I}{A+B}}{1-\dfrac{1}{2}\left[\dfrac{2I}{A+B}\right]},$$

whence writing $$\delta=\frac{2I}{A+B},$$

we get $$i=\frac{\delta}{1-\frac{1}{2}\delta}=\delta+\frac{\delta^2}{2}+\frac{\delta^3}{4}+\dots,$$

which agrees with the correct equation

$$i=\delta+\frac{\delta^2}{2}+\frac{\delta^3}{6},$$

as far as the term involving δ^2.

If the net rate is i and the gross rate is i' then it is logical to expect that $i=i'(1-t)$, where t is the rate of tax incurred in the year.

On this basis i' might be taken as $\dfrac{i}{1-t}$, i.e. as

$$\frac{\dfrac{2I}{1-t}}{A+B-I}=\frac{2I'}{A+B-I'},$$

and this is the formula generally used. It is possible, however, to make out a case for the alternative formula $\frac{2I'}{A+B-I'}$, on the following lines:

If income tax is considered as a deduction from the ordinary income throughout the year then

$$A(1+i')+(\overline{B-A-I}-\overline{I'-I})\bar{s}_{\overline{1}|}=B,$$

or

$$A(1+i')+(B-A-I')(1+\tfrac{1}{2}i')=B,$$

or

$$i'=\frac{2I'}{A+B-I'}.$$

It really depends upon what assumptions are made, and since in deriving the formula $i=\frac{2I}{A+B-I}$ it was assumed that interest was received in one sum at the end of the year, it is perhaps illogical to assume that income-tax payments are spread over the year. As already stated, the two formulae

$$i=\frac{2I}{A+B-I} \text{ for the net rate of interest,}$$

and

$$i'=\frac{2I'}{A+B-I} \text{ for the gross rate of interest,}$$

are those which in practice are adopted by assurance companies.

Example 11·8

An office transacts both ordinary and industrial business. In the year 1946 the gross interest income was £360,000, upon which tax of £50,000 was paid. The tax is charged wholly to the ordinary branch.

Given the following data find the net rate of interest earned on the funds of the ordinary branch, assuming the gross interest earnings of £360,000 are apportioned so that the gross yields on the industrial and ordinary funds are identical.

	Industrial	Ordinary	Total
Funds as at 1 January 1946	2,500,000	5,000,000	7,500,000
Premium income	350,000	500,000	850,000
Claims and surrenders	150,000	250,000	400,000
Expenses of management	100,000	50,000	150,000
Interest	—	—	360,000
Income tax	—	50,000	50,000

Using the notation of Example 11·7, A, in the industrial branch, is £2,500,000. B is A plus the premiums, plus I, less claims and surrenders, less expenses of managements. Hence the gross yields will be calculated as follows, working for convenience in £10,000's.

	Industrial	Ordinary
A	250	500
$B-I$	260	520
$A+B-I$	510	1020

The amount of gross interest must be in the same proportion as the denominators of the expressions used in calculating the gross rates of interest, i.e. in the ratio 1 : 2. Hence the interest on the ordinary fund is £240,000. It will be noted that it is not necessary to know the actual interest in order to find the value of $A+B-I$.

The net yield on the ordinary branch is therefore

$$\frac{2\,[240{,}000-50{,}000]}{10{,}200{,}000}$$

$$= \cdot 037255$$

$$= £3 \cdot 73\,\%.$$

CHAPTER 12

CONSTRUCTION OF TABLES

12·1. Introductory

Although virtually any compound interest problem likely to arise in practice could be solved by the knowledge that the amount of 1 at the end of n years at an effective rate of interest of i per annum is $(1+i)^n$ it will be obvious that much time and labour can be saved if prepared tables of some of the elementary functions are available at various rates of interest. Many such tables have already been prepared but it is instructive to consider the principles which govern the method of their construction, as these principles are common to the preparation of all actuarial tables and are indeed more easily grasped in the comparatively simple case of the compound interest table than in the more complicated types of tables which are used in other branches of actuarial science.

12·2. Factors affecting the choice of method

Two factors which affect the preparation of a set of tables of any kind are:

(*a*) the use to which the tables will be put,
(*b*) the availability or otherwise of mechanical aids for their preparation.

The first of these is obviously the more important and on it will depend decisions as to

(i) the functions to be tabulated,
(ii) the arrangement of these functions in the published tables,
(iii) the range of values of the variables for which functions are to be tabulated,
(iv) the number of significant figures to be retained in the tables.

The second factor is unlikely to be of great practical importance as it will be rare that a set of tables has to be constructed without the full and powerful aid of modern calculating machinery. The two factors are further discussed with particular reference to compound interest problems in the following sections.

12·3. Compound interest tables: general considerations

The uses to which a set of compound interest tables can be put may be classified as:

(*a*) General—that is to say the tables should contain values of such functions as are likely to be required in the solution of compound interest problems in general.

(*b*) Particular—that is to say tables containing such functions as are likely to be required in some particular business or profession, for example, a table of Bond Values for the Stockbroker, or a table showing the division of the payments of an annuity into principal and interest for a Building Society.

In a general set of tables the following points will have to be considered:

(i) The functions to be tabulated will naturally include $(1+i)^n$, v^n, $a_{\overline{n}|}$ and $s_{\overline{n}|}$. A table of $\dfrac{1}{a_{\overline{n}|}}$ may also be useful $\left(\text{or alternatively a table of } \dfrac{1}{s_{\overline{n}|}}\text{: it is not necessary to tabulate both, since } \dfrac{1}{a_{\overline{n}|}} = \dfrac{1}{s_{\overline{n}|}} + i\right)$.

In some forms of actuarial work values of $v^{n+\frac{1}{2}}$ are often required and these might be included. In order to make the tables applicable to problems involving nominal rates of interest the values of $i^{(m)}$ and $d^{(m)}$ for varying values of m should be tabulated and possibly also values of $\dfrac{i}{i^{(m)}}$ or $\dfrac{i}{d^{(m)}}$.

(ii) The arrangement of the tables is to some extent a matter of personal taste. The choice is clearly a grouping by function, or a grouping by rate of interest. That is to say, the tables may comprise either a set of values of $(1+i)^n$ at different values of i and so on, or they may collect together the values of $(1+i)^n$, v^n, and so on at one rate of interest, and follow that by a similar set of tables at the next tabular rate of interest. Modern preference is for grouping by rate of interest as this probably minimizes the chance of error in referring to the tables for isolated values of a required function. It is also more convenient in dealing with a problem where only one rate of interest is involved but where possibly several functions at that rate are required.

(iii) The range of values of the variables is mainly a matter of common sense. For example, since a table of $(1+i)^n$ will often be used for nominal as well as for effective rates, it should be regarded more generally as a table of the values of $\left(1+\frac{i^{(m)}}{m}\right)^{mn}$ and by considering the values of i and m likely to be required in practice, it will be easier to fix the range over which the table should extend. The most common nominal rates met with in practice are those convertible half-yearly, quarterly, or monthly. If therefore the lowest annual rate of interest which it is considered is likely to arise in practice is, say, 1 %, the set of tables should begin with $i = \cdot 00083$ so that problems involving a nominal rate of interest of 1 % convertible monthly can be solved. Functions could be tabulated at rates of interest progressing by $\frac{1}{12}$ % up to the limit of the highest annual rate of interest likely to arise. On the other hand if it were thought that the tables were unlikely to be used for problems involving rates of interest convertible more frequently than quarterly, the first value of i for which functions need be tabulated would be $\cdot 0025$. The interval between successive values of i would probably be fixed at $\frac{1}{8}$ % in such a case.

The range of values given to n would be conditioned first by the fact that it is rare for a financial transaction to last for a period so long as 100 years, and second by the consideration that, if the very low rates of interest are to be used as nominal rates, very long terms may be involved. For example, at a nominal rate convertible monthly, a transaction involving a period of 20 years would involve functions for $n=240$. It is true that any given value could be deduced by simple relationships, such as

$$(1+i)^{m+n}=(1+i)^m(1+i)^n,$$

but this is inconvenient and there is much to be said in practice for extending the range of tabular values at low rates of interest. Rates of interest over, say, 5 % however are unlikely to be required as nominal rates and a more restricted range of values of n may suffice.

(iv) the number of significant figures to be retained depends so much on the use to which the tables are to be put that no general ruling can be given. It is probably quite sufficient to have six significant figures in tables not intended for a specific purpose where higher accuracy is required.

If the tables are required for a specific purpose then of course the problems are simpler. For example, a Building Society requiring a table showing the division of the payments of an annuity into principal and interest will start by knowing the rate of interest at which it grants such loans, how frequently it is convertible and the maximum term for which it grants loans. Similarly it will know the average loan granted and whether it requires the division of the payments for this sum to be accurate to pence or rounded off to some larger amount, and this will determine the number of places of decimals to which the work must be carried out.

12·4. Aids to construction

Before discussing methods of construction in detail it may be useful to give a brief description of the types of multiplying machines, which are usually available to assist in constructing tables. The common multiplying machine consists basically of three parts—a fixed keyboard on which, by depressing keys or some similar device, a number can be registered, and a rotating mechanism which, when turned by hand or by electricity, causes the number registered on the keyboard to appear in the product register, this latter part being moveable. For example, if it were desired to multiply 5678 by 1234, the first step would be to register 5678 on the keyboard. The rotating mechanism would then be revolved 4 times and the result (4×5678) would appear in the product register. If the product register were now moved one place to the right and the mechanism revolved thrice the result would be that 30×5678 would be added to the product already shown, so that the register would now give the answer to 34×5678. Moving the register one further step to the right and rotating the mechanism twice would give 234×5678 and so on.

This is the simplest form of machine. More elaborate models may include refinements such as a device whereby the answer appearing in the product register is automatically transferred to the keyboard at the end of any operation, or a double product register, one part of which (Register A say), can be cleared at the end of each operation, while the other part (Register B say), records an accumulated total of all the operations performed. For example, it might be desired to form simultaneously a table of the values of $(1+i)^n$ and $s_{\overline{n}|}$. If a machine with an accumulating register were available one would register $(1+i)$ on the keyboard and multiply by 1. Product register A would now show $(1+i)$ and product register B would also show $(1+i)$. The automatic transfer device would clear register A, transferring the answer to the keyboard, and on multiplying by $(1+i)$ register B would now show the accumulated total $(1+i)+(1+i)^2$ and A would show the value of $(1+i)^2$ itself. On clearing as before and again multiplying by $(1+i)$ register B would show $(1+i)+(1+i)^2+(1+i)^3$ and A would show $(1+i)^3$, and in this way the two tables would be constructed simultaneously. The speed of operation of such a machine in trained hands is very great and even without these refinements the ease with which complicated calculations can be performed on modern multiplying machines has made some of the methods of constructing tables, developed in an age when logarithms were the main aid to calculation, seem now to be very laborious.

12·5. Methods of construction

Whatever aids to calculation are available it is clearly desirable to construct tables by a method which will

(a) involve the minimum of work in carrying out the process of calculation,
(b) require as little checking as possible,
(c) involve the minimum chance of error during the construction.

For these reasons it is usual to try to devise what is known as a 'Continued Process'—that is to say a process in which each successive value is derived directly from the immediately preceding one. To check such a table it should, in theory, be necessary to check, by some independent process, only the final value calculated. If it is correct, and if it has been derived directly from all the preceding values, its correctness should prove, apart from compensating errors, the correctness of the whole table. In practice, however, it is usual to calculate check values by independent means at more frequent intervals throughout the table. This serves the dual purpose of preventing a mistake being carried on over a long series of calculations, and also of preventing an accumulative error due to the use of a restricted number of decimal places. For example, if a table of $\log(1+i)^n$ were required it could easily be constructed by starting with $\log(1+i)$ and adding $\log(1+i)$ to each previous value. If the work were being carried out to five decimal places the value of $\log(1+i)$ for $i = \cdot 0255$ would be taken as ·00966 and successive additions would give $\log(1+i)^{10}$ as ·09660, whereas the true value to five decimal places is ·09663. This could be overcome by remembering to add 1 in the last decimal place to every second, fifth, eighth, ..., value, but the periodic check values are useful in ensuring that this has been done.

A 'Continued Process' therefore involves three things.

(*a*) An *initial value* on which the subsequent values depend.

(*b*) A *working formula* which connects successive values of the function to be calculated.

(*c*) A *check formula* which enables check values of the function to be calculated independently.

For example, if a table at $2\frac{1}{2}\%$ were required of the paid-up policies which could be granted after 1, 2, ..., 20 years premiums had been paid under a 20-year leasehold policy and if a table of values of $a_{\overline{n}|}$ were available the work could be carried out thus:

Initial value $\qquad {}_{20}W_{\overline{20}|} = \dfrac{a_{\overline{20}|}}{a_{\overline{20}|}} = 1.$

Working formula

$$\begin{aligned} {}_tW_{\overline{20}|} &= \frac{a_{\overline{t}|}}{a_{\overline{20}|}} \\ &= \frac{(1+i)\,a_{\overline{t+1}|} - 1}{a_{\overline{20}|}} \\ &= (1+i)\,{}_{t+1}W_{\overline{20}|} - \frac{1}{a_{\overline{20}|}} \\ &= {}_{t+1}W_{\overline{20}|} - \left(\frac{1}{a_{\overline{20}|}} - i_{t+1}W_{\overline{20}|}\right). \end{aligned}$$

Check formula $\qquad {}_tW_{\overline{20}|} = \dfrac{a_{\overline{t}|}}{a_{\overline{20}|}}.$

It will be noted that the terminal value of ${}_{20}W_{\overline{20}|}$ has been chosen as the 'initial value', and that the table has been constructed by working backwards from it. This device is often used in constructing tables and is frequently the simplest method. The work could be arranged in tabular form to be carried out quite readily even if no calculating aids were available, thus:

Duration t	${}_tW_{\overline{20}|}$	$\cdot025 \times (1)$	$\dfrac{1}{a_{\overline{20}|}}$	(3) − (2)
	(1)	(2)	(3)	(4)
20	1·	·025	·06415	·03915
19	·96085	·02402	·06415	·04013
18	·92072	·02302	·06415	·04113
17	·87959	·02199	·06415	·04216
16	·83743	·02094	·06415	·04321
15	·79422	—	—	—

The schedule is self-explanatory except that the value of ${}_{19}W_{\overline{20}|}$ is found by subtracting the amount in column (4) at duration 20 from ${}_{20}W_{\overline{20}|}$. The value at duration 18 is similarly derived from the data at duration 19 and so on. Check values would be inserted at say quinquennial intervals from the check formula. The value of $\frac{a_{\overline{15}|}}{a_{\overline{20}|}}$ is ·79423 and the virtual agreement of this with the value calculated in the schedule checks both that value and all the work up to that point.

If tables of v^n and a multiplying machine were available, particularly an electrically operated one, it would be very much quicker simply to put $1/a_{\overline{20}|}$ on the keyboard as a constant and, without clearing the machine, multiply successively by v, v^2, v^3, ..., v^{20}. The amounts in the product register after successive multiplications would then be $\frac{a_{\overline{1}|}}{a_{\overline{20}|}}$, $\frac{a_{\overline{2}|}}{a_{\overline{20}|}}$, ..., and so on as required. Once again check values should be inserted and the work verified as it progressed.

There is obviously scope for ingenuity in devising continued methods of constructing tables, and the student should devise his own methods of constructing tables of the common functions, such as $s_{\overline{n}|}$, $a_{\overline{n}|}$, etc., using methods suitable for multiplying machines and also adapting the formulae for use if no such aids are available.*

12·6. Checking of tables

The most satisfactory check, and the only one which would probably satisfy the author of tables which were to be published for general use, is to have the work performed independently in duplicate and the results compared. Apart from this, however, there are three types of check which may be put on the work:

(*a*) the automatic check of a continued process,

(*b*) a visual check,

(*c*) a summation check.

* The simplest working formulae will be found to be conveniently expressed as follows:

$$s_{\overline{n}|}=(1+i)\,s_{\overline{n-1}|}+1$$

$$a_{\overline{n}|}=(1+i)\,a_{\overline{n+1}|}-1.$$

So far as the continued process is concerned errors may arise, even when the check values inserted in the working are reproduced, for the following reasons:

(1) A compensating error in arithmetic. For example, if in the schedule in § 12·5 the value at duration 18 had been taken as ·92062 and the value in column (4) wrongly calculated as ·04103 the subsequent values would be correct. Such errors are rare but they do sometimes occur.

(2) It may be overlooked that while part of the process is continued the whole may not be. For example in forming the table of log $(1+i)^n$ in § 12·5 the whole process is a continued one. But if a table of values of $(1+i)^n$ were to be formed by this method it would involve taking the anti-logarithms of the logarithms calculated, and this being an entirely separate process, the agreement of any given value of $(1+i)^n$ with the value calculated independently would prove nothing about the remainder of the table.

(3) In all continued processes which employ calculating machines there is always the liability that a correct answer on the machine may be copied down wrongly. As the correct answer remains on the machine and is used by it in the subsequent working, the periodic check values will not disclose such an error.

A visual check is very useful in detecting errors of transcription as in (3) above. For example suppose that the values of $(1{\cdot}05)^n$ have been calculated on a machine and transcribed as follows:

Term n	$(1{\cdot}05)^n$
20	2·6533
21	2·7860
22	2·9523
23	3·0715
24	3·2251

An examination of the first differences will show that their successive values are ·1327, ·1663, ·1192, ·1536 and this irregular progression at once suggests that the value of $(1{\cdot}05)^{22}$ is too large. In fact there has been an error of transcription and the true value is

2·9253. Substituting this, the differences run ·1327, ·1393, ·1462, ·1536—an obvious improvement. This type of check is easily applied and is most useful. It will not disclose the true value but it will usually reveal which value requires to be examined further for error.

A summation check is also useful for detecting errors of transcription. For example if a table of $s_{\overline{n}|}$ has been prepared on a calculating machine by the continued process

$$s_{\overline{n}|}=(1+i)\,s_{\overline{n-1}|}+1$$

then an error of transcription might be detected by summing the calculated values of $s_{\overline{n}|}$. Since

$$s_{\overline{n}|}=\frac{(1+i)^n-1}{i},\quad \sum_1^n s_{\overline{t}|}=\frac{1}{i}\sum_1^n (1+i)^t-\frac{n}{i}=\frac{\ddot{s}_{\overline{n}|}-n}{i},$$

and the calculated value of this expression should agree with the value found by adding the tabulated values of $s_{\overline{n}|}$. This type of check, applied to small ranges of a table, is often useful in localizing a suspected error but it is of course not infallible as it will not disclose compensating errors.

12·7. A useful list of the main tables existing at the date of publication of the work is contained in the Institute of Actuaries' *Text-Book on Compound Interest and Annuities-Certain* by R. Todhunter (fourth edition, revised by R. C. Simmonds and T. P. Thompson). It is to be feared that at the moment many of these tables are out of print and unavailable.

A few tables of the commoner functions extracted from *Actuarial Tables for Examination Purposes* are appended to this work for the convenience of students.

ANSWERS TO THE EXERCISES

Note. These answers are not complete solutions. They provide numerical answers which should enable the accuracy of students' work to be checked. In addition lines of approach are indicated by which solutions to some of the more difficult examples may most readily be obtained.

EXERCISES 2

2·1 (*a*) £37·24. (*b*) £36·79 (*c*) £49·98.

2·2 (*a*) £224·37. (*b*) £267·39. (*c*) £284·71.

2·3 ·00014.

2·4 £673·54.

2·5 £0·54.

2·6 4¼%.

EXERCISES 4

4·1

Annuity payable	Interest convertible			
	Yearly	Half-yearly	Quarterly	Momently
Yearly	15·622	15·556	15·523	15·489
Half-yearly	15·777	15·712	15·679	15·646
Quarterly	15·854	15·790	15·757	15·724
Momently	15·932	15·868	15·836	15·803

4·2 £39·67.

4·3 £5507·25.

4·4 $\dfrac{a^3}{(2a-b)^2}\left[2a-b-(b-a)\log_e\dfrac{a}{b-a}\right]$.

4·5 £809·10.

4·6 4%.

4·7 This problem should be solved by considering:

(*a*) the amount of the fund when it suffices to meet future payments at the rate of £ $(100+5n)$ per annum,

(*b*) at what stage the rate of interest changes.

It will be found that when there are 10 payments to be made the fund is £1930. Hence up to and including the 20th payment the amounts paid are 10% of the amount of the fund at the beginning of the year and the rate of interest is 4%. Hence if X is the fund

$$X(\cdot 94)^{20}=205a_{\overline{10}|}+5\,\frac{\ddot{a}_{\overline{10}|}-10v^{10}}{\cdot 03}\quad\text{at } 3\,\%$$

leading to $X=$ £6653·20.

EXERCISES 5

5·1 (a) £481·71. (b) £359·46 (c) £85·41.
(d) £4104·30.

5·2 (a) £581·71. (b) £359·46. (c) £185·41.
(d) £4104·30.

5·3 (a) £439·31.
(b) Principal £252·24. Interest £187·07. Loan outstanding £3150.

5·4 The amount borrowed is £1246·22 repayable by 20 instalments. *B* earns £4·67%.

5·5 This is a complicated problem which can be solved only by trial and error. The difficulty is to discover at what stage interest on the total loan, including amounts advanced under (*a*), is first less than the next instalment due. At the beginning of the *t*th year, if the original loan is *X*, the loan then outstanding is $X(1{\cdot}04)^{t-1} - \frac{s_{\overline{t}|} - t}{\cdot 04}$ at 4%. If this amount be represented by *Y* then we have the relations

$$t - 1 < \cdot 04Y \leqslant t$$

and

$$\sum_{t}^{20} (t - \cdot 04Y)(1{\cdot}03)^{20-t} = Y.$$

It will be found that $t = 6$, leading to $Y = 132{\cdot}78$ and $X = 122{\cdot}14$.

EXERCISES 6

6·1 £0·68%

6·2 £131·94.

6·3 (a) $\dfrac{s^{j}_{\overline{n}|}}{1 + is^{j}_{\overline{n}|}}$; (b) $\dfrac{s^{j}_{\overline{n+1}|} - \dfrac{1+i}{1+j}}{\dfrac{1+i}{1+j} + is^{j}_{\overline{n+1}|}}$.

6·4 £790.

6·5 Assuming it is appropriate to value new commitments at 4½% the new premium must be calculated at not more than 2½% effective.

EXERCISES 7

7·1 £102·49.

7·2 £7379·71.

7·3 5%.

7·4 20.

7·5 (a) £118·14. (b) £100·68.

EXERCISES 8

8·1 £8698.

8·2 The stock is worth £52,800 and the value at 4 % of the outstanding instalments is £52,762. The offer is therefore very slightly in the assurance company's favour.

8·3 $4\frac{3}{4}$%.

8·4 £1142·50.

8·5 £225,213.

8·6 (*a*) £106·95. (*b*) £4·43.

EXERCISES 9

9·1 (*a*) £1,569,000. (*b*) £1,758,000.

9·3 The term is 12 years almost exactly. The price per cent is £97·80.

9·4 The term is 31 years, the final capital payment being 2·819 %. The price is £108·28.

9·5 6·27 %.

9·6 Using the notation of §9·4

$$f(t+1) = \frac{[10{,}000 - {\cdot}025F(t)]\ 1{\cdot}01 - {\cdot}025F(t)}{1{\cdot}05}$$

and
$$F(t+1) = F(t) - f(t+1)$$

whence it may be shown that

$$f(t+1) = \frac{1{\cdot}10025}{1{\cdot}05} f(t)$$

and
$$f(1) = 4833.$$

In 14 years the amount repaid is $4833 s_{\overline{14|}}$ at rate $\dfrac{{\cdot}05025}{1{\cdot}05} = £93{,}674$. The payment required in the 15th year is £6891.

9·7 If $F(t)$ = loan outstanding at start of tth year and $f(t)$ = amount of loan repaid at par after t years then

$$X = {\cdot}04F(t) + {\cdot}02F(t) \times 1{\cdot}25 + f(t)$$

and
$$F(t+1) = F(t) - {\cdot}02F(t) - f(t)$$

whence
$$F(t+1) = F(t)\,(1{\cdot}045) - X$$

and as $F(0) = 1{,}000{,}000$ and $F(20) = 0$ it follows that at $4\frac{1}{2}$%

$$1{,}000{,}000\,(1{\cdot}045)^{20} - X s_{\overline{20|}} = 0$$

whence
$$X = £76{,}876.$$

If interest were yearly the value of the loan would be $76{,}876 a_{\overline{20|}}$ at 3% (i.e. £1,143,700). The capital payments in each year, C_t, say are

$$76{,}876 - \cdot 04\,\{1{,}000{,}000\,(1\cdot 045)^t - \cdot 04 \times 76{,}876\, s_{\overline{t|}}^{\cdot 045}\}$$
$$= 76{,}876 - 40{,}000\,(1\cdot 045)^t + 3075\, s_{\overline{t|}},$$

These can be valued directly by evaluating $\sum_{0}^{19} v^{t-1} C_t$ at 3%. Deducting this amount from the whole value the value of the interest is found to be 383,150, assuming that interest is paid yearly.

The value with half-yearly interest is therefore

$$1{,}143{,}700 + 383{,}150\,(s_{\overline{1|}}^{(2)} - 1)$$
$$= £1{,}146{,}553.$$

EXERCISES 10

10·1 From the equations $A = K + \frac{5}{4}(C - K)$

and $$A - 14 = K + \frac{5\,(\cdot 625)}{4}(C - K)$$

it follows that $$A = 117\cdot 467.$$

Hence at 4% $$5\cdot 5 a_{\overline{n|}} + 110 v^n \geqslant 117\cdot 467$$

and $$n \geqslant 9.$$

10·2 £40,170.

10·3 Issue price = 100·97%.

All bonds drawn in the first 10 years yield 3% or more, and no bond drawn thereafter yields as much as 3%; the probability is therefore $\frac{1}{2}$.

10·4 The net yield on the loan at the present market price is $2\frac{1}{2}$% convertible half-yearly. The present value of the three offers at this rate are:

(i) £$106 v^{\frac{1}{12}}$ at $1\frac{1}{4}$%. (ii) £105.25. (iii) £105.

Hence offer (i) is the most advantageous.

10·5 £92·10.

10·6 A is found to be £114·92. If Y calculated on a 3% basis then clearly X will earn 3% net since he is merely paying to Y the same amount as he himself should set aside out of each interest payment to write down the value of his loan.

If Y calculates at 4% the present value of his receipts

$$= k \sum_{1}^{12} v^t \left[1 - \frac{1\cdot 5\,(1\cdot 05)^{20}\, s_{\overline{t-1|}}}{60\cdot 401} \right]$$

and of his payments

$$= 4\cdot 92 \left[\sum_{1}^{11} v^t \frac{(1\cdot 5)\,(1\cdot 05)^{20+t-1}}{60\cdot 401} + \frac{v^{12} \times 3\cdot 8588}{60\cdot 401} \right],$$

i.e. $k \times$ value at 4% of interest at unit rate on the loan outstanding and $4{\cdot}92 \times$ value at 4% of future capital payments.

By the usual methods the value at 4% of interest of 1% is

$$7a_{\overline{11}|} + 3{\cdot}8588\,(1{\cdot}05)\,v^{12} - 60{\cdot}401 = 3{\cdot}453$$

and the value of the capital is therefore

$$63{\cdot}854 - 5 \times 3{\cdot}453 = 46{\cdot}589.$$

K is therefore $4{\cdot}92 \times \dfrac{46{\cdot}589}{100 \times 3{\cdot}453}$, i.e. ·664, and *A*'s net yield is therefore

$$\frac{4{\cdot}125 - {\cdot}664}{114{\cdot}92} = 3{\cdot}012\,\%.$$

COMPOUND INTEREST TABLES

Constants	
Function	**Value**
i	·005 000
$i^{(2)}$	·004 994
$i^{(4)}$	·004 991
$i^{(12)}$	·004 989
δ	·004 988
$(1+i)^{\frac{1}{2}}$	1·002 497
$(1+i)^{\frac{1}{4}}$	1·001 248
$(1+i)^{\frac{1}{12}}$	1·000 416
v	·995 025
$v^{\frac{1}{2}}$	·997 509
$v^{\frac{1}{4}}$	·998 754
$v^{\frac{1}{12}}$	·999 584
d	·004 975
$d^{(2)}$	·004 981
$d^{(4)}$	·004 984
$d^{(12)}$	·004 987
$i/i^{(2)}$	1·001 248
$i/i^{(4)}$	1·001 873
$i/i^{(12)}$	1·002 290
i/δ	1·002 498
$i/d^{(2)}$	1·003 748
$i/d^{(4)}$	1·003 123
$i/d^{(12)}$	1·002 706
$\log_{10}(1+i)$	·002 166 1

n	$(1+i)^n$	v^n	$s_{\overline{n}\rvert}$	$a_{\overline{n}\rvert}$	$(a_{\overline{n}\rvert})^{-1}$	n
1	1·005 00	·995 02	1·000 0	0·995 0	1·005 000	1
2	1·010 03	·990 07	2·005 0	1·985 1	0·503 753	2
3	1·015 08	·985 15	3·015 0	2·970 2	·336 672	3
4	1·020 15	·980 25	4·030 1	3·950 5	·253 133	4
5	1·025 25	·975 37	5·050 3	4·925 9	·203 010	5
6	1·030 38	·970 52	6·075 5	5·896 4	·169 595	6
7	1·035 53	·965 69	7·105 9	6·862 1	·145 729	7
8	1·040 71	·960 89	8·141 4	7·823 0	·127 829	8
9	1·045 91	·956 10	9·182 1	8·779 1	·113 907	9
10	1·051 14	·951 35	10·228 0	9·730 4	·102 771	10
11	1·056 40	·946 61	11·279 2	10·677 0	·093 659	11
12	1·061 68	·941 91	12·335 6	11·618 9	·086 066	12
13	1·066 99	·937 22	13·397 2	12·556 2	·079 642	13
14	1·072 32	·932 56	14·464 2	13·488 7	·074 136	14
15	1·077 68	·927 92	15·536 5	14·416 6	·069 364	15
16	1·083 07	·923 30	16·614 2	15·339 9	·065 189	16
17	1·088 49	·918 71	17·697 3	16·258 6	·061 506	17
18	1·093 93	·914 14	18·785 8	17·172 8	·058 232	18
19	1·099 40	·909 59	19·879 7	18·082 4	·055 303	19
20	1·104 90	·905 06	20·979 1	18·987 4	·052 666	20
21	1·110 42	·900 56	22·084 0	19·888 0	·050 282	21
22	1·115 97	·896 08	23·194 4	20·784 1	·048 114	22
23	1·121 55	·891 62	24·310 4	21·675 7	·046 135	23
24	1·127 16	·887 19	25·432 0	22·562 9	·044 321	24
25	1·132 80	·882 77	26·559 1	23·445 6	·042 652	25
26	1·138 46	·878 38	27 691 9	24·324 0	·041 112	26
27	1·144 15	·874 01	28·830 4	25·198 0	·039 686	27
28	1·149 87	·869 66	29·974 5	26·067 7	·038 362	28
29	1·155 62	·865 33	31·124 4	26·933 0	·037 129	29
30	1·161 40	·861 03	32·280 0	27·794 1	·035 979	30
31	1·167 21	·856 75	33·441 4	28·650 8	·034 903	31
32	1·173 04	·852 48	34·608 6	29·503 3	·033 895	32
33	1·178 91	·848 24	35·781 7	30·351 5	·032 947	33
34	1·184 80	·844 02	36·960 6	31·195 5	·032 056	34
35	1·190 73	·839 82	38·145 4	32·035 4	·031 215	35
36	1·196 68	·835 64	39·336 1	32·871 0	·030 422	36
37	1·202 66	·831 49	40·532 8	33·702 5	·029 671	37
38	1·208 68	·827 35	41·735 4	34·529 9	·028 960	38
39	1·214 72	·823 23	42·944 1	35·353 1	·028 286	39
40	1·220 79	·819 14	44·158 8	36·172 2	·027 646	40
41	1·226 90	·815 06	45·379 6	36·987 3	·027 036	41
42	1·233 03	·811 01	46·606 5	37·798 3	·026 456	42
43	1·239 20	·806 97	47·839 6	38·605 3	·025 903	43
44	1·245 39	·802 96	49·078 8	39·408 2	·025 375	44
45	1·251 62	·798 96	50·324 2	40·207 2	·024 871	45
46	1·257 88	·794 99	51·575 8	41·002 2	·024 389	46
47	1·264 17	·791 03	52·833 7	41·793 2	·023 927	47
48	1·270 49	·787 10	54·097 8	42·580 3	·023 485	48
49	1·276 84	·783 18	55·368 3	43·363 5	·023 061	49
50	1·283 23	·779 29	56·645 2	44·142 8	·022 654	50
60	1·348 85	·741 37	69·770 0	51·725 6	·019 333	60
70	1·417 83	·705 30	83·566 1	58·939 4	·016 967	70
80	1·490 34	·670 99	98·067 7	65·802 3	·015 197	80
90	1·566 55	·638 34	113·310 9	72·331 3	·013 825	90
100	1·646 67	·607 29	129·333 7	78·542 6	·012 732	100

n	$(1+i)^n$	v^n	$s_{\overline{n}\vert}$	$a_{\overline{n}\vert}$	$(a_{\overline{n}\vert})^{-1}$	n
1	1·007 50	·992 56	1·000 0	0·992 6	1·007 500	1
2	1·015 06	·985 17	2·007 5	1·977 7	0·505 632	2
3	1·022 67	·977 83	3·022 6	2·955 6	·338 346	3
4	1·030 34	·970 55	4·045 2	3·926 1	·254 705	4
5	1·038 07	·963 33	5·075 6	4·889 4	·204 522	5
6	1·045 85	·956 16	6·113 6	5·845 6	·171 069	6
7	1·053 70	·949 04	7·159 5	6·794 6	·147 175	7
8	1·061 60	·941 98	8·213 2	7·736 6	·129 256	8
9	1·069 56	·934 96	9·274 8	8·671 6	·115 319	9
10	1·077 58	·928 00	10·344 3	9·599 6	·104 171	10
11	1·085 66	·921 09	11·421 9	10·520 7	·095 051	11
12	1·093 81	·914 24	12·507 6	11·434 9	·087 451	12
13	1·102 01	·907 43	13·601 4	12·342 3	·081 022	13
14	1·110 28	·900 68	14·703 4	13·243 0	·075 512	14
15	1·118 60	·893 97	15·813 7	14·137 0	·070 736	15
16	1·126 99	·887 32	16·932 3	15·024 3	·066 559	16
17	1·135 44	·880 71	18·059 3	15·905 0	·062 873	17
18	1·143 96	·874 16	19·194 7	16·779 2	·059 598	18
19	1·152 54	·867 65	20·338 7	17·646 8	·056 667	19
20	1·161 18	·861 19	21·491 2	18·508 0	·054 031	20
21	1·169 89	·854 78	22·652 4	19·362 8	·051 645	21
22	1·178 67	·848 42	23·822 3	20·211 2	·049 477	22
23	1·187 51	·842 10	25·001 0	21·053 3	·047 498	23
24	1·196 41	·835 83	26·188 5	21·889 1	·045 685	24
25	1·205 39	·829 61	27·384 9	22·718 8	·044 016	25
26	1·214 43	·823 43	28·590 3	23·542 2	·042 477	26
27	1·223 54	·817 30	29·804 7	24·359 5	·041 052	27
28	1·232 71	·811 22	31·028 2	25·170 7	·039 729	28
29	1·241 96	·805 18	32·260 9	25·975 9	·038 497	29
30	1·251 27	·799 19	33·502 9	26·775 1	·037 348	30
31	1·260 66	·793 24	34·754 2	27·568 3	·036 274	31
32	1·270 11	·787 33	36·014 8	28·355 7	·035 266	32
33	1·279 64	·781 47	37·284 9	29·137 1	·034 320	33
34	1·289 23	·775 65	38·564 6	29·912 8	·033 431	34
35	1·298 90	·769 88	39·853 8	30·682 7	·032 592	35
36	1·308 65	·764 15	41·152 7	31·446 8	·031 800	36
37	1·318 46	·758 46	42·461 4	32·205 3	·031 051	37
38	1·328 35	·752 81	43·779 8	32·958 1	·030 342	38
39	1·338 31	·747 21	45·108 2	33·705 3	·029 669	39
40	1·348 35	·741 65	46·446 5	34·446 9	·029 030	40
41	1·358 46	·736 13	47·794 8	35·183 1	·028 423	41
42	1·368 65	·730 65	49·153 3	35·913 7	·027 845	42
43	1·378 91	·725 21	50·521 9	36·638 9	·027 293	43
44	1·389 26	·719 81	51·900 9	37·358 7	·026 768	44
45	1·399 68	·714 45	53·290 1	38·073 2	·026 265	45
46	1·410 17	·709 13	54·689 8	38·782 3	·025 785	46
47	1·420 75	·703 85	56·100 0	39·486 2	·025 325	47
48	1·431 41	·698 61	57·520 7	40·184 8	·024 885	48
49	1·442 14	·693 41	58·952 1	40·878 2	·024 463	49
50	1·452 96	·688 25	60·394 3	41·566 4	·024 058	50
60	1·565 68	·638 70	75·424 1	48·173 4	·020 758	60
70	1·687 15	·592 72	91·620 1	54·304 6	·018 415	70
80	1·818 04	·550 04	109·072 5	59·994 4	·016 668	80
90	1·959 09	·510 44	127·879 0	65·274 6	·015 320	90
100	2·111 08	·473 69	148·144 5	70·174 6	·014 250	100

Constants

Function	Value
i	·007 500
$i^{(2)}$	·007 486
$i^{(4)}$	·007 479
$i^{(12)}$	·007 474
δ	·007 472
$(1+i)^{\frac{1}{2}}$	1·003 743
$(1+i)^{\frac{1}{4}}$	1·001 870
$(1+i)^{\frac{1}{12}}$	1·000 623
v	·992 556
$v^{\frac{1}{2}}$	·996 271
$v^{\frac{1}{4}}$	·998 134
$v^{\frac{1}{12}}$	·999 378
d	·007 444
$d^{(2)}$	·007 458
$d^{(4)}$	·007 465
$d^{(12)}$	·007 470
$i/i^{(2)}$	1·001 871
$i/i^{(4)}$	1·002 808
$i/i^{(12)}$	1·003 433
i/δ	1·003 745
$i/d^{(2)}$	1·005 621
$i/d^{(4)}$	1·004 683
$i/d^{(12)}$	1·004 058
$\log_{10}(1+i)$	·003 245 1

Constants	
Function	Value
i	·010 000
$i^{(2)}$	·009 975
$i^{(4)}$	·009 963
$i^{(12)}$	·009 954
δ	·009 950
$(1+i)^{\frac{1}{2}}$	1·004 988
$(1+i)^{\frac{1}{4}}$	1·002 491
$(1+i)^{\frac{1}{12}}$	1·000 830
v	·990 099
$v^{\frac{1}{2}}$	·995 037
$v^{\frac{1}{4}}$	·997 516
$v^{\frac{1}{12}}$	·999 171
d	·009 901
$d^{(2)}$	·009 926
$d^{(4)}$	·009 938
$d^{(12)}$	·009 946
$i/i^{(2)}$	1·002 494
$i/i^{(4)}$	1·003 742
$i/i^{(12)}$	1·004 575
i/δ	1·004 992
$i/d^{(2)}$	1·007 494
$i/d^{(4)}$	1·006 242
$i/d^{(12)}$	1·005 408
$\log_{10}(1+i)$	·004 321 4

n	$(1+i)^n$	v^n	$s_{\overline{n}\rvert}$	$a_{\overline{n}\rvert}$	$(a_{\overline{n}\rvert})^{-1}$	[illegible]
1	1·010 00	·990 10	1·000 0	0·990 1	1·010 000	
2	1·020 10	·980 30	2·010 0	1·970 4	0·507 512	
3	1·030 30	·970 59	3·030 1	2·941 0	·340 022	
4	1·040 60	·960 98	4·060 4	3·902 0	·256 281	
5	1·051 01	·951 47	5·101 0	4·853 4	·206 040	
6	1·061 52	·942 05	6·152 0	5·795 5	·172 548	
7	1·072 14	·932 72	7·213 5	6·728 2	·148 628	
8	1·082 86	·923 48	8·285 7	7·651 7	·130 690	
9	1·093 69	·914 34	9·368 5	8·566 0	·116 740	
10	1·104 62	·905 29	10·462 2	9·471 3	·105 582	1
11	1·115 67	·896 32	11·566 8	10·367 6	·096 454	1
12	1·126 83	·887 45	12·682 5	11·255 1	·088 849	1
13	1·138 09	·878 66	13·809 3	12·133 7	·082 415	1
14	1·149 47	·869 96	14·947 4	13·003 7	·076 901	1
15	1·160 97	·861 35	16·096 9	13·865 1	·072 124	1
16	1·172 58	·852 82	17·257 9	14·717 9	·067 945	1
17	1·184 30	·844 38	18·430 4	15·562 3	·064 258	1
18	1·196 15	·836 02	19·614 7	16·398 3	·060 982	1
19	1·208 11	·827 74	20·810 9	17·226 0	·058 052	1
20	1·220 19	·819 54	22·019 0	18·045 6	·055 415	2
21	1·232 39	·811 43	23·239 2	18·857 0	·053 031	2
22	1·244 72	·803 40	24·471 6	19·660 4	·050 864	2
23	1·257 16	·795 44	25·716 3	20·455 8	·048 886	2
24	1·269 73	·787 57	26·973 5	21·243 4	·047 073	2
25	1·282 43	·779 77	28·243 2	22·023 2	·045 407	2
26	1·295 26	·772 05	29·525 6	22·795 2	·043 869	2
27	1·308 21	·764 40	30·820 9	23·559 6	·042 446	2
28	1·321 29	·756 84	32·129 1	24·316 4	·041 124	2
29	1·334 50	·749 34	33·450 4	25·065 8	·039 895	2
30	1·347 85	·741 92	34·784 9	25·807 7	·038 748	3
31	1·361 33	·734 58	36·132 7	26·542 3	·037 676	3
32	1·374 94	·727 30	37·494 1	27·269 6	·036 671	3
33	1·388 69	·720 10	38·869 0	27·989 7	·035 727	3
34	1·402 58	·712 97	40·257 7	28·702 7	·034 840	3
35	1·416 60	·705 91	41·660 3	29·408 6	·034 004	3
36	1·430 77	·698 92	43·076 9	30·107 5	·033 214	3
37	1·445 08	·692 00	44·507 6	30·799 5	·032 468	3
38	1·459 53	·685 15	45·952 7	31·484 7	·031 761	3
39	1·474 12	·678 37	47·412 3	32·163 0	·031 092	3
40	1·488 86	·671 65	48·886 4	32·834 7	·030 456	4
41	1·503 75	·665 00	50·375 2	33·499 7	·029 851	4
42	1·518 79	·658 42	51·879 0	34·158 1	·029 276	4
43	1·533 98	·651 90	53·397 8	34·810 0	·028 727	4
44	1·549 32	·645 45	54·931 8	35·455 5	·028 204	4
45	1·564 81	·639 06	56·481 1	36·094 5	·027 705	4
46	1·580 46	·632 73	58·045 9	36·727 2	·027 228	4
47	1·596 26	·626 46	59·626 3	37·353 7	·026 771	4
48	1·612 23	·620 26	61·222 6	37·974 0	·026 334	4
49	1·628 35	·614 12	62·834 8	38·588 1	·025 915	4
50	1·644 63	·608 04	64·463 2	39·196 1	·025 513	5
60	1·816 70	·550 45	81·669 7	44·955 0	·022 244	6
70	2·006 76	·498 31	100·676 3	50·168 5	·019 933	7
80	2·216 72	·451 12	121·671 5	54·888 2	·018 219	8
90	2·448 63	·408 39	144·863 3	59·160 9	·016 903	9
100	2·704 81	·369 71	170·481 4	63·028 9	·015 866	10

n	$(1+i)^n$	v^n	$s_{\overline{n}\vert}$	$a_{\overline{n}\vert}$	$(a_{\overline{n}\vert})^{-1}$	n
1	1·012 50	·987 65	1·000 0	0·987 7	1·012 500	1
2	1·025 16	·975 46	2·012 5	1·963 1	0·509 394	2
3	1·037 97	·963 42	3·037 7	2·926 5	·341 701	3
4	1·050 95	·951 52	4·075 6	3·878 1	·257 861	4
5	1·064 08	·939 78	5·126 6	4·817 8	·207 562	5
6	1·077 38	·928 17	6·190 7	5·746 0	·174 034	6
7	1·090 85	·916 72	7·268 0	6·662 7	·150 089	7
8	1·104 49	·905 40	8·358 9	7·568 1	·132 133	8
9	1·118 29	·894 22	9·463 4	8·462 3	·118 171	9
10	1·132 27	·883 18	10·581 7	9·345 5	·107 003	10
11	1·146 42	·872 28	11·713 9	10·217 8	·097 868	11
12	1·160 75	·861 51	12·860 4	11·079 3	·090 258	12
13	1·175 26	·850 87	14·021 1	11·930 2	·083 821	13
14	1·189 95	·840 37	15·196 4	12·770 6	·078 305	14
15	1·204 83	·829 99	16·386 3	13·600 5	·073 526	15
16	1·219 89	·819 75	17·591 2	14·420 3	·069 347	16
17	1·235 14	·809 63	18·811 1	15·229 9	·065 660	17
18	1·250 58	·799 63	20·046 2	16·029 5	·062 385	18
19	1·266 21	·789 76	21·296 8	16·819 3	·059 455	19
20	1·282 04	·780 01	22·563 0	17·599 3	·056 820	20
21	1·298 06	·770 38	23·845 0	18·369 7	·054 438	21
22	1·314 29	·760 87	25·143 1	19·130 6	·052 272	22
23	1·330 72	·751 47	26·457 4	19·882 0	·050 297	23
24	1·347 35	·742 20	27·788 1	20·624 2	·048 487	24
25	1·364 19	·733 03	29·135 4	21·357 3	·046 822	25
26	1·381 25	·723 98	30·499 6	22·081 3	·045 287	26
27	1·398 51	·715 05	31·880 9	22·796 3	·043 867	27
28	1·415 99	·706 22	33·279 4	23·502 5	·042 549	28
29	1·433 69	·697 50	34·695 4	24·200 0	·041 322	29
30	1·451 61	·688 89	36·129 1	24·888 9	·040 179	30
31	1·469 76	·680 38	37·580 7	25·569 3	·039 109	31
32	1·488 13	·671 98	39·050 4	26·241 3	·038 108	32
33	1·506 73	·663 69	40·538 6	26·905 0	·037 168	33
34	1·525 57	·655 49	42·045 3	27·560 5	·036 284	34
35	1·544 64	·647 40	43·570 9	28·207 9	·035 451	35
36	1·563 94	·639 41	45·115 5	28·847 3	·034 665	36
37	1·583 49	·631 52	46·679 4	29·478 8	·033 923	37
38	1·603 29	·623 72	48·262 9	30·102 5	·033 220	38
39	1·623 33	·616 02	49·866 2	30·718 5	·032 554	39
40	1·643 62	·608 41	51·489 6	31·326 9	·031 921	40
41	1·664 16	·600 90	53·133 2	31·927 8	·031 321	41
42	1·684 97	·593 48	54·797 3	32·521 3	·030 749	42
43	1·706 03	·586 16	56·482 3	33·107 5	·030 205	43
44	1·727 35	·578 92	58·188 3	33·686 4	·029 686	44
45	1·748 95	·571 77	59·915 7	34·258 2	·029 190	45
46	1·770 81	·564 71	61·664 6	34·822 9	·028 717	46
47	1·792 94	·557 74	63·435 4	35·380 6	·028 264	47
48	1·815 35	·550 86	65·228 4	35·931 5	·027 831	48
49	1·838 05	·544 06	67·043 7	36·475 5	·027 416	49
50	1·861 02	·537 34	68·881 8	37·012 9	·027 018	50
60	2·107 18	·474 57	88·574 5	42·034 6	·023 790	60
70	2·385 90	·419 13	110·872 0	46·469 7	·021 519	70
80	2·701 49	·370 17	136·118 8	50·386 7	·019 847	80
90	3·058 81	·326 92	164·705 0	53·846 1	·018 571	90
100	3·463 40	·288 73	197·072 3	56·901 3	·017 574	100

Constants	
Function	Value
i	·012 500
$i^{(2)}$	·012 461
$i^{(4)}$	·012 442
$i^{(12)}$	·012 429
δ	·012 423
$(1+i)^{\frac{1}{2}}$	1·006 231
$(1+i)^{\frac{1}{4}}$	1·003 110
$(1+i)^{\frac{1}{12}}$	1·001 036
v	·987 654
$v^{\frac{1}{2}}$	·993 808
$v^{\frac{1}{4}}$	·996 899
$v^{\frac{1}{12}}$	·998 965
d	·012 346
$d^{(2)}$	·012 384
$d^{(4)}$	·012 403
$d^{(12)}$	·012 416
$i/i^{(2)}$	1·003 115
$i/i^{(4)}$	1·004 675
$i/i^{(12)}$	1·005 716
i/δ	1·006 237
$i/d^{(2)}$	1·009 365
$i/d^{(4)}$	1·007 800
$i/d^{(12)}$	1·006 758
$\log_{10}(1+i)$	·005 395 0

Constants	
Function	Value
i	·015 000
$i^{(2)}$	·014 944
$i^{(4)}$	·014 916
$i^{(12)}$	·014 898
δ	·014 889
$(1+i)^{\frac{1}{2}}$	1·007 472
$(1+i)^{\frac{1}{4}}$	1·003 729
$(1+i)^{\frac{1}{12}}$	1·001 241
v	·985 222
$v^{\frac{1}{2}}$	·992 583
$v^{\frac{1}{4}}$	·996 285
$v^{\frac{1}{12}}$	·998 760
d	·014 778
$d^{(2)}$	·014 833
$d^{(4)}$	·014 861
$d^{(12)}$	·014 879
$i/i^{(2)}$	1·003 736
$i/i^{(4)}$	1·005 608
$i/i^{(12)}$	1·006 857
i/δ	1·007 481
$i/d^{(2)}$	1·011 236
$i/d^{(4)}$	1·009 358
$i/d^{(12)}$	1·008 107
$\log_{10}(1+i)$	·006 466 0

n	$(1+i)^n$	v^n	$s_{\overline{n}\mid}$	$a_{\overline{n}\mid}$	$(a_{\overline{n}\mid})^{-1}$	n
1	1·015 00	·985 22	1·000 0	0·985 2	1·015 000	1
2	1·030 23	·970 66	2·015 0	1·955 9	0·511 278	2
3	1·045 68	·956 32	3·045 2	2·912 2	·343 383	3
4	1·061 36	·942 18	4·090 9	3·854 4	·259 445	4
5	1·077 28	·928 26	5·152 3	4·782 6	·209 089	5
6	1·093 44	·914 54	6·229 6	5·697 2	·175 525	6
7	1·109 84	·901 03	7·323 0	6·598 2	·151 556	7
8	1·126 49	·887 71	8·432 8	7·485 9	·133 584	8
9	1·143 39	·874 59	9·559 3	8·360 5	·119 610	9
10	1·160 54	·861 67	10·702 7	9·222 2	·108 434	10
11	1·177 95	·848 93	11·863 3	10·071 1	·099 294	11
12	1·195 62	·836 39	13·041 2	10·907 5	·091 680	12
13	1·213 55	·824 03	14·236 8	11·731 5	·085 240	13
14	1·231 76	·811 85	15·450 4	12·543 4	·079 723	14
15	1·250 23	·799 85	16·682 1	13·343 2	·074 944	15
16	1·268 99	·788 03	17·932 4	14·131 3	·070 765	16
17	1·288 02	·776 39	19·201 4	14·907 6	·067 080	17
18	1·307 34	·764 91	20·489 4	15·672 6	·063 806	18
19	1·326 95	·753 61	21·796 7	16·426 2	·060 878	19
20	1·346 86	·742 47	23·123 7	17·168 6	·058 246	20
21	1·367 06	·731 50	24·470 5	17·900 1	·055 865	21
22	1·387 56	·720 69	25·837 6	18·620 8	·053 703	22
23	1·408 38	·710 04	27·225 1	19·330 9	·051 731	23
24	1·429 50	·699 54	28·633 5	20·030 4	·049 924	24
25	1·450 95	·689 21	30·063 0	20·719 6	·048 263	25
26	1·472 71	·679 02	31·514 0	21·398 6	·046 732	26
27	1·494 80	·668 99	32·986 7	22·067 6	·045 315	27
28	1·517 22	·659 10	34·481 5	22·726 7	·044 001	28
29	1·539 98	·649 36	35·998 7	23·376 1	·042 779	29
30	1·563 08	·639 76	37·538 7	24·015 8	·041 639	30
31	1·586 53	·630 31	39·101 8	24·646 1	·040 574	31
32	1·610 32	·620 99	40·688 3	25·267 1	·039 577	32
33	1·634 48	·611 82	42·298 6	25·879 0	·038 641	33
34	1·659 00	·602 77	43·933 1	26·481 7	·037 762	34
35	1·683 88	·593 87	45·592 1	27·075 6	·036 934	35
36	1·709 14	·585 09	47·276 0	27·660 7	·036 152	36
37	1·734 78	·576 44	48·985 1	28·237 1	·035 414	37
38	1·760 80	·567 92	50·719 9	28·805 1	·034 716	38
39	1·787 21	·559 53	52·480 7	29·364 6	·034 055	39
40	1·814 02	·551 26	54·267 9	29·915 8	·033 427	40
41	1·841 23	·543 12	56·081 9	30·459 0	·032 831	41
42	1·868 85	·535 09	57·923 1	30·994 1	·032 264	42
43	1·896 88	·527 18	59·792 0	31·521 2	·031 725	43
44	1·925 33	·519 39	61·688 9	32·040 6	·031 210	44
45	1·954 21	·511 71	63·614 2	32·552 3	·030 720	45
46	1·983 53	·504 15	65·568 4	33·056 5	·030 251	46
47	2·013 28	·496 70	67·551 9	33·553 2	·029 803	47
48	2·043 48	·489 36	69·565 2	34·042 6	·029 375	48
49	2·074 13	·482 13	71·608 7	34·524 7	·028 965	49
50	2·105 24	·475 00	73·682 8	34·999 7	·028 572	50
60	2·443 22	·409 30	96·214 7	39·380 3	·025 393	60
70	2·835 46	·352 68	122·363 8	43·154 9	·023 172	70
80	3·290 66	·303 89	152·710 9	46·407 3	·021 548	80
90	3·818 95	·261 85	187·929 9	49·209 9	·020 321	90
100	4·432 05	·225 63	228·803 0	51·624 7	·019 371	100

n	$(1+i)^n$	v^n	$s_{\overline{n}\rvert}$	$a_{\overline{n}\rvert}$	$(a_{\overline{n}\rvert})^{-1}$	n
1	1·017 50	·982 80	1·000 0	0·982 8	1·017 500	1
2	1·035 31	·965 90	2·017 5	1·948 7	0·513 163	2
3	1·053 42	·949 29	3·052 8	2·898 0	·345 067	3
4	1·071 86	·932 96	4·106 2	3·830 9	·261 032	4
5	1·090 62	·916 91	5·178 1	4·747 9	·210 621	5
6	1·109 70	·901 14	6·268 7	5·649 0	·177 023	6
7	1·129 12	·885 64	7·378 4	6·534 6	·153 031	7
8	1·148 88	·870 41	8·507 5	7·405 1	·135 043	8
9	1·168 99	·855 44	9·656 4	8·260 5	·121 058	9
10	1·189 44	·840 73	10·825 4	9·101 2	·109 875	10
11	1·210 26	·826 27	12·014 8	9·927 5	·100 730	11
12	1·231 44	·812 06	13·225 1	10·739 5	·093 114	12
13	1·252 99	·798 09	14·456 5	11·537 6	·086 673	13
14	1·274 92	·784 36	15·709 5	12·322 0	·081 156	14
15	1·297 23	·770 87	16·984 4	13·092 9	·076 377	15
16	1·319 93	·757 62	18·281 7	13·850 5	·072 200	16
17	1·343 03	·744 59	19·601 6	14·595 1	·068 516	17
18	1·366 53	·731 78	20·944 6	15·326 9	·065 245	18
19	1·390 45	·719 19	22·311 2	16·046 1	·062 321	19
20	1·414 78	·706 82	23·701 6	16·752 9	·059 691	20
21	1·439 54	·694 67	25·116 4	17·447 5	·057 315	21
22	1·464 73	·682 72	26·555 9	18·130 3	·055 156	22
23	1·490 36	·670 98	28·020 7	18·801 2	·053 188	23
24	1·516 44	·659 44	29·511 0	19·460 7	·051 386	24
25	1·542 98	·648 10	31·027 5	20·108 8	·049 730	25
26	1·569 98	·636 95	32·570 4	20·745 7	·048 203	26
27	1·597 46	·625 99	34·140 4	21·371 7	·046 791	27
28	1·625 41	·615 23	35·737 9	21·987 0	·045 482	28
29	1·653 86	·604 65	37·363 3	22·591 6	·044 264	29
30	1·682 80	·594 25	39·017 2	23·185 8	·043 130	30
31	1·712 25	·584 03	40·700 0	23·769 9	·042 070	31
32	1·742 21	·573 98	42·412 2	24·343 9	·041 078	32
33	1·772 70	·564 11	44·154 4	24·908 0	·040 148	33
34	1·803 72	·554 41	45·927 1	25·462 4	·039 274	34
35	1·835 29	·544 87	47·730 8	26·007 3	·038 451	35
36	1·867 41	·535 50	49·566 1	26·542 8	·037 675	36
37	1·900 09	·526 29	51·433 5	27·069 0	·036 943	37
38	1·933 34	·517 24	53·333 6	27·586 3	·036 250	38
39	1·967 17	·508 34	55·267 0	28·094 6	·035 594	39
40	2·001 60	·499 60	57·234 1	28·594 2	·034 972	40
41	2·036 63	·491 01	59·235 7	29·085 2	·034 382	41
42	2·072 27	·482 56	61·272 4	29·567 8	·033 821	42
43	2·108 53	·474 26	63·344 6	30·042 1	·033 287	43
44	2·145 43	·466 11	65·453 2	30·508 2	·032 778	44
45	2·182 98	·458 09	67·598 6	30·966 3	·032 293	45
46	2·221 18	·450 21	69·781 6	31·416 5	·031 830	46
47	2·260 05	·442 47	72·002 7	31·858 9	·031 388	47
48	2·299 60	·434 86	74·262 8	32·293 8	·030 966	48
49	2·339 84	·427 38	76·562 4	32·721 2	·030 561	49
50	2·380 79	·420 03	78·902 2	33·141 2	·030 174	50
60	2·831 82	·353 13	104·675 2	36·964 0	·027 053	60
70	3·368 29	·296 89	135·330 8	40·177 9	·024 889	70
80	4·006 39	·249 60	171·793 8	42·879 9	·023 321	80
90	4·765 38	·209 85	215·164 6	45·151 6	·022 148	90
100	5·668 16	·176 42	266·751 8	47·061 5	·021 249	100

Constants	
Function	Value
i	·017 5
$i^{(2)}$	·017 424
$i^{(4)}$	·017 386
$i^{(12)}$	·017 361
δ	·017 349
$(1+i)^{\frac{1}{2}}$	1·008 712
$(1+i)^{\frac{1}{4}}$	1·004 347
$(1+i)^{\frac{1}{12}}$	1·001 447
v	·982 801
$v^{\frac{1}{2}}$	·991 363
$v^{\frac{1}{4}}$	·995 672
$v^{\frac{1}{12}}$	·998 555
d	·017 199
$d^{(2)}$	·017 274
$d^{(4)}$	·017 311
$d^{(12)}$	·017 336
$i/i^{(2)}$	1·004 356
$i/i^{(4)}$	1·006 539
$i/i^{(12)}$	1·007 996
i/δ	1·008 725
$i/d^{(2)}$	1·013 106
$i/d^{(4)}$	1·010 914
$i/d^{(12)}$	1·009 454
$\log_{10}(1+i)$	·007 534 4

Constants	
Function	Value
i	·02
$i^{(2)}$	·019 901
$i^{(4)}$	·019 852
$i^{(12)}$	·019 819
δ	·019 803
$(1+i)^{\frac{1}{2}}$	1·009 950
$(1+i)^{\frac{1}{4}}$	1·004 963
$(1+i)^{\frac{1}{12}}$	1·001 652
v	·980 392
$v^{\frac{1}{2}}$	·990 148
$v^{\frac{1}{4}}$	·995 062
$v^{\frac{1}{12}}$	·998 351
d	·019 608
$d^{(2)}$	·019 705
$d^{(4)}$	·019 754
$d^{(12)}$	·019 786
$i/i^{(2)}$	1·004 975
$i/i^{(4)}$	1·007 469
$i/i^{(12)}$	1·009 134
i/δ	1·009 967
$i/d^{(2)}$	1·014 975
$i/d^{(4)}$	1·012 469
$i/d^{(12)}$	1·010 801
$\log_{10}(1+i)$	·008 600 2

n	$(1+i)^n$	v^n	$s_{\overline{n}\rvert}$	$a_{\overline{n}\rvert}$	$(a_{\overline{n}\rvert})^{-1}$	
1	1·020 00	·980 39	1·000 0	0·980 4	1·020 000	
2	1·040 40	·961 17	2·020 0	1·941 6	0·515 050	
3	1·061 21	·942 32	3·060 4	2·883 9	·346 755	
4	1·082 43	·923 85	4·121 6	3·807 7	·262 624	
5	1·104 08	·905 73	5·204 0	4·713 5	·212 158	
6	1·126 16	·887 97	6·308 1	5·601 4	·178 526	
7	1·148 69	·870 56	7·434 3	6·472 0	·154 512	
8	1·171 66	·853 49	8·583 0	7·325 5	·136 510	
9	1·195 09	·836 76	9·754 6	8·162 2	·122 515	
10	1·218 99	·820 35	10·949 7	8·982 6	·111 327	1
11	1·243 37	·804 26	12·168 7	9·786 8	·102 178	1
12	1·268 24	·788 49	13·412 1	10·575 3	·094 560	1
13	1·293 61	·773 03	14·680 3	11·348 4	·088 118	1
14	1·319 48	·757 88	15·973 9	12·106 2	·082 602	1
15	1·345 87	·743 01	17·293 4	12·849 3	·077 825	1
16	1·372 79	·728 45	18·639 3	13·577 7	·073 650	1
17	1·400 24	·714 16	20·012 1	14·291 9	·069 970	1
18	1·428 25	·700 16	21·412 3	14·992 0	·066 702	1
19	1·456 81	·686 43	22·840 6	15·678 5	·063 782	1
20	1·485 95	·672 97	24·297 4	16·351 4	·061 157	2
21	1·515 67	·659 78	25·783 3	17·011 2	·058 785	2
22	1·545 98	·646 84	27·299 0	17·658 0	·056 631	2
23	1·576 90	·634 16	28·845 0	18·292 2	·054 668	2
24	1·608 44	·621 72	30·421 9	18·913 9	·052 871	2
25	1·640 61	·609 53	32·030 3	19·523 5	·051 220	2
26	1·673 42	·597 58	33·670 9	20·121 0	·049 699	2
27	1·706 89	·585 86	35·344 3	20·706 9	·048 293	2
28	1·741 02	·574 37	37·051 2	21·281 3	·046 990	2
29	1·775 84	·563 11	38·792 2	21·844 4	·045 778	2
30	1·811 36	·552 07	40·568 1	22·396 5	·044 650	3
31	1·847 59	·541 25	42·379 4	22·937 7	·043 596	3
32	1·884 54	·530 63	44·227 0	23·468 3	·042 611	3
33	1·922 23	·520 23	46·111 6	23·988 6	·041 687	3
34	1·960 68	·510 03	48·033 8	24·498 6	·040 819	3
35	1·999 89	·500 03	49·994 5	24·998 6	·040 002	3
36	2·039 89	·490 22	51·994 4	25·488 8	·039 233	3
37	2·080 69	·480 61	54·034 3	25·969 5	·038 507	3
38	2·122 30	·471 19	56·114 9	26·440 6	·037 821	3
39	2·164 74	·461 95	58·237 2	26·902 6	·037 171	3
40	2·208 04	·452 89	60·402 0	27·355 5	·036 556	4
41	2·252 20	·444 01	62·610 0	27·799 5	·035 972	4
42	2·297 24	·435 30	64·862 2	28·234 8	·035 417	4
43	2·343 19	·426 77	67·159 5	28·661 6	·034 890	4
44	2·390 05	·418 40	69·502 7	29·080 0	·034 388	4
45	2·437 85	·410 20	71 892 7	29·490 2	·033 910	4
46	2·486 61	·402 15	74·330 6	29·892 3	·033 453	4
47	2·536 34	·394 27	76·817 2	30·286 6	·033 018	4
48	2·587 07	·386 54	79·353 5	30·673 1	·032 602	4
49	2·638 81	·378 96	81·940 6	31·052 1	·032 204	4
50	2·691 59	·371 53	84·579 4	31·423 6	·031 823	5
60	3·281 03	·304 78	114·051 5	34·760 9	·028 768	6
70	3·999 56	·250 03	149·977 9	37·498 6	·026 668	7
80	4·875 44	·205 11	193·772 0	39·744 5	·025 161	8
90	5·943 13	·168 26	247·156 7	41·586 9	·024 046	9
100	7·244 65	·138 03	312·232 3	43·098 4	·023 203	10

n	$(1+i)^n$	v^n	$s_{\overline{n}\vert}$	$a_{\overline{n}\vert}$	$(a_{\overline{n}\vert})^{-1}$	n
1	1·022 50	·978 00	1·000 0	0·978 0	1·022 500	1
2	1·045 51	·956 47	2·022 5	1·934 5	0·516 938	2
3	1·069 03	·935 43	3·068 0	2·869 9	·348 445	3
4	1·093 08	·914 84	4·137 0	3·784 7	·264 219	4
5	1·117 68	·894 71	5·230 1	4·679 5	·213 700	5
6	1·142 83	·875 02	6·347 8	5·554 5	·180 035	6
7	1·168 54	·855 77	7·490 6	6·410 2	·156 000	7
8	1·194 83	·836 94	8·659 2	7·247 2	·137 985	8
9	1·221 71	·818 52	9·854 0	8·065 7	·123 982	9
10	1·249 20	·800 51	11·075 7	8·866 2	·112 788	10
11	1·277 31	·782 90	12·324 9	9·649 1	·103 637	11
12	1·306 05	·765 67	13·602 2	10·414 8	·096 017	12
13	1·335 44	·748 82	14·908 3	11·163 6	·089 577	13
14	1·365 48	·732 34	16·243 7	11·895 9	·084 062	14
15	1·396 21	·716 23	17·609 2	12·612 2	·079 289	15
16	1·427 62	·700 47	19·005 4	13·312 6	·075 117	16
17	1·459 74	·685 05	20·433 0	13·997 7	·071 440	17
18	1·492 59	·669 98	21·892 8	14·667 7	·068 177	18
19	1·526 17	·655 23	23·385 3	15·322 9	·065 262	19
20	1·560 51	·640 82	24·911 5	15·963 7	·062 642	20
21	1·595 62	·626 72	26·472 0	16·590 4	·060 276	21
22	1·631 52	·612 92	28·067 6	17·203 4	·058 128	22
23	1·668 23	·599 44	29·699 2	17·802 8	·056 171	23
24	1·705 77	·586 25	31·367 4	18·389 0	·054 380	24
25	1·744 15	·573 35	33·073 2	18·962 4	·052 736	25
26	1·783 39	·560 73	34·817 3	19·523 1	·051 221	26
27	1·823 52	·548 39	36·600 7	20·071 5	·049 822	27
28	1·864 54	·536 32	38·424 2	20·607 8	·048 525	28
29	1·906 50	·524 52	40·288 8	21·132 3	·047 321	29
30	1·949 39	·512 98	42·195 3	21·645 3	·046 199	30
31	1·993 25	·501 69	44·144 7	22·147 0	·045 153	31
32	2·038 10	·490 65	46·137 9	22·637 7	·044 174	32
33	2·083 96	·479 86	48·176 0	23·117 5	·043 257	33
34	2·130 85	·469 30	50·260 0	23·586 8	·042 397	34
35	2·178 79	·458 97	52·390 8	24·045 8	·041 587	35
36	2·227 82	·448 87	54·569 6	24·494 7	·040 825	36
37	2·277 94	·438 99	56·797 4	24·933 7	·040 106	37
38	2·329 20	·429 33	59·075 4	25·363 0	·039 428	38
39	2·381 60	·419 89	61·404 6	25·782 9	·038 785	39
40	2·435 19	·410 65	63·786 2	26·193 5	·038 177	40
41	2·489 98	·401 61	66·221 4	26·595 1	·037 601	41
42	2·546 01	·392 77	68·711 3	26·987 9	·037 054	42
43	2·603 29	·384 13	71·257 4	27·372 0	·036 534	43
44	2·661 86	·375 68	73·860 6	27·747 7	·036 039	44
45	2·721 76	·367 41	76·522 5	28·115 1	·035 568	45
46	2·783 00	·359 32	79·244 3	28·474 4	·035 119	46
47	2·845 61	·351 42	82·027 3	28·825 9	·034 691	47
48	2·909 64	·343 69	84·872 9	29·169 5	·034 282	48
49	2·975 11	·336 12	87·782 5	29·505 7	·033 892	49
50	3·042 05	·328 73	90·757 6	29·834 4	·033 518	50
60	3·800 13	·263 15	124·450 4	32·749 0	·030 535	60
70	4·747 14	·210 65	166·539 6	35·082 1	·028 505	70
80	5·930 15	·168 63	219·117 6	36·949 8	·027 064	80
90	7·407 96	·134 99	284·798 1	38·444 9	·026 011	90
100	9·254 05	·108 06	366·846 5	39·641 7	·025 226	100

Constants

Function	Value
i	·022 5
$i^{(2)}$	·022 375
$i^{(4)}$	·022 313
$i^{(12)}$	·022 271
δ	·022 251
$(1+i)^{\frac{1}{2}}$	1·011 187
$(1+i)^{\frac{1}{4}}$	1·005 578
$(1+i)^{\frac{1}{12}}$	1·001 856
v	·977 995
$v^{\frac{1}{2}}$	·988 936
$v^{\frac{1}{4}}$	·994 453
$v^{\frac{1}{12}}$	·998 148
d	·022 005
$d^{(2)}$	·022 127
$d^{(4)}$	·022 189
$d^{(12)}$	·022 230
$i/i^{(2)}$	1·005 594
$i/i^{(4)}$	1·008 398
$i/i^{(12)}$	1·010 271
i/δ	1·011 208
$i/d^{(2)}$	1·016 844
$i/d^{(4)}$	1·014 023
$i/d^{(12)}$	1·012 146
$\log_{10}(1+i)$	·009 663 3

Constants	
Function	Value
i	·025
$i^{(2)}$	·024 846
$i^{(4)}$	·024 769
$i^{(12)}$	·024 718
δ	·024 693
$(1+i)^{\frac{1}{2}}$	1·012 423
$(1+i)^{\frac{1}{4}}$	1·006 192
$(1+i)^{\frac{1}{12}}$	1·002 060
v	·975 610
$v^{\frac{1}{2}}$	·987 730
$v^{\frac{1}{4}}$	·993 846
$v^{\frac{1}{12}}$	·997 944
d	·024 390
$d^{(2)}$	·024 541
$d^{(4)}$	·024 617
$d^{(12)}$	·024 667
$i/i^{(2)}$	1·006 211
$i/i^{(4)}$	1·009 327
$i/i^{(12)}$	1·011 407
i/δ	1·012 449
$i/d^{(2)}$	1·018 711
$i/d^{(4)}$	1·015 577
$i/d^{(12)}$	1·013 491
$\log_{10}(1+i)$	·010 723 9

n	$(1+i)^n$	v^n	$s_{\overline{n}\rceil}$	$a_{\overline{n}\rceil}$	$(a_{\overline{n}\rceil})^{-1}$	n
1	1·025 00	·975 61	1·000 0	0·975 6	1·025 000	
2	1·050 63	·951 81	2·025 0	1·927 4	0·518 827	
3	1·076 89	·928 60	3·075 6	2·856 0	·350 137	
4	1·103 81	·905 95	4·152 5	3·762 0	·265 818	
5	1·131 41	·883 85	5·256 3	4·645 8	·215 247	
6	1·159 69	·862 30	6·387 7	5·508 1	·181 550	
7	1·188 69	·841 27	7·547 4	6·349 4	·157 495	
8	1·218 40	·820 75	8·736 1	7·170 1	·139 467	
9	1·248 86	·800 73	9·954 5	7·970 9	·125 457	
10	1·280 08	·781 20	11·203 4	8·752 1	·114 259	
11	1·312 09	·762 14	12·483 5	9·514 2	·105 106	
12	1·344 89	·743 56	13·795 6	10·257 8	·097 487	
13	1·378 51	·725 42	15·140 4	10·983 2	·091 048	
14	1·412 97	·707 73	16·519 0	11·690 9	·085 537	
15	1·448 30	·690 47	17·931 9	12·381 4	·080 766	
16	1·484 51	·673 62	19·380 2	13·055 0	·076 599	
17	1·521 62	·657 20	20·864 7	13·712 2	·072 928	
18	1·559 66	·641 17	22·386 3	14·353 4	·069 670	
19	1·598 65	·625 53	23·946 0	14·978 9	·066 761	
20	1·638 62	·610 27	25·544 7	15·589 2	·064 147	
21	1·679 58	·595 39	27·183 3	16·184 5	·061 787	21
22	1·721 57	·580 86	28·862 9	16·765 4	·059 647	22
23	1·764 61	·566 70	30·584 4	17·332 1	·057 696	23
24	1·808 73	·552 88	32·349 0	17·885 0	·055 913	24
25	1·853 94	·539 39	34·157 8	18·424 4	·054 276	25
26	1·900 29	·526 23	36·011 7	18·950 6	·052 769	26
27	1·947 80	·513 40	37·912 0	19·464 0	·051 377	27
28	1·996 50	·500 88	39·859 8	19·964 9	·050 088	28
29	2·046 41	·488 66	41·856 3	20·453 5	·048 891	29
30	2·097 57	·476 74	43·902 7	20·930 3	·047 778	30
31	2·150 01	·465 11	46·000 3	21·395 4	·046 739	31
32	2·203 76	·453 77	48·150 3	21·849 2	·045 768	32
33	2·258 85	·442 70	50·354 0	22·291 9	·044 859	33
34	2·315 32	·431 91	52·612 9	22·723 8	·044 007	34
35	2·373 21	·421 37	54·928 2	23·145 2	·043 206	35
36	2·432 54	·411 09	57·301 4	23·556 3	·042 452	36
37	2·493 35	·401 07	59·733 9	23·957 3	·041 741	37
38	2·555 68	·391 28	62·227 3	24·348 6	·041 070	38
39	2·619 57	·381 74	64·783 0	24·730 3	·040 436	39
40	2·685 06	·372 43	67·402 6	25·102 8	·039 836	40
41	2·752 19	·363 35	70·087 6	25·466 1	·039 268	41
42	2·821 00	·354 48	72·839 8	25·820 6	·038 729	42
43	2·891 52	·345 84	75·660 8	26·166 4	·038 217	43
44	2·963 81	·337 40	78·552 3	26·503 8	·037 730	44
45	3·037 90	·329 17	81·516 1	26·833 0	·037 268	45
46	3·113 85	·321 15	84·554 0	27·154 2	·036 827	46
47	3·191 70	·313 31	87·667 9	27·467 5	·036 407	47
48	3·271 49	·305 67	90·859 6	27·773 2	·036 006	48
49	3·353 28	·298 22	94·131 1	28·071 4	·035 623	49
50	3·437 11	·290 94	97·484 3	28·362 3	·035 258	50
60	4·399 79	·227 28	135·991 6	30·908 7	·032 353	60
70	5·632 10	·177 55	185·284 1	32·897 9	·030 397	70
80	7·209 57	·138 70	248·382 7	34·451 8	·029 026	80
90	9·228 86	·108 36	329·154 2	35·665 8	·028 038	90
100	11·813 72	·084 65	432·548 6	36·614 1	·027 312	100

n	$(1+i)^n$	v^n	$s_{\overline{n}\vert}$	$a_{\overline{n}\vert}$	$(a_{\overline{n}\vert})^{-1}$	n
1	1·027 50	·973 24	1·000 0	0·973 2	1·027 500	1
2	1·055 76	·947 19	2·027 5	1·920 4	0·520 718	2
3	1·084 79	·921 84	3·083 3	2·842 3	·351 832	3
4	1·114 62	·897 17	4·168 0	3·739 4	·267 421	4
5	1·145 27	·873 15	5·282 7	4·612 6	·216 798	5
6	1·176 77	·849 78	6·427 9	5·462 4	·183 071	6
7	1·209 13	·827 04	7·604 7	6·289 4	·158 997	7
8	1·242 38	·804 91	8·813 8	7·094 3	·140 958	8
9	1·276 55	·783 36	10·056 2	7·877 7	·126 941	9
10	1·311 65	·762 40	11·332 8	8·640 1	·115 740	10
11	1·347 72	·741 99	12·644 4	9·382 1	·106 586	11
12	1·384 78	·722 13	13·992 1	10·104 2	·098 969	12
13	1·422 87	·702 81	15·376 9	10·807 0	·092 533	13
14	1·461 99	·684 00	16·799 8	11·491 0	·087 025	14
15	1·502 20	·665 69	18·261 8	12·156 7	·082 259	15
16	1·543 51	·647 87	19·764 0	12·804 6	·078 097	16
17	1·585 96	·630 53	21·307 5	13·435 1	·074 432	17
18	1·629 57	·613 66	22·893 4	14·048 8	·071 181	18
19	1·674 38	·597 23	24·523 0	14·646 0	·068 278	19
20	1·720 43	·581 25	26·197 4	15·227 3	·065 672	20
21	1·767 74	·565 69	27·917 8	15·792 9	·063 319	21
22	1·816 35	·550 55	29·685 6	16·343 5	·061 186	22
23	1·866 30	·535 82	31·501 9	16·879 3	·059 244	23
24	1·917 63	·521 48	33·368 2	17·400 8	·057 469	24
25	1·970 36	·507 52	35·285 8	17·908 3	·055 840	25
26	2·024 55	·493 94	37·256 2	18·402 3	·054 341	26
27	2·080 22	·480 72	39·280 8	18·883 0	·052 958	27
28	2·137 43	·467 85	41·361 0	19·350 8	·051 677	28
29	2·196 21	·455 33	43·498 4	19·806 2	·050 489	29
30	2·256 60	·443 14	45·694 6	20·249 3	·049 384	30
31	2·318 66	·431 28	47·951 2	20·680 6	·048 355	31
32	2·382 42	·419 74	50·269 9	21·100 3	·047 393	32
33	2·447 94	·408 51	52·652 3	21·508 8	·046 493	33
34	2·515 26	·397 57	55·100 2	21·906 4	·045 649	34
35	2·584 43	·386 93	57·615 5	22·293 3	·044 856	35
36	2·655 50	·376 58	60·199 9	22·669 9	·044 111	36
37	2·728 52	·366 50	62·855 4	23·036 4	·043 410	37
38	2·803 56	·356 69	65·583 9	23·393 1	·042 748	38
39	2·880 66	·347 14	68·387 5	23·740 2	·042 123	39
40	2·959 87	·337 85	71·268 1	24·078 1	·041 532	40
41	3·041 27	·328 81	74·228 0	24·406 9	·040 972	41
42	3·124 91	·320 01	77·269 3	24·726 9	·040 442	42
43	3·210 84	·311 44	80·394 2	25·038 4	·039 939	43
44	3·299 14	·303 11	83·605 0	25·341 5	·039 461	44
45	3·389 86	·295 00	86·904 2	25·636 5	·039 007	45
46	3·483 09	·287 10	90·294 0	25·923 6	·038 575	46
47	3·578 87	·279 42	93·777 1	26·203 0	·038 164	47
48	3·677 29	·271 94	97·356 0	26·474 9	·037 772	48
49	3·778 42	·264 66	101·033 3	26·739 6	·037 398	49
50	3·882 32	·257 58	104·811 7	26·997 2	·037 041	50
60	5·092 25	·196 38	148·809 1	29·222 7	·034 220	60
70	6·679 26	·149 72	206·518 4	30·919 4	·032 342	70
80	8·760 85	·114 14	282·212 9	32·212 9	·031 043	80
90	11·491 18	·087 02	381·497 6	33·199 2	·030 121	90
100	15·072 42	·066 35	511·724 4	33·951 0	·029 454	100

Constants

Function	Value
i	·027 5
$i^{(2)}$	·027 313
$i^{(4)}$	·027 221
$i^{(12)}$	·027 159
δ	·027 129
$(1+i)^{\frac{1}{2}}$	1·013 657
$(1+i)^{\frac{1}{4}}$	1·006 805
$(1+i)^{\frac{1}{12}}$	1·002 263
v	·973 236
$v^{\frac{1}{2}}$	·986 527
$v^{\frac{1}{4}}$	·993 241
$v^{\frac{1}{12}}$	·997 742
d	·026 764
$d^{(2)}$	·026 946
$d^{(4)}$	·027 037
$d^{(12)}$	·027 098
$i/i^{(2)}$	1·006 828
$i/i^{(4)}$	1·010 254
$i/i^{(12)}$	1·012 542
i/δ	1·013 688
$i/d^{(2)}$	1·020 578
$i/d^{(4)}$	1·017 129
$i/d^{(12)}$	1·014 834
$\log_{10}(1+i)$	·011 781 8

Constants	
Function	Value
i	·03
$i^{(2)}$	·029 778
$i^{(4)}$	·029 668
$i^{(12)}$	·029 595
δ	·029 559
$(1+i)^{\frac{1}{2}}$	1·014 889
$(1+i)^{\frac{1}{4}}$	1·007 417
$(1+i)^{\frac{1}{12}}$	1·002 466
v	·970 874
$v^{\frac{1}{2}}$	·985 329
$v^{\frac{1}{4}}$	·992 638
$v^{\frac{1}{12}}$	·997 540
d	·029 126
$d^{(2)}$	·029 341
$d^{(4)}$	·029 450
$d^{(12)}$	·029 522
$i/i^{(2)}$	1·007 445
$i/i^{(4)}$	1·011 181
$i/i^{(12)}$	1·013 677
i/δ	1·014 926
$i/d^{(2)}$	1·022 445
$i/d^{(4)}$	1·018 681
$i/d^{(12)}$	1·016 177
$\log_{10}(1+i)$	·012 837 2

n	$(1+i)^n$	v^n	$s_{\overline{n}\vert}$	$a_{\overline{n}\vert}$	$(a_{\overline{n}\vert})^{-1}$	n
1	1·030 00	·970 87	1·000 0	0·970 9	1·030 000	
2	1·060 90	·942 60	2·030 0	1·913 5	0·522 611	
3	1·092 73	·915 14	3·090 9	2·828 6	·353 530	
4	1·125 51	·888 49	4·183 6	3·717 1	·269 027	
5	1·159 27	·862 61	5·309 1	4·579 7	·218 355	
6	1·194 05	·837 48	6·468 4	5·417 2	·184 598	
7	1·229 87	·813 09	7·662 5	6·230 3	·160 506	
8	1·266 77	·789 41	8·892 3	7·019 7	·142 456	
9	1·304 77	·766 42	10·159 1	7·786 1	·128 434	
10	1·343 92	·744 09	11·463 9	8·530 2	·117 231	
11	1·384 23	·722 42	12·807 8	9·252 6	·108 077	
12	1·425 76	·701 38	14·192 0	9·954 0	·100 462	
13	1·468 53	·680 95	15·617 8	10·635 0	·094 030	
14	1·512 59	·661 12	17·086 3	11·296 1	·088 526	
15	1·557 97	·641 86	18·598 9	11·937 9	·083 767	
16	1·604 71	·623 17	20·156 9	12·561 1	·079 611	
17	1·652 85	·605 02	21·761 6	13·166 1	·075 953	
18	1·702 43	·587 39	23·414 4	13·753 5	·072 709	
19	1·753 51	·570 29	25·116 9	14·323 8	·069 814	
20	1·806 11	·553 68	26·870 4	14·877 5	·067 216	
21	1·860 29	·537 55	28·676 5	15·415 0	·064 872	
22	1·916 10	·521 89	30·536 8	15·936 9	·062 747	
23	1·973 59	·506 69	32·452 9	16·443 6	·060 814	
24	2·032 79	·491 93	34·426 5	16·935 5	·059 047	
25	2·093 78	·477 61	36·459 3	17·413 1	·057 428	
26	2·156 59	·463 69	38·553 0	17·876 8	·055 938	
27	2·221 29	·450 19	40·709 6	18·327 0	·054 564	
28	2·287 93	·437 08	42·930 9	18·764 1	·053 293	
29	2·356 57	·424 35	45·218 9	19·188 5	·052 115	
30	2·427 26	·411 99	47·575 4	19·600 4	·051 019	
31	2·500 08	·399 99	50·002 7	20·000 4	·049 999	
32	2·575 08	·388 34	52·502 8	20·388 8	·049 047	
33	2·652 34	·377 03	55·077 8	20·765 8	·048 156	
34	2·731 91	·366 04	57·730 2	21·131 8	·047 322	
35	2·813 86	·355 38	60·462 1	21·487 2	·046 539	35
36	2·898 28	·345 03	63·275 9	21·832 3	·045 804	36
37	2·985 23	·334 98	66·174 2	22·167 2	·045 112	37
38	3·074 78	·325 23	69·159 4	22·492 5	·044 459	38
39	3·167 03	·315 75	72·234 2	22·808 2	·043 844	39
40	3·262 04	·306 56	75·401 3	23·114 8	·043 262	
41	3·359 90	·297 63	78·663 3	23·412 4	·042 712	41
42	3·460 70	·288 96	82·023 2	23·701 4	·042 192	42
43	3·564 52	·280 54	85·483 9	23·981 9	·041 698	43
44	3·671 45	·272 37	89·048 4	24·254 3	·041 230	44
45	3·781 60	·264 44	92·719 9	24·518 7	·040 785	45
46	3·895 04	·256 74	96·501 5	24·775 4	·040 363	46
47	4·011 90	·249 26	100·396 5	25·024 7	·039 961	47
48	4·132 25	·242 00	104·408 4	25·266 7	·039 578	48
49	4·256 22	·234 95	108·540 6	25·501 7	·039 213	49
50	4·383 91	·228 11	112·796 9	25·729 8	·038 865	50
60	5·891 60	·169 73	163·053 4	27·675 6	·036 133	60
70	7·917 82	·126 30	230·594 1	29·123 4	·034 337	70
80	10·640 89	·093 98	321·363 0	30·200 8	·033 112	80
90	14·300 47	·069 93	443·348 9	31·002 4	·032 256	90
100	19·218 63	·052 03	607·287 7	31·598 9	·031 647	100

n	$(1+i)^n$	v^n	$s_{\overline{n}\rvert}$	$a_{\overline{n}\rvert}$	$(a_{\overline{n}\rvert})^{-1}$	n
1	1·035 00	·966 18	1·000 0	0·966 2	1·035 000	1
2	1·071 23	·933 51	2·035 0	1·899 7	0·526 400	2
3	1·108 72	·901 94	3·106 2	2·801 6	·356 934	3
4	1·147 52	·871 44	4·214 9	3·673 1	·272 251	4
5	1·187 69	·841 97	5·362 5	4·515 1	·221 481	5
6	1·229 26	·813 50	6·550 2	5·328 6	·187 668	6
7	1·272 28	·785 99	7·779 4	6·114 5	·163 544	7
8	1·316 81	·759 41	9·051 7	6·874 0	·145 477	8
9	1·362 90	·733 73	10·368 5	7·607 7	·131 446	9
10	1·410 60	·708 92	11·731 4	8·316 6	·120 241	10
11	1·459 97	·684 95	13·142 0	9·001 6	·111 092	11
12	1·511 07	·661 78	14·602 0	9·663 3	·103 484	12
13	1·563 96	·639 40	16·113 0	10·302 7	·097 062	13
14	1·618 69	·617 78	17·677 0	10·920 5	·091 571	14
15	1·675 35	·596 89	19·295 7	11·517 4	·086 825	15
16	1·733 99	·576 71	20·971 0	12·094 1	·082 685	16
17	1·794 68	·557 20	22·705 0	12·651 3	·079 043	17
18	1·857 49	·538 36	24·499 7	13·189 7	·075 817	18
19	1·922 50	·520 16	26·357 2	13·709 8	·072 940	19
20	1·989 79	·502 57	28·279 7	14·212 4	·070 361	20
21	2·059 43	·485 57	30·269 5	14·698 0	·068 037	21
22	2·131 51	·469 15	32·328 9	15·167 1	·065 932	22
23	2·206 11	·453 29	34·460 4	15·620 4	·064 019	23
24	2·283 33	·437 96	36·666 5	16·058 4	·062 273	24
25	2·363 24	·423 15	38·949 9	16·481 5	·060 674	25
26	2·445 96	·408 84	41·313 1	16·890 4	·059 205	26
27	2·531 57	·395 01	43·759 1	17·285 4	·057 852	27
28	2·620 17	·381 65	46·290 6	17·667 0	·056 603	28
29	2·711 88	·368 75	48·910 8	18·035 8	·055 445	29
30	2·806 79	·356 28	51·622 7	18·392 0	·054 371	30
31	2·905 03	·344 23	54·429 5	18·736 3	·053 372	31
32	3·006 71	·332 59	57·334 5	19·068 9	·052 442	32
33	3·111 94	·321 34	60·341 2	19·390 2	·051 572	33
34	3·220 86	·310 48	63·453 2	19·700 7	·050 760	34
35	3·333 59	·299 98	66·674 0	20·000 7	·049 998	35
36	3·450 27	·289 83	70·007 6	20·290 5	·049 284	36
37	3·571 03	·280 03	73·457 9	20·570 5	·048 613	37
38	3·696 01	·270 56	77·028 9	20·841 1	·047 982	38
39	3·825 37	·261 41	80·724 9	21·102 5	·047 388	39
40	3·959 26	·252 57	84·550 3	21·355 1	·046 827	40
41	4·097 83	·244 03	88·509 5	21·599 1	·046 298	41
42	4·241 26	·235 78	92·607 4	21·834 9	·045 798	42
43	4·389 70	·227 81	96·848 6	22·062 7	·045 325	43
44	4·543 34	·220 10	101·238 3	22·282 8	·044 878	44
45	4·702 36	·212 66	105·781 7	22·495 5	·044 453	45
46	4·866 94	·205 47	110·484 0	22·700 9	·044 051	46
47	5·037 28	·198 52	115·351 0	22·899 4	·043 669	47
48	5·213 59	·191 81	120·388 3	23·091 2	·043 306	48
49	5·396 06	·185 32	125·601 8	23·276 6	·042 962	49
50	5·584 93	·179 05	130·997 9	23·455 6	·042 634	50
60	7·878 09	·126 93	196·516 9	24·944 7	·040 089	60
70	11·112 83	·089 99	288·937 9	26·000 4	·038 461	70
80	15·675 74	·063 79	419·306 8	26·748 8	·037 385	80
90	22·112 18	·045 22	603·205 0	27·279 3	·036 658	90
00	31·191 41	·032 06	862·611 7	27·655 4	·036 159	100

Constants

Function	Value
i	·035
$i^{(2)}$	·034 699
$i^{(4)}$	·034 550
$i^{(12)}$	·034 451
δ	·034 401
$(1+i)^{\frac{1}{2}}$	1·017 349
$(1+i)^{\frac{1}{4}}$	1·008 637
$(1+i)^{\frac{1}{12}}$	1·002 871
v	·966 184
$v^{\frac{1}{2}}$	·982 946
$v^{\frac{1}{4}}$	·991 437
$v^{\frac{1}{12}}$	·997 137
d	·033 816
$d^{(2)}$	·034 107
$d^{(4)}$	·034 254
$d^{(12)}$	·034 352
$i/i^{(2)}$	1·008 675
$i/i^{(4)}$	1·013 031
$i/i^{(12)}$	1·015 942
i/δ	1·017 400
$i/d^{(2)}$	1·026 175
$i/d^{(4)}$	1·021 781
$i/d^{(12)}$	1·018 859
$\log_{10}(1+i)$	·014 940 3

Constants	
Function	Value
i	·04
$i^{(2)}$	·039 608
$i^{(4)}$	·039 414
$i^{(12)}$	·039 285
δ	·039 221
$(1+i)^{\frac{1}{2}}$	1·019 804
$(1+i)^{\frac{1}{4}}$	1·009 853
$(1+i)^{\frac{1}{12}}$	1·003 274
v	·961 538
$v^{\frac{1}{2}}$	·980 581
$v^{\frac{1}{4}}$	·990 243
$v^{\frac{1}{12}}$	·996 737
d	·038 462
$d^{(2)}$	·038 839
$d^{(4)}$	·039 029
$d^{(12)}$	·039 157
$i/i^{(2)}$	1·009 902
$i/i^{(4)}$	1·014 877
$i/i^{(12)}$	1·018 204
i/δ	1·019 869
$i/d^{(2)}$	1·029 902
$i/d^{(4)}$	1·024 877
$i/d^{(12)}$	1·021 537
$\log_{10}(1+i)$	·017 033 3

n	$(1+i)^n$	v^n	$s_{\overline{n}\vert}$	$a_{\overline{n}\vert}$	$(a_{\overline{n}\vert})^{-1}$
1	1·040 00	·961 54	1·000 0	0·961 5	1·040 000
2	1·081 60	·924 56	2·040 0	1·886 1	0·530 196
3	1·124 86	·889 00	3·121 6	2·775 1	·360 349
4	1·169 86	·854 80	4·246 5	3·629 9	·275 490
5	1·216 65	·821 93	5·416 3	4·451 8	·224 627
6	1·265 32	·790 31	6·633 0	5·242 1	·190 762
7	1·315 93	·759 92	7·898 3	6·002 1	·166 610
8	1·368 57	·730 69	9·214 2	6·732 7	·148 528
9	1·423 31	·702 59	10·582 8	7·435 3	·134 493
10	1·480 24	·675 56	12·006 1	8·110 9	·123 291
11	1·539 45	·649 58	13·486 4	8·760 5	·114 149
12	1·601 03	·624 60	15·025 8	9·385 1	·106 552
13	1·665 07	·600 57	16·626 8	9·985 6	·100 144
14	1·731 68	·577 48	18·291 9	10·563 1	·094 669
15	1·800 94	·555 26	20·023 6	11·118 4	·089 941
16	1·872 98	·533 91	21·824 5	11·652 3	·085 820
17	1·947 90	·513 37	23·697 5	12·165 7	·082 199
18	2·025 82	·493 63	25·645 4	12·659 3	·078 993
19	2·106 85	·474 64	27·671 2	13·133 9	·076 139
20	2·191 12	·456 39	29·778 1	13·590 3	·073 582
21	2·278 77	·438 83	31·969 2	14·029 2	·071 280
22	2·369 92	·421 96	34·248 0	14·451 1	·069 199
23	2·464 72	·405 73	36·617 9	14·856 8	·067 309
24	2·563 30	·390 12	39·082 6	15·247 0	·065 587
25	2·665 84	·375 12	41·645 9	15·622 1	·064 012
26	2·772 47	·360 69	44·311 7	15·982 8	·062 567
27	2·883 37	·346 82	47·084 2	16·329 6	·061 239
28	2·998 70	·333 48	49·967 6	16·663 1	·060 013
29	3·118 65	·320 65	52·966 3	16·983 7	·058 880
30	3·243 40	·308 32	56·084 9	17·292 0	·057 830
31	3·373 13	·296 46	59·328 3	17·588 5	·056 855
32	3·508 06	·285 06	62·701 5	17·873 6	·055 949
33	3·648 38	·274 09	66·209 5	18·147 6	·055 104
34	3·794 32	·263 55	69·857 9	18·411 2	·054 315
35	3·946 09	·253 42	73·652 2	18·664 6	·053 577
36	4·103 93	·243 67	77·598 3	18·908 3	·052 887
37	4·268 09	·234 30	81·702 2	19·142 6	·052 240
38	4·438 81	·225 29	85·970 3	19·367 9	·051 632
39	4·616 37	·216 62	90·409 1	19·584 5	·051 061
40	4·801 02	·208 29	95·025 5	19·792 8	·050 523
41	4·993 06	·200 28	99·826 5	19·993 1	·050 017
42	5·192 78	·192 57	104·819 6	20·185 6	·049 540
43	5·400 50	·185 17	110·012 4	20·370 8	·049 090
44	5·616 52	·178 05	115·412 9	20·548 8	·048 665
45	5·841 18	·171 20	121·029 4	20·720 0	·048 262
46	6·074 82	·164 61	126·870 6	20·884 7	·047 882
47	6·317 82	·158 28	132·945 4	21·042 9	·047 522
48	6·570 53	·152 19	139·263 2	21·195 1	·047 181
49	6·833 35	·146 34	145·833 7	21·341 5	·046 857
50	7·106 68	·140 71	152·667 1	21·482 2	·046 550
60	10·519 63	·095 06	237·990 7	22·623 5	·044 202
70	15·571 62	·064 22	364·290 5	23·394 5	·042 745
80	23·049 80	·043 38	551·245 0	23·915 4	·041 814
90	34·119 33	·029 31	827·983 3	24·267 3	·041 208
100	50·504 95	·019 80	1237·623 7	24·505 0	·040 808

n	$(1+i)^n$	v^n	$s_{\overline{n}\vert}$	$a_{\overline{n}\vert}$	$(a_{\overline{n}\vert})^{-1}$	n
1	1·045 00	·956 94	1·000 0	0·956 9	1·045 000	1
2	1·092 03	·915 73	2·045 0	1·872 7	0·533 998	2
3	1·141 17	·876 30	3·137 0	2·749 0	·363 773	3
4	1·192 52	·838 56	4·278 2	3·587 5	·278 744	4
5	1·246 18	·802 45	5·470 7	4·390 0	·227 792	5
6	1·302 26	·767 90	6·716 9	5·157 9	·193 878	6
7	1·360 86	·734 83	8·019 2	5·892 7	·169 701	7
8	1·422 10	·703 19	9·380 0	6·595 9	·151 610	8
9	1·486 10	·672 90	10·802 1	7·268 8	·137 574	9
10	1·552 97	·643 93	12·288 2	7·912 7	·126 379	10
11	1·622 85	·616 20	13·841 2	8·528 9	·117 248	11
12	1·695 88	·589 66	15·464 0	9·118 6	·109 666	12
13	1·772 20	·564 27	17·159 9	9·682 9	·103 275	13
14	1·851 94	·539 97	18·932 1	10·222 8	·097 820	14
15	1·935 28	·516 72	20·784 1	10·739 5	·093 114	15
16	2·022 37	·494 47	22·719 3	11·234 0	·089 015	16
17	2·113 38	·473 18	24·741 7	11·707 2	·085 418	17
18	2·208 48	·452 80	26·855 1	12·160 0	·082 237	18
19	2·307 86	·433 30	29·063 6	12·593 3	·079 407	19
20	2·411 71	·414 64	31·371 4	13·007 9	·076 876	20
21	2·520 24	·396 79	33·783 1	13·404 7	·074 601	21
22	2·633 65	·379 70	36·303 4	13·784 4	·072 546	22
23	2·752 17	·363 35	38·937 0	14·147 8	·070 682	23
24	2·876 01	·347 70	41·689 2	14·495 5	·068 987	24
25	3·005 43	·332 73	44·565 2	14·828 2	·067 439	25
26	3·140 68	·318 40	47·570 6	15·146 6	·066 021	26
27	3·282 01	·304 69	50·711 3	15·451 3	·064 719	27
28	3·429 70	·291 57	53·993 3	15·742 9	·063 521	28
29	3·584 04	·279 02	57·423 0	16·021 9	·062 415	29
30	3·745 32	·267 00	61·007 1	16·288 9	·061 392	30
31	3·913 86	·255 50	64·752 4	16·544 4	·060 443	31
32	4·089 98	·244 50	68·666 2	16·788 9	·059 563	32
33	4·274 03	·233 97	72·756 2	17·022 9	·058 745	33
34	4·466 36	·223 90	77·030 3	17·246 8	·057 982	34
35	4·667 35	·214 25	81·496 6	17·461 0	·057 270	35
36	4·877 38	·205 03	86·164 0	17·666 0	·056 606	36
37	5·096 86	·196 20	91·041 3	17·862 2	·055 984	37
38	5·326 22	·187 75	96·138 2	18·050 0	·055 402	38
39	5·565 90	·179 67	101·464 4	18·229 7	·054 856	39
40	5·816 36	·171 93	107·030 3	18·401 6	·054 343	40
41	6·078 10	·164 53	112·846 7	18·566 1	·053 862	41
42	6·351 62	·157 44	118·924 8	18·723 5	·053 409	42
43	6·637 44	·150 66	125·276 4	18·874 2	·052 982	43
44	6·936 12	·144 17	131·913 8	19·018 4	·052 581	44
45	7·248 25	·137 96	138·850 0	19·156 3	·052 202	45
46	7·574 42	·132 02	146·098 2	19·288 4	·051 845	46
47	7·915 27	·126 34	153·672 6	19·414 7	·051 507	47
48	8·271 46	·120 90	161·587 9	19·535 6	·051 189	48
49	8·643 67	·115 69	169·859 4	19·651 3	·050 887	49
50	9·032 64	·110 71	178·503 0	19·762 0	·050 602	50
60	14·027 41	·071 29	289·498 0	20·638 0	·048 454	60
70	21·784 14	·045 90	461·869 7	21·202 1	·047 165	70
80	33·830 10	·029 56	729·557 7	21·565 3	·046 371	80
90	52·537 11	·019 03	1145·269 0	21·799 2	·045 873	90
100	81·588 52	·012 26	1790·856 0	21·949 8	·045 558	100

Constants

Function	Value
i	·045
$i^{(2)}$	·044 505
$i^{(4)}$	·044 260
$i^{(12)}$	·044 098
δ	·044 017
$(1+i)^{\frac{1}{2}}$	1·022 252
$(1+i)^{\frac{1}{4}}$	1·011 065
$(1+i)^{\frac{1}{12}}$	1·003 675
v	·956 938
$v^{\frac{1}{2}}$	·978 232
$v^{\frac{1}{4}}$	·989 056
$v^{\frac{1}{12}}$	·996 339
d	·043 062
$d^{(2)}$	·043 536
$d^{(4)}$	·043 776
$d^{(12)}$	·043 936
$i/i^{(2)}$	1·011 126
$i/i^{(4)}$	1·016 720
$i/i^{(12)}$	1·020 461
i/δ	1·022 335
$i/d^{(2)}$	1·033 626
$i/d^{(4)}$	1·027 970
$i/d^{(12)}$	1·024 211
$\log_{10}(1+i)$	·019 116 3

Constants	
Function	Value
i	·05
$i^{(2)}$	·049 390
$i^{(4)}$	·049 089
$i^{(12)}$	·048 889
δ	·048 790
$(1+i)^{\frac{1}{2}}$	1·024 695
$(1+i)^{\frac{1}{4}}$	1·012 272
$(1+i)^{\frac{1}{12}}$	1·004 074
v	·952 381
$v^{\frac{1}{2}}$	·975 900
$v^{\frac{1}{4}}$	·987 877
$v^{\frac{1}{12}}$	·995 942
d	·047 619
$d^{(2)}$	·048 200
$d^{(4)}$	·048 494
$d^{(12)}$	·048 691
$i/i^{(2)}$	1·012 348
$i/i^{(4)}$	1·018 559
$i/i^{(12)}$	1·022 715
i/δ	1·024 797
$i/d^{(2)}$	1·037 348
$i/d^{(4)}$	1·031 059
$i/d^{(12)}$	1·026 881
$\log_{10}(1+i)$	·021 189 3

n	$(1+i)^n$	v^n	$s_{\overline{n}\vert}$	$a_{\overline{n}\vert}$	$(a_{\overline{n}\vert})^{-1}$	n
1	1·050 00	·952 38	1·000 0	0·952 4	1·050 000	1
2	1·102 50	·907 03	2·050 0	1·859 4	0·537 805	2
3	1·157 63	·863 84	3·152 5	2·723 2	·367 209	3
4	1·215 51	·822 70	4·310 1	3·546 0	·282 012	4
5	1·276 28	·783 53	5·525 6	4·329 5	·230 975	5
6	1·340 10	·746 22	6·801 9	5·075 7	·197 017	6
7	1·407 10	·710 68	8·142 0	5·786 4	·172 820	7
8	1·477 46	·676 84	9·549 1	6·463 2	·154 722	8
9	1·551 33	·644 61	11·026 6	7·107 8	·140 690	9
10	1·628 89	·613 91	12·577 9	7·721 7	·129 505	10
11	1·710 34	·584 68	14·206 8	8·306 4	·120 389	11
12	1·795 86	·556 84	15·917 1	8·863 3	·112 825	12
13	1·885 65	·530 32	17·713 0	9·393 6	·106 456	13
14	1·979 93	·505 07	19·598 6	9·898 6	·101 024	14
15	2·078 93	·481 02	21·578 6	10·379 7	·096 342	15
16	2·182 87	·458 11	23·657 5	10·837 8	·092 270	16
17	2·292 02	·436 30	25·840 4	11·274 1	·088 699	17
18	2·406 62	·415 52	28·132 4	11·689 6	·085 546	18
19	2·526 95	·395 73	30·539 0	12·085 3	·082 745	19
20	2·653 30	·376 89	33·066 0	12·462 2	·080 243	20
21	2·785 96	·358 94	35·719 3	12·821 2	·077 996	21
22	2·925 26	·341 85	38·505 2	13·163 0	·075 971	22
23	3·071 52	·325 57	41·430 5	13·488 6	·074 137	23
24	3·225 10	·310 07	44·502 0	13·798 6	·072 471	24
25	3·386 35	·295 30	47·727 1	14·093 9	·070 952	25
26	3·555 67	·281 24	51·113 5	14·375 2	·069 564	26
27	3·733 46	·267 85	54·669 1	14·643 0	·068 292	27
28	3·920 13	·255 09	58·402 6	14·898 1	·067 123	28
29	4·116 14	·242 95	62·322 7	15·141 1	·066 046	29
30	4·321 94	·231 38	66·438 8	15·372 5	·065 051	30
31	4·538 04	·220 36	70·760 8	15·592 8	·064 132	31
32	4·764 94	·209 87	75·298 8	15·802 7	·063 280	32
33	5·003 19	·199 87	80·063 8	16·002 5	·062 490	33
34	5·253 35	·190 35	85·067 0	16·192 9	·061 755	34
35	5·516 02	·181 29	90·320 3	16·374 2	·061 072	35
36	5·791 82	·172 66	95·836 3	16·546 9	·060 434	36
37	6·081 41	·164 44	101·628 1	16·711 3	·059 840	37
38	6·385 48	·156 61	107·709 5	16·867 9	·059 284	38
39	6·704 75	·149 15	114·095 0	17·017 0	·058 765	39
40	7·039 99	·142 05	120·799 8	17·159 1	·058 278	40
41	7·391 99	·135 28	127·839 8	17·294 4	·057 822	41
42	7·761 59	·128 84	135·231 8	17·423 2	·057 395	42
43	8·149 67	·122 70	142·993 3	17·545 9	·056 993	43
44	8·557 15	·116 86	151·143 0	17·662 8	·056 616	44
45	8·985 01	·111 30	159·700 2	17·774 1	·056 262	45
46	9·434 26	·106 00	168·685 2	17·880 1	·055 928	46
47	9·905 97	·100 95	178·119 4	17·981 0	·055 614	47
48	10·401 27	·096 14	188·025 4	18·077 2	·055 318	48
49	10·921 33	·091 56	198·426 7	18·168 7	·055 040	49
50	11·467 40	·087 20	209·348 0	18·255 9	·054 777	50
60	18·679 19	·053 54	353·583 7	18·929 3	·052 828	60
70	30·426 43	·032 87	588·528 5	19·342 7	·051 699	70
80	49·561 44	·020 18	971·228 8	19·596 5	·051 030	80
90	80·730 37	·012 39	1594·607 3	19·752 3	·050 627	90
100	131·501 26	·007 60	2610·025 2	19·847 9	·050 383	100

INDEX

[NOTE: *Page references in Roman type relate to the main text, those in italics to the illustrative examples at the end of each chapter*]